Stories OF Faith AND Courage
FROM THE
KOREAN WAR

Stories OF Faith AND Courage
FROM THE
KOREAN WAR

LARKIN SPIVEY

GOD & COUNTRY
PRESS

Contents

Maps

Acknowledgments

I AM grateful to all veterans of the Korean War for their heroic service to Korea and to America. I especially thank those veterans and their family members who graciously shared their stories for this book. John McCurry is one of those veterans. John has been especially helpful with his recollections, notes, and insights into every aspect of this conflict. He is a member of my church, a good friend, and an invaluable consultant.

Capt. Randy Cash, USN (Ret.), the historian of the Navy Chaplain Corps, played a large role in this work by sharing his own knowledge and the amazing archives of the Navy Chaplain School. Also, as has been the case for many years, the Naval War College was one of my great resources, and I particularly thank Alice Juda, Julie Zecher, and the other members of the NWC Library staff for their generous support.

My daughter, Catherine-Alexa Spivey Rountree has been my primary research assistant, gathering information for this book. Her familiarity with military matters, the history of the period, and Internet sources has been invaluable. I also thank Rebecca Randall and Bob Bardo for their professional and tireless work in editing. Dale Anderson and Rick Steele of AMG Publishers have provided encouragement and professional guidance throughout this project, as they have for the entire *Battlefields & Blessings* series.

I especially thank my wife, Lani, for her loving support of my writing efforts and her own special input. She has been an ever-present advisor and a constant source of insight into the spiritual aspects of the veterans' stories contained in this book.

Finally, and most importantly, I acknowledge Jesus Christ as my Lord and Savior, and I acknowledge him as the cause for which I write. When I came to him after a lifetime of religious skepticism, he changed my heart and my life. I hope his person and his lifesaving message shine through in these stories.

Introduction

THIS BOOK is a daily devotional written from a somewhat unusual spiritual perspective. By showing the power of faith under the extreme conditions of war, I hope to inform and inspire readers about deeper possibilities in their own lives. Believers and skeptics alike will be challenged by these stories of faith, doubt, courage, and renewal in times of adversity. Additionally, I intend to demonstrate to Korean War veterans their ultimate accomplishments during this frustrating conflict and the historical significance of their heroic service.

The Korean War has been called the "Forgotten War" for obvious reasons. Historically, it fell between the glorious victory of World War II and the controversy-filled conflict of Vietnam. There was no victory celebration when the Korean War ended, because it ended in a virtual stalemate where it began. The war was unpopular but not subject to the kind of controversy that came a decade later in Vietnam. Most Americans viewed the Korean War as a necessary evil brought on by the overt Communist invasion that started it. Even after the cease-fire in 1953, neither side was satisfied. Both have remained on a war footing ever since with recurring border incidents and bellicose threats. As I write this Introduction, the leaders of North Korea are threatening the South with use of nuclear weapons. Unlike World War II, most of the US population was not greatly affected by the Korean War, and so, when hostilities ceased, young, war-torn South Korea quickly faded from public consciousness in America.

Over the decades since the war, however, an amazing story has unfolded. South Korea's impressive economic growth has gradually placed it among the world's most developed industrial countries. Few other countries have exceeded its increase in per capita output since the early 1960s. Ever-larger portions of the South Korean population have benefitted from this rising prosperity.

The growth of Christianity in modern South Korea has been equally rapid. From modest beginnings (about 2 percent of the population in 1945), the Christian community in South Korea has grown to more than twelve million believers, or one-third of the population. The capital, Seoul, boasts ten of the eleven largest Christian congregations in the world. An amazing by-product of the growth of Christianity has been the upsurge in missionary activity. South Korea now sends abroad more missionaries than any other nation except the United States.

South Korea's phenomenal story since the end of the Korean War should be a source of great pride to the military men and women who made it possible. The so-called "Forgotten War" may have ended in frustration and controversy as America's first war not "won." However, the freedom of South Korea was restored and guaranteed for the future. Korean War veterans can be exceedingly proud of their role in shaping this history.

On a personal note, this book has been a continuation of the spiritual journey I have undertaken over the past five years with AMG Publishers, writing for the *Battlefields & Blessings* series. After the arduous process of completing devotionals based on World War II and the Vietnam War, I was somewhat reluctant to undertake a book about the Korean War. To my great satisfaction, however, I found the task as interesting and rewarding as either of the others, and Korean War veterans just as inspiring. In this book I have more often relied on the veterans' own words and deeds to speak for themselves, with less sermonizing on my part and, I hope, a wider range of spiritual insight. A glance at the Table of Contents will show that the devotionals in this book are grouped by month, generally corresponding to chronological phases of the war. Each month includes an historical overview and most have maps to orient the reader. Readers are also invited to peruse the two indexes to find stories related to individuals (Index of Names) and to specific subject areas (Topical Index). The many photographs throughout the book usually include specific credits. If credits do not appear, the photos are either my own or provided by the subject of the story.

Closeup of Korean War Memorial,
Washington, DC

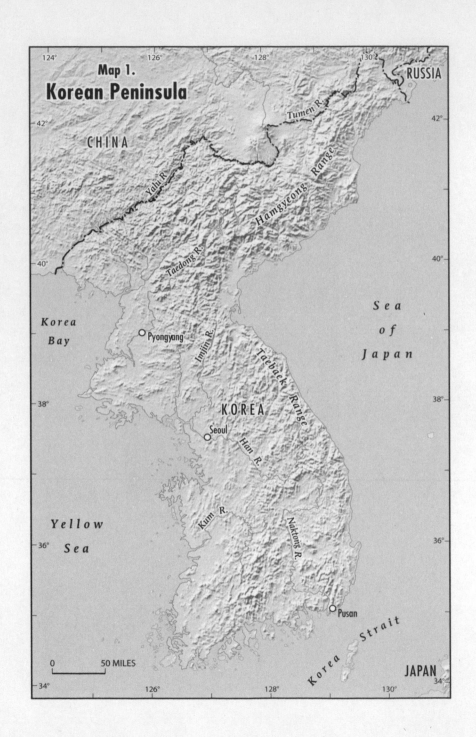

Map 1.
Korean Peninsula

RUSSIA

CHINA

Tumen R.

Hamgyeong Range

Yalu R.

Taedong R.

Korea
Bay

Pyongyang

Imjin R.

Sea
of
Japan

Taebaek Range

KOREA

Seoul

Han R.

Kum R.

Naktong R.

Yellow
Sea

Pusan

0   50 MILES

Korea Strait

JAPAN

THE KOREA STORY

THE HISTORY of Korea has been shaped by its unique geography. Placed strategically between more powerful neighbors, it has been the crossroads of conflict in East Asia for centuries. The entire area of the Korean peninsula is about eighty-five thousand square miles, the approximate size of Utah. It extends about six hundred miles from north to south and varies in width from one hundred to two hundred miles. The northern border is formed by the Yalu and Tumen rivers and is shared mostly with China and, for a short distance in the extreme east, with Russia. The other border is its long coastline on the Korea Bay and Yellow Sea to the west, the Korea Strait to the south, and the Sea of Japan to the east. Japan itself lies only about a hundred miles across the Korea Strait.

The entire country is mountainous, dominated by the Hamgyeong range in the northeast and the Taebaek range projecting south along the rugged eastern coast. Some rivers thus drain to the west, forming gentler hills and valleys before emptying into the Yellow Sea, while others drain to the south into the Korea Strait. Agriculture and fishing have always been important and have been concentrated along the western valleys and coast. The best harbors are also found on the western and southern coasts in spite of extreme tidal ranges.

Korea's early history is one of warring kingdoms, consolidated for the first time under one monarch in the seventh century. For hundreds of years a unique Korean culture and language developed in the so-called Hermit Kingdom, as the peninsula maintained its isolation and independence from powerful neighbors. The strongest cultural influences came from China, including the introduction of the Buddhist religion in the fourth century and Confucianism in the thirteenth century.[1]

By the late 1800s a rapidly modernizing Japan turned a covetous eye toward its neighbor across the Korea Strait. After a war between Japan and China in 1894–95, the Japanese left troops in Korea and began to dominate the region militarily and politically. Japan fought a war with Russia in 1904–05 to thwart Russian ambitions in Manchuria and Korea.

With little protest from the outside world, Japan overtly annexed Korea in 1910 and disbanded the Korean army, commencing more than three decades of strict colonial rule. In the process of exploiting Korean resources and labor, Japan did much to modernize Korea, building roads, bridges, railroads, and factories. Unfortunately, Japan's rule was repressive, dealing harshly with resistance and imposing Japanese customs and procedures on Korean society.

Tradition has it that Christianity came to Korea in 1794. A young Korean named Lee Seung-hoon was baptized in China, then returned to Korea to begin spreading his new faith.[2] When missionaries came later, they found an existing network of believers and a grassroots movement already in existence, giving Christianity an impetus it would not have had if introduced by foreigners. Nevertheless, the young Christian community suffered severe persecutions during the 1800s at the hand of suspicious rulers.

A group of Protestant missionaries came to Korea in the 1880s, including Horace Underwood, Henry Appenzeller, and Horace Allen. These men would be influential over many decades in spreading the gospel, starting modern schools, and translating the Bible into the Korean language. Allen was a doctor and established Korea's first modern hospital in Seoul. His work was instrumental in changing the anti-Christian policies of the nation and in opening the door for other missionaries to follow.

These early missionaries were effective in using the indigenous leadership to expand a self-governing and self-supporting Christian community in Korea. During the Japanese occupation, Christianity grew further in influence and filled the spiritual needs of a repressed people. A writer for the *Christian Science Monitor* described this period in Korean history:

> *The Korean people, in desperate straits, were hungry for what the preachers had to offer. Some native Christians were imprisoned by the Japanese for pro-independence activities, including refusing to worship Japan's emperor. Missionaries were seen as supporting the movement.*[3]

Samuel Moffett, a Presbyterian missionary, was actually expelled in 1939 because he refused to send his students to Shinto shrines. The Christians in Korea would face increasing difficulties as the Japanese occupation became even more brutal during World War II, and even more severe disruptions would occur after the war as Communist Russia took control of the northern half of the country.

The Power of Scripture

ROBERT THOMAS was a missionary to China when he first learned about Korea and heard God's call to take Bibles to that country. In 1866 he joined an American merchant-marine expedition on its way to Pyongyang, taking with him a supply of National Bible Society Bibles. As their schooner, the *General Sherman*, sailed up the Taedong River, he gave the books away at every opportunity. As they moved further inland, however, there were more and more warnings from the people to turn back as the local rulers were suspicious of the foreigners and wanted no contact with them. The expedition was finally stopped by an attack that destroyed the schooner. Thomas is reported to have thrown Bibles during the attack to the people on shore, shouting, *"Jesus, Jesus!"*[4]

Varying accounts of what followed the attack have evolved over the years. One story is told that Thomas and the rest of the crew were taken into custody and sentenced to death. When Thomas faced the executioner, he knelt down humbly and asked the man to accept his last Bible. After taking it, the executioner carried out the death sentence.[5]

Shortly after this incident, the governor issued an edict that anyone found with one of these Bibles would be arrested. Many of the books were gathered and destroyed, although some found their way into people's homes—where they were torn up and used as wallpaper. Some who read this "wallpaper" out of curiosity were moved by the Holy Spirit to accept Jesus Christ as their Savior. Even Thomas's executioner became a Christian and, with other new believers, formed one of the first Christian congregations in what is now North Korea.

> . . . you have known the holy Scriptures, which are able to make you wise for salvation through faith in Christ Jesus. ~2 Timothy 3:15

These early Korean believers had no resources or support—there were no cathedrals or ministers. Their only spiritual guide was the written Word of God, which proved, by itself, adequate to teach, convict, and save. With their faith and their Bibles they had what was most important—a fact worth remembering if we face challenges within our own churches.

Even on Sunday

AFTER SPENDING his early years in Manchuria, Kim Eun Kook returned with his parents in 1938 to their home village near Pyongyang, Korea, where he soon started third grade in the local school. On his first day, he noticed a large white flag flying from the flagpole—with a big red circle in the middle. He didn't know what it represented, but soon learned that it was the flag of Japan.

At his first assembly, a teacher addressed the students in Japanese, which few understood. Then, one of the student leaders barked out a command, and everyone faced the same direction. Then, at the second command, everyone bowed at the waist. Joining with the others, Kim later found out they were facing east and bowing to the Japanese emperor in his Imperial Palace in Tokyo. In his classroom a large Japanese flag hung over the blackboard, and banners on the wall said, *"Long Live the Emperor"* and *"Long Live the Invincible Imperial Forces."* On one wall there was a large map of China with part of it colored red and little Japanese flag pins stuck in many of the cities.

Kim also found Sundays to be different from those in his past. His whole family was used to getting up early to prepare for church. They were Presbyterians, and since Kim's mother was the church pianist, they always went early so she could rehearse with the choir. Now, however, Kim had to leave his parents to attend a school assembly, timed every Sunday to interfere with church services. There the students heard a lecture by the Japanese principal followed by an hour of calisthenics, effectively barring them from church attendance. When she learned of this, Kim's grandmother hissed, *"Like leeches. The Japanese won't leave the children alone, even on Sundays."*[6]

Like other totalitarian regimes, wartime Japan found Christians and their faith a threat. To change a whole culture, they focused on the most impressionable members. Jesus understood the vulnerability of children and was always protective of them. He was particularly harsh in his condemnation of those who would abuse their innocence:

> But if anyone causes one of these little ones who believe in me to sin, it would be better for him to have a large millstone hung around his neck and to be drowned in the depths of the sea.
> ~Matthew 18:6

Lost Names

ON FEBRUARY 11, 1940, Kim Eun Kook and his fellow students went to school as usual. However, their teacher was waiting as they entered the classroom. He stood ominously facing the class as one student started a fire in the stove and another called the roll. Then, without looking up, he read from a paper announcing that the day had come when each student had to change his name—from Korean to Japanese. He dismissed the students so they could go with their families to the police station and formally register their new names.

As Kim trudged home through the snow, he kept thinking to himself, *I am going to lose my name; I am going to lose my name; we are all going to lose our names.*[7]

At home he found his father dressed in native Korean clothes, usually reserved for special occasions such as weddings and funerals. He was also wearing a black arm band. Together, father and son went to the police station where they joined a long line. Once inside, Kim's father took a piece of paper out of his pocket and handed it to the clerk. The clerk glanced at the paper and then dutifully wrote the name "Iwamoto" in the large ledger before him.

As they left the police station, Kim asked his father what the name meant. His father said, *"Foundation of Rock . . . on this rock I will build my church."* As Kim looked at him questioningly, he added, *"It is from the Bible."*[8]

Remaining strong in their faith, Kim and his family did not lose their identity as Koreans or as Christians. God knew their real names and did not abandon them. In spite of every effort by the Japanese to erase their culture and religion, their knowledge of who they were and to whom they belonged remained strong.

> For you created my inmost being; you knit me together in my mother's womb. ~Psalm 139:13
>
> And even the very hairs of your head are all numbered. ~Matthew 10:30
>
> He calls his own sheep by name and leads them out. ~John 10:3

Tell the Emperor

BY NOON on February 11, 1940, every pupil in Kim Eun Kook's class had registered their Japanese names with the local police. Back at school the teacher told them everyone would then go to the nearby Shinto shrine to announce their new names to the emperor. The shrine was a little wooden structure built recently on a hillside outside the village with a gabled roof, tended by a middle-aged, balding Japanese priest.

> I myself will gather the remnant of my flock out of all the countries where I have driven them and will bring them back to their pasture, where they will be fruitful and increase in number. ~Jeremiah 23:3

The small group struggled up the icy stone steps and assembled before the shrine, kneeling with bowed heads. When the priest came out, the teacher gave him the list with each student's Japanese name to be reported to the emperor. The priest, dressed in a purple and white robe and hat, then turned and read each name aloud, bowing each time. In a sing-song voice he went through a series of chants to complete the ceremony.

Later Kim, his father, and his grandfather held another ceremony at the village's nearby cemetery. There, they saw twenty or thirty other locals like them standing before the graves of their ancestors. The grandfather unwrapped a bundle he had been carrying under his arm, taking out three cups and a bottle of rice wine. After handing each a cup, he poured the wine, which they then emptied onto the graves. He poured again, and they drank—three generations of Korean men in "communion" with the past and the traditions of their own culture.[9]

In biblical times another culture was on the verge of extinction. In the fifth century BC the Assyrian empire defeated Israel, destroyed Jerusalem, and exiled the Jews to Babylon as slaves. Even through this tribulation, however, the Jewish people remained faithful to God and were eventually restored to their land.

Through decades of Japanese occupation, war, and then Communist control, a strong remnant has also remained in Korea, faithful to their Christian heritage. Those in South Korea have been obviously blessed. We can only pray that their fellow Christians in North Korea will be rewarded eventually for the persecution they have endured in the name of Jesus Christ.

Japanese Troops enter Korea c. 1904 (KoreanHistory.info)

Korean resistance early 1900s (KoreanHistory.info)

Thirty-Six Years

IN 1945 the Korean people knew little about the actual state of World War II. There were always rumors, but their only "news" came from Japanese radio, which told them nothing of the invasion of Okinawa or the destruction of Hiroshima and Nagasaki by atomic bombs. There was excitement in the air, however, on August 14 when the Japanese police told the people to listen to their radios at noon the next day. The emperor was going to speak for the first time with an important announcement about the war.

> The Spirit of the Lord is on me, because he has anointed me to preach good news to the poor. He has sent me to proclaim freedom for the prisoners and recovery of sight for the blind, to release the oppressed . . . ~Luke 4:18

At the appointed hour Kim Eun Kook, his mother, and his grandparents gathered in their home around the radio. Kim's father was absent, imprisoned in an internment camp for his activities with the resistance movement. They listened to the Japanese national anthem, and then heard the emperor's voice crackling over the airwaves, as Kim translated for his family. He could not believe what he was hearing. As everyone looked at him in bewilderment, he jumped into his grandfather's arms, shouting, *"Japan has surrendered to the Americans!"*[10]

With tears streaming down his face, the grandfather grabbed a knife from the kitchen and took Kim to his room. There, he plunged the knife into a section of the wall, cutting away the wallpaper and plaster. He pulled out a small wooden box containing several bundles wrapped in oiled paper. Opening one, he handed Kim a neatly-folded Korean flag, saying to him, *"It's yours now. Go and fly it. We are free!"*[11]

Later, Kim's mother would pray, *"For thirty-six years, Lord, for thirty-six long years, we have been praying for this day, and the day has come at last. You have blessed us with our freedom this day. Lord, keep us in your grace and guide us in this uncertain time."*[12]

Favorite Prayer

Young Harry Truman in uniform (Truman Library)

HARRY TRUMAN was not an overtly spiritual man. However, he was sustained throughout his presidency by a firm faith learned in his childhood. In his presidential papers there is a handwritten prayer on White House stationery with the following penciled note attached:

The prayer on this page has been said by me—by Harry S. Truman—from high school days, as a window washer, bottle duster, floor scrubber in an Independence, Mo., drugstore, as a timekeeper on a railroad contract gang, as an employee of a newspaper, as a bank clerk, as a farmer riding a gang plow behind four horses and mules, as a fraternity official learning to say nothing at all if good could not be said of a man, as public official judging the weaknesses and shortcomings of constituents, and as President of the United States of America. (dated 8/15/50)[13]

The prayer itself is an earnest appeal for God's guidance in all things and a model of humility:

Oh! Almighty and Everlasting God, Creator of the Heaven, Earth and the Universe:
Help me to be, to think, to act what is right, because it is right; make me truthful, honest and honorable in all things; make me intellectually honest for the sake of right and honor and without thought of reward to me. Give me the ability to be charitable, forgiving and patient with my fellowmen—help me to understand their motives and their shortcomings—even as Thou understandest mine!
Amen, Amen, Amen[14]

But when you pray, go into your room, close the door and pray to your Father, who is unseen. Then your Father, who sees what is done in secret, will reward you. And when you pray, do not keep on babbling like pagans, for they think they will be heard because of their many words. Do not be like them, for your Father knows what you need before you ask him.
~Matthew 6:6–8

To me, notable are the things the President did *not* ask for in his prayer: success, victory, or even his own good health. Although we can bring every concern to God and he hears all our prayers, I believe he is especially pleased to hear a simple, earnest appeal for honesty and patience toward others.

A Moral Code

PRESIDENT HARRY TRUMAN was asked about his views on morals and ethics. He first addressed the importance of faith in God and life after death. He then mentioned the great religious teachers of history, concluding that, *"Jesus Christ was the greatest teacher of them all—not only ancient but modern,"* and that our moral code *"comes from ancient Israel and the Sermon on the Mount."*[15] This "sermon" by Jesus is found in chapters 5 through 7 of Matthew. Speaking to his followers on a mountainside, Jesus gave them—and all mankind—radically new standards of morality:

> *Blessed are the meek (5:5).*
> *Blessed are those who hunger and thirst for righteousness (5:6).*
> *Blessed are the merciful (5:7).*
> *Blessed are the peacemakers (5:9).*
> *You have heard that it was said,*
> *"Do not murder . . ." But I tell you that anyone who is angry with his brother will be subject to judgment (5:21–22).*
> *You have heard that it was said, "Do not commit adultery." But I tell you that anyone who looks at a woman lustfully has already committed adultery with her in his heart (5:27–28).*
> *You have heard that it was said, "Eye for eye, and tooth for tooth." But I tell you, Do not resist an evil person (5:38–39).*
> *You have heard that it was said, "Love your neighbor and hate your enemy." But I tell you: Love your enemies and pray for those who persecute you (5:43–44).*
> *When you give to the needy, do not announce it with trumpets (6:2).*
> *When you pray, go into your room, close the door and pray to your Father, who is unseen (6:6).*
> *Do not store up for yourselves treasures on earth . . . But store up for yourselves treasures in heaven (6:19–20).*
> *Do not worry . . . Who of you by worrying can add a single hour to his life (6:25, 27)?*
> *Do not judge, or you too will be judged (7:1).*

Finally, Jesus' sermon included a simple command that serves as the basis for all human interaction, known simply as the "Golden Rule."

> So in everything, do to others what you would have them do to you, for this sums up the Law and the Prophets.
> ~Matthew 7:12

Three Years to Root

GEN. PAIK SUN-YUP was considered by many high-ranking American officers to be the best operational commander in the Republic of Korea (ROK) Army. At age thirty he led the First ROK Division through the difficult early stages of the war, and then went on to command a corps and eventually reach the highest level as chief of staff of the army. In spite of his great success, the Korean officer never forgot his humble beginnings and a near-disaster that almost cut his life short at age six.

> Let the little children come to me, and do not hinder them, for the kingdom of God belongs to such as these.
> ~Mark 10:14

Paik was born in 1920 to a desperately poor family in the small rural hamlet of Tokhung. When he was five years old, his mother moved their small family to Pyongyang in hopes of improving their impoverished condition. For a year, Paik, his mother, sister, and brother lived in a room that measured six-by-six feet, often without food to eat. As they neared starvation, the mother decided on a drastic course. She took her three children to the Taedong River bridge and told them they were going to jump together to their deaths. Paik was only six, but he never forgot what happened at the bridge.

> *My sister was eleven, and she quickly understood what we were doing. She looked up at Mom and appealed to her with wisdom outstripping her tender years. "It takes a tree three years to put down solid roots, and we've been here for only a year," she sobbed. "Let's wait two more years, and if we don't make it, then we can go through with this."*[16]

The often surprising wisdom of children is captured in the expression, *"Out of the mouths of babes . . ."* Jesus borrowed this phrase from the Old Testament as he responded to priests and scribes criticizing a group of children singing his praise in the temple: *"Yea, have ye never read, Out of the mouth of babes and sucklings thou hast perfected praise?"* (Matthew 21:16 KJV) Jesus often extolled the special wisdom of children and urges us to cling to simple truths with a childlike fervor. It was this grasp of a simple truth on the part of an eleven-year-old girl that brought clarity to a mother and saved Paik Sun Yup and his family.

Reward

AS THE US Armed Forces were cut back during the post-World War II years, promotion in every military service became slow and uncertain. Sensing a certain amount of frustration and even preoccupation with this situation, a senior officer in the Navy Chaplain Corps wrote a pointed article stressing the higher calling of service to the nation and to God:

> His work will be shown for what it is, because the Day will bring it to light. It will be revealed with fire, and the fire will test the quality of each man's work. If what he has built survives, he will receive his reward. If it is burned up, he will suffer loss; he will himself be saved, but only as one escaping through the flames.
> ~1 Corinthians 3:13–15

> To give unstintingly of time and talent to your religious ministry is of major importance. In this extremely materialistic age, our only hope lies in a right relationship with God. It is the chaplain's high calling to remind men of this right relationship and to demonstrate successfully a deeply religious life at its highest levels. In fulfilling this high calling, the chaplain will exalt his place as God's ambassador.
>
> How pitiful it would be to see a servant of God bitter and resentful because the temporary and passing rewards of this life did not come to him. We work for one Master—God! He will reward our unselfish efforts far beyond our hopes or dreams.
>
> To quote Thomas à Kempis: "Carry the cross patiently, and with perfect submission; and in the end it shall carry you."[17]

Chaplains and ministers are not unlike the rest of us, having a certain amount of worldly ambition and need for recognition. We can each benefit from this advice by striving to keep these things from dominating our lives. A thoughtful person will always question his or her own motives. *Am I doing this deed for myself, or for God?* Sometimes the answer to this question can be extremely difficult to

Shipboard church service (US Navy)

discern. When in doubt, I pray earnestly God will use my work to bring glory to his kingdom, even if it is motivated by my selfish and fallen nature.

Korean Service

HORACE UNDERWOOD devoted his life to serving the Korean people. The son and grandson of Presbyterian missionaries, he graduated from college in New York in 1939 and returned to Seoul to teach at the Chosen Christian College. During World War II, he joined the US Navy and served throughout the war as a Japanese and Korean language officer.

> Whoever wants to become great among you must be your servant, and whoever wants to be first must be your slave—just as the Son of Man did not come to be served, but to serve, and to give his life as a ransom for many.
> ~Matthew 20:26–28

When North Korea invaded the South in 1950, Underwood went back into the navy to help the Allied war effort with his expertise in the Korean language and geography. He was one of the few Americans to know anything about the harbor at Inchon and the treacherous Han River currents, having sailed along the Korean coast during his childhood. He helped plan the Inchon amphibious landing and was one of the first to go ashore in that operation.[18] On September 19, 1950, he swam across the Han River at night with a Marine reconnaissance party to scout enemy defenses in advance of an armored attack the next day.[19] For his military actions he was awarded the Bronze Star and the Legion of Merit.

After the Korean War, Underwood returned to Yonsei University as a professor of education and was instrumental in building the university's international education program. He was honored by the Korean Society in 2002 with the prestigious Van Fleet Award. His citation stated in part, *"No living American can match Horace G. Underwood's unique and continuing contribution to Korea and to U.S.–Korea relations."*[20] Underwood's amazing career epitomizes Christian service and the effort of countless dedicated men and women over the past century to build a vibrant Christian community in this often war-torn nation.

Respect for Authority

IN 1950 a senior naval officer delivered a speech to the citizens of Salem, Massachusetts, warning of the threat to America posed by the spread of Communism at home and abroad. His talk focused on the issues of authority and discipline. The source of our nation's problems may not be the same today, but this call to age-old values is as relevant now as ever:

One of the shrewdest weapons our enemy now employs is an insidious appeal against authority. Speaking as self-styled liberals, his agents . . . seek to make us scorn all forms of discipline as being un-democratic and un-American. Nothing, of course, can be further from the truth. Obedience to and respect for duly constituted authority is a basic duty of all citizens of a democracy. It is born in the home where we must honor our father and mother. It is carried to the schools where we even raise the teacher on a dais to overlook and command her charges. The corner policeman must have our respect and obedience as he guards our homes and shepherds our children through the dangers of traffic. We find it in court where we all, regardless of our station, rise to pay our respects to the majesty of the law.[21]

For the grace of God that brings salvation has appeared to all men. It teaches us to say "No" to ungodliness and worldly passions, and to live self-controlled, upright and godly lives in this present age, while we wait for the blessed hope—the glorious appearing of our great God and Savior, Jesus Christ . . . These, then, are the things you should teach. Encourage and rebuke with all authority.
~Titus 2:11–13, 15

This officer saw a clear threat to America's fundamental values posed by international Communism at that time in history. Whether our nation has been victimized over the years by this kind of conspiracy or has merely suffered from a self-inflicted decline of morality, there has clearly been a loss of respect for authority in general throughout American culture. Neither parents, nor teachers, nor policemen, nor judges receive the respect they once did.

My son is a public school teacher and deals too often with disrespectful students who are the unfortunate products of families with a lack of respect in the home. It is at the basic level of family and church that the values needed for a cohesive society must be taught and practiced. Discipline and respect should always remain at the forefront of those values.

Poor to Rich

WHILE STILL in seminary, Harold Berger joked that when he finished his training, someone would probably hand him ten hymnals and tell him to go find a church. In fact, a mission board gave him his first job in 1931—to start a church from scratch. He later recalled, *"They didn't even give me the hymnals."*[22] Times were hard for him and his family as he struggled through the depression years. Later, as a Veterans Administration hospital chaplain, Berger reflected on those lean years:

> *In those days we were poor, very poor. There were occasions when we counted the few pennies which represented all the money we had. There was not a crust of bread to eat. But we never went hungry. Inevitably the Lord supplied our needs; often in an astounding manner. Yes, those were difficult but happy years when we leaned hard on the staff of the Good Shepherd.*[23]

Then Jesus said to his disciples, "I tell you the truth, it is hard for a rich man to enter the kingdom of heaven. Again I tell you, it is easier for a camel to go through the eye of a needle than for a rich man to enter the kingdom of God."

When the disciples heard this, they were greatly astonished and asked, "Who then can be saved?" Jesus looked at them and said, "With man this is impossible, but with God all things are possible."

~Matthew 19:23–26

Then, thinking about his relative prosperity after World War II, he tried to explain the danger that comes from more and more disposable income:

> *The means it provides for easy and carefree living unburdened by financial concern can prove a stumbling block or a pitfall to the servant of God. It can instill one with a false sense of security. It may subtly fill one with more regard for the welfare of the body than the security of the soul. A friend once confided to a Christian mother regarding her successful son, "John is certainly getting on in the world." To which the thoughtful mother replied: "Which world?"*[24]

This is a cautionary tale for every Christian today. Our consumer society is highly focused on the things of this world, and no one is immune to the drumbeat of appeals to conscious and unconscious desires. Realizing we all fall prey to these physical and emotional demands, we are more than ever dependent on a Savior who understands our weaknesses and lifts us out of them, in spite of ourselves.

Before the Throne

SLEET WAS falling on a cold winter night as the chaplain and his wife finally climbed into a warm bed after a long day. At 2:15 a.m. the telephone rang with an urgent message—the chaplain was needed at the hospital.

As the VA hospital chaplain in Danville, Illinois, Harold Berger was used to this kind of telephone call. Still, it happened to be Christmas Eve, and the weather was miserable. He had to get up and make his way over dark, icy streets to reach the bedside of a well-loved patient named Fred. During this late-night ordeal, the chaplain actually had thoughts of the shepherds who had journeyed through the darkness to be in the stable by the bedside of their newborn King. In spite of the inconvenience, his situation seemed somehow an appropriate observance of Jesus' birthday.

> Let us then approach the throne of grace with confidence, so that we may receive mercy and find grace to help us in our time of need.
> ~Hebrews 4:16

Fred had endured months of suffering from a long illness, but his mind was clear. He was a gentleman of the old school and, in spite of his pain, was always considerate of the doctors, nurses, and many friends who came to visit. In fact, he more often gave a sympathetic ear to their problems rather than voice his own. Fred was, above all, a Christian. Every day he read his Bible and prepared himself for whatever was to come. Unfortunately, he passed away during the night—but not before he received the comfort of friendship and prayer. Chaplain Berger made a poignant observation based on Christ's promise to every faithful follower: *"For him it was truly a Merry Christmas, not before the manger of the Christ-Child, but before the throne of God."*[25]

Keeping Our Republic

Pres. Truman speaking(Truman Library)

I N A SPEECH to church leaders in September of 1951 President Harry Truman elaborated on the extent to which religion has played a role in the national life of America:

It is said that when Benjamin Franklin left the Constitutional Convention he was asked, "What have you given us?" He answered, "A republic, if you can keep it." Millions of Americans since then have believed that the keeping of our Republic depends upon keeping the deep religious convictions on which it was founded. From the worship and teachings of the synagogues and churches of our land, have come a moral integrity, a concern for justice and human welfare, a sense of human equality, a love of human freedom, and a practice of brotherhood which are necessary to the life of our national institutions.[26]

John Adams also addressed this theme soon after the US Constitution was adopted. He believed that overpowering human passions such as avarice, ambition, and greed were capable of piercing even the strongest constitutional limits. In light of this, he stated, *"Our Constitution was made for a moral and religious people. It is wholly inadequate to the government of any other."*[27]

> I will put my law in their minds and write it on their hearts. I will be their God, and they will be my people.
> ~Jeremiah 31:33

Our founders and succeeding generations of Americans have believed that America needs more than good laws. A free society needs citizens imbued with the *urge* to do good, who are also governed by objective moral constraints. People without such constraint will always find ways to circumvent the laws and the Constitution. A business school graduate applying for a job was asked recently if he believed in moral absolutes. Reflecting his secular education, he quickly and emphatically replied, "No." He was then asked, *"Then how do we know you won't cheat our customers?"*[28] He had no answer.

Television

DURING THE Korean War era, television was beginning to gain popularity as a news and entertainment medium. Statistics showed that 59 percent of urban families owned television sets. Navy chaplain wrote an article bemoaning the fact that so little of the programming in the new industry addressed religious subjects. He challenged other chaplains to use the medium to present the Christian message:

> Whoever of you loves life and desires to see many good days, keep your tongue from evil and your lips from speaking lies. Turn from evil and do good; seek peace and pursue it. The eyes of the LORD are on the righteous and his ears are attentive to their cry.
> ~Psalm 34:12–15

I think the apostle Paul would have been awed by the miracle of electronic communication—to send pictures and sermons through the air; to reproduce the voices and figures of saints long since gone—would have left him awestruck, but not for long. If these media had been given to him in his day, perhaps we would have fewer of his wonderful letters, but we would have had more Christians sooner. I think Paul would have dedicated himself most reverently to each of the new ways of communicating, that we might use it for the Glory of God. In that spirit we call upon you to join with us in rededication to the great task before us, astonished and grateful that the means to serve so widely have been placed in our hands.

The chaplain's time is valuable, but so too the chaplain must take time to use this most modern means of communicating to the families, the home churches, and the American and foreign communities, the story of the religious man in uniform. Thus, the message of the brotherhood of man and Father-hood of God can be proclaimed and television made the tool of Almighty God. Chaplains, use television![29]

A pastor in the World War II era likened the power of radio to that of prayer, with a message from one person permeating the ether to thousands of others around the world simultaneously. The same imagery applies to television, amplified even further by its visual content. Few of us are called to produce Christian programming for television. It is our duty, instead, to be discerning in what we watch, supporting what little there is that seeks to make us better and wiser, while shunning the myriad appeals to our fallen nature. We can assign television a wholesome place in God's kingdom by choosing wisely what we watch.

Sanctuary

DURING THE Korean War an article was published to help navy chaplains understand their role in the newly-enacted military justice system. In official court martial proceedings it was the responsibility of line officers to serve as members of the court and as trial and defense counsels and the responsibility of commanding officers to administer non-judicial punishment. For the system to work, however, there was a need for unofficial mediation on the part of chaplains:

> *He can explore, probably better than any other officer, the background of the difficulty. Many times he will discover that the basic cause of the breakdown of the individual's discipline lies in some perplexity, trouble, or worry at home. Many of these cases can be solved by the advice of the chaplain and the co-operation of the commanding officer. Thus, discipline is preserved, and the offender rehabilitated. Chaplains in these and other disciplinary situations should be mindful that the new Code recognizes that a person who is perplexed, troubled, or confused, needs "sanctuary."*
>
> *It is necessary for him to be able to talk and to talk confidentially without fear of disclosure by the person in whom he confides. In many situations the chaplain can, through the confidence placed in him, redirect the efforts of young men and help them to straighten out their lives.*[30]

As parents, most of us believe that our children can and should talk to us about their problems. However, we have to remember we are also their final disciplinary authority. Just like Marines and sailors in trouble, teenagers sometimes need "sanctuary." They need a sympathetic ear and a calm voice that can give advice without judgment. At times, a minister or family counselor may fill this role. More often another Christian adult who is a friend of the family and friend to the children will be able to offer this kind of safe haven. This is another powerful reason we need to have Christian friends and to be Christian friends to others—young and old alike. Is there someone for whom you can be a sanctuary? Do you have your own sanctuary?

> We do have such a high priest, who sat down at the right hand of the throne of the Majesty in heaven, and who serves in the sanctuary, the true tabernacle set up by the Lord, not by man.
> ~Hebrews 8:1–2

Plain Talk

THE DICTIONARY defines the word *abstraction* as *"the act of considering something in terms of general qualities or characteristics, apart from concrete realities."* We use abstract terms every day, such as justice and honor, to express complex concepts. Our religious language can be especially prone to this kind of language. In an article for other Korean War-era clergy, a chaplain cited a hypothetical example of what one minister might say to another: *"The vicarious atonement makes justification possible; but justification must precede sanctification."*[31] The other minister might have had no problem decoding this message, but the average person would have a lot of difficulty. In the article, the chaplain went on to make an appeal to other chaplains for more down-to-earth language in their presentation of the gospel:

> When I came to you, brothers, I did not come with eloquence or superior wisdom as I proclaimed to you the testimony about God. For I resolved to know nothing while I was with you except Jesus Christ and him crucified.
> ~1 Corinthians 2:1–2

> *People like to think concretely. Abstractions are up in the air; we need to bring them down to earth where the people are and think. We should tie our abstractions to people and things. Plain talk helps our abstractions put on work clothes and walk in our world; it shows the people how to put on grace, mercy, courage in their own lives. Our product, the Word of God, is so important we must use plain talk.*[32]

This is excellent advice today not only for ministers but for all who want to be effective in sharing the gospel with others. Many abstract words such as *grace, sin,* and *salvation* are deeply meaningful to Christians. However, unbelievers need plainer words and concrete examples. The apostle Paul was the greatest advocate for this kind of simplicity. Addressing the difficult subject of speaking in tongues, he said, *"Unless you speak intelligible words with your tongue, how will anyone know what you are saying? . . . In the church I would rather speak five intelligible words to instruct others than ten thousand words in a tongue"* (1 Corinthians 14:9, 19). In all situations Paul relied on the simple truths embodied in the ultimate concrete example: the life and death of Jesus Christ.

My Bible

LOUIS LOCHNER won the 1939 Pulitzer Prize for his reporting from Nazi Germany during the early stages of World War II. As chief of the Berlin bureau of the Associated Press, he voluntarily remained at his post when the war started and was arrested when the United States entered the war. After spending months in a Nazi prison camp, he returned home to the United States in 1942 to continue his brilliant career, reporting for NBC, lecturing, and writing books about Germany. He also returned to his Christian roots by writing articles for religious periodicals.[33] One of his essays was filled with advice for Christians on how to give tangible evidence of their faith in Christ. He told, as an example, a poignant story about a woman in a train station:

> But as for you, continue in what you have learned and have become convinced of, because you know those from whom you learned it, and how from infancy you have known the holy Scriptures, which are able to make you wise for salvation through faith in Christ Jesus.
> ~2 Timothy 3:14–15

> *In 1945 I entered Berlin with the very first American troops. The scenes of destruction, of a paralyzed economy, and especially of human suffering which I then witnessed have been indelibly engraven upon my soul. One day I walked to the railway station in which thousands upon thousands of hapless refugees were milling around who had been cruelly driven from their homes by the Russians and Poles in contravention of all humanitarian principles. I walked about among them, observing their dilapidated clothing, their paltry possession of but one suitcase or traveling bag each.*
> *Amidst all the turmoil, the crying of children, the lamentation of oldsters, I noticed a white-haired grandmother sitting on her travel bag, and reading. When I stepped nearer, I saw that she was reading her Bible, poring over the Sermon on the Mount. Here was an example of time and place where nobody except a zealous atheist would have scoffed when he saw the old lady. She was deeply engrossed in what she was reading, and I could not but observe how several of her fellow refugees sitting within hearing distance were visibly impressed as she said to me, quite simply, "My Bible is the one thing that keeps up my spirit in all the misery that has come upon me and my family."[34]*

When we see how the Bible can bring peace in the midst of the most tragic circumstances imaginable, we gain confidence that it will also provide comfort in our own troubles. No matter what dark place we are in, we will always find a beam of light in Holy Scripture.

Doctors of Music

LOUIS LOCHNER, the 1939 Pulitzer Prize-winning journalist and author, wrote an article explaining the Christian's responsibility for developing his or her God-given talents.

I believe that it is our duty as Christians to accept the challenge which God throws out to us by endowing us with natural talent . . . and to develop that talent to the glory of God and the benefit of our fellow-man.[35]

It is good to praise the Lord and make music to your name, O Most High, to proclaim your love in the morning and your faithfulness at night, to the music of the ten-stringed lyre and the melody of the harp.
~Psalm 92:1–3

Lochner was especially interested in music and observed that many doctors are blessed with musical talents above and beyond their professional skills in medicine:

A physician may be and often is an excellent musician. As professions go, I believe more medical men play instruments as amateurs than do men in any other calling. Think of the edification, the spiritual uplift that this physician can give to his fellow-men if he lets them have the benefit of his mastery of his hobby! And think how he can beautify the services of his church![36]

Lochner's comments could have been written for my own church, where two of my best friends, who also happen to be doctors, lead worship services with their music. Joe Jarrett and Frank Sloan bring *"edification and spiritual uplift"* to Trinity Episcopal Church every Sunday by using the God-given talents they have patiently and diligently developed to the benefit of their fellow Christians and to the glory of God.

Joe Jarrett and Frank Sloan lead music

Loneliness

A Dutch sailor was rescued after thirty-seven days adrift on a life-raft in the Atlantic. Ravaged by hunger and thirst, burned by the sun and wind, endangered by vulture-like sharks, he exclaimed that lonesomeness was his greatest ordeal.[37]

A CHAPLAIN told this story to illustrate the overpowering effect of loneliness when a person has no contact with other human beings. Having lived as a man, Jesus Christ was well aware of the heartache that comes with such separation. The chaplain cited a poem that conveys the profound loneliness endured by our Lord:

Alone in the barren desert
With the prowling beasts of prey,
Alone with the evil Temptor
Whom He met and held at bay.

Alone on a windswept mountain
Where He went apart for rest,
Alone with His heavenly Father
To lie on His loving breast.

Alone in the olive garden
Where His holy hands were bound,
Alone in the hall of judgment
Where His head with thorns was crowned.

Alone on a skull-like hilltop
Where His precious blood was shed,
Yea, alone He trod the winepress
In the sinner's place and stead.[38]

> And surely I am with you always, to the very end of the age.
> ~Matthew 28:20

There are times when each of us will experience loneliness due to separation or loss of loved ones. When this happens, we need to remember the One who understands this kind of pain better than anyone who ever lived. Jesus suffered the most profound loneliness possible when he walked this earth yet was sustained by the one relationship that never failed him. His heavenly Father was always there when he needed him, just as he is for us. Jesus endured human loneliness to reassure us we are never separated from the One who loves us most.

O'Hare

WHILE READING a magazine for Korean War veterans, I found a fascinating article explaining how Chicago's airport got its name. Butch O'Hare was the son of a famous Chicago lawyer who worked for Al Capone, testified against him in court, and was then killed by the mob in a blaze of gunfire.[39] His son, Butch, received an appointment to the Naval Academy and graduated in 1937 to become a pilot in the US Navy.

On February 20, 1942, O'Hare was flying combat air patrol defending his aircraft carrier, *USS Lexington,* from Japanese air attacks. When his wingman's guns jammed, he found himself alone against a formation of eight bombers headed for his ship. His actions are best described in the Medal of Honor citation awarded for his heroic deed:

> David said to the Philistine, "You come against me with sword and spear and javelin, but I come against you in name of the Lord Almighty, the God of the armies of Israel, whom you have defied.
> ~1 Samuel 17:45

Without hesitation, alone and unaided, he repeatedly attacked this enemy formation, at close range in the face of intense combined machine-gun and cannon fire. Despite this concentrated opposition, Lieutenant O'Hare, by his gallant and courageous action, his extremely skillful marksmanship in making the most of every shot of his limited amount of ammunition, shot down five enemy bombers and severely damaged a sixth before they reached the bomb release point. As a result of his gallant action—one of the most daring, if not the most daring, single action in the history of combat aviation—he undoubtedly saved his carrier from serious damage.[40]

Butch O'Hare was the US Navy's first ace of World War II and the first naval aviator to receive the Medal of Honor. In 1949 Chicago's Orchard Depot Airport was renamed O'Hare International Airport in his honor. At the west end of Terminal Two a restored Grumman F4F Wildcat is on permanent display in honor of the hero who gave the airport its name.

Opening of Japanese railroad (Govt. of Japan)

Train station in Seoul c. 1920 (KoreanHistory.Info)

A Mother's Strength

KATIE KRAMER lost two brothers in two wars. Her three children, however, knew little, until after her death in 2006, of the heartache she suffered for many years. Then, while cleaning out her attic, one of her sons discovered three boxes with her most important treasures. All the children got together to examine the contents. One box contained memorabilia from her husband of forty-two years, who had died of cancer in 1990. The other two boxes were labeled "George" and "Chuck" for her two brothers.

> She speaks with wisdom, and faithful instruction is on her tongue. She watches over the affairs of her household and does not eat the bread of idleness. Her children arise and call her blessed; her husband also, and he praises her.
> ~Proverbs 31:26–28

The children learned that Chuck had been killed on the *USS Arizona* at Pearl Harbor. The box contained his medals and a letter from President Franklin D. Roosevelt. He was their mom's older brother, and the two siblings were very close. They found letters back and forth among family members expressing the love and concern of a close-knit family. One was signed by their mother.

The other box contained information about their mom's younger brother, George. There was a high school yearbook and family photos, including many of their mother as a young girl. They also found a Western Union telegram announcing that George was killed in action in Korea and a letter of condolence from President Harry Truman. Also in the box were a Silver Star and a Purple Heart.

Katie Kramer's children had always known their mother to be a strong woman with a deep faith in God. Still, they were deeply touched by the evidence of so much tragedy, about which they had known so little, in her life. Her son, Bill, said,

> For my mom, I gained a profound admiration. She was a woman of courage and strength; one who devoted herself to her children and husband always with a sense of stubborn pride that the trials of this world would not defeat her. Her faith in God and her devotion to the ones she loved could not be denied. I shall be forever grateful to my Creator that Katie Kramer was my mom.[41]

Purple Heart

WHEN KATIE KRAMER died in 2006, her children learned some amazing family history. Her two brothers had died eleven years apart in two separate wars. In boxes hidden away in the attic her children found memorabilia that she had cherished, including two Purple Hearts, one awarded to an older brother who died on the *USS Arizona* in World War II, and a second to a younger brother who died in combat in Korea. They also found a letter signed by Secretary of the Navy Frank Pace, Jr., stating:

> *The medal, which you will receive in a short time, is of slight intrinsic value, but rich with the tradition for which Americans have so gallantly given their lives ever since the days of George Washington, whose profile and coat of arms adorn the medal.*[42]

> Keep watch over yourselves and all the flock of which the Holy Spirit has made you overseers. Be shepherds of the church of God, which he bought with his own blood. ~Acts 20:28

The Purple Heart medal is the oldest award given to members of the US military, and dates to the Revolutionary War. Washington instituted the Badge of Military Merit, a heart-shaped emblem made of purple silk, edged with a silver-colored binding, embroidered with the word "Merit." The heart was chosen to symbolize courage and devotion, while the color purple was selected because it would stand out on any uniform.[43] In 1932 the present design and name "Purple Heart" were adopted. Since World War II this award has been the only military personal decoration not requiring a nomination process. It is earned and automatically awarded to those wounded (including those killed) in action.

The Purple Heart may have little intrinsic value itself, but it does represent the incalculable value of blood spilled in defense of our nation. Of all who ever lived, our Savior, Jesus Christ, understands this kind of sacrifice. I believe he has a special blessing for the men and women who wear this medal for having given their own blood.

Purple Heart medal (US Govt.)

Acronyms

ACRONYMS ARE big in the military, helping servicemen and women remember simple things under stress. Every officer learns SMEAC, the five-paragraph operations order, used by squad leaders and division commanders alike to explain a new mission: Situation, Mission, Execution, Administration and logistics, Command and control. Amazingly, President Harry Truman likened maneuvers in politics to military tactics with his own version of SMEAC:

> Be careful that you do not forget the Lord your God, failing to observe his commands, his laws and his decrees that I am giving you this day.
> ~Deuteronomy 8:11

> *In the first paragraph you make an estimate of the enemy.*
> *In the second paragraph you make an estimate of your own condition.*
> *In the third paragraph you decide what you are going to do.*
> *The fourth paragraph—you set up your logistics and supply sources to carry out what you are going to do.*
> *And in the fifth paragraph, you tell where you are going to be so that everybody can reach you.*
> *That is all there is to politics.*[44]

There is, of course, a lot more to politics and the five-paragraph order than what President Truman mentions. Still, this little acronym can give anyone a framework for organizing others in a new undertaking.

Over the centuries, Christians have also become adept at formulating their own acronyms to remind themselves of important truths and duties. Some of my favorites:

> *ACTS—Adoration, Contrition, Thanksgiving, Supplication (how we pray)*
> *BIBLE—Basic Instructions Before Leaving Earth*
> *BUSY—Being Under Satan's Yoke*
> *JOY—Jesus First, Others Second, Yourself Last*
> *NUTS—Never Underestimate The Spirit*
> *PUSH—Pray Until Something Happens*
> *WWJD—What Would Jesus Do?*
> *WWYD—What Will You Do? (Now that you know what Jesus would do)*[45]

Susan McDonald, a good friend in my church, gave me my most useful acronym, to help keep the middle books of the New Testament straight: G.E. PHILCO—Galatians, Ephesians, Philippians, Colossians. The older I get, the more I lean on these little memory aids.

The Buck Stops

"PASSING THE buck" is an old expression for shifting responsibility to someone else. It is thought to have been originally a poker term. Tradition has it that poker players at one time used a buck-handled knife as a marker designating the dealer. If one person did not wish to deal he could "pass the buck" to the next player.

"The Buck Stops Here!" sign belonging to Pres. Harry Truman (Truman Library)

One of President Harry Truman's friends had a little desk sign made for him at the Federal Reformatory in El Reno, Oklahoma, that said, *The BUCK STOPS here.*" It was a perfect fit for the man and the job, and Truman proudly displayed it on his desk in the Oval Office. He referred to it in public statements on many occasions. At the National War College in 1952 he said, *"You know, it's easy for the Monday morning quarterback to say what the coach should have done, after the game is over. But when the decision is up before you—and on my desk I have a motto which says 'The Buck Stops Here'—the decision has to be made."*[46] In his farewell address in 1953 he asserted the same idea: *"The President— whoever he is—has to decide. He can't pass the buck to anybody."*[47]

Making decisions and taking responsibility were admirable traits of this president and a great example to others. We should each have a desk sign with the same message. Anyone in a leadership role has responsibilities that should not be shifted to others.

> If we claim to be without sin, we deceive ourselves and the truth is not in us. If we confess our sins, he is faithful and just and will forgive us our sins and purify us from all unrighteousness. ~1 John 1:8–9

The same is true on a more personal level. Scripture tells us, *"Christ Jesus came into the world to save sinners"* (1 Timothy 1:15). Our first step toward Jesus has to be taking responsibility for our own shortcomings. Only when we acknowledge our fallen nature to ourselves and confess our sins to Jesus will we be ready to receive him into our hearts. When it comes to our own salvation, the buck truly stops here.

Vocabulary

THE MARINE lexicon has many unusual words derived from the Corps' history of foreign and seagoing service. To overstressed recruits it's like learning another language. A female Marine of the Korean War era took some literary license to give a sample of new words women recruits had to make part of their vocabulary in a hurry:[48]

> For I will give you words and wisdom that none of your adversaries will be able to resist or contradict. ~Luke 21:15

ALL HANDS. *Everyone, excepting only the certifiably infirm and the dearly departed.*

ASHORE. *The world beyond Marine Corps Recruit Depot, Parris Island.*

BOONDOCKS. *The "field." A swamp or forest primeval where boots get bitten by insects.*

BULKHEAD. *A wall, against which frustrated boots may pound their empty heads.*

BOOTS. *Recruits in training.*

BUNK. *A bed, a sack, a rack on which boots' aching bodies may rest when given permission.*

DECK. *Floor; a level surface on which to place sore feet when ordered to "hit the - - - -."*

FALL IN. *Assemble at designated areas as fast as your blisters will allow.*

FIELD DAY. *The sanitization of a living space by hand, mop, and/or toothbrush.*

G.I. PARTY. *A group celebration of the virtues of hygienic living.*

HEAD. *Bathroom area. Improperly referred to as a "latrine" in the US Army.*

JUNK ON THE BUNK. *An organized display on one's rack of all gear in one's possession.*

POLICE. *Spruce up, as in "police the area" around the barracks whether or not it needs it.*

REVEILLE. *When the USMC wants boots to get out of their bunks before daybreak.*

SCIVVIES. *Whatever you wear under your uniform that males are never allowed to see.*

SQUARE AWAY. *Bring perfect order to your gear, living space, or thought patterns.*

TURN TO. *Get moving, begin, get your posterior in motion.*

Every human endeavor seems to develop its own unique vocabulary. Christians in particular need to keep this in mind as they speak in the presence of nonbelievers. We need to use words easy to understand without a background in theology.

Pride

A WRITER described the amazing changes he saw come over Marine recruits as they neared the end of boot camp:

The boots were marching sharply, feeling better psychologically, passing their tests, and beginning to believe that they were actually going to make it. They were developing a certain savoir faire about their circumstances, and with that came an increase in confidence and self-esteem. They are becoming a unit . . . a company of near-Marines who sense that they are about to be inducted in the ranks of "The Best."[49]

One of the primary objectives of boot camp is to instill pride in each new class of Marines. The trials and tribulations of recruit training build toward the ultimate award of the Globe and Anchor insignia. There is no feeling of pride to compare with that moment when a drill instructor says, *"Well done, Marine."*

Pride in the Marine Corps has been an important part of my life. However, as a Christian, I have found the subject troubling. Searching the Bible, I find sixty-three references to the word "pride," and not one speaks of it favorably.[50] We learn that *"Patience is better than pride"* (Ecclesiastes 7:8) and *"Pride goes before destruction"* (Proverbs 16:18). In spite of this, we are concerned about our children's self-esteem and feel good about ourselves when we are occasionally recognized for a job well done. Is pride a bad thing, or not?

> For it is by grace you have been saved, through faith—and this not from yourselves, it is the gift of God—not by works, so that no one can boast.
> ~Ephesians 2:8–9

Theologians could argue this question, but I believe God is okay with our feelings of satisfaction over our achievements—with one great exception. There is no room for pride in our relationship with God himself. He has provided for our salvation, and one of the great errors we commit is striving to make ourselves worthy in his sight. When we try to work our way to God, or take pride in our status, we are negating the value of his grace and the sacrifice of his Son.

To a Mother

THE MOTHER of a Marine read an article in the *Milwaukee Journal* describing Marine Corps training methods. Concerned that they were trying to eliminate all traces of individuality, she wrote a pointed letter to President Truman, stating in part:

> Everyone who competes in the games goes into strict training. They do it to get a crown that will not last; but we do it to get a crown that will last forever. Therefore I do not run like a man running aimlessly; I do not fight like a man beating the air.
> ~1 Corinthians 9:25–26

> *If we would give our dogs the same treatment, the officers of the Humane Society would prosecute us. When the boys enlist they know the training will be tough, but they think they will be treated like human beings. They forget these boys each have an immortal soul. They want these boys of ours to be soulless beasts with no personality.*
> "What shall it profit a man if he gain the whole world and lose his own soul?" (Matthew 16:26). Is this a Christian country?[51]

As might be expected, the White House sent this letter to Headquarters, Marine Corps, for an answer. The Director of Public Information wrote back on behalf of the Commandant, explaining the need for tough training to build the combat effectiveness and *esprit de corps* for which the Marine Corps has always been famous. He then addressed the spiritual issues raised by the mother:

> *As far as the spiritual well-being of our men is concerned, the Marine Corps realizes that fighting men must keep with them the religious principles learned at home. Marines who command have a deep and abiding regard for the spiritual lives of the men. We are assisted in performing our religious duties by a valiant, self-sacrificing and respected corps of Navy chaplains. Divine services at sea or on a lonely island may be amid strange surroundings, but the prayers and hymns are the same. Although our men may be dressed in dungarees, instead of their "Sunday best," they are, for the most part, the same men who would be going to church were they at home.*
> *It has been said that there are no atheists in foxholes nor in the gun turrets of our fighting ships at sea. In our training or on the battlefield, Marines turn to God in no uncertain manner.*
> *Mrs. _____, You need not fear for the young man entrusted to our care.[52]*

Perseverance

A YOUNG WOMAN Marine described the rigors of recruit training in the Korean War era:

(USMC)

Boot camp was hell. Running all the time. We never walked, it seemed. DIs who acted like they hated us. Food that was not like mother used to make. Shots and physicals. Sand fleas that chewed tender parts of your body. Ironing and pressing our fatigues till the creases would cut butter. It was hard but we made it. I feel sorry for those girls who couldn't tough it out . . . They have never known their strength and true grit.[53]

I have never met a person who completed Marine Corps boot camp who didn't feel he or she benefited from the experience. Not that they would want to do it again. The hard things we do in life are usually not fun at the time and are seen to be beneficial only in retrospect. Marine recruits eventually realize they are able to function under the pressure of combat due to the rigorous training they endured earlier. It is true that we get stronger when we endure and overcome any challenge.

When we experience our hard times, it is important to realize that these are also training opportunities—if we use them to draw closer to God. He doesn't cause our problems, but he is always there to help us through them. And if we learn to lean on him more completely, then there is no crisis that can't eventually be a blessing. The apostle Paul endured his own tribulations, and gave us God's perspective on human suffering and the greatest encouragement ever conceived to persevere in our trials.

> We rejoice in the hope of the glory of God. Not only so, but we also rejoice in our sufferings, because we know that suffering produces perseverance; perseverance, character; and character, hope. And hope does not disappoint us, because God has poured out his love into our hearts by the Holy Spirit, whom he has given us. ~Romans 5:2–5

A Pretty Piece of Cloth

WHEN JOHN GLENN reported to First Marine Air Wing at K-3 Airbase near P'ohang, Korea, he found an area typical of wartime Korea: barren hills, low buildings and huts, and people bundled up against the bitter cold, walking or biking wherever they had to go. The somber scene made separation from his family all the more poignant.

Glenn was keenly aware he would miss his daughter Lyn's sixth birthday. As the day approached he wrote her a heartfelt letter to explain why he was away, in words that a six-year-old could understand. Trying to describe Communist aggression, he told her, *"It's a little like when you play house with some of the other girls. It's no fun if one of the children always insists on being the boss and tells everyone what to do all the time, is it?"*[54] On a more positive note, he explained to his daughter what America stands for—reminding her of the flag:

> *Our flag represents all the things we believe our country should be. It means that children can go to school, the mothers and fathers can have homes and raise their children the way they want, and live the lives they choose. So when you see our flag, think of that. The flag is not just a pretty piece of cloth to look bright and make a nice decoration. It stands for all those things I've been talking about that make our country, the United States, so different and better.*[55]

Warriors have great reverence for the symbol of what they fight for—in this case, the flag of our nation. The symbol of our faith is even more meaningful in what it represents. The cross of our Savior depicts the means of his execution while reminding us his death was not the end of the story—but the beginning of his reign in heaven. As warriors for Jesus we look to the cross for inspiration that we, too, will rise in the face of whatever difficulty we meet.

> For Christ did not send me to baptize, but to preach the gospel—not with words of human wisdom, lest the cross of Christ be emptied of its power. For the message of the cross is foolishness to those who are perishing, but to us who are being saved it is the power of God.
> ~1 Corinthians 1:17–18

Not to Be Discouraged

PRESIDENT HARRY TRUMAN received many letters, including praise, criticism, and requests of every kind. He was a noted letter writer himself and tried to answer much of his own correspondence. It was also his nature to give advice. On one occasion he heard from a woman who was disappointed her son could not get a navy commission. Truman wrote to her:

> Have I not commanded you? Be strong and courageous. Do not be terrified; do not be discouraged, for the LORD your God will be with you wherever you go.
> ~Joshua 1:9

A long time ago I was refused entrance to both Annapolis and West Point because I couldn't see. Years after that I was instrumental in helping to organize a National Guard battery—that was in 1905. When the First World War came along, due to the fact that I had done a lot of studying, I was made a first lieutenant in the 129th Field Artillery in battery "F." I attended the Fort Sill, Oklahoma, school of fire control and several other special schools. Finally I became a battery commander and an instructor in the field Artillery firing for the regiment and the brigade.

After the First World War, I organized the first Reserve Officers Association in the United States and became its President. Luckily, or unluckily, I then got into a political career, and you know the result. So you tell that son of yours not to be discouraged because he can't get exactly what he wants now. The thing is to take the next best, make the most of it, and you never can tell what will happen.[56]

These words from an American president should encourage every young person. Everyone has disappointments, many painful. In the long run, however, it's not the disappointments that matter. What matters is what we do next. As an aspiring actress, my daughter, Anastasia, auditioned unsuccessfully many times. However, she never lost heart and never stopped learning. Her perseverance led to many great theater, movie, and television roles.

An oft-heard expression among Christians is, "When God closes one door, he opens another." Our faith that God is in control gives us the confidence to face our disappointments with courage and resolve, and the optimism to always hope for something better.

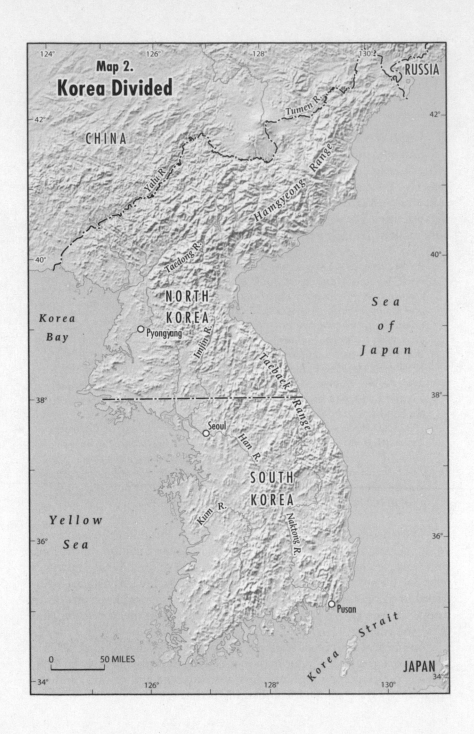

Map 2.
Korea Divided

124° 126° 128° 130°

RUSSIA

Tumen R.

42°

CHINA

Yalu R.

Hamgyeong Range

40°

Taedong R.

NORTH
KOREA

○ Pyongyang

Imjin R.

Korea
Bay

Sea
of
Japan

Taebaek Range

38°

○ Seoul

Han R.

SOUTH
KOREA

Kum R.

Yellow
Sea

Naktong R.

36°

○ Pusan

Korea Strait

0   50 MILES

JAPAN

34°

WORLD WAR II

A S THE JAPANESE invaded China in 1937, they sought to further
solidify Korea as an integral part of their expanding empire. Korea's
key strategic position, raw materials, and manpower were all important
to Japan's ambitions. An important part of this shift was an overt effort
to virtually extinguish Korean culture. The Japanese language was sub-
stituted for Korean in the education system, and Koreans were made to
adopt Japanese names. The Japanese even tried to impose their state religion on the Korean people, forcing them to worship at Shinto shrines and
pay reverence to the emperor.[57]

These efforts to eradicate Korean culture continued and intensified
after the outbreak of World War II under an ever harsher Japanese
wartime administration. Agricultural and industrial production increased
to support the war effort. After having little success with voluntary recruit-
ment, the Japanese conscripted thousands of Korean men for military service, mostly as laborers. Women were conscripted as virtual sex slaves,
referred to euphemistically as "comfort women."

On December 1, 1943, the war-weary people of Korea received their
first words of encouragement from the outside world as President Franklin
Roosevelt, Prime Minister Winston Churchill, and Generalissimo Chiang
Kai-shek met in Cairo, Egypt, to clarify the Allies' war aims toward Japan.
They issued the following statement: "The aforesaid three great powers,
mindful of the enslavement of the people of Korea, are determined that
in due course Korea shall become free and independent."[58]

Korea was never a theater of conflict during World War II and was
consequently given relatively little attention by Allied war planners. In
August 1945, however, a few days after the atomic bombs were dropped
on Hiroshima and Nagasaki, Russia declared war on Japan and invaded
Manchuria and Korea. With no military presence in Korea, US officials
proposed the 38th parallel as an arbitrary demarcation line between US
and Russian zones to facilitate the surrender of Japanese forces. At the
time, the line was meant to be temporary, and only later took on a formal
permanence. The line itself was completely arbitrary, cutting across roads,
rivers, and boundaries, and separating the more industrial north from the
primarily agricultural south.

The first US military forces, under Lt. Gen. John Hodge, arrived in September 1945 to face a country in chaos. As the Japanese technicians and administrators were expelled, the infrastructure of the country practically collapsed.[59] General Hodge had to provide aid and maintain order until some kind of international resolution could be reached about Korea's political future. After direct negotiations with the Soviets failed, the United States submitted the Korean problem to the United Nations in 1947.

Within months the UN General Assembly recognized Korea's independence and provided for the establishment of a national government and withdrawal of occupation forces. A UN commission then went to Korea to supervise elections in May 1948. The Soviet Union rejected the UN action and did not admit the commission to the Soviet-occupied zone. In the south a National Assembly was elected and the Republic of Korea was established with Syngman Rhee as its first president. Within less than a month the Communist regime in the North proclaimed the Democratic People's Republic of Korea under Kim Il Sung. Both governments claimed authority over all Korea.

US occupation forces were withdrawn from South Korea by June 1949 except for a few military advisors, shifting the burden of reconstruction to the Department of State. The missionary community also resumed its work in the country, continuing its own unique contribution to the developing nation. A Department of State official in South Korea explained:

> *Since the 1880s, missionaries have been laying the groundwork for the adoption of Western standards of government, economy, and religion. By 1950 the physical evidence of their presence was staggering. From the Yalu to Pusan could be found the hospitals, schools, colleges, universities, churches, and cathedrals built by the labors of their converts. In Seoul alone there were 190 Protestant churches, while in Pyongyang . . . there were once forty thousand Christians.[60]*

By 1950, a South Korean army had been formed but was lightly equipped due to US fears the Rhee government might be overly aggressive in its desire to forcefully reunify the country. The Soviets had no such reservations in North Korea where a well-equipped, mechanized army was put into place.

Men of Strong Faith

ADMIRAL CHESTER NIMITZ commanded the US Pacific fleet during World War II and was the principal architect of the greatest naval victory in US history. At Midway in 1942 his small fleet of three aircraft carriers met and defeated an immense Japanese armada bent on destroying those carriers. Due to the skill of the US airmen, great decision making, and an amazing sequence of fortunate events, this battle was rightfully called the "Miracle of Midway."

Nimitz was promoted to the rank of Fleet Admiral in 1944, the first naval officer to wear five stars. In 1951 he wrote an article for *Guideposts* magazine explaining the nature of Communism and the response required from free nations to oppose it. In the article he emphasized the spiritual nature of the struggle:

> Surely this great nation is a wise and understanding people. What other nation is so great as to have their gods near them the way the Lord our God is near us whenever we pray to him? And what other nation is so great as to have such righteous decrees and laws as this body of laws I am setting before you today?
> ~Deuteronomy 4:6–8

Our strongest attributes are our spiritual and moral principles. Thoughtful men regardless of race or creed are coming to the conclusion in ever increasing numbers that only through a great religious revitalization will emerge the answers to the world problems of today.

Again we must fully train and equip ourselves with emphasis on spiritual and moral lines—before America can take (the) complete offensive in a battle for our way of life. The preservation of our way of life depends on men of strong faith.[61]

John Adams, one of our great Founding Fathers, said, *"Our Constitution was made only for a moral and religious people. It is wholly inadequate to the government of any other."*[62] Nimitz is echoing this truth for a later generation of Americans. America does indeed have spiritual roots that go back to its founding, and these roots have always served as the basis for her cohesion and strength. Men and women of strong faith are as vital to this nation today as ever.

In His Will

THE REV. ROBERT RAYBURN was surprised and shocked when he was recalled to active duty for the Korean War. He had served as a chaplain in Europe during World War II and had already experienced the loneliness and heartache of wartime separation from his family. In 1950 he was content and happily pastoring the College Church at Wheaton, Illinois, when the summons came. As an "inactive" reservist he had been assured that he would be the very last to be called in a national emergency, and he greeted the notice with a certain amount of resentment. Had he not already done his part in military service to the nation?

Upon reporting for active duty at Camp Carson, Colorado, Rayburn was further assured that he did not have to worry about going overseas in the near future. He made all the arrangements to bring his family to Colorado, and, on the day of the move, received further orders to the Far East. Again, he could not understand why this was happening to him. There seemed to be so many other chaplains who had never served overseas.

> And he who searches our hearts knows the mind of the Spirit, because the Spirit intercedes for the saints in accordance with God's will. And we know that in all things God works for the good of those who love him, who have been called according to his purpose.
> ~Romans 8:27–28

During the long sea voyage to Korea, the chaplain did some serious praying and soul-searching. It wasn't long before the Holy Spirit began working on his heart. He had preached often that God did not make mistakes in directing the lives of his followers. His thoughts went back again and again to Romans 8:28, as he began to see more clearly that he had been called *"according to his purpose."* He knew that, even if a person had everything he wanted, but was not in God's will, he would be miserable. He also knew, on the other hand,

He may be sitting in the mud of a Korean rice paddy without any comforts or conveniences, far from those who are dear to him on earth and his heart will be singing a glad song if he is conscious of the fact that he is in the Lord's will, where the Lord wants him to be.[63]

Koreans with Japanese Army in Manchuria c. 1930 (Govt. of Japan)

Allied leaders meet in Cairo, 1943 (National Archives)

Clerks

AS AN OFFICIAL in the US Information Service, John Caldwell had the task of explaining the American way of life to the people of Korea. With ten provincial centers and more than three hundred Korean employees he coordinated a multitude of programs, including displays and movies designed by experts in Washington. Regardless of the resources and expertise devoted to these programs, he learned that nothing equaled the importance of the people doing their jobs in-country:

> *I have become convinced, from my experiences in China and Korea, that the clerk or stenographer is in the final analysis more important than the Secretary of State or even the President. In his or her daily life, the clerk or stenographer will make friends or enemies for America. Regardless of the merit of our product, the final acceptance of it will depend upon the people who carry it abroad.*[64]

Any person in business will echo these sentiments. Millions of dollars and vast amounts of expertise may be invested to create a great store, product, or service. Success or failure, however, depends on the lowest-paid person on the payroll—the clerk who interacts with the public. Business leaders ignore this fact at their own peril. They must focus their attention on their main people—the ones on the front line.

This fact should be a source of inspiration to all who work in God's kingdom. The clergy and other church leaders have their roles. It is the ordinary members of the church, however, who work and play in the outside world. As we do this, we gain standing among other people who share our joys and frustrations. Every day we have the opportunity to represent Christ to the world by the way we live our lives and the compassion we show others. There is much to be done in God's service, but there is no greater work than this.

> And now, O Israel, what does the LORD your God ask of you but to fear the LORD your God, to walk in all his ways, to love him, to serve the LORD you God with all your heart and with all your soul?
> ~Deuteronomy 10:12

Guarantor

IN 1948 JOHN CALDWELL was a State Department official assigned as Deputy Director of the new US Information Service (USIS) in Korea. It was his mission to explain American culture to the Korean people through radio, movies, exhibits, language classes, and written material. The USIS headquarters was in Seoul, occupying a four-story building in the center of the city. The centerpiece of the facility was an eighteen-thousand-volume library open to the public. Even though many of the Koreans could not read the books or magazines, they enjoyed leafing through them and looking at the pictures. Students also used the library for academic purposes.

> Having believed, you were marked in him with a seal, the promised Holy Spirit, who is a deposit guaranteeing our inheritance until the redemption of those who are God's possession—to the praise of his glory.
> ~Ephesians 1:13–14

Caldwell was especially proud of his library's policy of free circulation, mirroring how this was done in America. This was a revolutionary concept to the Koreans who operated their own libraries on the Japanese model, learned during the occupation. Anyone wanting to see a book had to go through an attendant. Caldwell was warned that letting books go out on loan would result in prohibitive losses. He felt strongly, however, that the books best served their purpose circulating in homes and classrooms. To solve the problem, he instituted a "guarantor" system:

> *In the Orient, a guarantor is part of both business and academic routine. A guarantor is one who recommends another and guarantees that the individual recommended will not steal and will make good. Following this pattern, our borrowers' cards carried a place where a guarantor signed, agreeing to pay for the book if it were lost or stolen.*[65]

Amazingly, God also has a guarantor system for those who accept the gospel of salvation. For those who believe in his Son, Jesus Christ, he gives the Holy Spirit as a guarantee of what is to come and a taste of what that future will be like. We cannot imagine the blessings that await us in the next life, but we get a sense of what it will be like through the Holy Spirit working within us now.

Wisdom

IN HIS FIRST address to Congress in 1945 President Truman asked for help and cooperation from the elected leaders of the nation and from the American people. He also asked for God's guidance, repeating the prayer of King Solomon: *"Give therefore thy servant an understanding heart to judge thy people, that I may discern between good and bad; for who is able to judge this thy so great a people?"* (1 Kings 3:9 KJV).[66]

Looking back four years later, as he prepared his State of the Union message for the Eighty-First Congress, he recalled receiving the cooperation he had asked for but only for so long as the war lasted. Afterward, he felt he had been subject to unreasonable vilification by Congress, columnists, and commentators. As a preamble to his speech, he made a series of notes for himself cataloguing many of these grievances. Wisely, he ultimately chose not to include these notes in his speech. Still, they have been preserved and give a valuable insight into the spiritual nature of a great, but controversial, president:

> *Now all I want to do is to carry out that people's mandate. I only want peace in the world and a fair deal for every part of the population of this great nation. I want your help and cooperation. You have learned that the people do not believe in the kept press and the paid radio and that they have no patience with the man who lets a poll be his conscience.*
>
> *We have the greatest republic in the world if we remember that the people elect us to do what we think is right and not what some pollster or misguided editorial writer tells us to do. I pray (to) God constantly for guidance. I hope you will do that too. Then this great country which God has chosen to lead the world to peace and prosperity will succeed in that undertaking.*[67]

Give me now wisdom and knowledge, that I may go out and come in before this people: for who can judge this thy people, that is so great?
~2 Chronicles 1:10 (KJV)

President Truman also quoted another great Bible passage asking God for wisdom to lead a great people:

Sacred Birds

CRANES ARE a revered species of bird throughout much of Asia. The sarus crane (*Grus antigone*) can reach a height of six feet and is the tallest flying bird on Earth. Its name in some cultures is synonymous with goodness, and, since it mates for life, it has become a symbol for virtue and fidelity. The crane was a holy messenger for the Hindu deity Vishnu and inspired the great Indian epic called the *Ramayana,* beloved throughout southern Asia. Outside the Hall of Supreme Harmony in Beijing two majestic bronze cranes stand majestically, symbolizing long life and good fortune. The species has been long protected by Hindus and Buddhists wherever their cultures have spread.[68]

> And God said, "Let the water teem with living creatures, and let birds fly above the earth across the expanse of the sky." So God created the great creatures of the sea and every living and moving thing with which the water teems, according to their kinds, and every winged bird according to its kind. And God saw that it was good. ~Genesis 1:20–21

Two of the great crane species, the red-crowned (*Grus japonensis*) and white-naped (*Grus vipio*) have migrated down the Korean peninsula for centuries, taking advantage of the tranquil wetland areas of the Chorwon Basin and the Imjin and Han rivers. These migratory patterns were unfortunately disrupted completely by the outbreak of hostilities in these areas during the Korean War. The area that became known as the "Iron Triangle," bordered by Pyonggang, Kumhwa, and Chorwon, was actually the scene of some of the most bitter fighting of the war. This violence shattered the silent sanctuary and still waters needed by the great birds and many were killed for food by a desperate and starving population of refugees.

The folly of mankind that almost killed off some of God's most beautiful creatures would eventually bring them back, unintentionally—the subject of another story. Amazingly, the cranes would survive the devastation of war.

Crane

Accidental Sanctuary

WHEN THE Korean War cease-fire took effect on July 27, 1953, the guns fell mercifully silent along the battle-scarred front line, which cut diagonally across the peninsula from one coast to the other. Under the agreement the forces pulled back two thousand meters from the line, creating a buffer zone of four thousand meters, or about two-and-a-half miles. This left an area with an unknown quantity of unexpended ordnance and minefields guarded by hundreds of thousands of troops who continued to regard each other suspiciously, only from a greater distance. Over many decades, the Korean Demilitarized Zone (DMZ) has gradually taken on another function unnoticed by most of the world, but described by naturalist Peter Matthiessen:

> He makes springs pour water into the ravines; it flows between the mountains. They give water to all the beasts of the field; the wild donkeys quench their thirst. The birds of the air nest by the waters; they sing among the branches.
> ~Psalm 104:10–12

> *Since a region from which Homo sapiens has been excluded is inevitably hospitable to other species, what had been created, in effect, was a no-man's land several miles across and 149 miles long (about 375 square miles altogether), with streams and springs that remained open all winter—the most fiercely protected wildlife sanctuary anywhere on earth, and an accidental paradise for the great cranes.*[69]

Since the combatants in the war were generally unaware of the departure of the majestic birds, their return was also little noticed. During the 1960s naturalists began to see small numbers of red-crowned and white-naped cranes wintering along the Imjin River and the Panmunjom Valley, and by the 1970s, both species had returned in large numbers to the Chorwon Basin. Some of the most bitterly contested terrain ever fought over had finally become an ideal habitat for Asia's most respected creatures. A professor of environmental biology at the Korean National University has observed something profoundly symbolic about this phenomenon: *"In Korea, too, turumi (the crane) is well known to bring long life and good fortune . . . And now—because they are most numerous in the border region where so many young men died—the crane is our symbol of peace."*[70]

Ingenuity

IVAN BENNETT was the Chief of Far East Command Chaplains early in the Korean War and was known for his ingenuity in working with senior officers on Gen. Douglas MacArthur's staff. One of his first projects was to get an English-Korean language hymnbook published for chaplains in the war zone. After running into a stone wall trying to get funds from the staff for printing, he tried a different approach. He went directly to Gen. MacArthur and proposed a foreword to the hymnbook that the general would sign. When Gen. MacArthur agreed to this, Bennett went back to the staff officer in charge of the pursestrings and suggested it might be a good idea to have a hymnal to go with the general's foreword. Amused and somewhat chagrined, the officer said, *"Okay, Chaplain, you've got me again."*[71]

There is always room for a little ingenuity in doing God's work—in this case, even appealing to the lesser instincts of certain individuals. Chaplain Bennett knew the general's pride and the staff officer's fear would both come into play to achieve a worthwhile goal. The apostle Paul reached a similar conclusion as he sought to carry forward the gospel to different kinds of people, including Jews and Gentiles, educated and uneducated, etc. As he explained to the church in Corinth, he tried to be like the people he encountered so he could identify with them and have the greatest influence with each. This may strike some as slightly unethical, unless the object of Paul's effort is understood: to save people's souls. He said, *"I am compelled to preach. Woe to me if I do not preach the gospel!"* (1 Corinthians 9:16).

> Though I am free and belong to no man, I make myself a slave to everyone, to win as many as possible. To the Jews I became like a Jew, to win the Jews. To those under the law I became like one under the law . . . so as to win those under the law. To those not having the law I became like one not having the law . . . so as to win those not having the law. To the weak I became weak. I have become all things to all men so that by all possible means I might save some.
> ~1 Corinthians 9:19–22

Pushing Back

BETWEEN WORLD WAR II and the Korean War, Bruce Livingston served in China as a noncommissioned officer with the Fifth Marines. One of his first duties was guarding coal trains running from northern China to Peking (now called Beijing). Coal was a valuable commodity everywhere in this war-torn country devastated and depleted of resources.

On one of his first runs Livingston couldn't help but notice a group of young Chinese boys running alongside the train making obscene gestures and shouting insults at him. In irritation, he threw lumps of coal at the ill-mannered urchins. He continued this exchange until he noticed that each of the boys had a bag and was carefully picking up each piece of coal he threw. He had to laugh as he realized the point of their abuse.[72]

> He causes his sun to rise on the evil and the good, and sends rain on the righteous and the unrighteous. If you love those who love you, what reward will you get? ~Matthew 5:45–46

I think I observed the same kind of clever manipulation recently when my two-year-old granddaughter had a meltdown while traveling in the car with her parents and grandparents. There was no apparent reason for the temper tantrum, and there was little success in pacifying it. This pointless behavior was, however, very successful in commanding the undivided attention of four adults for a good part of the journey.

In our everyday lives we often run into irritating situations and people. Our tendency as human beings is to push back against those who are ill-mannered or ill-intentioned, responding in kind to their actions. As Christians, however, we are called to look beyond this kind of behavior. Jesus admonished us, *"If someone strikes you on the right cheek, turn to him the other also"* (Matthew 5:39), which isn't necessarily a passive acceptance of abuse. When we make a positive effort to better understand another's motives, we can see their actions from a new perspective and perhaps find the basis for a better relationship. Also, when we are able to view others as God's fallen children, like ourselves, it is hard to be too angry at any irritating behavior.

Prisoner of the Law

SOON OK LEE was born in northern Korea three years before the start of the Korean War. Her father had fought for Korea's independence with Kim Il Sung, and became a privileged member of North Korean society. The girl attended the best schools and was brought into the Communist Party at an early age. Before she was thirty, she attained a supervisory position in a major distribution center. She married a respected teacher, had one child, and functioned diligently within the system in which she had been indoctrinated from childhood. She said, *"Every moment, awake or asleep, I devoted to the Party. I never questioned the Party's doctrine, but accepted it as absolute fact."*[73]

The ground in her world took a sudden shift in 1986 when she was put in charge of distributing a special fabric imported from China for use in making fashionable jackets patterned after one worn by Kim Jong Il, the dictator's son. The head of the KGB-like Public Security Bureau asked for twice the allotted amount, and Soon Ok refused the request, trying to fairly carry out her duties. Within a few days, she was arrested in her office, placed on a train with armed guards, and delivered to prison in Chongjin. She soon learned she was accused of accepting bribes and showing favoritism. Since there was no evidence against her, a torture-filled interrogation began for the stated purpose of eliciting a confession. For fourteen months she was threatened, beaten, nearly suffocated, made to stand in freezing conditions without clothes for hours, and deprived of sleep and food.

> For in my inner being I delight in God's law; but I see another law at work in the members of my body, waging war against the law of my mind and making me a prisoner of the law of sin at work within my members. ~Romans 7:22–23

As this ordeal continued, her belief system and faith in Communism began to crumble. Hatred grew within her toward a system that could so unfairly single out one person for unlimited abuse in order to cover up the crimes of others. Her hatred would sustain her through years of imprisonment as she sought something to fill this terrible void within her.

The Believers

AS A NORTH Korean citizen, Soon Ok Lee learned at an early age that there was only one supreme authority in the land: Kim Il Sung. Any form of religious belief that threatened the absolute power of the dictator was suppressed and persecuted. *"All my life,"* Soon Ok said, *"I had been taught that religion was like a drug. I learned in school that religion paralyzes human creativity and logic. I was well trained to never think about God's existence."*[74] In spite of her anti-religious upbringing, when Soon Ok Lee faced the depravity of her life in prison, she discovered a spark of interest about God somewhere inside herself. In despair and frustration she began to look upward and cry, *"Why are you doing this to me?"*[75]

> My heart says of you,
> "Seek his face!" Your
> face, LORD, I will seek.
> ~Psalm 27:8

In the North Korean prison system Soon Ok Lee found herself among Christians and other religious believers for the first time. The life of these people was worse than that of the other prisoners because the guards were given incentives to make them recant their beliefs. They were given the worst abuse and most dangerous jobs.

As she observed these people Soon Ok began to notice certain profound differences in their behavior from that of the others. It was not uncommon for prisoners to lie about each other to the authorities to gain favor or shift the blame for their mistakes. However, the Christians never did this. Not only did they never falsely accuse others, many of them instead took the blame for others. She also saw many singled out for special beatings. She was amazed that many of them continued to pray and sing hymns throughout these ordeals. She never saw one of them recant his or her beliefs.

As she watched the faith of these Christians in action, Soon Ok began to ask herself: *"What did they see, and what am I missing?"*[76]

Our Favorite Guard

EDDY MCCABE enlisted in the Marine Corps out of high school in 1948. In June 1950 he was with the Second Marines at Camp Lejeune, North Carolina, when his entire regiment was reassigned to the First Division. Within weeks his unit boarded transport ships in San Diego, California, bound for Japan and Korea. It was a tearful scene on the docks as the ships pulled away, with families waving goodbye and everyone singing *Auld Lang Syne*.

As his ship pulled into Kobe, Japan, McCabe witnessed an amazing incident. It was one of those incredible coincidences that almost defy belief. A member of his unit named Olawski spotted a Japanese worker on the dock. As soon as he could, he left the ship, found the worker, and, as everyone watched, gave the man a big hug. They then spent some time together laughing and talking. McCabe and the other Marines were mystified. They knew Olawski had been captured during World War II shortly after Pearl Harbor and had spent the entire war in a Japanese prisoner-of-war (POW) camp. They couldn't comprehend the scene of goodwill playing out on the dock between someone who had suffered as a POW and a Japanese civilian. Later, the answer was revealed as Olawski explained:

> A kind man benefits himself, but a cruel man brings trouble on himself. ~Proverbs 11:17
>
> Be kind and compassionate to one another, forgiving each other, just as in Christ God forgave you. ~Ephesians 4:32

> *That guy was our favorite guard in the prison camp I was in during World War II. He'd always try to get us a little extra food, some smokes, things like that. There are Americans who are alive today because of that guy.* [77]

Most stories from Japanese POW camps tell of brutal treatment. The Japanese military code did not tolerate surrender within their own ranks, and enemy troops that surrendered to them consequentially got little respect. It is uplifting to hear evidence that, in spite of this, not all kindness and goodwill had disappeared.

Integration

ENDING RACIAL segregation in America was a long and difficult process. The military services were at the forefront of this struggle, often reflecting the crosscurrents of attitudes within the nation as a whole. In general, the Armed Forces have successfully led the way in breaking down these longstanding barriers to racial desegregation.

> You are all sons of God through faith in Christ Jesus ... There is neither Jew nor Greek, slave nor free, male nor female, for you are all one in Christ Jesus.
> ~Galatians 3:26, 28

During World War II black Americans were inducted into the services but then served in segregated units. Even after President Harry Truman issued Executive Order 9981 in 1948 declaring *"there shall be equality of treatment and opportunity for all persons in the armed forces without regard to race or color,"*[78] full integration of military units took years to accomplish. There were instances, however, when it happened immediately.

Marine General Victor Krulak recalled his experience commanding a logistical unit at Camp Pendleton in 1948. The order came down from the Secretary of the Navy specifying that, *"Henceforward, no member of the Naval Service shall be promoted, reduced, billeted, messed, disciplined or otherwise administered in regard to race, color or creed."*[79]

So far as Krulak was concerned, this meant simply that segregation was over. Within his command there was one black unit, the Depot Company. He immediately reassigned every man but one out of the company into other units. He said, *"That was it. Throughout the Corps it was the same. We were integrated and that's all there was to it. I don't remember it being a problem in Korea."*[80] Actually, the Korean War would be the first time black and white Marines served together in combat units. Old attitudes did not always disappear quickly, but the military continued to lead the way in reducing racial barriers in America.

Black Marine

BOB SMITH was a young black man who wanted a military career and a "man's life." He enlisted in the Marine Corps in 1949. Even though the services were officially desegregated the year before, racial attitudes did not change overnight. He went to a black boot camp at Camp Lejeune, North Carolina, where black noncommissioned officers (NCOs) were in charge. There were, however, no black officers.

In the units he served with, Smith found prejudice among Marines, both white and black. There were black Marines who banded together and stirred up trouble. There were whites who continued to resist racial mixing. He commented, *"I've served with plenty of Marines, black and white, who I've thought were idiots. I've tried to stay away from these people."*[81]

Soldiers man machine gun (National Archives)

Since he was a career Marine, Smith was assigned duty as a fire team leader in the newly-organized Seventh Marines, training for deployment to Korea in 1950. Some of the reservists in his team had a problem at first with a black man being in charge. This changed as he proved his ability and asserted his authority. In fact, he saw more division between regulars and reservists than he did between the races. The regulars, or old-timers, always stuck together, regardless of race. He particularly recalled several liberties spent off-base with other regulars, black and white, before going off to war. Eventually, racial consciousness would practically disappear among all ranks, as combat proved to be the big equalizer of racial attitudes:

> *On the twenty-ninth of August we left the States for Korea. It was there that we found out we were going to have a lot more trouble with the North Koreans and Chinese than we'd had with each other. And when we got to the Chosin, we were to have more trouble with the weather than anything else.*[82]

> Pray for those who persecute you, that you may be sons of your Father in heaven. He causes his sun to rise on the evil and the good, and sends rain on the righteous and the unrighteous.
> ~Matthew 5:44–45

Obligations

It is not enough to congratulate ourselves upon the religious spirit of our forebears. We must ask ourselves if we truly believe the things which they believed. We must examine our conduct to see whether we are carrying out in our daily lives the ideals we profess.[83]

Faith by itself, if it is not accompanied by action, is dead. ~James 2:17

IN SPEAKING to a group of Christian church-going men, President Harry Truman reviewed the religious basis of America's founding. He told them it was good to look back at those beginnings and to rededicate themselves to those ideals. However, he went on to discuss what this rich heritage means for those living now:

> *Our religious heritage imposes great obligations upon us. It does not permit us to be self-satisfied and complacent. Indeed, if we accept the faith which has been handed down to us, our task as a Nation is much more difficult. We cannot be satisfied with things as they are. We must always be striving to live up to our beliefs and to make things better in accordance with the divine commandments.*
>
> *The people of Israel, you will remember, did not, because of their covenant with God, have an easier time than other nations. Their standards were higher than those of other nations and the judgment upon them and their shortcomings were more terrible. A religious heritage, such as ours, is not a comfortable thing to live with. It does not mean that we are more virtuous than other people. Instead, it means that we have less excuse for doing the wrong thing—because we are taught right from wrong.*
>
> *We must remember that the test of our religious principles lies not in what we say, not only in our prayers, or even in living blameless personal lives—but in what we do for others.*
>
> *We must remember that in his ministry on Earth, Jesus delivered His strongest condemnation against those who were superficially and publicly good. The scribes and the Pharisees He attacked were the respectable people of His day.*
>
> *If we are to respond to our religious heritage, we must be guided by the principle of charity—charity in the biblical sense of love for one's fellow man. This is the greatest virtue, without which other virtues are of little worth.*
>
> *We must work for morality in public and in private life. You can't make an honest man by law. He has to be raised by the rules of the 20th chapter of Exodus, and the Sermon on the Mount, if he has the right moral fiber to become an ethical public or private citizen.*[84]

Citizen-Soldier

GLEN SCHROEDER voluntarily joined the US Navy in 1945. However, by the time he completed boot camp and Hospital Corps School, World War II was over. At the time of his discharge he joined the inactive reserve, returned home, and resumed his education. Four years later, he was attending Oregon State University when he received the big manila envelope in the mail with orders to active duty for service in the Korean War.

To further compound his consternation, Schroeder was sent to Combat Corpsman School at Camp Pendleton, California, for duty with the Marines. Practically all naval casualties at that time were being suffered by corpsmen with Marine units. When he did arrive in Korea in March 1951, he was assigned to an engineer unit in the First Marine Division where he found himself frequently on or ahead of the front lines and often under enemy fire. He treated dozens of wounded Marines and was himself wounded by shrapnel. When asked about his time in Korea, he would eventually reply, *"I have visited Hell."*[85]

> Each of you should look not only to your own interests, but also to the interests of others.
> ~Philippians 2:4

After his wartime experience Schroeder returned to civilian life and college with a new attitude. He was no longer a carefree college kid. For the first time, he was serious about his studies and plans for the future. His professors and friends noticed the change. Ultimately, he earned a doctorate degree in education and devoted a distinguished career to teaching and educational administration.

Schroeder always felt that his time in the navy contributed to his success. He would say, *"I have yet to talk to a combat corpsman who is not proud of that service."*[86] He is representative of the thousands of reservists who had their lives interrupted by the Korean War, who served honorably, and then returned to their civilian lives. America is still blessed to have such citizen-soldiers who, at great personal sacrifice, answer their nation's call in times of need.

Bad Advice

JOE BROWN joined the navy in 1949, and on the advice of his uncle, volunteered for Hospital Corpsman School. After sixteen weeks of medical training, he was assigned to a naval hospital, where he experienced the kind of duty he and his uncle had anticipated. Then, however, war broke out in Korea, and he found himself transferred to the Fleet Marine Force as a corpsman. With a lot of medical training but practically no infantry skills he was shipped to Korea, where he was assigned to a rifle platoon in the Second Battalion, Fifth Marines.

> You must not mention "the oracle of the LORD" again, because every man's own word becomes his oracle and so you distort the words of the living God, the LORD Almighty, our God.
> ~Jeremiah 23:36

With the Marines, Brown led the hard existence of an infantryman in the field under combat conditions. He had many occasions to recall the advice of his uncle, who had told him, "Corpsmen had the best living quarters and best meals in the navy—the duty stations were nice; quarters were good; food was good; and the liberty was port and starboard."[87] Unfortunately, this advice came from a man who had been stationed at Bayonne, New Jersey, for the duration of World War II. Brown recalled,

You can imagine the loving thoughts I had of him while eating cold beans from a tin can, on top of a mountain or while taking a lunch break near a rice paddy in a country over 10,000 miles from home. When attached to Marines on the front line of a combat zone, "nice" and "good" are two words that are not apropos when describing a corpsman's life.[88]

We have all led and been led astray by well-meaning but flawed advice. In the spiritual realm this can happen from an inaccurate or incomplete understanding of God's Word. A pastor whom I respect told me that Scripture should be interpreted in light of *all* Scripture. That is, we need to be careful about citing a particular passage to prove a point. As laymen, we do well when we stick to the simple truths of the gospel message when advising others, while leaving complex theological issues to the true experts.

Gentler Forces

IN FEBRUARY 1950, law enforcement officials from around the nation assembled at the Justice Department in Washington, DC, to address the problem of increasing crime. President Harry Truman shared his views with the group. He told them that the fundamental basis for our laws is found in the biblical books of Exodus and Matthew—the Ten Commandments and the Sermon on the Mount. He explained that these form the moral basis for our rights and responsibilities and need to be emphasized. He warned his audience and future generations, *"If we don't have the proper fundamental moral background, we will finally wind up with a totalitarian government which does not believe in rights for anybody except the state."*[89]

After discussing various issues related to law enforcement in the nation, he turned to what he called the *"gentler forces"* that needed to be brought to bear (and still do) on the prevention and cure of crime. He mentioned the home, education, and religion. However, he put special emphasis on one area in particular—the raising of children:

> Fix these words of mine in your hearts and minds; tie them as symbols on your hands and bind them on your foreheads. Teach them to your children, talking about them when you sit at home and when you walk along the road, when you lie down and when you get up.
> ~Deuteronomy 11:18 19

The most important business in this nation—or any other nation, for that matter—is raising and training children. If those children have the proper environment at home, and educationally, very, very few of them ever turn out wrong. I don't think we put enough stress on the necessity of implanting in the child's mind the moral code under which we live.[90]

These words have never been truer than today. Complaints are heard constantly about our school systems, and many of these complaints are justified. Unfortunately, the problem with our children's education goes deeper than the schools. Moral values have to be learned first in the home. This requires God-fearing parents who teach right and wrong by word and example. President Truman gives us a timeless reminder of the vital role of the family and the importance of the Bible as the foundation of our moral values.

Letter of the Law

TO IMPRESS his girlfriend, Raymond Cesaretti enlisted in the navy after high school. When he completed the paperwork, the recruiter told him to go home and wait for further orders. Back at home, he learned that two of his good friends had just joined the Marine Corps. Impulsively, again, he packed his bags and went to San Francisco to find the Marine recruiting station, where he enlisted once more. This time there was no delay. Within days he found himself at the Marine Corps Recruit Depot, San Diego, otherwise known as "boot camp."

Within a few weeks Cesaretti received an official letter from the US Navy ordering him to *"report for induction."* In a quandary, he tried to approach his drill instructor (DI). Knocking on the office door, he heard, *"Go back to where you belong or you will be scrubbing the parade ground with a toothbrush!"*[91] After several more attempts, he finally stood before the DI with his letter. After reading it, the instructor broke out laughing and gave the confused recruit the guidance he was seeking: *"Get the h--- outa here!"*[92]

> Woe to you, teachers of the law and Pharisees, you hypocrites! You clean the outside of the cup and dish, but inside they are full of greed and self-indulgence . . . You are like whitewashed tombs, which look beautiful on the outside but on the inside are full of dead men's bones and everything unclean.
> ~Matthew 23:25, 27

The next day all the DIs got a good laugh from Cesaretti's letter, figuring the Marine Corps had put one over on the navy. In somewhat typical Marine fashion, a complex legal problem was solved—by ignoring it. Cesaretti went on with his training and ultimately to combat duty with the First Marine Division in Korea.

Jesus also had a pronounced tendency to downplay the importance of the letter of the law. After miraculously restoring sight to a man blind from birth, he was chastised by the Pharisees for performing such an act on the Sabbath. Jesus did not hold back his criticism for anyone who would focus on the legalities of a situation while disregarding the physical and spiritual well-being of someone in need.

Fear

FROM THE day Ralph Fly was assigned to the Fleet Marine Force (FMF) he began to worry. His father had persuaded him to join the navy as a way to avoid going to Korea. Unfortunately this strategy didn't work out. After twenty weeks of Hospital Corpsman School and an internship in a naval hospital, he was assigned to Marine boot camp. He said, *"My feelings were mixed. Sometimes I was feeling euphoric. I had heard so much about the wonders of FMF Corpsmen, their training, their exploits, and their bonding to their Marine platoon. But I also had feelings of dread."*[93]

> The LORD is my light and my salvation—whom shall I fear? ~Psalm 27:1
>
> I sought the LORD and he answered me; he delivered me from all my fears. ~Psalm 34:4
>
> When I am afraid, I will trust in you. In God, whose word I praise, in God I trust; I will not be afraid. What can mortal man do to me? ~Psalm 56:3–4

His training gave him all the skills necessary to be an effective corpsman and to survive on the battlefield. However, his training did not relieve the fears of dying and death that would be with him throughout his tour of duty in combat. He later explained, *"What I learned in Korea is that no matter how well-trained you are, survival is a matter of luck."* Even though his combat training served him well, he felt there was no way to prepare for the random paths of incoming bullets and shells. *"Marines used to say, 'I don't worry about those that have my name on them. I worry about the ones that say, 'To Whom it May Concern.'"*[94]

Fear is a natural reaction to danger. It can even be useful when it encourages prudent precautions. When it becomes pervasive or debilitating, however, we have a trust issue. I sometimes forget that God is all-powerful and in control of all things. He may not protect me from every danger, but he promises to be with me no matter what happens. And, ultimately, he has prepared a place for each of us with him. We can trust his promises. They are not sent randomly or "To Whom it May Concern." They all have our individual names on them.

The Word

HENRY OPPENBORN was very confused on the morning of July 6, 1950. The young soldier was stationed in Japan and a few nights before had listened to President Harry Truman announce on the radio that US ground troops would not be committed to the war in Korea. At 5 a.m. that morning he was rudely awakened to find his unit frantically preparing for immediate deployment. A few days later he disembarked from a ship at Pusan and soon found himself in a defensive position forty miles south of Seoul. Within hours he saw a column of North Korean troops, four abreast, advancing toward his unit in *the longest line you ever saw.*[95]

> In the beginning was the Word, and Word was with God, and the Word was God. He was with God in the beginning.
> ~John 1:1-2

To go from peacetime garrison duty in Japan to frontline combat in Korea was a drastic change in fortune for this and every other soldier who went to Korea in the summer of 1950. Military men and women have always faced such disruptions, often caused by rapidly changing political events. During one of my Marine Corps assignments my unit was often on alert for deployment to some trouble spot in the world. We would load our equipment and board trucks for the embarkation port—only to return to base when things cooled down. The troops coined their own somewhat sacrilegious phrase to describe these frequent reversals: *"In the beginning was the word . . . and then the word was changed."*

This lament seems to capture the frustration we all feel at times when things don't go the way we expect. We are often irritated when unforeseen events interrupt our plans, big or small. When these "interruptions" occur we need to remember that God is in control of events and may have plans different from our own. When certain doors are closed to us, we need to pray for confidence and discernment to recognize the new one he will inevitably open. As we continue to pray, God will reveal his purpose for us, and we will eventually see the wisdom of his plan.

US troops welcomed in Seoul c. 1950 (US Navy)

US Sailors in Korea (US Navy)

Juche

AS THE SUPREME leader of North Korea, Kim Il Sung not only reshaped the political and economic landscape of a nation, he also undertook to reshape the nature of the people themselves. During the 1950s and 60s he introduced his own collectivist philosophical system called *Juche*. Borrowing from Marx, Lenin, Stalin, Mao, and Confucius, his ideology stressed national self-reliance and sought to distance North Korea from all outside influences by stressing internal solidarity under his sole authority. Under this "system" the people were expected to be self-disciplined and unified, and willing to live lives of sacrifice and austerity—which they have done out of necessity rather than ideological purity.

> You shall have no other gods before me. You shall not make for yourself an idol in the form of anything in heaven above or on the earth beneath or in the waters below. You shall not bow down to them or worship them. ~Exodus 20:3–5

As in all Communist countries, religious belief posed a threat to this system, since faith in another authority could not be tolerated. Kim Il Sung therefore took steps to eradicate Christianity. He closed the churches, banned the Bible, and sent countless Christians into prison camps. He even appropriated Christian imagery to glorify himself. As one defector recounted:

> *Stormy seas were said to be calmed when sailors clinging to a sinking ship sang songs in praise of Kim Il Sung. He caused trees to bloom and snow to melt. If Kim Il Sung was God, then Kim Jong Il was the son of God. Like Jesus Christ, Kim Jong Il's birth was said to have been heralded by a radiant star in the sky and the appearance of a beautiful rainbow.*[96]

We can hardly grasp the immensity of evil required to indoctrinate an entire population in such propaganda from infancy to old age, and we are incredulous that so many people could gullibly accept such blatant forms of thought control. We are incredulous until we consider the pervasive influence of mass media in our own culture. Is there an American form of *Juche* at work to displace our own religious faith, only by more sophisticated and subtle means?

A Walk through Scripture

IN THE SPRING 1950 issue of the *Navy Chaplains Bulletin* an inspirational piece was published illustrating the majesty of God's kingdom as revealed successively through the major themes of the Bible:

> All scripture is God-breathed. ~2 Timothy 3:16

With the Holy Spirit as my guide, I entered the wonderful temple of Christianity:

I entered at the portico of Genesis, walked down through the Old Testament and galleries, where pictures of Noah, Abraham, Moses, Joseph, Isaac and Daniel were hung on the walls.

I passed into the music rooms of Psalms, where the Spirit swept the keyboard of nature until it seemed that every reed and pipe in God's great organ responded to the tuneful hand of David, the sweet singer of Israel.

I entered the chamber of Ecclesiastes, where the voice of the preacher was heard; and into the conservatory of Sharon, where the Lily of the Valley's sweet-scented spices filled and perfumed my life.

I entered the business office of Proverbs, and then into the observatory room of the Prophets, where I saw telescopes of various sizes, pointed to far-off events, but all concentrated on the Bright and Morning Star.

I entered the audience room of the King of kings, and caught a vision of His glory from the standpoint of Matthew, Mark, Luke, and John; passed into the Acts of the Apostles where the Holy Spirit was doing his work in the formation of the infant Church.

Then into the Correspondence Room, where sat Paul, Peter, James, and John penning their Epistles.

I stepped into the throne room of Revelation, where towered the glittering peaks, and got a vision of the King sitting upon the throne in all His glory, and I cried:

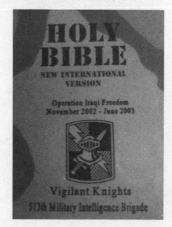

> *"All hail the power of Jesus' name,*
> *Let angels prostrate fall,*
> *Bring forth the royal diadem*
> *And crown Him Lord of all."*[97]

Ministers in War

IN 1950, Rear Admiral Stanton Salisbury, the Chief of Navy Chaplains, gave an address to the National Council of Churches about the nature of Christian ministry in the Armed Forces. He stressed that it is always inclusive, in that military chaplains are there for everyone. The chaplain does have certain ecclesiastical and denominational duties, such as church, burial, and memorial services, but he is also there as an ever-present help to all, *"Christian and non-Christian, Protestant and non-Protestant, believer and unbeliever, just and unjust."*

> Therefore, since we are surrounded by such a great cloud of witnesses, let us throw off everything that hinders and the sin that so easily entangles, and let us run with perseverance the race marked out for us. Let us fix our eyes on Jesus, the author and perfecter of our faith.
> ~Hebrews 12:1–2

He is at hand when they become ill; he will be at hand at the scene of any accident almost as soon as the doctor and the crash crews; he will give lectures on the true way of life; he will provide means of securing knowledge of culture, education, and advancement; and by personal example the chaplain will be the living representative of Him whom we call Master.

The need may be for a word of encouragement; for a courageous example in time of moral danger; for a kindly word of consolation to the loved ones of those lost in action; for the prayer offered as the warrior enters the land of eternal peace; for the sympathy extended to parents and relatives when the last sad word must be given; and for all the other ministries which mark the life of the Christian way.

The chaplain serves all: the faithful followers of our Lord; those who may falter at times; and those who may know not the true way. No matter where or when, he represents Christianity to the best of his ability. In fact, the chaplain is, in truth, a missionary to the largest and most representative mission field in the world today.[98]

Pastors and lay people today can take a cue from military chaplains, past and present. Often, in our churches, we tend to focus on the faithful while paying less attention to those outside the church. Every Christian is called to be not only a faithful member of the body of Christ but also a courageous missionary, reaching out in a troubled world to those who need our Savior most.

Feedback

CHAPLAIN JOSEPH LOPER was assigned to the Recruit Training Command at Great Lakes, Illinois, in early 1949 and considered this duty *"the most important work a chaplain can do, and as representing the most effective type of spiritual ministry in the Navy."*[99] For each company of recruits, he or another chaplain gave an introductory class, wrote letters to every parent, and then, as part of the training curriculum, gave a series of six lectures ranging from general responsibilities to sex education.

The chaplain was always concerned about improving these lectures but felt it difficult to get unbiased feedback from the men. He suspected they were saying only what he wanted to hear. By coincidence, at one point in his assignment, his own son went through the Great Lakes training program after enlisting in the navy. Since his son had always been brutally frank with his father, the chaplain thought he could rely on him for an honest appraisal of the chaplain's lectures.

His son told him, *"We consider them the best lectures we have. The boys usually don't get sleepy when the chaplain talks."*[100] Based on his son's feedback, the chaplain reported that, *"Such is one recruit's honest reaction to the chaplain and his work. In the opinion of this writer, who is both a Reserve chaplain and the father of a seaman recruit, the recruit chaplains are doing a wonderful job in serving the spiritual needs of the men."*[101]

> Have I not written thirty sayings for you, sayings of counsel and knowledge, teaching you true and reliable words, so that you can give sound answers to him who sent you? ~Proverbs 22:20–21

An objective observer might wonder just how "brutally frank" these comments from a son to his father were. Each of us needs honest feedback from those under our authority, and it is not easy to get. We have to encourage openness and honesty from our children and employees, even while realizing it poses risks for them and us. The truth can sometimes be painful. Since we will never be effective as leaders without regular doses of reality, it is up to us to seek out and even reward the honest feedback we need.

The Church Sent Me

IT WAS AN unusual setting for divine services. The Navy Club bar in Kaohsiung, Taiwan, showed evidence of heavy partying the night before. The room was decorated with a mixture of brightly colored flags, hanging in various states of disarray. Band instruments littered the stage, where musicians had played rhythmic tunes a few hours earlier for dancing sailors and local girls. The bar itself was in the back of the room where the usual display of liquor bottles had been mercifully hidden from sight—more for purposes of security than religious sensitivity. A music stand had been appropriated for a podium, and the service was accompanied by hymns from a tape recorder.

> And I say also unto thee, that thou art Peter, and upon this rock I will build my church; and the gates of hell shall not prevail against it.
> ~Matthew 16:18 (KJV)

The strains of "Holy, Holy, Holy" seemed to cleanse the air somewhat, as twenty-five white-clad seamen and officers from the US tanker in port sang together with Chaplain Leslie Brandt in worship. For some reason, the ship's captain had declined the chaplain's offer of shipboard services, necessitating the offbeat venue. After the service, the sailors expressed their thanks to the chaplain for being in a place where they least expected to be able to go to church. One sailor asked, *"What are you doing in this hole?"* He responded, *"Your church sent me to you."*[102]

Chaplain Brandt was part of the Lutheran Service Center, stationed in Keelung, Taiwan, during the Korean War. Since ships were also visiting Kaohsiung, he went to that port to offer his services whenever he could. Like missionaries of every period in time, he brought the Word of God to men who needed it in faraway places under difficult circumstances. As he explained, *"The gates of hell shall not prevail . . . even when we carry the Gospel of Christ to its very threshold."*[103]

Blessed

CHAPLAIN EMIL KAPAUN joined the Eighth Cavalry Regiment in Japan in early 1950, for what he expected to be a peacetime assignment. One of his first duties was to deliver a series of five fifteen-minute morning meditations over the US Far East Radio Network, broadcasting to Japan, Okinawa, and parts of China. Prophetically, he chose the Beatitudes from Matthew's Gospel as the theme for his talks, foreshadowing what would be his own experience in the near future in combat and as a prisoner of war:

> Blessed are the peacemakers, for they will be called sons of God.
> ~Matthew 5:9

Explaining this verse, Kapaun actually gave a description of what his own performance would be like under the stress of combat a few months later:

> *The peace which God gives is a gift which exists even in suffering, in want, and even in time of war. People who try to promote peace and love among their fellow men are peacemakers in the true sense of the word. And the people who try to bring the peace of God to souls are peacemakers of a higher order.*[104]

> Blessed are those who are persecuted because of righteousness, for theirs is the kingdom of heaven. ~Matthew 5:10

Speaking first about the persecution of early Christians, he brought the theme back to the present and again foreshadowed his own future as a prisoner:

> *We can surely expect that in our own lives there will come a time when we must make a choice between being loyal to our faith or giving allegiance to something else which is either opposed to or not in alliance with our faith. O God, we ask of Thee to give us the courage to be ever faithful to Thee.*[105]

In his final meditation, the chaplain stressed forgiveness for those who offend us. Within months his belief in those words would be tested. Could he forgive the brutality brought on himself and his fellow soldiers by his captors? Could he live up to his own words explaining Matthew's Gospel? Kapaun would pass every test, heroically representing his faith to friend and foe alike under the worst conditions imaginable.

All Clear

AS OPEN WARFARE broke out on the Korean peninsula in 1950, an army chaplain wrote an article reminiscing how Americans had so recently looked forward to peaceful times heralded by the end of World War II. Comparing this postwar optimism to the feeling of relief a soldier or sailor gets when the "all clear" is sounded after an air raid, he said, *"On the sixth anniversary of the signing of the surrender documents on board the battleship Missouri, America still waits and, from all indications will wait a long time, for the 'all clear' signal to be sounded."*[106]

> O LORD God Almighty, how long will your anger smolder against the prayers of your people?... Restore us, O God Almighty; make your face shine upon us, that we may be saved.
> ~Psalm 80:4, 7

Lamenting the start of another war and the wider threat of Communist insurgencies around the world, the chaplain expressed concern that America was actually closer to a "red alert" than a stand-down. He concluded somberly, *"The 'all clear' may never be heard during our lifetime. But that fact relieves no individual of the responsibility of praying to God for a special measure of His grace to measure up properly to the obligations we should assume."*[107]

Over the following decades, these words have proved prophetic. Even the eventual fall of the Soviet Union did not bring tranquility to the world, as new threats to peace have continued to arise. Apparently, humankind is destined to endure conflict, at both the personal and international levels. If we are waiting for a final solution to the problems that bring these conflicts about, we are waiting in vain. For most of us, our primary recourse is as the chaplain suggested above—prayer. We should pray constantly to God for purity in our own hearts and the self-discipline to overcome our own sins of pride, suspicion, and greed. After dealing with our own weaknesses, Christians can then tackle the problems of the world one person at a time.

Japanese flag comes down (National Archives)

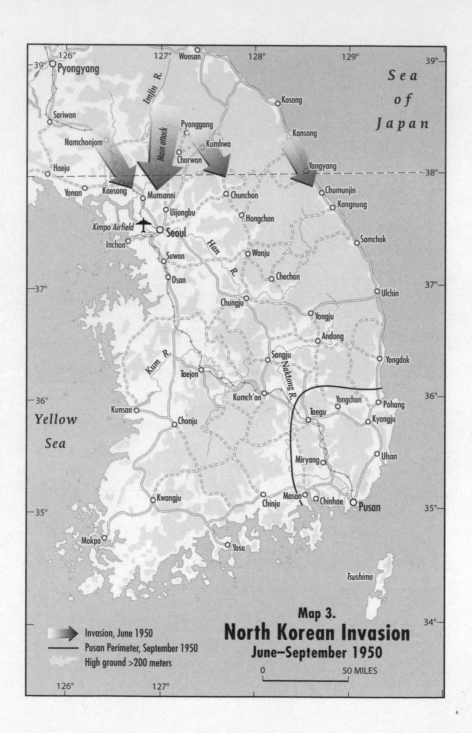

Map 3.
North Korean Invasion
June–September 1950

Invasion, June 1950
Pusan Perimeter, September 1950
High ground >200 meters

0   50 MILES

INVASION

B Y THE SUMMER of 1950, all US forces were withdrawn from South Korea except for a small cadre of about five hundred officers and men of the US Korean Military Advisory Group (KMAG). By then the fledgling Republic of Korea (ROK) Army consisted of eight understrength divisions with about one hundred thousand undertrained men.[108] Despite repeated requests by South Korean President Syngman Rhee and his government for more equipment, the new army lacked tanks, heavy artillery, and combat aircraft. The American policy was to leave an ROK Army strong enough to repel an invasion but not strong enough to launch one itself.[109]

Across the demilitarized zone, the Russians had shown no such reluctance to fully equip Kim Il Sung's North Korean People's Army (NKPA). With twelve divisions, 150 T-34 tanks, heavy artillery, aircraft, and an estimated three thousand Soviet advisors, the NKPA was a potent force. About a third of its troops were veterans who had fought with the Communist forces in the Chinese civil war and therefore had recent combat experience.[110]

In Japan, Gen. Douglas MacArthur continued to preside over the post-World War II reconstruction with a depleted occupation force. The Eighth Army, commanded by Lt. Gen. Walton "Johnnie" Walker and consisting of the First Cavalry, Seventh, Twenty-Fourth, and Twenty-Fifth Divisions, was understrength and undersupplied due to postwar cutbacks and was scattered throughout Japan performing peacetime garrison duties. There were no war plans for US military intervention on the Korean peninsula.

In the early hours of June 25, 1950, the tanks and infantry of the North Korean People's Army poured across the demilitarized zone behind a curtain of artillery fire. The four-pronged invasion was spaced across the entire peninsula with the main thrust in the east along the Uijongbu Corridor toward Seoul. Inexplicably, the ROK Army was caught completely by surprise. Frontline units were depleted by large numbers that had been furloughed to help with the summer harvest, and many officers were not present. Some units, like the First ROK Division fought effectively but were forced to withdraw when flanking units were overrun.

More devastating than the element of surprise, however, were the tanks. The South Koreans had no weapons to stop them. Within days the NKPA had taken Seoul and forced the Rhee government to flee to the south.

In Washington, President Harry Truman and his administration reacted vigorously to the unfolding disaster in Korea. Secretary of State Dean Acheson immediately brought the issue before the United Nations, where the Security Council, in the absence of the Soviet representative, unanimously passed a resolution condemning the invasion. President Truman authorized commitment of US forces, stating, "The attack upon Korea makes it plain beyond all doubt that Communism has passed beyond the use of subversion to conquer independent nations and will now use armed invasion and war."[111] American forces would eventually be followed by forces from fifteen other nations, all under the command of General McArthur, headquartered in Japan.

The first US force to reach Korea was an infantry battalion of the Twenty-Fourth Division, named Task Force Smith for its commander Lt. Col. Charles Bradley Smith. As this unit arrived in Pusan on July 1, North Korean-led elements were crossing the Han River, south of Seoul, and only two ROK divisions were offering organized resistance. The small American force took position north of Osan but were overrun and routed in the first US engagement of the war on July 5. The NKPA advance continued relentlessly south.

Other Twenty-Fourth Division units landed at Pusan and were committed piecemeal into the deteriorating battle. Within two weeks two US regiments were shattered with little accomplished.[112] General MacArthur issued orders to deploy the entire Eighth Army to Korea despite a lack of combat readiness and scarcity of transportation. On July 20, a determined effort was made to hold Taejon, a key city on the Kum River about midway between Seoul and Pusan. Again, the ROK and US forces were overwhelmed by a well-coordinated infantry and armor assault. In the action, Maj. Gen. William Dean, the Twenty-Fourth Division commander, was wounded and captured. Simultaneously, Chonju to the south of Taejon was taken, and on the east coast the North Korean advance moved further south threatening Pohang. By August 1, the Eighth Army had been forced back to the last feasible line of defense in South Korea, the Naktong River, running north-south a few miles west of Taegu.

Perspective

P EOPLE WERE affected by the outbreak of war in Korea in different ways. Matt Akers was with the Marine detachment on a large ship based on the East Coast. As the Captain's orderly he was knowledgeable about the Captain's activities on and off the ship. One night at 2:00 a.m. he was awakened by the officer of the day frantically searching for the Captain. An urgent message had come in ordering the ship to Korea. Fortunately, the orderly knew where to go.

> Now that you have been set free from sin and have become slaves to God, the benefit you reap leads to holiness, and the result is eternal life. For the wages of sin is death, but the gift of God is eternal life in Christ Jesus our Lord.
> --Romans 6:22–23

Soon thereafter, Akers found his boss ashore, somewhat inebriated, in the company of a lady friend. After several cups of black coffee, they headed back to the ship. As Akers described it, he was driving "like a bat out of hell" when he was stopped by a policeman. He tried to explain the reason for his haste as the captain mumbled away in the back seat about going to war again. The policeman was pretty amused at the situation and finally said, *"Take off, Marine, but take it easy. You don't want to get killed before you get to the war."*[113]

This story reminded me of a scene in the movie *Butch Cassidy and the Sundance Kid*. With the posse closing in and their backs to a cliff over a raging river, Butch announced that they had to jump. Sundance replied that he couldn't swim. Butch roared with laughter and answered, *"What? Are you crazy? The fall'll probably kill you!"*

Both of these stories are lessons in perspective. Our present troubles always have a larger context. Our larger and ultimate context as Christians is eternity. It doesn't matter whether the span of our lives is long or short, we know that eventually there will be an end. No matter what risks or hardships we face now, we have the security of an ultimate place in God's eternal kingdom. There is no crisis we cannot endure with this certain knowledge.

In Control

HENRY LITVIN joined the Naval Reserve while a pre-med student at the University of Pennsylvania. By June 1950 he had completed medical school and a two-year internship to become a fully-qualified doctor. Expecting to go on active duty with the navy, he was shocked to get orders to Second Battalion, Fifth Marines, at Camp Pendleton, California. Up until that moment, he had no idea the navy provided doctors to the Marine Corps. And he soon learned the Marines were going to war, this time in Korea.

Litvin was ready to practice medicine but not to fight a war. He didn't consider himself the outdoor type, having never been a Boy Scout or even on a camping trip. He got a lot of ridicule at first for his distinctly unmilitary bearing. Even though he felt like a fish out of water with no prior military experience, he was confident in his abilities. He felt—as do most doctors who have recently completed an internship—they can cure any sickness and heal any wound. The word "omnipotent" or "cocky" might have described his attitude, until he came face to face with reality:

> Trust in the LORD with all your heart and lean not on your own understanding; in all your ways acknowledge him, and he will make your paths straight. ~Proverbs 3:5–6

> *But I was to get my comeuppance, and in the worst way possible. To see so many of those young Marines die without being able to help them was the most heartbreaking experience of my life.*[114]

It can be profoundly moving to realize for the first time or any time, that we are not in control of events. We plan, prepare, and do our best, but often see an outcome we didn't expect or want. Amazingly, it is in these difficult moments we find potential for spiritual growth. When we are able to concede that God is in control or consciously turn control over to him, we relieve ourselves of the burden of trying to be perfect. Only in this way can we accept our fallen nature as human beings and our need for comfort and guidance from the only One who is truly "omnipotent."

Extreme Disadvantages

AFTER THE fall of Seoul on June 28, 1950, President Harry Truman ordered US ground forces into Korea. Leading the way was an understrength battalion of the Twenty-First Regiment consisting of two infantry companies with supporting weapons. This meager force landed in Pusan on July 2 and made its way north by train, reaching Osan a few days later. Chaplain Carl Hudson had joined the regiment only two weeks earlier, like everyone else, expecting a peacetime assignment. However, he now found himself with combat troops in the middle of a war zone.

It was raining heavily on the morning of July 5, when Hudson and a few other men wandered off their hilltop position and found an abandoned hut for shelter to prepare breakfast. A little while later they heard the sound of an approaching vehicle. Hudson glanced out the front door—and found himself staring directly at a North Korean tank. As he and the others scurried out the back, the tank's machine guns riddled the hut.

> For in the day of trouble he will keep me safe in his dwelling; he will hide me in the shelter of his tabernacle and set me high upon a rock.
> ~Psalm 27:5

For the next seven hours the US troops fought a losing battle against overwhelming North Korean tank and infantry attacks. Hudson moved around the battlefield in the rain and mud doing his best to pray for the wounded and console the dying. Finally ordered back, only about half the original force eventually linked up with friendly units. For Hudson, this was only the first taste of combat at the beginning of a thirteen-month tour of wartime duty.

Reflecting later on his experiences in Korea, Hudson said, *"I am glad God called me to serve our men in Korea. I think some of the best times were under extreme disadvantages like these."*[115]

The chaplain's comment should inspire us to reconsider our own setbacks and heartaches. They are never pleasant while we are in the midst of them. However, every problem or crisis presents a unique opportunity to grow closer to God and to show others the power of faith in action. How we deal with adversity says a lot more about our faith than do our words.

Underestimating the Enemy

AS THE NORTH Korean invasion continued, units of the US Twenty-Fourth Infantry Division began arriving in Korea from Japan. Rumors abounded as to what lay ahead. One platoon leader tried to reassure his troops by telling them, *"You've been told repeatedly that this is a police action, and that is exactly what it is going to be."*[116] He assured them they would be back in Sasebo, Japan, within a few weeks. One soldier was heard to boast to another, *"As soon as those North Koreans see an American uniform over here, they'll run like hell."*[117]

> And no wonder, for Satan himself masquerades as an angel of light. It is not surprising, then, if his servants masquerade as servants of righteousness.
> ~2 Corinthians 11:14–15

This cocky attitude evaporated quickly when the North Korean advance struck the hastily-formed American lines at Osan. The World War II-era rocket launchers in the hands of the US troops were inadequate to stop the Soviet T-34 tanks. The enemy infantry, armed with modern weapons, deployed methodically and enveloped the American positions. An ordered withdrawal turned into a rout. News of this catastrophe spread quickly, as one soldier described it, *"like a cancer into the combat morale of all troops moving to the front."*[118] Overconfidence and underestimation of the enemy had taken their toll.

Failing to understand the power of the enemy is not only a military failure. The fact that Christians do the same is no accident. C. S. Lewis has given us a masterful portrait of Satan's tactics to make himself appear trivial from a human perspective. In *The Screwtape Letters* a senior devil instructs his nephew:

> *I do not think you will have much difficulty in keeping the patient (human subject) in the dark. The fact that "devils" are predominantly comic figures in the modern imagination will help you. If any faint suspicion of your existence begins to arise in his mind, suggest to him a picture of something in red tights, and persuade him that since he cannot believe in that he therefore cannot believe in you.*[119]

Christians often fall into the trap of underestimating the power of evil in the world and in their lives. We are able to grasp what we are up against only by reading and contemplating God's Word.

First US troops arrive in Korea (Dept. of Defense)

UN Security Council votes June 1950 (NY Times)

He Stayed Behind

HERMAN FELHOELTER was ordained a Catholic priest in 1939 and served as an army chaplain during World War II, earning a Bronze Star for combat service. After the war, he pastored a church in Cincinnati for several years and then went back on active duty in time to go to Korea with the first troops to see action there. As a chaplain with the Nineteenth Infantry Regiment, he provided aid and comfort to his men during the battle for Taejon and was with them when they were forced to retreat before the overwhelming North Korean advance.

> I have been crucified with Christ and I no longer live, but Christ lives in me. The life I live in the body, I live by faith in the Son of God, who loved me and gave himself for me.
> ~Galatians 2:20

On July 16, 1950, Felhoelter was with a group of one hundred soldiers trying to regain friendly lines after the enemy had cut the main supply route. Burdened with thirty wounded men, progress was painstakingly slow moving cross-country over rugged terrain. At one point, they reached the top of a hill where they could see the enemy closing in on them. The chaplain convinced those able to walk to go ahead, while he volunteered to stay behind with the wounded. Looking back from a distant hill, the men who escaped saw the chaplain praying with the wounded men as they were all surrounded and killed by enemy soldiers. Eleven days after the start of the war and on the day before his thirty-seventh birthday, Felhoelter became the first chaplain killed in action during the Korean War. For his heroic service he was posthumously awarded the Distinguished Service Cross.

A few days before his death, the heroic chaplain wrote home, *"Don't worry, Mother. God's will be done. I feel good to know the power of your prayers accompanying me. I am not comfortable in Korea (that is impossible here) but I am happy in the thought that I can help some souls who need help. Keep your prayers going upward."*[120]

A Man Crying

CECILIA ANN SULKOWSKI was an army nurse with the first Mobile Army Surgical Hospital (MASH) unit sent to Korea in July 1950. Arriving in Pusan, her team occupied a school building with a dirt floor and immediately began treating wounded coming from the front lines. It was a traumatic experience seeing her first casualties of war. She was especially dismayed at the men who seemed broken down mentally:

These men would cry. They had seen their buddies falling, and to see a man cry anytime is hard. They'd reach out to you. From the timbre of their voice, the way they were sitting, very dejected, you knew they wanted and needed to talk to somebody. You'd sit on their cot or squat by it, and hold their hand. You mostly listened. Let them talk, let them get it out of their system, and tell them that you understand what has happened to them, why they're feeling the way they are.[121]

The wounded soldiers treated in the MASH units and able to unburden themselves in this way were fortunate in one respect. Men (and women in some cases) have a tendency to suppress emotions such as anger, guilt, or extreme sadness. In combat there is often no time to process these feelings, and they have to be stuffed down deep inside. Many combat veterans never have the chance or realize the necessity to bring these feelings out into the open. They subsequently are burdened with symptoms of depression, anger, and even thoughts of suicide. Since the Vietnam era this condition has been labeled Post-Traumatic Stress Disorder (PTSD), and a lot of progress has been made in counseling techniques to help overcome it.

> Come to me, all you who are weary and burdened, and I will give you rest. Take my yoke upon you and learn from me, for I am gentle and humble in heart, and you will find rest for your souls. For my yoke is easy and my burden is light.
> ~Matthew 11:28–30

In my own experience with veterans I have learned the even greater importance of addressing the spiritual dimension of the problem. In Jesus Christ veterans from every war have found the answer to dealing with emotional problems they are incapable of fixing themselves. Jesus above all others understands pain and suffering and stands ready to heal the wounds and lift the burdens that afflict us, not only in war but in every aspect of our lives.

East Meets West

WHEN CDR. Walter Peck and Lt. Won Dong Lee met for the first time, they found they had something in common: they were both Presbyterian ministers. Peck was a navy chaplain with the First Marine Division, while Lee was a newly assigned chaplain with the First Regiment, Korean Marine Corps. During their first meeting the American learned some interesting things about his Korean counterpart.

> There is one body and one Spirit—just as you were called to one hope when you were called— one Lord, one faith, one baptism; one God and Father of all, who is over all and through all and in all. ~Ephesians 4:4–6

Lee had his first contact with Christianity at age eighteen, when he met Presbyterian missionaries in his hometown and read the literature they gave him. He became a Christian while his country was still under Japanese occupation during World War II and, as a result, found himself under constant surveillance. The police often entered his home to question him and search for evidence of subversive behavior. After the war, he attended Chosun Theological College and was ordained a Presbyterian minister in 1948. He served as pastor of a Presbyterian church in Yangpyeong until he entered military service as one of seven chaplains with the Korean Marine Corps.

Lee explained that within his regiment there was a mixture of men who were religious and nonreligious, but, like all good chaplains, he felt it his duty to minister to all. He found that even those who were not Christian respected his work and ministry. He also made a prophetic statement to his American friend:

> I believe that one day Christianity will be the dominant religion throughout Korea. It is the one cause in which both my people and the North Koreans can always find a common devotion. As a matter of fact, I am sure that loyalty to our Christ by all the peoples of the world would solve all the conflicts and difficulties that face us today.[122]

Sixty years later, Jesus Christ is more than ever the one unifying figure who could bring this divided nation back together. On the day the shackles of Communism eventually fall off, the Christians of North and South Korea will be at the forefront, bringing reconciliation and healing to a people with many old wounds.

Thank You

CHONG SUK was a seven-year-old Korean girl living in a small village south of Seoul. She didn't understand too much about the Korean War except that all the men were gone, and she was always hungry. She went to school and helped her mother during the day and spent her nights in an underground bunker for protection. Her first contact with Americans came one day as someone ran through the village shouting, *"Yankees are here!"* She ran with all the other children to the top of a nearby hill where she saw two GIs standing beside a jeep, apparently on some kind of survey mission. From her youthful perspective they seemed exceptionally big and dirty.

> Let the word of Christ dwell in you richly as you teach and admonish one another with all wisdom, and as you sing psalms, hymns and spiritual songs with gratitude in your hearts to God.
> ~Colossians 3:16

One day at school her teacher announced that American soldiers had brought food for them. It was memorable because the pangs of hunger were a constant reality for the Korean children and their families. They all received powdered milk from large barrels with "U.S.A." stamped on top. They drank milk until their stomachs ached and then had powdered milk pancakes. Even though their digestive systems suffered from a new food source, they were forever grateful for this unexpected gift.

Chong Suk added "Dickman" to her name when she later married a career American soldier and had children of her own. Her son and son-in-law served their country in the Armed Forces of the United States. Speaking from experience, she strongly affirms the value of American efforts to help others around the world in the midst of strife. Of America's efforts on behalf of the Korean people, she says:

> *I write this memory now, as a U. S. citizen . . . to thank all the men who served in Korea. You changed our lives. We did not know who you were, where the United States was, or why you had to be there. We only knew you as our guardian angels.*[123]

Korean girl with baby
(National Archives)

The Fighting Preacher

LOGAN WESTON always wanted to be a minister. In 1941 he was in his third year of Bible college when his life was turned upside down for the first time. He was drafted into the army to fight as an infantryman and was assigned to combat duty in the Solomon Islands campaign and in Burma with Merrill's Marauders. Although he was highly decorated for bravery as a soldier, he earned the nickname of "The Fightin' Preacher" from his men, because of his openly religious nature.

> Trust in the LORD and do good; dwell in the land and enjoy safe pasture. Delight yourself in the LORD and he will give you the desires of your heart. Commit your way to the LORD; trust in him.
> ~Psalm 37:3–5[125]

After the war Weston returned to Bible college and eventually became a pastor at a small church in rural Pennsylvania. Soon, however, he felt a calling to return to military service as a chaplain. An army recruiter told him to apply first for active duty and then request a branch transfer from the infantry to the chaplain corps. Once on active duty, however, he was informed by the US Army Chief of Chaplains that a recent change to the regulations made him one year too old for transfer to the chaplaincy. He would remain in the infantry and see combat again—this time in Korea. Still affectionately known as "The Fightin' Preacher," he led his men both militarily and spiritually through some of the bitterest fighting of the war. Wounded three times in one battle, he returned to duty to complete his assignment.

In August 1951, a war-weary soldier met his family on the tarmac of the Pittsburgh airport. He saw his thirteen-month-old son for the first time and realized his two-and-a-half-year-old didn't even recognize him. Of this homecoming he said:

> *I could scarcely believe that I was home with my family, my beautiful wife and two handsome boys. The horrors and bloodshed of battle in Korea seemed so far away, almost like a dream. But as in World War II, I knew I had survived not because of my own skill and cunning, but because of the grace of an ever present, all-knowing, all-powerful, loving God. We got down on our knees and thanked Him for His protection, His guidance, and His many wonderful blessings right there on the tarmac, in public, at the Pittsburgh Airport.*[124]

Prayers under Fire

LOGAN WESTON was an infantry officer sustained through two wars by a firm faith in Jesus Christ. Reflecting on his duty as a platoon leader with Merrill's Marauders during World War II, he remembered the many opportunities he had to renew his faith as the Lord guided and protected him. He learned that God not only wanted his best efforts, but he also wanted his trust.[126]

> For he will command his angels concerning you to guard you in all your ways; they will lift you up in their hands, so that you will not strike your foot against a stone.
> ~Psalm 91:11–12

In Korea, Logan was a company commander with the Twenty-Fifth Division fighting in the Pusan Perimeter. Early on August 3, 1950, he was wounded painfully in his right thigh as his unit was attacked by North Korean forces near Masan. Staying with his men, he was wounded a second and a third time, all the while directing his defensive fires and, at one point, leading a counterattack to clear enemy troops from his lines.

As the attacks subsided, he let himself be helped off the hill to an aid station, where medics bandaged his wounds and put him into an ambulance. Even then, the ambulance came under fire, and bullets began ripping holes through its sides. As the vehicle sped out of range of the enemy fire, Logan's thoughts turned to the one place he had always found comfort:

God comforted me in my pain as each bounce of the ambulance sent a jolt of pain through my arm where the muscle was so badly torn. I struggled to breathe, my lungs filled with blood from the chest wound. I thanked the generosity of our Lord in sparing my life and giving me the strength to do my duty.[127]

Treating Wounded near Pusan (USMC)

Where Are You?

DURING THE battle at Chindong-ni, Logan Weston was wounded three times, refused evacuation, and continued to lead his men in the bitter fight until he collapsed from loss of blood. He was loaded into an ambulance with other wounded men to run a gauntlet of fire to a rear-area hospital.

As Weston lay on the litter inside the careening ambulance, he could hear the sound of gunfire over the noise of the engine. As small-arms fire clanged on the side of the vehicle, he began to see sunlight through bullet holes opening above him. In severe pain from wounds to his arm, leg, and chest, he drifted in and out of consciousness. One bullet had punctured his right lung and, as it filled with blood, each breath became an agony of pain. He slowly became aware that his comrades in the ambulance were as bad off as himself when blood from another soldier began dripping onto his face from above.

> He lifted me out of the slimy pit, out of the mud and mire; he set my feet on a rock and gave me a firm place to stand. He put a new song in my mouth, a hymn of praise to our God.
> ~Psalm 40:2–3

Weston had been a devout Christian all his life, and his faith had seen him through many other crises. Once again, in the midst of pain and fear in a speeding ambulance, he cried out to his heavenly Father:

> "Oh God, where are you?" I prayed. In an instant, my mind was flooded with a quiet peace. Even in my agony, I somehow knew that Jesus Christ was there with me, comforting me. Once again, I could rest assured that my life was in His hands.[128]

Weston would later be awarded the Distinguished Service Cross. His actions that day were credited with stopping an enemy attack that could have overwhelmed his regimental headquarters. He was forever thankful his Savior had been there when he needed him most.

Let Down

WHEN THE door of the C-47 opened, Bud Biteman looked out on a desolate scene. Before him lay a large open area of pastureland with an adobe hut, stacks of boxes, scattered pup tents, and six widely dispersed F-51 Mustangs that had arrived a few days before. In July 1950, Taegu "Air Base" was an air base in name only. The only runway was a forty-five-hundred-foot dirt strip with potholes and soft spots. There were no amenities. For the moment Biteman was disappointed, thinking that war should somehow be more organized than this. He described his thoughts at that moment:

> As I looked around at the bleak, nonexistent facilities at Taegu, I wondered if I hadn't arrived in Korea too soon; maybe I could go out and come in again after they had things arranged more in the fashion that I had been led to expect![129]

> I give you this charge: Preach the Word; . . . correct, rebuke and encourage—with great patience and careful instruction . . . Keep your head in all situations, endure hardship, do the work of an evangelist, discharge all the duties of your ministry.
> ~2 Timothy 4:1–2, 5

Biteman's disappointment faded into irrelevance as he began flying combat missions in support of beleaguered US and Korean ground forces. He and his fellow pilots learned to make do with what they had in order to get a vital job done.

This airman's experience brings to mind a similar disappointment of my own. I don't remember exactly what I expected of Boy Scout camp, but I found it definitely not a summer retreat. In my first separation from home I experienced hot weather, a tent, and few amenities. This little disappointment also resolved itself as I joined in the activities. Making friends and earning merit badges became more significant than the sleeping accommodations.

I think these stories are relevant to how we perceive our churches. It is easy to get disappointed with our pastors and sometimes inadequate facilities when we forget the nature of the church's mission. When we fully focus on our responsibility to share the good news of the gospel with others, issues of our own comfort and convenience fade away. Being fed by our churches is not our first concern. Our job as followers of Jesus Christ is to feed others.

War

ALBERT PROVOST joined the navy at age eighteen and served on a destroyer during World War II. In 1948 he transferred to the army and served two tours in Korea where he called in air strikes to protect his fellow soldiers. As a sailor and soldier, he saw a lot of violence in war. He was also gratified to see a lot of compassion as well.

> And we know that in all things God works for the good of those who love him, who have been called according to his purpose. ~Romans 8:28

His fondest memory of Korea was helping others in need. While in Pusan, he and some other soldiers met a Catholic priest trying to rebuild a church while caring for a group of homeless children. The soldiers found the priest and children in a desperate state, living in the open on pallets. Provost organized a collection to put a roof on the church and build a dormitory for the orphans. *"We also diverted a few supplies,"* he recalled. *"But the Koreans did most of the labor."*[130] He was particularly proud he was able to pay for the twelve Stations of the Cross adorning the interior of the refurbished church. Of the whole project, he later said, *"Things like that happened every day, hundreds of times during the war."*[131]

In his little classic, *The Screwtape Letters*, C. S. Lewis makes a similar point about war. Through the voice of a senior devil instructing his junior, Lewis gives us Satan's perspective:

> I must warn you not to hope too much from a war. Of course war is entertaining. We may hope for a good deal of cruelty and unchastity. But, if we are not careful, we shall see thousands turning in this tribulation to the Enemy (God, from his point of view), while tens of thousands who do not go so far as that will nevertheless have their attention diverted from themselves to values and causes which they believe to be higher than the self.[132]

Provost demonstrated Lewis' thesis perfectly, showing compassion to others in a combat zone. How easy it is to frustrate Satan when we elevate our sights! Turning to God and away from ourselves, we can bring light to dark places, always relying on the certain knowledge that God can redeem any human condition, including war.

Death March

Herbert Lord
(Salvation
Army)

S ALVATION ARMY Commissioner Herbert Lord was prominent among a group of seventy noncombatant prisoners forced to suffer through the infamous Tiger Death March across North Korea in 1950. One member of the party was an aged Russian woman who came to the point of collapse. Lord tried his best to help her along and even put a rope around her waist and pulled her behind him. Finally, however, she fell beside the road and couldn't get up. The guards forced the rest of the party to move on, and the woman was never seen again.

At that moment, Herbert Lord's faith hit its lowest point. It was snowing and bitterly cold. He had no coat and no hope. He didn't seem able to help or save himself, much less anyone else. Was life even worth such a struggle? At that moment, at the highest point of his discouragement and despair, the words of the Twenty-Third Psalm leapt into his mind, particularly the line, *"Thou preparest a table before me in the presence of mine enemies"* (v. 5).

> Why are you downcast, O my soul? Why so disturbed within me?
> Put your hope in God, for I will yet praise him, my Savior and my God. ~Psalm 42:5-6

As he trudged along in the snow, this thought was followed by another that was even more amazing: *"And then, like the sound of a group of trumpeters breaking forth into a paean of praise, there came to mind the chorus: I carried a heavy burden, But it rolled away; There's a melody in my heart today."*[133]

This was, for Herbert Lord, the *"deepest spiritual experience"* and climax of the so-called *"death march."* Through all the pain and disappointment to follow, he never again allowed himself to lose faith or hope.

Do You Believe?

THE NORTH KOREAN guard stood menacingly over Herbert Lord with a gun in his hand. As the guard started throwing questions at him the thought flashed through Lord's mind that this could be the end of his life:

"Do you believe there is a God?" inquired the Korean.

Lord understood the question perfectly, and firmly replied, "Yes."

"You are an intelligent, educated man and yet you really believe there is a God?"

"Yes," came the unflinching reply again.

"And do you believe that this God answers prayer?"

"Yes."

"Well, we'll prove it. I am going to stand behind you, and I want you to pray to God and ask him to tell you in which hand I am holding this gun."

"I refuse to offer such a prayer," declared Lord. "God is not a conjuror."

"And yet you believe He answers prayer?"

"Yes, and I am praying now."

"For what?"

"That he will give me grace not to lose my temper with you, and that if you decide to use your gun that I may die like a Christian gentleman."[134]

After hearing Lord's reply, the guard walked away in silence. The irresistible force of the guard's logic had broken on the immovable object of Commissioner Lord's clear conviction. There was nothing else to say. When confronted with seemingly logical objections, every Christian can rest in the assurance that logic does not change lives. Faith in Jesus Christ does.

> The mocker seeks wisdom and finds none . . . Evil men will bow down in the presence of the good, and the wicked at the gates of the righteous. ~Proverbs 14:6, 19

Words

LARRY ZELLERS was a newly-married Methodist minister teaching in a little mission school at Kaesong when the Korean War broke out. He was taken prisoner by North Koreans on June 25, 1950. After several years of captivity and many unforgettable moments, his fellow prisoner and Salvation Army commissioner, Herbert Lord, asked him if he would eventually write about his experience.

"*No, Commissioner, I'm afraid not,*" he replied.

"*Why not?*"

"*Commissioner, there are no words to describe what we have been through.*"

"*That is ridiculous! There are words for every human emotion and every experience. If you haven't found them yet, then it means that either your vocabulary isn't large enough, or you haven't thought about it enough, or you haven't felt deeply enough about it. If you dedicate yourself to the task, you will find the right words!*"[135]

Based on this conversation, Zellers did find the words to write a uniquely insightful book describing his ordeal as a prisoner of war. Words are the building blocks of language and, as such, are the necessary tools of a writer. With the right words, we are able to communicate our thoughts and emotions to others. God also used words to reveal himself in Holy Scripture, showing us how to know and follow him. He finally and completely embodied his message for mankind in the person of his Son, Jesus Christ. Jesus is the Word of God in human form and the complete communication of who God is to the world.

> In the beginning was the Word, and the Word was with God, and the Word was God. He was with God in the beginning. Through him all things were made; without him nothing was made that has been made. In him was life, and that life was the light of men. The light shines in the darkness, but the darkness has not understood it. The Word became flesh and made his dwelling among us. We have seen his glory, the glory of the One and Only, who came from the Father, full of grace and truth.
> ~John 1:1–5, 14

Inquisition

LARRY ZELLERS received special attention from the North Korean interrogators. Although he was a Methodist missionary when captured, he had served in the military in World War II, making him a special target for "reeducation." The interrogations went on endlessly:

> I was in the hands of people who were not content merely to control the body; they wanted the mind and heart as well. They had the training to make us pay dearly for thoughts and attitudes that were not "correct." These people felt that they were doing us a favor when they caused us all forms of deprivation: loss of freedom, controlled starvation, controlled fatigue, controlled fear, controlled confusion, confinement. The purpose was to assist us in learning the "truth," according to their definition of it.
>
> "But Larry, we want you to learn the truth freely. We could force you to agree with us, but we want you to see the truth from your heart. This way you can have a clear conscience."
>
> "But I don't agree with you," I said.
>
> "We understand that. You are poisoned by capitalistic thinking. But we want you to see the truth on your own so that you will have a clear conscience. When you do, you will thank us for our efforts on your behalf."[136]

This insight into Communist thinking reminds us of one of the great evils of history, perpetrated in the name of Christianity. The Inquisition was conducted in Spain during the 1400s ostensibly to purge heresy from the Roman Catholic Church. The horrors inflicted on people with the "wrong beliefs" had no bounds because the inquisitors believed that torture was for the *benefit* of a heretic if it succeeded in saving his soul.

> Then Jesus said to them, "Give to Caesar what is Caesar's and to God what is God's." ~Mark 12:17

This kind of evil is possible when absolute power rests in the hands of ideological zealots. Intense religious belief is usually a good thing—when practiced individually. It cannot be forced down the throats of others. In America, we benefit from the wisdom of our Founding Fathers and a tradition that generally separates issues of conscience from politics. Although this line is not easy to draw, this imperfect separation works to give us better government and purer religion.

A Real War

THE FIFTH CAVALRY Regiment was committed to battle early in the Korean War, even though it was understrength and ill-prepared to face the determined advance of the North Korean army. Overconfident in the beginning, the men had to taste the bitter pill of defeat, suffering heavy casualties and forced retreats. These depressing circumstances began to take their toll on morale, as disillusionment with the war set in.

Nineteen-year-old Pvt. James Lutze was with Headquarters Company, Fifth Cavalry, and experienced these setbacks firsthand. He expressed his feelings in a letter home:

> The question on the lips of the G.I. over here is, "What are we fighting for?"
>
> This is no "police job" as Mr. Truman says, it is a real war, but not the kind most people at home can realize. We are fighting [against] men who can live for a week in the mountains with just a little bag of rice. Where we have to travel by road they travel over the mountains and beat us to where we are going.
>
> About half the members of our battalion have been killed or wounded. Among the latter is our battalion commander and six other officers including my section leader.
>
> Well, we withdrew again last night for about 10 miles and again the enemy knew we were moving, because they shelled the road. It's an old saying here on the lines that if you kill one Korean, there are 10 more to take his place.
>
> In closing all I can say is this: give us reinforcements, or pull out what is left of us—which isn't many.[137]

In a confused and confusing world, those of us who follow Jesus Christ can also become discouraged by the apparent strength of our opposition. The forces of secularization seem to be advancing on all fronts. The advantage we have, however, is the certain knowledge of "what we are fighting for." Each of us has a mission to fulfill in building up God's kingdom. We also have the advantage of knowing that victory is certain—that his kingdom will prevail over every power of this world.

Now I know that the LORD saves his anointed; he answers him from his holy heaven with the saving power of his right hand. Some trust in chariots and some in horses, but we trust in the name of the LORD our God. ~Psalm 20:6–7

She Was a Blessing!

EARLY IN THE Korean War, crewmembers of the *USS Heron* (AMS-18) rescued a little dog from starvation, fearing it might wind up as food for people who were themselves destitute and starving. They named the dog "Dozo," the Japanese word for "please," and smuggled her aboard their small minesweeper. They tried to keep her presence secret, but it was not long before the officers found out about their stowaway. To their amazement the captain not only liked the new addition but also accepted Dozo as a crewmember.

> God made the wild animals according to their kinds, the livestock according to their kinds, and all the creatures that move along the ground according to their kinds. And God saw that it was good. ~Genesis 1:25

Dozo made it her job to visit every space on the ship on a regular basis. She was seen at the bridge, pilot house, engine room, radio shack, and wardroom. She slept with the sailors in the crew quarters. The cooks made sure she was well fed. She was on deck in subzero weather during mine sweeping operations, braving stormy seas and enemy fire alongside the rest of the crew. Of their canine friend, one officer said:

She loved and respected every person on that ship. She exuded happiness everywhere she went. She loved life and provided joy in others' lives. Dozo was more than pleasing: she was a blessing![138]

So many of us can say the same thing about our own pets—they are truly blessings in our lives. They don't ask for much as they selflessly give us their affection. In good times and bad they are there beside us with a constant demeanor trying to cheer us up. Like us, they are God's creatures put on the earth according to his own purpose. They fulfill that purpose through their love and obedience, bringing a small taste of God's unconditional love into our daily lives.

(National Archives)

Howitzer firing near Pusan (National Archives)

Frontline church service (USArmy)

Volunteers

AS THE NAVY expanded to meet the manpower needs of the Korean War, a call went out to the reserve establishment seeking volunteers for active duty. The response was gratifying, especially within the Chaplain Corps, as applications came in from every naval district in the United States plus Scotland, Japan, and Alaska. It was remarked at the time:

> It was he who gave
> some to be apostles,
> some to be prophets,
> some to be evangelists,
> and some to be pastors
> and teachers, to prepare
> God's people for works
> of service, so that the
> body of Christ may be
> built up until we all reach
> unity in the faith and in
> the knowledge of the
> Son of God.
> ~Ephesians 4:11–13

The Chief of Chaplains notes with some surprise and a great deal of humility that so many of those who have applied are veteran chaplains—men with years of experience in the Navy and in the ministry. It would seem that these distinguished clergymen who did such a splendid job during World War II could be expected, short of all-out mobilization, to rest awhile on their hard-won laurels. However, it is these older ministers and priests with more than a touch of grey in their temples and a stride that is not as vigorous as it once was, who are responding so generously. They are not only ready, but willing, to leave large and prosperous churches to follow the youth of the nation into the training camps, the combatant ships, the foreign stations, and into the smoke and dust of battle. Once more they march with their men. Once more the uniform of Navy blue and gold is broken out. The blue may be a bit faded and the gold a little tarnished, but the heart it covers is as stout as ever.[139]

During the Korean War reservists from the Army, Navy, and Marine Corps returned to active duty, many with service in World War II. In many cases these men and women left secure careers and tranquil family lives to go halfway around the world to an uncertain fate. In every national emergency since Lexington and Concord, America has been blessed with men and women who have answered such calls to duty. We see the same today, as regulars and reservists alike deploy repeatedly to the Middle East to fight for our nation in a protracted conflict. We thank them for their unselfish service and pray that God blesses everyone who wears the uniform and goes into harm's way for our benefit.

God's PIO

FATHER PATRICK O'CONNOR went to Korea as a priest-correspondent for a Catholic news service and was humorously dubbed by his contemporaries "God's PIO." In military parlance of the time, the Public Information Officer (PIO) was the officer on staff responsible for public and press relations.

During his time in the Korean War, Father O'Connor probably held more religious services than any unit chaplain due to the fact he was not assigned to one command and was able to move about freely. Every morning, no matter where he was, he shared morning worship with whoever was nearby. He heard confession from paratroopers before a jump, soldiers on the march, and infantrymen about to go on patrol. His presence was always welcome since there were never enough unit chaplains to minister to the thousands of troops in need.

On one occasion, Father O'Connor was asked about the spiritual state of the soldiers. He said:

It reflects directly the spiritual health of the nation. The good are very good; the careless are very careless. War has awakened a number of men to the question of their own destiny and eternal salvation. But even war has failed to do so for some.[140]

Many live as enemies of the cross of Christ. Their destiny is destruction, their god is their stomach, and their glory is in their shame. Their mind is on earthly things. But our citizenship is in heaven. And we eagerly await a Savior from there, the Lord Jesus Christ.
~Philippians 3:18–20

The priest's comments are timeless and thought provoking. In my case, a war did awaken me to questions about my destiny, but not to the matter of eternal salvation. I think this is what Father O'Connor means by "careless." If a person is not seeking answers or thinks he has the answers, he is indeed on a careless path. To go along in life thinking one is the master of his fate requires a callous disregard for the realities of the world we live in. I unfortunately had to go a long way before finally realizing I was not as good a person as I thought I was, and that I was also incapable of making myself better. It shouldn't take a war to awaken us to our need for forgiveness and a change of heart. We know we have a God who hears us, forgives us, and has a divine destiny in store for each of us. Carelessness regarding our eternal fate is not an option.

Combat Fatigue

LT. ADDISON TERRY was with the Twenty-Seventh Regiment when it first deployed to Korea and was in the middle of many battles to hold the Pusan Perimeter. As an artillery forward observer he and his small team of two enlisted men were frequently under fire from enemy small arms, mortars, and artillery. One day while in an exposed position expecting an enemy attack, one of his men began to show signs of nervousness.

> Do not be afraid of any man, for judgment belongs to God.
> ~Deuteronomy 1:17

As darkness fell, the eighteen-year-old private began to moan quietly in the foxhole he shared with Terry. The lieutenant tried to ignore this behavior, hoping it would pass. However, it got worse. The soldier began to plead to be sent to the rear and was unable to comprehend that this was out of the question. Anyone moving around at night was likely to be shot by another nervous soldier on the line. Instead he began rocking back and forth and his moan turned into a wail. His teeth were chattering as he broke into a cold sweat. After this went on for some time, he gasped, *"I am going to leave. I don't care if I get court-martialed. I ain't gonna sit here and get killed!"*[141]

As the soldier moved to jump out of the foxhole, Terry wrestled him to the ground and held him down for several minutes as he writhed furiously to break free. Finally, he gave up and began to cry pitifully. This went on for the rest of the night. The next day, the lieutenant decided that instead of disciplinary action he would quietly arrange a transfer and a replacement for the soldier. His only feeling was one of compassion:

> *It twisted my heart out to see what this dirty war had done to him. (He was) a normal healthy boy. The kind who at this minute were tinkering with Model A's back in the States. Boys like this one were having dates, drinking Cokes, working on the farms, playing golf, working at soda fountains.*[142]

The lieutenant could have used harsh disciplinary measures to deal with this case of apparent extreme fear. Instead, he administered a more Christ-like justice. He considered the extenuating circumstances and made allowance for the human weaknesses that can cause each of us to stumble.

SOP

EARLY IN THE Korean War the commanding general of the Fleet Marine Force Pacific published a Standing Operating Procedure (SOP) for chaplains. In Korean combat areas, duties to be performed by the regimental chaplain were spelled out in great detail:

> —He obtains information as soon as possible from S-1 (personnel officer) as to the location of the regimental cemetery. He provides for the proper religious rites in the burial of deceased personnel. When practicable an individual picture of each grave with the appropriate chaplain standing by in benediction should be taken, so that families may secure copies if desired.
>
> —He establishes and maintains contact with the regimental collecting section, and the battalion aid stations. He establishes and maintains contact with field hospitals in support of the regiment. He and other chaplains should visit daily the field hospitals, communicating with the parents of the wounded, relative to their condition. The unit chaplain's battle station during combat will most generally be the battalion or regimental aid station.
>
> —He performs divine services as prescribed by the commanding officer, whenever and wherever practicable. He will make special effort to insure that chaplains are present whenever companies or battalions come out of the front lines to go into rest or reserve areas and also when reserve companies or battalions are about to move into the front lines.[143]

Leave these men alone! Let them go! For if their purpose or activity is of human origin, it will fail. But if it is from God, you will not be able to stop these men; you will only find yourselves fighting against God.
~Acts 5:38–39

These specific duties addressed the chaplain's role in ministering to the dead, the wounded, and the healthy members of the command. His duties regarding the spiritual welfare of these troops were more difficult to specify, but were summed up as follows: "*Common sense in the rapidly changing conditions of battle, initiative for which there is no substitute, and the reminder to pursue the goal of 'bringing men to God and God to men' under all conditions, are the constant criteria for every chaplain.*"[144]

Navy chaplains with the Marines have always had the difficult task of trying to please God and Marine commanding officers at the same time—two very demanding chains of command. The priority was clear, however, in this SOP from the Korean War. The spiritual needs of the men came first.

Life Goes On

VINCENT WALSH was a machinist's mate on the *USS Beatty*, one of four destroyers operating together out of Yokosuka, Japan, in support of naval forces off the coast of Korea. At times his ship was assigned to a carrier task force as part of the escort screen, and at other times operated close to shore, escorting minesweepers and engaging North Korean targets with naval gunfire. After an extended deployment the *Beatty* returned to Yokosuka for replenishment.

In addition to some welcome shore leave, Walsh received a backlog of mail from buddies back home. He was amazed to read that their lives seemed so unaffected by the war—as if they didn't even know there was one. They wrote mostly about their jobs, paychecks, and chances for promotion. He didn't think too much about this until he returned home:

> First he said, "Sacrifices and offerings, burnt offerings and sin offerings you did not desire, nor were you pleased with them" (although the law required them to be made). Then he said, "Here I am, I have come to do your will." He sets aside the first to establish the second. And by that will, we have been made holy through the sacrifice of the body of Jesus Christ once for all.
> ~Hebrews 10:8–10

After I got out I began to resent it, because nobody seemed to know we'd ever been there. People didn't care about the war. They weren't thinking about it. They just put it out of their minds. We were just ignored. Eventually I got over my resentment.[145]

Since the end of World War II, the United States has engaged in a series of wars where the vast majority of its citizens have been unaffected by the fighting. Korea, Vietnam, Iraq, and Afghanistan have been fought by servicemen and their families, with little disruption to the daily lives of most others on the home front. Sometimes this sacrifice is appreciated, sometimes it is ignored. With few exceptions, our soldiers do not resent this burden, but accept it willingly. These patriotic Americans stand ready to give everything for their nation. Their fellow citizens should be equally prepared to sacrifice something for them and their nation's cause.

Robes

CAPT. JOHN ZIMMERMAN took command of the Navy Chaplain School as the Navy was expanding to support the Korean War effort. Chaplains were being recalled to active duty from all over the country from a wide range of backgrounds:

> I have become all things to all men so that by all possible means I might save some. I do all this for the sake of the gospel, that I may share in its blessings.
> ~1 Corinthians 9:22–23

The mix of chaplains was interesting. Although we had many who had had previous service in World War II, we also had youngsters with no previous training. They came to us from many denominations, some of whom had never known another denomination. You would get, for example, a Baptist from Texas who had never seen a Roman Catholic, rooming with a Boston or a New York Roman Catholic whose only training from kindergarten had been in Catholic schools. And they suddenly discovered they were both human beings.[146]

As these newly-trained chaplains were sent out to the fleet and Marine units, many of the Protestants from more informal churches expressed disinterest in the communion and altar kits and the vestments recommended for their use, expressing their resolve to hold services according to their own customs. Often, however, these chaplains learned a different lesson in practice:

Even if it was not their custom to wear any vestments, to stand up there as another officer often caused the men to see the stripes and not the cross. And we found that they themselves chose to wear a robe so that they were standing there in a distinct way, not separating themselves from the men, but eliminating any difference between the minister and the congregation.[147]

Chaplain Corps insignia (US Navy)

Although these young chaplains found robes necessary to overcome distinctions in military rank, many young pastors today lean away from robes and vestments because they seem to separate them from their congregations. This trend toward informality strives to make many churches more accessible to seekers—and more meaningful to a new generation of believers. Whatever our traditions, we know that Jesus is concerned with what is in our hearts—not with what we wear or what congregation we belong to.

Refugee Seminary

THE CHOSUN PRESBYTERIAN Seminary in Seoul was the only institution in Korea licensed by the government to confer the Bachelor of Divinity degree. When Seoul was taken by the North Koreans at the beginning of the war, the faculty and students of the seminary became refugees, fleeing to the south with vast numbers of their fellow citizens. Soon, however, the school was reconstituted on a hillside overlooking Pusan. Five professors and one hundred seventy students assembled there to live and hold classes in tents and makeshift buildings contributed by US military personnel. Financial aid to help keep the school going came from nearby units, as well as from church groups back in the States.

> I know your deeds, your hard work and perseverance. I know . . . that you have tested those who claim to be apostles but are not, and have found them false. You have persevered and have endured hardships for my name, and have not grown weary.
> ~Revelation 2:2–3

In spite of their primitive living conditions and meager rations, this heroic little group continued the important work of preparing Christian ministers for service to their country. One group of students even asked for help in obtaining Greek New Testaments, which they received and used for a class studying Greek Scripture.

Chaplain Richard Barnes with the First Marine Air Wing was one of the American officers who helped the seminary get established and gave one of the first commencement addresses. He had some observations on the state of Christianity in Korea:

> The whole of South Korea is filled with amazing stories, stories which should thrill the church at home, concerning the ability of this infant church to absorb punishment, and adapt itself to disruption and chaotic conditions.[148]

During the war years Christians in North and South Korea suffered greatly from the ravages of war, reminiscent of the early church in Europe and Asia. Fortunately, dedicated men and women persevered through the hard times in Korea just as their Christian forebears did in ancient times. From these tribulations we have seen one of the most dynamic Christian societies in the world spring forth.

Couldn't Save Them All

LIFE IN A Mobile Army Surgical Hospital (MASH) was often an unending procession of wounded. The doctors and nurses worked twelve-hour shifts, often without a break, never knowing when or if the flow would stop. The nurses would go from man to man giving what aid they could along with an encouraging word. No matter how busy they were they tried to stop and talk to every patient. They knew their efforts were appreciated, but they never seemed to have

> But the one who received the seed that fell on good soil is the man who hears the word and understands it. He produces a crop, yielding a hundred, sixty or thirty times what was sown. ~Matthew 13:23

enough time. One of the nurses, Cecilia Ann Sulkowski, said, "That was the hard part, not being able to give each one as much time as they really needed. You had to move on."[149]

Unfortunately, there was also a lot of regret over the many lives lost in spite of heroic effort to save them. In looking back on this experience Sulkowski commented,

> *There are experiences in your life that you wouldn't mind reliving. I don't think I want to relive those months at the beginning of the Korean War. At this stage in my life, my system wouldn't take it. I'd be sitting there and instead of giving those men care, I'd be crying with them. As Army nurses, we had a job to do, and that was to take care of our boys. Most of the nurses cherish their service time, feel sadness about it too, at the many young people we took care of and couldn't help. As much as we tried, we couldn't save them all.*[150]

Christians who take evangelism seriously experience the same sense of inadequacy. Sometimes it seems we can't even save one, much less all. It is important to remember that it isn't up to us to "save" anyone. Only God does that. All we can do is play our part in sharing the gospel when appropriate and setting a Christian example. How we live is more important than what we say. Our job is to plant seeds wherever we can, and to rest in the assurance that God will water them in his time.

Wounded brought to MASH (National Archives)

Hand Guns

EARLY IN THE Korean War the Marines learned some hard lessons about nighttime security. During Chinese attacks men were bayonetted in their sleeping bags, and some were even captured as enemy troops dragged them away like bagged game. Word of this soon filtered back to the Officers' Basic School at Quantico, Virginia, where Lt. Bruce Livingston was undergoing training. A Korean veteran on staff strongly suggested he obtain a handgun to take to Korea, since officers were only issued the M-1 carbine, a lightweight rifle. Livingston was able to heed this advice when his father gave him a German Luger 9mm pistol he had brought home from World War I. Livingston kept this weapon by his side every night, even though he fortunately never had to fire it from inside a sleeping bag.[151]

Bruce Livingston

One of my weapons instructors once discussed the relative merits of rifles and handguns, pointing out a simple truth: *"A rifle is obviously a superior weapon in every way . . . unless you're fighting in a phone booth."* With a pistol's small size and simple operation, there is a time and place where it has the advantage.

There have been times I felt as if I were in a phone booth with the wrong weapon— during religious discussions with unchurched friends. Even though I knew the truth of the gospel, I still felt I was losing the theological argument. At such times, I have learned to go to a simpler weapon: my own story. When you tell someone what has happened in your life, there is little room for argument. A brief explanation of what you were like before Jesus and what you are like since Jesus can have a profound effect on someone who puts up barriers. Just keep it simple, keep it short, and— make it heartfelt.

> When I came to you, brothers, I did not come with eloquence or superior wisdom as I proclaimed to you the testimony about God. For I resolved to know nothing while I was with you except Jesus Christ and him crucified.
> ~1 Corinthians 2:1–2

Respect

MARINE SECOND Lt. Joe Owen took charge of a group of new recruits, regulars, and reservists to prepare for combat duty in Korea. It was not an easy task. For several weeks he pushed these men to the limit, running the hills of Camp Pendleton, California, and drilling constantly on their weapons. Although he had begun to sense some progress, he was dismayed when his company commander told him at noon one day that he wanted to inspect his men the next morning. Owen knew this would be a problem.

> Here is a trustworthy saying: If anyone sets his heart on being an overseer, he desires a noble task. Now the overseer must be above reproach.
> ~1 Timothy 3:1–2

Conducting several preliminary inspections that afternoon, Owen could tell he was in trouble. Most of his men had not even been to boot camp and had no idea of how to detail clean their weapons or to prepare their uniforms and equipment for a formal inspection. After doing all he could, he went home that night with a sense of impending disaster.

The next morning, as he walked down the company street, he found his men lined up for the inspection. As he went from man to man, he was astounded to see that a transformation had taken place. Weapons were presented crisply, uniforms were immaculate, and answers to his questions were firm and direct. When the company commander arrived, this performance was repeated. He was almost in shock when he finally heard the skipper say, "Well done."

Later, the lieutenant thanked his platoon sergeant for doing such a great job. The sergeant replied, *"It was the men, Lieutenant. They stayed up all night. They wanted to make you look good. The men are afraid of you. But they were afraid they might lose you, too. They think you'll take care of them."*[152]

Any leader will accomplish only so much by relying on the authority of his position. Only when he earns the true respect of those under him will he see them go the extra distance to accomplish a difficult task or reach a lofty goal.

Goodbye

SEPTEMBER 1, 1950, First Battalion, Seventh Marines, formed up on the docks at San Diego with full combat gear. As the individual units began filing aboard the *USS Okanogan*, men with families were allowed to break ranks to say their final goodbyes. Lt. Joe Owen found his wife, Dorothy, and gave her a clumsy embrace, encumbered by his field transport pack and weapon. As a going away present she gave him an envelope filled with pictures of herself and the children. He placed the photos carefully inside his helmet. They both fought back tears and tried to smile bravely as they held each other and wondered when they would be together again. Dorothy stayed on the dock long after her Marine had gone aboard. She and the other wives waved handkerchiefs as the ship pulled away from the dock and bagpipes played the "Marines' Hymn."[153]

> A wife of noble character who can find? She is worth far more than rubies. Her husband has full confidence in her and lacks nothing of value. She brings him good, not harm, all the days of her life . . . Her children arise and call her blessed; her husband also, and he praises her.
> ~Proverbs 31:10–12, 28

This is a sad but familiar scene from every war. Saying goodbye to loved ones is never easy, but when soldiers and sailors depart for war there is a level of anxiety and sadness that is hard to imagine for those who have not experienced it. In addition to the worry, wives suddenly assume total responsibility for their households. Every issue with the children, home, and finances becomes theirs to solve alone. During the Korean War, irregular mail, often weeks behind time, was the only contact with husbands halfway around the world in places with unpronounceable names.

Marine says goodbye (USMC)

God bless these brave women who were as important to the war effort in Korea as any combat infantryman. God bless the wives of every era and especially those of today who shoulder these unimaginable burdens, serving their husbands, their children, and their nation in the most important role of all.

Battle Hymn

AS THE PRISONERS of Camp No. 5 in North Korea gathered to acknowledge Easter in March 1951, they had every reason to be despondent. Many were sick, all were malnourished, and death claimed the weakest each day. As the ragtag, bearded, and dirty group of prisoners gathered, there were men of many different faiths and even some who were not Christians. Chaplain Emil Kapaun gave the message, talking earnestly about the suffering and crucifixion of Jesus Christ. The men present had been through a lot and perhaps could better relate to the kind of suffering Christ endured as the chaplain's words inspired them to persevere in their determination to endure and survive.

> When the perishable has been clothed with the imperishable, and the mortal with immortality, then the saying that is written will come true: "Death has been swallowed up in victory." . . . Thanks be to God! He gives us the victory through our Lord Jesus Christ.
> ~1 Corinthians 15:54, 57

This spirit of inspired determination was captured in the words of a famous hymn this forlorn and bedraggled group of men chose to sing during that Easter service in a POW camp—the "Battle Hymn of the Republic":[154]

Mine eyes have seen the glory of the coming of the Lord;
He is trampling out the vintage where the grapes of wrath are stored;
He hath loosed the fateful lightning of His terrible swift sword;
His truth is marching on.

I have seen Him in the watch-fires of a hundred circling camps;
They have builded Him an altar in the evening dews and damps;
I can read His righteous sentence by the dim and flaring lamps;
His day is marching on.

He has sounded forth the trumpet that shall never call retreat;
He is sifting out the hearts of men before His judgment-seat;
Oh, be swift, my soul, to answer Him! Be jubilant, my feet;
Our God is marching on.

In the beauty of the lilies Christ was born across the sea,
With a glory in His bosom that transfigures you and me;
As He died to make men holy, let us die to make men free;
While God is marching on.

Glory! Glory! Hallelujah! Glory! Glory! Hallelujah!
Glory! Glory! Hallelujah! Our God is marching on.[155]

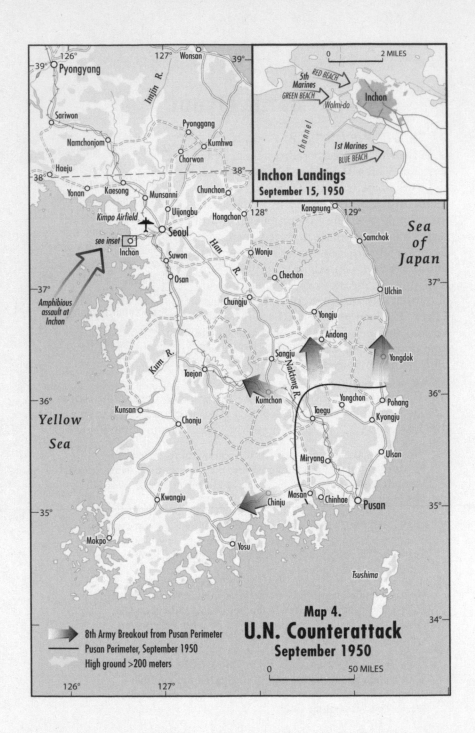

Inchon Landings
September 15, 1950

5th Marines
RED BEACH
GREEN BEACH
Wolmi-do
Inchon
1st Marines
BLUE BEACH
channel
0   2 MILES

Pyongyang
39°   126°   127°   Wonsan   39°
Imjin R.
Sariwon
Namchonjom
Pyonggang
Kumhwa
Chorwon
Haeju
38°   38°
Yonan   Kaesong   Munsanni   Chunchon
Uijongbu   Hongchon   128°
Kimpo Airfield   Kangnung   129°
Seoul   Samchok
see inset   Inchon   Han R.   Wonju   Sea
Suwon   of
37°   Osan   Chechon   Japan
Amphibious   Ulchin   37°
assault at
Inchon   Chungju   Yongju
Andong
Kum R.   Sangju   Yongdok
Taejon   Naktong R.   Pohang
36°   Kumchon   Yongchon   36°
Kunsan   Taegu   Kyongju
Chonju   Miryang   Ulsan
Yellow
Sea
Kwangju   Chinju   Masan   Chinhae   Pusan   35°
35°

Mokpo   Yosu

Tsushima
34°
Map 4.
U.N. Counterattack
September 1950

8th Army Breakout from Pusan Perimeter
Pusan Perimeter, September 1950
High ground >200 meters

0   50 MILES

126°   127°

COUNTERATTACK

B Y AUGUST 1, 1950, the Eighth Army had been forced back to positions east of the Naktong River. Lt. Gen. Walton Walker, Commander of the Eighth Army, ordered his forces on the southern flank to pull back eastward to Masan. As these dispositions were completed, the so-called "Pusan Perimeter" began to take shape. With more troops and interior lines of communication, the US forces finally began to contain the North Korean advance.

The US perimeter was roughly a fifty-by-one-hundred-mile area bounded on the west by the Naktong River and on the north by rugged mountains. In places, the line was thinly held, often by depleted units and combat-weary troops. However, reinforcements were starting to arrive, and the road and rail networks enabled rapid movement of troops and supplies within the stronghold. The British Twenty-Seventh Infantry Brigade deployed from Hong Kong in August, making the defenders finally a United Nations force.

Among the new units was the First Provisional Marine Brigade composed of the Fifth Marine Regiment with its own artillery, tank, and air support. F-4U Corsairs flying off aircraft carriers in nearby waters brought their unique brand of air power in close support of Marine ground units. During this crucial phase of the war, the Marines became the Eighth Army's "Fire Brigade," moving rapidly to a series of trouble spots on the perimeter.[156]

As the US forces were building up, the North Korean People's Army (NKPA) was becoming more and more extended and depleted due to combat losses. With ten effective divisions, the North Koreans tried desperately to penetrate the American defenses in their last bid for outright victory. Unwisely, they spread their effort over several fronts instead of massing for a concerted effort at any part of the thinly held perimeter. In the process, four NKPA divisions were severely depleted in separate unsuccessful advances. By late August the Americans were confidently holding their hard-won positions.

As intense fighting continued at key points around the Pusan Perimeter, Gen. Douglas MacArthur's staff planned for the long-anticipated counteroffensive, to be initiated by an amphibious landing at Inchon. An attack there would enable the early liberation of Seoul and decisively sever NKPA supply lines to the south. There were great risks, however, due to the geographic peculiarities of the landing site. The harbor at Inchon was only accessible through a narrow channel that could be mined or blocked, and a large tidal range left the harbor a vast mud flat for many hours of the day. General MacArthur considered these objections but brushed them aside, asserting that such an unlikely landing site only enhanced the element of surprise. The First Marine Division was assigned the mission of taking Inchon and continuing the attack on Seoul with the Seventh Infantry Division.

At 6:30 a.m. on September 15, the Third Battalion, Fifth Marines, stormed ashore on Wolmi-do, a little island dominating the harbor and connected to Inchon by a narrow causeway. Eleven hours later the rest of the Fifth Marines assaulted directly into the city of Inchon over the surrounding seawalls while the First Marines landed to the south to bypass and cut off the defenders in the city. Resistance was stiff at every point, but during the night the US troops reached their objectives and secured the beachhead. In the following days the Marines took Kimpo Airfield and continued the attack on Seoul against increasing resistance.

The Seventh Infantry Division landed administratively at Inchon and moved into blocking positions to the south to face the anticipated retreat of NKPA forces from the Pusan area.

Meanwhile, around the Pusan Perimeter, the Eighth Army mounted a series of attacks designed to break out of their encirclement, timed to coincide with the Inchon landings. After a week of heavy fighting, the NKPA began giving up their commanding positions around the perimeter. On all fronts US forces began advancing to the north, and on September 27 linked up with Inchon units at Osan.

After securing the beachhead, the Fifth Marines fought their way into Seoul from the east, while Col. Chesty Puller's First Marines crossed the Han River on September 24 directly into the southern outskirts of the city. Together with Seventh Division units, Seoul was taken after hard street-by-street fighting over the next four days. On September 29, General MacArthur, President Syngman Rhee, and a large group of military and civilian officials assembled in Seoul for a ceremony marking the restoration of the South Korean government in its original capital. General MacArthur declared the liberation of Seoul and asked for God's wisdom and strength to guide the Korean people. He then led the assembly in reciting the Lord's Prayer.[157]

Easter

EASTER IS significant to many people in different ways. To some it signifies the arrival of spring, flowers, and warm weather. To college students, it means spring break, often at a beach in a sunny place. To many resort communities, it is the first major tourist event of the year, with streets crowded by an influx of vacationers. For some families, it means a time to gather for church, in keeping with traditions from the past. In 1952, Chaplain Arthur Piepkorn wrote an article for military chaplains and servicemen and women to remind them about the true meaning of "The Queen of Holy Days":

> *Easter exists to remind the world that on an April Sunday morning some 1,920 years ago three worried women left their homes in Jerusalem in the pale darkness of the breaking dawn, to complete in secretive haste upon the corpse of Jesus of Nazareth the burial offices which the setting of the sun on the Friday evening before had interrupted. They had to return to their homes with their ointments and their spices unused, because the tomb was empty.*
>
> *This is the real meaning of Easter, that ever since that day men and women have known with absolute certainty of faith—*
>
> *That Jesus of Nazareth, who on Good Friday had been executed as a criminal, whose heart had been pierced by a soldier's spear, and the fact of whose death is beyond all doubt, was alive again less than thirty-six hours after they had buried Him, as He said He would be, and is alive today;*
>
> *That, accordingly, Jesus is what He claims to be, the Eternal Son of God, made man,*
>
> *That the message of Jesus is wholly and completely true, both as to the assurance of God's pardoning love and of His character-transforming grace; and*
>
> *That by His death Jesus has destroyed death and by His rising to life again has restored eternal life to all who are united with Him in His Church.*[158]

Long ago the apostle Paul summarized the same Easter message in a letter to his fellow Christians in the church at Corinth:

> For what I received I passed on to you as of first importance: that Christ died for our sins according to the Scriptures, that he was buried, that he was raised on the third day according to the Scriptures, and that he appeared to Peter, and then to the Twelve. ~1 Corinthians 15:3–5

Faith of Our Fathers

THE PRISONERS at Camp No. 5 endured the horrendous North Korean winter, suffering from malnutrition, untreated sickness, and exposure to extreme cold. The coming of spring seemed to bring a ray of hope with the warmth. Sixty men slowly gathered at 6 a.m. on March 25, 1951, to watch the sun rise and to celebrate Easter.[159] The half-starved, foul-smelling group gathered on the steps of an old, partially destroyed church with stark Korean mountains as a backdrop. As they sang a beautiful old hymn, the words seemed to pour out, expressing their deepest feelings:

North Korean POW camp
(National Archives)

Faith of our fathers, living still
In spite of dungeon, fire and sword,
O how our hearts beat high with joy
Whene'er we hear that glorious word!
Faith of our fathers! Holy faith!
We will be true to thee till death.

Our fathers, chained in prisons dark,
Were still in heart and conscience free;
And blest would be their children's fate,
If they, like them should die for thee.
Faith of our fathers! Holy faith!
We will be true to thee till death.

Faith of our fathers, we will strive
To win all nations unto thee;
And through the truth that comes from
    God
Mankind shall then indeed be free.
Faith of our fathers! Holy faith!
We will be true to thee till death![160]

Dear friends, do not be surprised at the painful trial you are suffering, as though something strange were happening to you. But rejoice that you participate in the sufferings of Christ, so that you may be overjoyed when his glory is revealed. ~1 Peter 4:12–13

And the God of all grace, who called you to his eternal glory in Christ, after you have suffered a little while, will himself restore you and make you strong, firm and steadfast. To him be the power for ever and ever. Amen. ~1 Peter 5:10–11

Sitting Ducks

S EPTEMBER 13, 1950, six destroyers steamed up Flying Fish Channel into the inner harbor at Inchon, two days before the arrival of the invasion force. Their job was to take station close to shore and engage the enemy batteries threatening the amphibious landings. To find the enemy positions, however, the ships had to expose themselves to almost point-blank fire. For this unusual mission they would become known as the "sitting ducks" of Inchon.

All the ships went in less than a mile from shore, and several much closer. One anchored directly off the southern face of Wolmi-do Island, while three passed through the narrow neck of the channel to the other side. Their three-eighths-inch thick steel hulls offered little protection from the shore guns. As hoped and feared, the enemy gunners could not resist these targets as they loomed before them. The shoreline came to life with a withering fusillade, and a furious duel commenced as the destroyers responded in kind. Three of the ships were hit and casualties taken, but they stayed in the fight. Carrier aircraft added their firepower to the fray.

> Grace and peace to you from God our Father and the Lord Jesus Christ, who gave himself for our sins to rescue us from the present evil age, according to the will of our God and Father, to whom be glory for ever and ever.
> ~Galatians 1:3–5

Tides permitting, the small task force continued its grim task for the next two days, finally in direct support of the invasion itself. The six destroyers were the *USS Mansfield, USS DeHaven, USS Henderson, USS Lyman K. Swenson, USS Gurke,* and *USS Collett.* All were awarded the Navy Unit Commendation for successfully completing their heroic mission. The award stated in part, *"Although sustaining casualties and numerous hits from the roaring enemy batteries, these ships refused to leave their assigned stations."*[161] Without their gallant effort, it is difficult to imagine the fate of the troop transports that would eventually follow them into the harbor. The Marines in the assault craft sustained relatively few casualties in the most dangerous phase of any amphibious operation, the ship-to-shore movement. The courageous sailors manning these Navy ships were the unsung heroes of the Inchon invasion.

To Sacrifice

WHILE WAITING aboard ship to go into combat on September 14, 1950, a young officer wrote his parents, *"If you catch yourself starting to worry, just remember that no one forced me to accept my commission in the Marine Corps."*[162] As a Naval Academy graduate, Lt. Baldomero Lopez sought the opportunity to lead men into combat. The day after he wrote this letter he did what he aspired to do by leading the second wave against the North Korean defenses

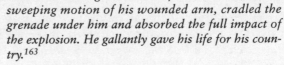

For whoever wants to save his life will lose it, but whoever loses his life for me will find it. What good will it be for a man if he gains the whole world, yet forfeits his soul? ~Matthew 16:25–26

at Inchon. He was the central figure in the iconic photograph of the Korean War, depicting a group of Marines scaling the seawall of the inner harbor.

Soon after going ashore, Lt. Lopez was wounded while trying to throw a grenade toward an enemy machine gun emplacement. Because of his wounds, the live grenade fell from his hand, and he was unable to pick it up. His selfless action to protect the men around him was later described in the Medal of Honor citation awarded to him posthumously:

Unable to grasp the hand grenade firmly enough to hurl it, he chose to sacrifice himself rather than endanger the lives of his men and, with a sweeping motion of his wounded arm, cradled the grenade under him and absorbed the full impact of the explosion. He gallantly gave his life for his country.[163]

Lopez is remembered by his family and friends as a happy and vibrant young man, filled with patriotism and highly motivated to serve his country. Among his high school classmates, he was voted the brightest. In his tragic death he took his place among America's greatest heroes, selflessly sacrificing his life in a worthy cause to save others.

Lt. Baldomero
Lopez (USMC)

Lt. Lopez leads Marines over the Inchon seawall (USMC)

In Support

GEORGE HENDERSON was a third-class petty officer on the *USS Henderson* when his ship steamed into Inchon Harbor to provide naval gunfire support to the invasion. With five other destroyers, the *USS Henderson* came in close to the beaches to bring naval guns to bear on the shore defenses. The ship anchored at 4:30 a.m. on September 15, and all guns commenced firing at 5:54 a.m. The young sailor described what he saw:

> *We started getting some fire from the enemy shore batteries and all the ships in the harbor returned fire, rapid fire. With our 5" guns and the cruisers' 8" guns, it was a sight that you could not believe. Within minutes it looked like a heavy fog had moved in and you could not see the shore. The rocket ship firing barrages of rockets was something you never forget.*[164]

Henderson also saw the landing craft approach the beaches: *"I watched the assault troops landing with binoculars and I remember the image of those young men going ashore. Within hours after the successful landing, as the tide ran out the water was a long way behind the beached landing craft."*[165]

> There are different kinds of gifts, but the same Spirit. There are different kinds of service, but the same Lord. There are different kinds of working, but the same God works all of them in all men.
> ~1 Corinthians 12:4–6

He noted that there was no way for those men to fall back once they reached the shore. A few days later, the captain of the ship gave the sailors a break from their duties and a special meal. Henderson enjoyed the food, but his mind kept returning to the men still fighting in and around Inchon. He said, *"I could not help wondering what our assault forces ashore were eating."*[166]

Henderson had great empathy for his brothers-in-arms, the infantrymen fighting to capture Inchon and Seoul. He was in a supporting role, but nevertheless took it seriously and did it competently.

We should each be so diligent in our work for God's kingdom. At times we will also be in supporting roles, helping others in some task. We should serve enthusiastically in whatever role we have. In the church, we are all vital members of the body of Christ, and the body will never get far if each individual part isn't working properly and fulfilling its role.

Readiness

IN THE EARLY days of the Korean War, naval chaplains were deploying to the combat zone in increasing numbers. The chief of chaplains wrote an open letter to the chaplain community addressing the need for constant readiness. On a personal level this meant taking care of family matters such as housing, insurance, and wills, both for themselves and for those serving under them. Professionally, there was a need for education and training in military and foreign affairs, specifically pertaining to the Far East and Korea. Above all, however, the chief felt the necessity of stressing spiritual readiness at all times:

> Be dressed and ready for service and keep your lamps burning, like men waiting for their master to return from a wedding banquet, so that when he comes and knocks they can immediately open the door for him. It will be good for those servants whose master finds them watching when he comes. ~Luke 12:35–37

> *These are days of deep concern for all men of good will. We do not attempt to prophesy the future, but once more a weary world is shaking under marching feet, and it may be that the dust clouds will obscure in some hearts the Son of Justice. We can best do our task by living from day to day. Too much concern about future things, which may or may not come to pass, will disquiet both ourselves and those who look to us for guidance. Let us trust implicitly in God, perform each labor, and meet each problem manfully, as becomes men of God. The seed of righteousness can never really want for anything. Let us always be charitable, but thirst after justice and not become blind, for there are many who follow us. Our weapons will be now, as always, those of the Spirit. The Everlasting Word of God is still a Flaming Sword, a guide, a beacon, an answer, a comfort. Use it well and we shall have no fear nor concern for the things that are expected of us all.*[167]

There are times each of us desperately needs help in focusing our attention on what is truly important. The chaplain has good advice, suggesting we think less about whatever is troubling us, while turning our attention instead to God's Word. There we can reacquaint ourselves with the eternal truths that put every care of this world in its proper perspective. With less preoccupation over what lies ahead and more immersion in Scripture, we can discern the guidance and comfort we truly need. Only when we have a firm hold on what is ultimately important will we be ready for whatever the world has in store.

Wounded

LT. BILL GLASGOW was a platoon leader with the Second Infantry Division fighting along the Naktong River. On September 17, 1950, he was wounded by a sniper's bullet while directing mortar fire on an enemy position. He described what it felt like:

> It picked me up and spun me completely around. There was this terrific burning feeling, like a hot poker going through me. My right side was on fire, the inside of my boots were soggy and there was blood all over my fatigues. I was lying on the ground in the open, between two groups of my men, and to this day I don't know how I did it but I got up and ran until I couldn't run anymore. When I collapsed I was pretty close to some of the men, and they put me on a poncho and carried me out of there.[168]

After a torturous journey by litter, jeep, and helicopter, Glasgow made it to a field hospital and eventually to Japan. The doctors told him the bullet that hit him went through his lung, spiraled down his rib cage and went through his liver and out of his back through a kidney. He was fortunate to have survived. He spent six months in a hospital and was not sent back to Korea.

When I get discouraged about things going wrong in my life, I think about the physical pain and realistic anxiety endured by Glasgow and other wounded warriors. However bad my mental anguish may be, it does not compare to a soldier's state of mind lying on a forlorn battlefield separated from loved ones, thinking he might be dying. My worst-case scenarios are usually not so dire. My problems can be solved or, more likely, will eventually solve themselves. God has expectations for each of us, but they do not include anxiety over the issues we deal with in our daily lives. He wants us to turn our problems into prayers and our worries into action on behalf of others and his kingdom.

> Do not be anxious about anything, but in everything, by prayer and petition, with thanksgiving, present your requests to God. And the peace of God, which transcends all understanding, will guard your hearts and your minds in Christ Jesus. ~Philippians 4:6–7

We Gotta Get Closer

PFC. WALTER MONEGAN was nineteen years old when he went into combat with the Second Battalion, First Marines, advancing on Seoul. As gunner on a 3.5-inch rocket launcher, also known as a bazooka, it was his job to engage enemy tanks. In the early morning of September 17, 1950, he got his first chance. As a North Korean armored column approached his unit, Monegan advanced with his weapon and, under heavy

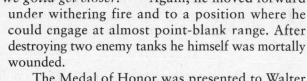

Have I not commanded you? Be strong and courageous. Do not be terrified; do not be discouraged, for the LORD your God will be with you wherever you go.
~Joshua 1:9

fire, destroyed the two lead tanks at a distance of less than fifty yards. The battle was over in fifteen minutes as other Marines routed the rest of the enemy column.

A few days later, at four in the morning, another force of enemy tanks broke through the lines of an adjacent unit, threatening to overrun the battalion command post. Monegan and two men carrying ammo for the rocket launcher made their way three hundred yards down a fire-swept hill to stop the attack. Sighting on the lead tank, he fired his first rocket, missing by a few yards. Showing the trait that had already made him a hero to his fellow Marines, he turned to his buddy and shouted over the din of the battle, *"We gotta get closer!"*[169] Again, he moved forward

under withering fire and to a position where he could engage at almost point-blank range. After destroying two enemy tanks he himself was mortally wounded.

The Medal of Honor was presented to Walter Monegan's widow, Elizabeth, and their infant son in Washington, DC, on February 8, 1952. The citation stated in part that his *"daring initiative, gallant fighting spirit and courageous devotion to duty were contributing factors in the success of his company."*[170]

Walter Monegan (USMC)

Truly, this young man gave his fellow Marines and all of us a lesson in courage. It is always easy to hang back at a safe distance. It is never easy to move closer to the source of the conflict or the root of the problem. God is always ready to help us tackle our problems head-on and to be the courageous men and women he wants us to be.

117

The Personal Touch

EARLY IN THE Korean War one chaplain wrote a moving article for others about his ministry, stressing the importance of personal relationships:

> *Wherever one human contacts another, as touching the deep and vital issues of life, there is an opportunity for service to God and man. We to whom men look and may rightly expect guidance and sympathy, counsel and aid in the spirit of the Master, should treasure each contact as a privilege and an opportunity.*
>
> *During the earthly ministry of our Lord, He never lost sight of the value of personal work. When others would have sent men and women on their way in blindness and pain, disappointment and sorrow, Jesus stopped to heal and bless, to guide and save by precept and example.*
>
> *Remember this, my brother—you may be a good preacher and you may have swayed hundreds Sunday after Sunday with your eloquence and logic, but when you have gone to your next assignment, men will cease to remember your texts or subjects. They may forget every sermon you preached, but they will not forget you, you as an individual worker, as a personal friend.*
>
> *Our ears should ever be open and our hearts responsive to the individual.*[171]

> You show that you are a letter from Christ, the result of our ministry, written not with ink but with the Spirit of the living God, not on tablets of stone but on tablets of human hearts.
> ~2 Corinthians 3:3

This minister's wise counsel is applicable not only to other ministers, but to the lay members of every church. Sometimes we become preoccupied with performing our various duties within the church and lose sight of the larger mission—taking the gospel to those in need outside the church. A Christian friend once explained to me, *"When doing 'church work,' we shouldn't lose sight of the 'work of the church.'"* In this kind of work, few are called to be missionaries or to preach on street corners. Rather, most of us are called, on a personal basis, to: *"Make a friend, be a friend, and bring a friend to Christ."* As we build a personal relationship with another person, we will have opportunities to witness by our deeds and our words the importance of Jesus Christ in our lives.

His Prayer Worked

JOE SALUZZI was a machine gunner with the Second Battalion, Seventh Marines, moving through the outskirts of Seoul. Suddenly his company came under a withering crossfire. His platoon leader went down, and then his platoon sergeant was killed nearby. Another member of his team was hit in the stomach as they both tried to get the machine gun into action. Then it was Saluzzi's turn. He felt the jarring impact of a bullet striking his chest. He described it as similar to someone hitting him with a baseball bat. The bullet cracked a rib, and he could hardly breathe. As he gasped for breath, time seemed to stand still for the young Marine:

> I crossed myself because I thought I was dying. I remember saying to myself, "God, please let me live. If you do, I'll go to Mass every Sunday and Holy Days of Obligation. I'll be a good Catholic 'til I die."[172]

As Saluzzi drifted in and out of consciousness, he was dimly aware he was alone on the battlefield. He spent a long night in the rubble, unable to cry out or to move. Heavy artillery fire fell all around him, but, miraculously, didn't hit him. Just after dawn the next morning he looked up to see four Korean children kneeling over him. They rolled Saluzzi onto a mat and started carrying him back to his lines in spite of rifle fire hitting all around them. Nothing stopped his little rescuers until they reached Joe's command post.

> The Lord stood at my side and gave me strength . . . And I was delivered from the lion's mouth. The Lord will rescue me from every evil attack and will bring me safely to his heavenly kingdom. To him be glory for ever and ever. Amen.
> ~2 Timothy 4:17–18

This was the end of the war for Saluzzi. Before he was evacuated, he gave one of the kids who saved him his watch, another his helmet. Whatever he had in his pockets, he gave to the other children. Somehow, his little band of unknown "saviors" had got him out. His prayers were answered.

He Changed Positions

DURING THE evening of September 25, 1950, Third Battalion, First Marines, came under an intense tank-led attack in the streets of Seoul. Pfc. Richard Hock from Milwaukee, Wisconsin, the son of a Marine, was behind a hastily-prepared barricade firing his M-1 rifle furiously. Suddenly, a man he didn't know dropped down beside him and asked if he had any spare ammunition. Hock knew he had extra bandoleers in his pack and crawled a few yards back to find it, while the other man took over his position and kept firing. At that moment, a North Korean T-34 tank fired an armor-piercing round that disintegrated a telephone pole in front of their position and almost decapitated the man firing from Hock's just-vacated position. Hock knew the man was dead before the body came to rest. The battle continued as the tank was destroyed by bazooka fire, and the Marines held their lines through the night.

> The Lord works out everything for his own ends . . . In his heart a man plans his course, but the Lord determines his steps. The lot is cast into the lap, but its every decision is from the Lord.
> ~Proverbs 16:4, 9, 33

Almost sixty years later, Hock retold this story and commented, "He changed positions with me and saved my life."[173]

When I saw the same kind of apparently random death on other battlefields, I questioned God's role in ordering such events. I have since come to believe that God does not direct the path of bullets or cause disasters. Bad things happen in this world as a result of human nature and natural forces. The world can be a dangerous place, and our Father in heaven does not guarantee our protection from all harm.

I also believe, however, God can change the course of events when it is his will to do so, and that he hears and answers our prayers. We should pray to understand his purpose and to be open to whatever plan he has in store for our lives. And we should never be afraid to ask for a miracle.

Dilemma

CORPSMAN BILL DAVIS was in his first attack across an open field near Uijongbu, when a member of his platoon fell to shrapnel wounds, bleeding profusely from a leg and arm. As mortar fire continued to fall around him, Davis applied battle dressings and tried to stop the bleeding. As he watched the rest of his platoon disappear over a dike, he faced his first dilemma as a corpsman. He knew his place was with his platoon, but he was afraid the wounded man would die if he didn't stay with him. He judged he should stay behind.

Evacuating the wounded (USMC)

Soon the battalion commander came on this scene and made a quick assessment. He showed the teenage corpsman how to mark the location of his casualty with an upended rifle and helmet, so that the stretcher bearers could find him and get him to an aid station. He then asked the corpsman his name and told him, *"You meant well, but your job is with your platoon. You'll make a good Marine, Corpsman Davis."*[174]

Sometimes our choices in life are difficult as we face our own dilemmas. We know we should turn to God for help, but for some reason we hesitate. Deep down we are programmed to solve our own problems, or perhaps the problems that trouble us seem too trivial for his concern. When we get in such a state, we must renew our confidence in God's faithfulness. He wants us to bring every concern to him, big and small. When we pray earnestly and listen to his voice, we get the direction we need while building the one relationship that will give us confidence to face whatever lies ahead.

> Show me your ways, O LORD, teach me your paths; guide me in your truth and teach me, for you are God my Savior, and my hope is in you all day long. Remember, O LORD, your great mercy and love. ~Psalm 25:4–6

Guilty Conscience

DON PLOOF had plans to become a monk. Instead of going to Catholic seminary, however, he went to Korea after being drafted into the army. At the time, he was a new and dedicated Christian. He had barely read the entire New Testament, but he prayed for hours every day. In recruit training he proved an excellent marksman even though he had serious qualms about using a weapon to kill another human being.

> My conscience is clear, but that does not make me innocent. It is the Lord who judges me. Therefore judge nothing before the appointed time; wait till the Lord comes. He will bring to light what is hidden in darkness and will expose the motives of men's hearts.
> ~1 Corinthians 4:4–5

Months later on a Korean battlefield, Ploof saw enemy soldiers for the first time. He had not even fired his rifle up until the moment he sighted two Chinese soldiers peering out of a foxhole across the barren landscape. He said, *"I was looking right into their faces when I pulled the trigger. I couldn't believe I was killing them."*[175] He later stood over their bodies and apologized for what he had done. He resolved to be killed himself before doing it again.

Unfortunately, circumstances did not allow the young soldier to stop being a soldier. Other battles followed, and he found himself killing enemy soldiers again and again. By the time he left Korea his new faith was in tatters. He buried the Catholic books he had brought with him to the war. He said, *"Now I was a murderer. Now I was a killer. I didn't want anything to do with God. I was angry that God would allow war to be possible."*[176]

This soldier's heartfelt anger was the product of a guilty conscience. He may have blamed God for the war, but he blamed himself for what he did in it. I have known soldiers in this condition who were able to find relief in only one place. By eventually turning back to God they found the forgiveness only he can give.

A Broader Vision

AS DIRECTOR of the Navy Chaplain School during the Korean War, Capt. John Zimmerman saw men from a wide variety of backgrounds coming into the service. Some were prior chaplains called back to active duty and some were newly-commissioned officers not long out of seminary.

> Of these, many had seen service in World War II in all branches of the Armed Forces. We had ex-Marines, ex-soldiers, ex-Air Force. We had one young chaplain who was an aviator with three Navy Crosses. We had one man who had the submarine dolphins (insignia). Chaplain George Fulfer had been a tail gunner in raids over Ploesti. They came to us from many denominations, some of whom had never known another denomination.[177]

Among these men practically every branch of Christianity was represented. Over time, however, denominational differences seemed to take on less significance as the men lived and worked together. They were also instructed to take a broader view:

> You are responsible for providing for the needs of everyone on board your ship or station. But on the other hand you are not in the Navy to make converts to your denomination. Those who come to you voluntarily and seek it, yes, of course. Do anything that you can to help them spiritually and guide them, but certainly you are not in the Navy to make new members of your denomination.[178]

As one chaplain from a very conservative church finished training, he remarked, "You know, we probably can't go back to our denomination. We now have a broader vision than our church taught, and we realize that there are other denominations with Christians."[179] Just as in World War II, these Korean War-era chaplains served as a strong force for ecumenism in the nation. These young ministers became close friends and, in combat, saw how insignificant denominational differences were to men who were hurt or fearful for their lives. They saw instead the uplifting and unifying effects of the gospel of Jesus Christ.

Make every effort to keep the unity of the Spirit through the bond of peace. There is one body and one Spirit— just as you were called to one hope when you were called—one Lord, one faith, one baptism; one God and Father of all, who is over all and through all and in all.
~Ephesians 4:3–6

God Saved Me

LEE CHAN SHIK was one of the most highly decorated soldiers in the South Korean army. He was also a devout Christian from a family of faithful believers. Extremely aggressive under fire, he was also noted as an officer concerned for his men and devoted to looking after them in every way he could. His first challenge in combat came in the battle for Hill 983, near Yanggu. He was leader of a thirty-two-man platoon, all older than him. After suffering several casualties from incoming artillery fire, he saw his men getting more and more nervous. He prayed fervently for his own resolve, and then encouraged his men: *"Just hit the ground when you hear the shells coming. Be ready to move quickly. Only the Maker knows our fate. Be brave!"*[180]

> Jesus said to them, "The kings of the Gentiles lord it over them . . . But you are not to be like that. Instead, the greatest among you should be like the youngest, and the one who rules like the one who serves.
> ~Luke 22:25–26

During the attack, Lee personally led assaults on a series of machine gun bunkers, praying each time for strength and accuracy as he went forward alone and threw grenades into the embrasures from close range. Each time he thanked God for his success. At one point, he described an especially intense mortar attack on his advancing unit:

> *As shells rained down, I hid myself behind rocks. One shell hit my backpack and my rib ever so slightly. Then it hit the ground right in front of my nose. It was a dud. If it had been live I would have been blown into a thousand pieces. I believed that God had saved me for better use later.*[181]

The spiritual convictions of this young Korean officer did not interfere with his effectiveness as a combat leader. Rather, his faith in God's ultimate protection enhanced his bravery under fire, and his compassion for his men inspired them to do the tough things he demanded. I was not a Christian while in combat, but believe strongly I would have been a better officer if I had been. These God-given qualities of confidence and compassion are what make each of us a better person and a more effective leader in every venue.

Rocket Fire

IN SEPTEMBER 1950 Bud Biteman was flying his F-51 Mustang on an interdiction mission northwest of Taegu along the Naktong River. He discovered a large body of North Korean troops crossing the river and, with the three other aircraft in his flight, began bombing and strafing runs to disrupt the enemy column. After several passes, he worked his way further upstream into a narrow canyon where he saw a group of North Korean soldiers pulling a truck across the river on a raft. With only seconds to react, he maneuvered his Mustang to line

Rocket Fire (US Air Force)

up with the target and fired all six of his five-inch rockets with a great *"whoosh!"* The explosion knocked the truck off the raft and sent a massive wall of water into the air directly in his own flight path. The narrow canyon prevented any kind of evasive maneuver. As Biteman flew through this self-induced hazard at 325 miles per hour, he felt a tremendous *"splat"* as he momentarily lost visibility. He described the sensation as similar to going through an automatic car wash. Fortunately, he made it through to clean air on the other side, safe *"except for a few more gray hairs."*[182]

An old military axiom warns pilots, *"Never bail out over an area you just bombed."* This episode might add a new one to the genre: *"Never create an explosion you have to fly through."*

When we see conflict coming, and there is little room to maneuver, maybe we should save our rockets for another day—or, in other words, keep our opinions to ourselves. This wisdom is summed up in a well-known biblical axiom conceived especially for husbands:

> My dear brothers, take note of this: Everyone should be quick to listen, slow to speak and slow to become angry, for man's anger does not bring about the righteous life that God desires.
> ~James 1:19–20

Sore Thumb

JACK WRIGHT served with Second Battalion, Fifth Marines, and told an interesting story about a man named A.C., his unit's only black Marine. One day they were moving by truck through mountainous terrain, when their convoy was stopped by small-arms fire from a nearby hill. The men dismounted, formed a skirmish line, and began assaulting the enemy position. As the attack moved forward, everyone noticed that A.C. was falling behind. He was the BAR (Browning Automatic Rifle) man and his firepower was needed. Finally the hill was taken, and, sometime later, A.C. appeared. Nothing was said, but everyone had a bad feeling about the performance of their only Negro.

> For he himself is our peace, who has made the two one and has destroyed the barrier, the dividing wall of hostility…His purpose was to create in himself one new man out of the two, thus making peace, and in this one body to reconcile both of them to God through the cross, by which he put to death their hostility.
> ~Ephesians 2:14–16

That night Wright's company was dug into defensive positions and came under attack. The North Koreans came at them from several sides in the darkness. In the noise and confusion, everyone heard the sound of the BAR. The first attack was stopped cold. As the night continued, the enemy continued attacking, and A.C. continued moving to the hottest area to respond. That night A.C.'s BAR was heard all over the hill.

When things finally quieted down, another Marine confronted A.C.: *"I'm not gonna mix no words. Yesterday, we couldn't get you up a hill to save ourself. Tonight you're all over the place. Now what's brung on the big change?"*

A.C. just grinned and replied, *"White boy, can't you tell the difference? In daytime I stand out like a sore thumb. At night, I got it made."*[183]

So that became the standard procedure in Wright's company. In daytime, A.C. hung back. At night he was at the front. There was no racial problem. There was no black or white. There were just Marines trying to get the job done and survive.

To Witness

DURING HIS internment Herbert Lord struggled to keep faith alive among his fellow prisoners. After his own uplifting experience of receiving God's assurance during the so-called "Tiger Death March" (see March 14), he tried to share his experience with all the others. Under the watchful eyes of the guards, he went from group to group, telling them, *"If you will bear with me, I want to give you a personal word."* Describing how God came to him on the road, he said, *"That text from the Twenty-Third Psalm cheered me tremendously—'I will fear no evil.' Remember it when we start off tomorrow. And now, bow your heads to say with me, 'The Lord's Prayer.'"*[184]

> You will receive power when the Holy Spirit comes on you; and you will be my witnesses in Jerusalem, and in all Judea and Samaria, and to the ends of the earth.
> ~Acts 1:8

Roman Catholics, Protestants, and even men of no religion said the comforting words reverently. Lord also said grace overtly over every meal no matter how meager or unappealing. On one occasion a guard appeared as he was bowing his head.

> *"What are you doing?"*
> *"I am thanking God for my food."*
> *"In the future you can thank me, I'm the one that gives it to you."*
> *"I do thank you for bringing it, but it is God who provides it."*[185]

Lord had said grace before meals since childhood. After this incident, he began saying it even over a cup of water. No matter what he received in the form of food or drink, he reflected, *"Every meal became a sacrament."*[186]

When we make a display of our faith it can have a powerful effect on others. Probably the simplest form of personal witness is to say grace in a public place. If you ever feel uncomfortable or embarrassed doing this, you might recall Commissioner Lord risking abuse and even torture for the simplest display of reverence. With his simple acts he inspired his fellow prisoners, and, over time, even won the respect of his guards.

Church Pennant

A SOLEMN, FIRM voice came over the ship's general announcing system, *"Raise the church pennant and lower the colors to half mast."* With that announcement, funeral services began aboard the *USS Bataan* for burial of a shipmate at sea.[187]

According to the US Flag Code, 4 U.S.C., Chapter 1, *"No other flag or pennant should be placed above or, if on the same level, to the right of the flag of the United States of America, except during church services conducted by naval chaplains at sea, when the church pennant may be flown above the flag during church services for the personnel of the Navy."*[188]

> A thousand will flee at the threat of one; at the threat of five you will all flee away, till you are left like a flagstaff on a mountaintop, like a banner on a hill.
> ~Isaiah 30:17

This provision of the law is rooted deeply in British and American naval tradition. History records a general order issued by Admiral David Farragut on April 26, 1862, aboard the flagship *Hartford* off the coast of New Orleans:

> *Eleven o'clock this morning is the hour appointed for all the officers and crews of the fleet to return thanks to Almighty God for His great goodness and mercy in permitting us to pass through the last two days with so little loss of life and blood. At that hour the church pennant will be hoisted on every vessel of the fleet, and their crews assembled will in humiliation and prayer make their acknowledgments therefor to the great Dispenser of all human events.*[189]

The church pennant is white, with a dark blue Latin cross. In 1975, the Secretary of the Navy further authorized a Jewish worship pennant depicting the emblem of the Jewish chaplaincy: the tablets of Moses and Star of David. Paying homage to the Almighty, the naval service still directs that these pennants, and only these, fly above that of the United States.

Church pennant (US Navy)

Prison Ministry

ONE OF THE most remarkable ministries of the Korean War was organized and led by a civilian Presbyterian missionary. Harold Voelkel was serving in South Korea when the war began in 1950. He was evacuated with his family to Japan where he met Ivan Bennett, the senior army chaplain in theater. Due to Voelkel's fluency in the Korean language, Bennett asked him to return to Korea to serve as a civilian auxiliary chaplain with the Republic of Korea (ROK) army.

> Keep on loving each other as brothers. Do not forget to entertain strangers, for by so doing some people have entertained angels without knowing it. Remember those in prison as if you were their fellow prisoners, and those who are mistreated as if you yourselves were suffering. ~Hebrews 13:1–3

Soon after landing at Inchon, however, Voelkel's ministry took an unexpected turn. After visiting a group of North Korean prisoners of war held in a prison near Seoul, he realized the need for pastoral care among these disoriented and discouraged men. They also seemed to respond to an American speaking the idiomatic (everyday) Korean language learned through twenty years of preaching in rural villages and schools.

Voelkel eventually went to the island of Koje-do, where more than one hundred thousand prisoners of war were held. Amazingly, he found many Christians among them. He organized Bible study groups and conducted thousands of evangelistic services for the duration of the war. He estimated that more than fifteen thousand made decisions for Christ during this time. When sixty thousand prisoners refused repatriation at the end of the war, many officials gave much of the credit to Voelkel's ministry. He later wrote of his work during that time:

> The ministry to the POWs has been the happiest and I believe the most fruitful ministry of my life. God has guided, protected, and prospered all along the way. He has kept His hand so manifestly and wonderfully on this work that at times I break out into laughter at the marvel of it all—God saving, training, and inspiring men to radiant Christian lives behind barbed wire. It is another of His holy surprises.[190]

Disappointment

DURING THE Korean War a nineteen-year-old soldier received a Dear John letter from his fiancée, announcing she had fallen in love with another man. In his poignant response the soldier wrote,

I never said I was the greatest guy on Earth; you did. Anyway, he's there. I'm here.

"Be careful," you tell me. "Take care." I almost laughed out loud. We wouldn't want to see me hurt, would we? There's no need to worry about me. I'll be all right . . . Do I say something brilliant like "may all your troubles be little ones?"

How about "if you ever need a friend?" That presumes a future.

There are 500,000 N. Koreans and Chinese on the other side of that hill bound and determined to make sure I don't have a future. Over here where your past is your last breath, your present is this breath, and your future is your next breath, you don't make too many promises. Which leaves me what?

Goodbye.[191]

> Then you will know that I am the Lord; those who hope in me will not be disappointed.
> ~Isaiah 49:23
>
> I will not leave you as orphans; I will come to you. Before long, the world will not see me anymore, but you will see me. Because I live, you also will live. On that day you will realize that I am in my Father, and you are in me, and I am in you. ~John 14:18–20

Two days later this soldier was killed in action charging an enemy machine gun position. We can only guess what part this painful rejection played in his untimely death. Despair could well have caused a lapse in judgment. Unfortunately, none of us is immune to this kind of emotional crisis. Every one of us will be left behind by loved ones who leave us for reasons sometimes good, sometimes bad. How many times do we hear of a person dying soon after the loss of a spouse?

Years ago, my wife, Lani, learned there is only one solution to this problem. As she tried to carry on with life after the death of her mother, she learned that when we have ourselves or our loved ones in the center of our life's circle, we are doomed to ultimate disappointment. Every human being we place in that position will at some point let us down or leave us. The only constant figure who will always be there is Jesus Christ. He will never reject us or leave us, and with him at the center of our lives, we will never be disappointed.

Fighting on the outskirts of Seoul (USMC)

Advance into Seoul (USMC)

Home

A KOREAN WAR-ERA chaplain discussed the challenges facing men and women in the Armed Forces during wartime and mentioned one that is sometimes overlooked—being separated from home:

> Only the naïve and ignorant fail to appreciate the shock of the breaking of the home bond in the case of many young men leaving home for the first time. Accustomed to the discipline, affection, and respect of a home, and a church, and a neighborhood, they become a mere unit in a vast military organization in a matter of so many hours.[192]

The chaplain also pointed out there are many young people with problems stemming from the absence of a stable home.

> The lack of the strong anchor of a good home tends to increase the drift that comes into the recruit's new life. Thus temptation acquires greater strength. Too often he is lured out of his loneliness into both moral difficulties and disciplinary troubles.[193]

This chaplain speaks from a bygone era and some of his words may seem naïve to us now. However, his stress on the influence of the home, for good or bad, in the lives of every person was justified then and is now. It is the home where we gain our identity and learn a sense of belonging. This identification with home and family is a strong theme we see running throughout the Bible. Jesus, however, sought to reorient our thinking on this subject. He encouraged his followers to seek another home that will last forever:

Do not let your hearts be troubled. Trust in God; trust also in me. In my Father's house are many rooms; if it were not so, I would have told you. I am going there to prepare a place for you. And if I go and prepare a place for you, I will come back and take you to be with me that you also may be where I am. You know the way to the place where I am going. ~John 14:1–4

Looking ahead to this future home, the apostle Peter considered himself and his fellow Christians *"aliens and strangers in the world"* (1 Peter 2:11). Although our earthly families and homes will always be important to us, we are clearly called to surrender our identification with the things of this world and receive an eternal identity as children of God.

We Suffered for Them

CHARLES HOUSE piloted a Corsair aircraft in the Marine Corps during the Korean War, flying off the *USS Badoeng Strait* in support of troops fighting ashore. He would often fly three missions a day, take a hot shower, put on a coat and tie for dinner, and play games in the wardroom until bedtime. Although his missions were as dangerous as anything imaginable, he described his role humbly: *"We were 'gentleman warriors.' We did not suffer the great hardships of the men on the ground. We only suffered for them, which inspired us to give them the best support we could."*[194]

Corsair takes off from USS *Badoeing Strait* (US Navy)

No one would consider a naval pilot's role in combat easy. The hazards of weather, enemy fire, and aircraft carrier operations made the daily lives of these pilots difficult and dangerous. This fact makes this young man's humility somewhat remarkable. He doesn't display the ego usually attributed to fighter pilots, but instead viewed his role as supporting others in worse circumstances than himself. He did not suffer the same hardships as did those on the ground, but he did what he could to help them.

This is a posture worthy of emulation by Christians. None of us will ever suffer to the extent our Savior did during his life and death. We can nevertheless suffer *for* him in countless ways every day. In whatever we do, we can pray harder, give more, and work longer to build up our churches and share his gospel. As we remember his suffering for us, we are inspired to suffer something for him as we give our best for his kingdom.

> For just as the sufferings of Christ flow over into our lives, so also through Christ our comfort overflows . . . And our hope for you is firm, because we know that just as you share in our sufferings, so also you share in our comfort.
> ~2 Corinthians 1:5, 7

Severe Apprehension

US FORCES had captured the small hill once and then been driven off by a massive Chinese counterattack. Robert Bryson and his fellow Marines in the First Battalion were given the job of retaking the hill. however, the attack was not going well, as a concentration of enemy mortar shells began falling among the Marines. Suddenly, something whizzed past Bryson's left shoulder, leaving a burning sensation. Reaching back, he felt a long tear in his uniform and blood seeping out. He recalled:

> I guess I realized I wasn't hurt that badly because I was still alive. I really wasn't that scared at that point. When a mortar hit, often there would be a whizzing sound. Pieces of shrapnel would whiz through the area and make a funny hissing sound.[195]

The young Marine's scariest moment, however, came shortly after being wounded. His unit began pulling back under the withering fire, and he found himself left behind with his captain and only two other men, guarding the retreat. He realized he was one of four men on one side of the hill, while hundreds of enemy soldiers were on the other side. In that moment he could only describe his feelings as *"severe apprehension."* He said, *"It was deep concern about the possibility of being captured. I would have certainly surrendered if I saw 300 guys come at me."*[196]

Sometimes it takes a greater danger to put our present trouble in perspective. Hamlet, in Shakespeare's great "To be, or not to be" soliloquy, contemplated the possibility of escaping the pain in his life: *"To die, to sleep—To sleep—perchance to dream. Ay, there's the rub! For in that sleep of death what dreams may come."*[197] Death is the greater danger anticipated by Hamlet and

> I pray also that the eyes of your heart may be enlightened in order that you may know the hope to which he has called you, the riches of his glorious inheritance in the saints. ~Ephesians 1:18

every other human being. Anyone without hope in the eternal future would have to face it with the "severe apprehension" of an isolated soldier or a melancholy prince.

Strongholds

THE ONE HUNDRED Eighty-Seventh Regimental Combat Team advance was stopped by heavy mortar and machine-gun fire from an enemy hilltop position. Artillery fire and air strikes were called on the hill with apparently devastating effect. However, when the smoke cleared, one could see that the hill was still in enemy hands. Under a continued cover of fire, infantry troops went into the attack, laboriously working their way up the hill. Chaplain Robert Rayburn watched the assault from a distance and finally saw the US soldiers sweep over the hill, securing the advance for the rest of the regiment.

As the chaplain observed this action, he was struck by similarities to warfare in the spiritual dimension. His unit had confronted an enemy stronghold that could not be ignored or bypassed. Some men were unfortunately lost in the attack, but the regiment could not have accomplished its mission if this threat had not been eliminated. Rayburn thought about the spiritual enemy that constantly seeks to establish strongholds within the lives of Christians. Satan covets these positions from which he can render the believer impotent and rob him or her of real victory—and make *"life something less than the joyous experience of fruitbearing for the glory of God which it should be."*[198]

We all know what our own weaknesses are and the ways we are tempted from the path God wants for us. Chaplain Rayburn reminds us these areas of our lives have to be confronted. We are in a constant spiritual battle that calls for courageous and resolute action on our part to deal with anything that separates us from God. The apostle Paul demonstrated a clear understanding of this kind of warfare when he wrote,

For though we live in the world, we do not wage war as the world does. The weapons we fight with are not the weapons of the world. On the contrary, they have divine power to demolish strongholds. We demolish arguments and every pretension that sets itself up against the knowledge of God, and we take captive every thought to make it obedient to Christ. ~2 Corinthians 10:3–5

Something in Common

BOB DOLAN was a forward observer with the Seventh Infantry Division on the front lines near Kumhwa. His job was to call and adjust artillery fire in support of his unit. He did his job during many brutal battles, and on one occasion called fire on his own position when it was being overrun by Chinese forces.

As a Korean War veteran, Dolan was asked many times after the war how he felt toward the Chinese, his enemies on the battlefield. He replied by telling a story about a young Chinese soldier. On many cold mornings, Dolan and the other American troops watched across the lines as a Chinese soldier came out into the open to play with his puppy. As the enemy soldier frolicked in the snow, he was completely vulnerable and apparently oblivious to the danger. Dolan recalled:

> He causes his sun to rise on the evil and the good, and sends rain on the righteous and the unrighteous. If you love those who love you, what reward will you get? ~Matthew 5:45–46

> *The bravery and playfulness of this Chinese soldier impressed me and the other American soldiers so much that no one fired upon him. We encouraged the newest arrivals to our camp to not fire as well. I guess we all felt good when we watched the soldier and the pup. We had something in common with that Chinese soldier, with the people we were fighting in hand-to-hand combat in a war. For those few days, it was the love of a puppy.*[199]

Sometimes it doesn't take much to break down our barriers. In another war, my attitude toward the enemy changed on the day I searched the body of a North Vietnamese soldier and found a photograph of his family. In that moment I realized we also had something in common—loved ones at home.

If soldiers can have such epiphanies on the battlefield, there is no reason we can't look beyond the obvious in our everyday lives. That person we know who seems so aloof or irritating has likable qualities hidden somewhere inside. When we look at every other human being as one of God's children, we find something in common that transcends all else in breaking down barriers—the love of a heavenly Father.

Leave None Behind

When I was in Korea, I was eighteen and a half and I didn't think I would live to be nineteen.[200]

DONALD MAGUIRE had his share of close calls while serving in combat with a Marine engineer company. His job was to operate a bulldozer, cutting roads and digging emplacements—often under fire. Enemy mortars were a constant threat, falling suddenly without warning. As he said, *"They came in just like rain."* One day, a bullet passed between his arm and body, penetrating the fuel tank mounted directly behind him. He was unhurt but realized there were several ways he could have died in that moment. Instead, he plugged the hole and continued with the job.

At one point in the war, the Marines on the line became isolated when a Chinese offensive pushed the US and Korean units back on either flank. Maguire had vivid memories of Gen. "Chesty" Puller coming up to the front to explain what was going on. The general said, *"We are going to advance to the rear. We are going back, and I don't want any Marines left here. Bring them all out."*[201] During a fighting withdrawal, the Marines took these instructions to heart. No wounded and no dead were left behind. Maguire did his part:

> *We brought out three guys that got hit with me on the dozer. They were with the infantry, and they got hit and were wounded, and we put them up on the deck of the dozer, and hauled them out with me, because we weren't going to leave them. We didn't want anybody to be left behind.*[202]

It's an important military principle to never leave a comrade on the battlefield. If Christians looked at their non-Christian friends in this way, we would have a more urgent view of evangelism. Do you want to go to heaven without your friends? If not, the time to act is now. Say something about your faith. Plant a seed. Don't leave them behind.

This is good, and pleases God our Savior, who wants all men to be saved and to come to a knowledge of the truth. For there is one God and one mediator between God and men, the man Christ Jesus.
~1 Timothy 2:3–5

God of the Weak

Gen. Wilbur
Brown (USMC)

BRIG. GEN. WILBUR BROWN was a former enlisted man who rose to general officer rank after commanding troops in combat during three wars. During the Korean War he addressed a group of Navy chaplains on the subject of what Marines expect from their chaplains. He began by recalling a short poem:

Men say you're the God of the wise and the good.
We know You're the God of the strong,
We hope You're the God of us blundering fools,
Who falter and stumble along.
The wise need so little, the good are all blessed,
Their strength to the strong You renew.
We hope there's a place in Your infinite plan
For the weak ones who have nothing but You.[203]

With this poem in mind, Brown explained to the chaplains some things about the men they would be serving:

In the Marine Corps you will encounter very few of the wise and the good. We do have some, most unaccountably, but if you encounter any of them, they will be no problem to you. Of those who will admit to being weak you will find very few. But there is a large percentage of those who claim to be strong who are just imitating those who really are. They are your main concern.[204]

In directing attention to the weak, the general was giving practical advice to the chaplains, and also highlighting the fundamental truth of the Christian gospel: *"Christ Jesus came into the world to save sinners"* (1 Timothy 1:15). Jesus was criticized by the religious leaders of his time for associating with disreputable people, but he was only going where he was needed. Then and now, he heals the wounded and broken-hearted. There is no room for him in a heart that is self-righteous or self-sufficient.

But God chose the foolish things of this world to shame the wise; God chose the weak things of the world to shame the strong. He chose the lowly things of this world and the despised things—and the things that are not—to nullify the things that are, so that no one may boast before him. It is because of him that you are in Christ Jesus, who has become for us wisdom from God—that is, our righteousness, holiness and redemption.

~1 Corinthians 1:27–30

Infinite Resources

A S A GROUP of chaplains prepared for combat duty in Korea, they listened intently to the advice of Wilbur Brown, a Marine Corps general and veteran of many battles. At one point the general's words took on an especially hard tone:

Chaplains of whatever brand of Christianity or Judaism that each of you represent, preach that death need not be feared. That is hard to believe. No one ever will believe it when it comes from a chaplain who has shown that he does not believe it himself. Battlefield experience has shown that cowardice on the part of chaplains does more harm to the Christianity that any such chaplain professes than twenty times their number of communist agitators preaching atheism could ever do.

Before and after battle when hardship is encountered it is necessary for the chaplain to set an example of fortitude. If he is a whining cry-baby, the men will turn from him. Maybe I am making a chaplain's job sound pretty tough. It is, but a chaplain is supposed to be sustained spiritually far more than any layman.

It is an awful responsibility that you have, gentlemen, but your resources are infinite. Remember the quotation, "If God be for us, who can be against us?"[205]

What then, shall we say in response to this? If God is for us, who can be against us? He who did not spare his own Son, but gave him up for us all—how will he not also, along with him, graciously give us all things? . . . Who shall separate us from the love of Christ? Shall trouble or hardship or persecution or famine or nakedness or danger or sword? . . . No, in all these things we are more than conquerors through him who loved us.
~Romans 8:31–32, 35, 37

This quotation is from the apostle Paul's epistle to the church in Rome (Romans 8:31). Amazingly, we see here a Marine officer using Paul's words to urge a group of religious leaders to remember the power of God. He knew they would not be able to successfully live up to the expectations placed on them using only their own resources.

We know these words are not just for the clergy. All Christians need to hear them and let them settle deeply into their souls. No matter what difficulties we face or how weak and powerless we feel, there are infinite resources available when we turn to our Father in heaven.

In Battle

BRIG. GEN. WILBUR BROWN continued his talk to chaplains about what to expect of themselves in battle. As Christians face the trials that go with standing up for their faith in a secular culture, his pointed remarks can be applied to every ordained and lay leader of the church:

> *We grade all of our officers and non-commissioned officers with one of four answers to the same question. "In time of war or national emergency, would you (a) Particularly desire this officer, (b) Be glad to have him, (c) Be willing to have him or (d) Prefer not to have him?" You will be marked on that question if you serve with Marines, and the marking will never be perfunctory. That evaluation of you will be made by very many people who will never record it on your record.*
>
> *In battle a chaplain must not show fear or shun danger. All men are more or less cowardly if they are normal. From my personal experience I can positively assure you that a man cannot die of fear, or I would have died long ago, and many times since. When fear is eating out your guts you have to call on your personal integrity to do for courage and face it down. Men all around you will be feeling the same fear as you.*
>
> *In battle a chaplain is a crutch to the weak, if he is strong. A broken crutch can never be patched up for further use. No one will ever again trust it.*[206]

These were hard words for young ministers to hear. By nature, Christians are forgiving and prone to overlooking the mistakes of others. However, these compassionate traits are generally not found in the unbelievers in this world. They are quick to judge the behavior of Christians. We may have only one opportunity to make an impression. Will we join in criticizing someone who is not present? Will we make a profane comment? Will we be silent when someone makes a joke about religion? Or, will we take advantage of a small opening to say something about the power of faith in our own life, or to give a brief witness about our life before and after Jesus?

In some cultures today, these would be life-or-death questions. For most of us, we only have to fear ridicule or rejection. But as General Brown said, *"A man cannot die of fear."* We will be judged by others and ultimately by God for the courage we summon in the midst of our own battles.

> But you, man of God, flee from all this, and pursue righteousness, godliness, faith, love, endurance and gentleness. Fight the good fight of the faith.
> ~1 Timothy 6:11–12

Chaplain holds roadside service (US Army)

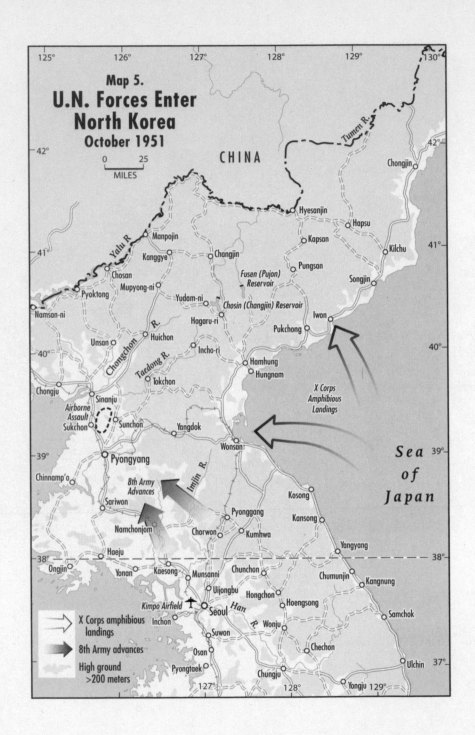

Map 5.
**U.N. Forces Enter
North Korea**
October 1951

0   25
MILES

CHINA

Tumen R.

Chongjin

Hyesanjin

Hapsu

Manpojin

Yalu R.

Kapsan

Kilchu

Kanggye

Changjin

Pungsan

Songjin

Chosan

Mupyong-ni

Fusen (Pujon)
Reservoir

Pyoktong

Yudam-ni

Chosin (Changjin) Reservoir

Iwon

Namsan-ni

Hagaru-ri

Pukchong

Unsan

Huichon

Incho-ri

Chongchon R.

Taedong R.

Hamhung

Hungnam

Tokchon

X Corps
Amphibious
Landings

Chongju

Sinanju

Airborne
Assault
Sukchon

Suchon

Yangdok

Wonsan

Pyongyang

Imjin R.

Sea
of
Japan

Chinnamp'o

8th Army
Advances

Sariwon

Kosong

Namchonjom

Pyonggang

Kansong

Chorwon

Kumhwa

Haeju

Yangyang

Ongjin

Yonan

Kaesong

Munsanni

Chunchon

Chumunjin

Kangnung

Uijongbu

Hongchon

Hoengson

Kimpo Airfield

Seoul

Han R.

Wonju

Samchok

Inchon

Suwon

Chechon

Osan

Pyongtaek

Chungju

Ulchin

Yongju

X Corps amphibious
landings

8th Army advances

High ground
>200 meters

MARCH TO THE YALU

THE CAPTURE of Inchon and Seoul and the breakout of the Eighth Army from the Pusan Perimeter were sudden and complete victories for the UN command. Unfortunately, an opportunity was missed to trap or destroy the North Korean People's Army (NKPA) between the Inchon and Pusan forces. The severely battered NKPA managed to withdraw north of Seoul with enough manpower to regroup and continue the fight.

Although the Truman administration and Gen. Douglas MacArthur were prepared to continue the war by invading North Korea, circumstances delayed an immediate advance. When the matter was taken before the United Nations, it wasn't until October 7, 1950, that a resolution was obtained, ambiguously stating, ". . . all appropriate steps be taken to ensure conditions of stability throughout Korea."[207] Although this was considered adequate sanction for further operations, General MacArthur's own plans created even more delays. He decided to pull the First Marine Division and Seventh Infantry Division out of the Seoul area, reload them aboard ships at Inchon, and send them around the coast to Wonsan. This movement was a logistical nightmare, tying up supply lines and shipping that would have enabled the Eighth Army to launch an immediate offensive.

At this same time, Communist China began voicing public concern over events in Korea. In September the Chinese Foreign Office declared that China would stand by the Korean people, and the Foreign Minister Zhou En-lai warned, "The Chinese people absolutely will not tolerate foreign aggression, nor will they supinely tolerate their neighbors being savagely invaded by the imperialists."[208] On October 3, a specific warning was sent through the Indian ambassador that China would intervene if UN forces entered North Korea. Unfortunately, US planners did not take these warnings seriously.

On October 9, General MacArthur issued a final call for the surrender of North Korean forces, advising that without an immediate response he would resume military action. On the same day, the First Cavalry Division crossed the 38th parallel north of Kaesong. The British Twenty-Seventh Commonwealth Brigade (with British and Australian units), the ROK First Division, and the US Twenty-Fourth Division took part in the advance. Enemy resistance was determined for the first week, but on

October 16 the NKPA lines at Kumchon collapsed, and the race was on for Pyongyang.

On the east coast, ROK units made rapid progress, reaching Wonsan October 10. They discovered that Wonsan harbor was effectively barred from naval operations by mine fields. Over two thousand mines of different types had been expertly laid under Soviet supervision. The landing of the First Marine Division and Seventh Infantry Divisions, designated X Corps, had to be delayed as a small fleet of minesweepers began the tedious process of clearing the harbor.

As the UN advance continued on all fronts, unknown to US intelligence agencies, eighteen divisions of the Chinese Thirteenth Army Group began crossing the Yalu River into North Korea. Moving at night, on foot, they remained completely undetected. An additional twelve divisions entrained from the Chinese province of Shandong, bound for Manchuria and then North Korea. In all, three hundred thousand Chinese troops were on the way to meet the UN advance.[209]

After heavy fighting on the outskirts of Pyongyang, the ROK First Division and the First Cavalry Division entered the North Korean capital largely unopposed on October 19 and 20. NKPA forces and the Communist government had abandoned a city already reduced to rubble by allied bombing. Also on October 20, the 187th Regimental Combat Team conducted the first airborne operation of the war, jumping into drop zones north of Pyongyang in the Sukchon-Sunchon area to cut off retreating enemy forces. The well-executed operation was unfortunately too late to bottle up significant numbers of NKPA units retreating ahead of the advance. As intelligence reports began to show NKPA forces well to the north of the Chongchon River, the Eighth Army continued in pursuit.

On October 25, the First Marine Division finally went ashore at Wonsan after steaming aimlessly at sea for over a week waiting for mines to be cleared. A few days later, the Seventh Infantry Division landed one hundred miles farther up the coast at Iwon. Both units advanced to the north toward the Yalu River against scattered resistance.

As UN forces in the east and west became more and more extended deep into the rugged terrain of North Korea, frigid Siberian air began to descend on troops poorly equipped for winter operations. Also, ominously, units began reporting the presence of Chinese soldiers on the battlefield. Again, these reports were ignored by higher headquarters.

Moral Courage

JUDGING THAT the North Korean army was in retreat, Gen. Douglas MacArthur ordered an all-out offensive on November 24, 1950, aimed at reaching the Yalu River and ending the war. On that day he spent five hours with Gen. Walton Walker at the front. He went from unit to unit and was notably cheerful about the army's prospects for success.

> I eagerly expect and hope that I will in no way be ashamed, but will have sufficient courage so that now as always Christ will be exalted in my body, whether by life or by death. ~Philippians 1:20

General Walker was not so cheerful and was unable to share his senior's optimistic outlook on the situation. In fact, he was feeling increasingly vulnerable as his units moved north toward enemy forces of unknown size. As he stood watching General MacArthur depart, he came to a decision. He turned, got into a jeep, and ordered the driver to take him to the nearby Twenty-Fourth Division command post. Once there, he gave the order to tell the regimental commander of the unit leading the attack, *"If he smells Chinese chow, pull back immediately."*[210] With those words, General Walker countermanded the orders he had received for an all-out offensive. He made the most difficult choice a military leader can face—to comply with a misguided order or to look after the safety of his men.

Examples of courage under fire are not unusual in combat. Some men rise to the occasion in spite of the physical danger. General Walker in this instance displayed a different kind of courage. He was not in the heat of battle and had to make a calm assessment of his situation and decide on a course of action that could ruin his career. It takes *moral* courage to choose a path because it is the right thing to do, in spite of possible adverse consequences for us. Our Savior displayed this kind of courage when he submitted himself to a torturous execution, knowing in advance how terrible it would be. We may never have to face what Christ faced, but we need this kind of courage to do his work in the world.

The Tunnel

AFTER THE Inchon landing, the North Korean army went into full retreat. Moving north, they took their prisoners with them, not wanting any to be repatriated. In late October, one hundred eighty survivors of a brutal march from Seoul to Pyongyang were put into open rail cars to continue the journey northward. After several days the train stopped in a tunnel near Sunchon. There, in groups of forty, the prisoners were herded from the train to a nearby embankment and shot with submachine guns.[211]

Lloyd Kreider was one of the American soldiers lined up to be shot. As he faced his executioners his senses were numb. He was too weak to walk, much less run away, and felt he was already close to death after being beaten and starved for more than a month. As the firing started, he dropped down into the ditch before being hit and was soon covered by another body. He was missed again by soldiers bayonetting survivors. Amazingly, he and one other soldier were left behind alive and were able to make it back to friendly lines.

> Dear friends, do not be surprised at the painful trial you are suffering, as though something strange were happening to you. But rejoice that you participate in the sufferings of Christ, so that you may be overjoyed when his glory is revealed.
> ~1 Peter 4:12–13

Afterward, Kreider seldom talked about his experience because he thought no one would understand it. He later said,

> Most people's troubles, they're petty. People think they have problems, but most people don't know what real suffering is. People like that aren't going to understand what I went through. They say, "Oh yeah, I know, I read about that." Well, you can read about it all you want, but you're not going to understand how it was.[212]

I was struck by this soldier's words as a pretty accurate description of how most of us relate to the suffering of our Lord and Savior. Yes, we've read all about it—we know what happened. But how are we ever going to truly understand? I don't believe any of us will ever completely understand what Jesus went through. We can only take the trials and tragedies confronting us in our daily lives as pale reminders of what he did for our sake.

Crossing the 38th parallel (US Army)

Infantry moves into North Korea (National Archives)

The Bell

ON OCTOBER 19, 1950, the northern advance of UN forces brought the First ROK Division to the outskirts of Pyongyang, the capital of Communist North Korea. That night the division commander, Gen. Paik Sun-yup, sent two officers across the Taedong River on a reconnaissance mission into the city. The next morning he was waiting anxiously for their report on enemy defenses when, from somewhere in the center of town, a single church bell began to peal boldly. Gen. Paik said, *"You could have knocked me over with a feather."*[213] He knew there had once been a sizable Christian community in Pyongyang, but it had not been in evidence since the Communist takeover in 1945. For five years the bells had been silent. The general said, *"It was as if the silent bell had found its tongue to announce to the world that Pyongyang was free at last. I cried shamelessly."*[214]

> But whenever anyone turns to the Lord, the veil is taken away. Now the Lord is the Spirit, and where the Spirit of the Lord is, there is freedom.
> ~2 Corinthians 3:16–17

Later, the general got the full story from his two officers. They had spent the night checking out key buildings in the downtown area. At dawn they slipped into a Christian church to hide. When they saw the church bell, however, they couldn't resist the temptation. Regardless of the danger, they were carried away with the drama of the moment. They were fearful they might arouse enemy soldiers, but, instead, were amazed to see the church begin to fill up with worshippers. From somewhere, a minister appeared, and an ad hoc worship service was held in the middle of the as yet unliberated city. The South Korean officers joined the service and were even asked to introduce themselves.

In explaining this touching scene to Gen. Paik, the two men proudly proclaimed that they were personally responsible for *"liberating Christianity"* in Pyongyang. The city was indeed free for a time. Even though this glimmer of liberty would not last, the faithfulness of this repressed community was a powerful witness to the world.

Communications

LT. CHARLES FORD was a new platoon leader with the 187th Regimental Combat Team when his platoon was given the job of leading an attack. He and his men were moving cautiously up a stream bed when they suddenly came under enemy fire. The soldiers dropped down among the rocks as machine gun bullets clipped the branches just above their heads. After a few moments Ford became conscious that everyone was looking to him for orders. Even though he had trained others in infantry tactics back in the States, his mind nevertheless seemed to go blank when he realized these bullets were aimed at him. He couldn't think of what to do.

Ford finally noticed his radio operator a short distance away and motioned for him to slide over. He made contact with his company commander, some distance to the rear, and told him of his plight. The company commander quickly gave him orders to deploy his men and get his own weapons into action. With a few words, the older officer galvanized the young lieutenant to put to use the knowledge he already had. He later said, *"If it had not been for that radio . . . I'd have been lying there frightened and unsure until someone had come to my rescue."*[215]

In the book of Ephesians, the apostle Paul eloquently describes the armor of God that Christians need in order to wage spiritual warfare against the powers of evil in the world. After describing each component of the armor and its purpose, he gives his final

> Be joyful always; pray continually; give thanks in all circumstances, for this is God's will for you in Christ Jesus.
> ~1 Thessalonians 5:16–18

and most important advice: *"And pray in the Spirit on all occasions"* (Ephesians 6:18). Just as the lieutenant needed communications with his company commander, Christians need a direct link to their source of instruction and inspiration. This link for us is prayer: Prayer that is deep and purposeful. Prayer that penetrates the confusion in our daily lives. We will never be effective warriors for our Lord and Savior unless we can communicate with him.

A Fine Line

GEN. PAIK SUN-YUP came upon an unfortunate scene on the outskirts of Pyongyang. He witnessed sniper fire that mortally wounded one of his platoon leaders in the First ROK Division. Then, in outrage, the rest of the platoon assaulted the building where the fire had come from. Suddenly two North Korean soldiers appeared in the doorway with their hands help up in surrender. However, the attacking soldiers opened fire, sending them scurrying for cover.

> You have heard that it was said to the people long ago, "Do not murder, and anyone who murders will be subject to judgment." But I tell you that anyone who is angry with his brother will be subject to judgment."
> ~Matthew 5:21–22

Gen. Paik took immediate action to halt the firing. Soon two fearful and starkly pallid prisoners were taken out of the building. The general reprimanded the men involved, even though they still almost glared with rage and frustration. They felt no sympathy for the men who had killed their lieutenant. Later, the general reflected on this incident:

There is a fine line in combat. One is often praised for crushing the enemy, yet it takes only a minor misjudgment for a combat situation to degenerate into barbarity. Courts and judges do not accompany infantrymen in combat. My view was that the crucible of combat can strip reason from men, if only momentarily.[216]

Gen. Paik Sun-yup (Dept. of Defense)

We often see civilization wear thin—and not just in wartime. Riots occur in this country and other places around the world that degenerate into looting sprees and even killing. Particularly in crowds, people can exhibit some very base human instincts, and these instincts do not seem to include compassion or mercy. As Christians, we may think ourselves immune to this kind of behavior. However, we need to remember that our Savior redefined morality for his followers. He was less concerned with our obedience to the law than with what is in our hearts. Our thoughtless and angry actions may not break the law, but they can wound others and separate us from God.

Sole Surviving Son

SGT. ROBERT WARD was a full-blooded Cherokee Indian whose two older brothers were killed during World War II, before he was old enough to enlist. When the Korean War started, he joined the Marine Corps and volunteered for combat duty. Soon after he arrived on the front lines, however, his mother wrote to the Commandant of the Marine Corps, requesting sole surviving son status for her son. The Commandant granted this request and sent orders to Korea transferring Ward to a desk job. He protested the assignment, feeling he was needed in his unit. He also believed in the war effort and the need to contain Communism before it spread to other countries. He wrote to his mother:

> Both the one who makes men holy and those who are made holy are of the same family. So Jesus is not ashamed to call them brothers. ~Hebrews 2:11

> *I went on the warpath for the right to do my bit to keep our people free and proud, and now I'm shackled to a useless job. I ask you, my mother, to free me so I can once again be free to help my boys. So, I ask of you the one thing your heart does not want to do—release me to fight. I'm no barracks-parade ground Marine—I'm a Cherokee Indian, and I'm happiest being miserable with my men up in those mountains.*[217]

Sgt. Ward's mother did relent to her son's pleas, and he was sent back to his platoon in Korea. She said, *"When men in our tribe say something, they mean it."*[218]

The law exempting sole surviving sons from combat duty was passed by Congress in 1948 in an effort to prevent a recurrence of World War II incidents where multiple brothers were lost in combat. The movie *Saving Private Ryan* was based on this theme. The United States and our military establishment today continue every effort to reduce the impact of combat service on any one family, recognizing the value of the family unit as the bedrock of our national strength.

Leadership

PVT. MICHAEL O'BRIEN enlisted in the Royal Marines at age seventeen. After training in England for more than a year he was sent to Japan for duty with the newly formed Forty-First Commando. At that time he had never heard the word *Korea*. For several months O'Brien and his fellow British Marines carried out raids along the northeastern coast of North Korea in support of United Nations operations. Landing in ten-man rubber boats, they destroyed bridges, railways, tunnels, and anything else that

British troops in Korea (Dept. of Defense)

would disrupt enemy supply lines to units farther south. When the US Marines landed at Wonsan, the British unit was reassigned to the First Marine Division for its advance north to the Chosin Reservoir.

O'Brien had reached Koto-ri when the Chinese onslaught came on November 28, 1950. His unit was given the difficult task of fighting north to Hagaru-ri to reinforce beleaguered units there and to defend a vital airstrip constructed during the advance. To reach Hagaru-ri the Royal Marines had to run a gauntlet of heavily defended hills and lost more than half their men. Reminiscing about his combat service in Korea, O'Brien later recalled the quality of leadership he had seen:

> 41st Commando in my mind was blessed with the best officers in the world. They would never ask us to do anything they could not do themselves. They lived in the same conditions we lived in. They landed alongside us in our raids. Our beloved Colonel Drysdale would land with us. We would follow him anywhere. That is what every one of us thought of our officers.[219]

Many books have been written on the subject of leadership, but this young Marine sums up the essence of it with few words. We are more likely to lead effectively when we share the workload and suffer the same difficulties as those serving under our leadership. Speaking to his disciples, Jesus put it even more succinctly:

The Son of Man did not come to be served, but to serve, and to give his life as a ransom for many. ~Matthew 20:28

Going to War

CHAPLAINS ON troop ships bound for Korea reported extensive interest in religious services. One noted that 75 percent of the men on board attended church during one voyage. Another reported, *"Daily services on the transport with men en route to battle areas during the Korean conflict were especially well attended and their responses were excellent. About fifty such services were held, with a total attendance of over 8,000."*[220] One chaplain held eleven services every Sunday en route to Pusan and distributed thousands of New Testaments and more than 2,500 copies of the complete Bible. There were also frequent baptisms aboard these ships as soldiers turned to Christianity to allay their fears.

> He calls his own sheep by name and leads them out. When he has brought out all his own, he goes on ahead of them, and his sheep follow him because they know his voice.
> ~John 10:3–4

Unfortunately, as one chaplain observed, *"There are atheists in foxholes."* At times piety was seen in direct proportion to imminent or perceived danger, with a noticeable drop off later. One chaplain who came home after serving with Marines noticed that, *"The sacraments became less important in the lives of the men back home than had been the case in Korea."*[221] One troop ship chaplain said, *"Going to Korea attendance at Holy Communion was very high; but on coming home, troops returning had again relapsed into the normal tendencies of home life."*[222] Sadly, men in uniform are no different from the rest of us—our piety is often proportional to the trouble we are in.

Most Christians seem to find they are often closest to God during the crises in their lives, when they are forced to lean more heavily on him. From this perspective, our trials and tribulations often turn into blessings by strengthening the most important relationship in our lives. However, we also need to remember the all-too-human tendency to turn away from him when things get better. If we want to hear God's voice when we need it most, we have to learn to seek it during the good times *and* the bad.

Morning Prayer

AS WAR was erupting in Korea in 1950, Capt. Maurice Sheehy, a chaplain in the Naval Reserve Chaplain Corps and head of religious education at Catholic University, wrote a poem to give daily encouragement to soldiers, sailors, and Marines going into harm's way:

A Morning Prayer

O Jesus, help me face today
With joy and hope. And help me pray.
If there are hours of dark despair
May I remember You are there.

By Thy strong hands please strengthen me
The splendor of God's will to see.
The light that gladdened childhood's hours
Must now bring forth Thy choicest flowers.

The crimson clouds at sunlit morn
Inspire my soul. New peace is born.
When love becomes the soul's sweet diet
Within my heart all else is quiet.

From hasty words deliver me
(They echo in eternity).
No riches of this world I seek
But Thy glad word in spirit meek.

Teach me the uses of the stars
And friendship's fine uplifting spars.
Rabboni, guide my faltering feet.
Into Thy arms and joy complete.

AMEN[223]

I will sing of your strength, in the morning I will sing of your love; for you are my fortress, my refuge in times of trouble. O my Strength, I sing praise to you; you, O God, are my fortress, my loving God. ~ Psalm 59:16–17

Facing Mecca

KOREAN WAR-ERA chaplains were either Catholic, Protestant, or Jewish, and all worked together, often across denominational lines, in performing their duties. When soldiers were in pain or fearing for their lives, the fine points of theology seemed to take on less importance. Unfortunately, modern chaplains face a more difficult task in achieving this degree of ecumenism due to the wider range of religions now represented, including Islam and Far Eastern religions, with complex differences in belief and practice.

> There will be trouble and distress for every human being who does evil: first for the Jew, then for the Gentile; but glory, honor and peace for everyone who does good: first for the Jew, then for the Gentile. For God does not show favoritism.
> ~Romans 2:9–11

An early example of an effort to bridge this gap can be found in 1951 aboard a US transport ship taking Turkish soldiers to Korea. The ship's chaplain, Lt. Leon Dickinson, made the effort to meet his counterpart and to assist him in different ways. Ali Ozyilmas was a Muslim holy man, commissioned into the Turkish army only ten days before the voyage, with little knowledge of how a chaplain was sup-

posed to work within a military unit. Lieutenant Dickinson took the opportunity to orient him to the ship and to help him understand his duties as a chaplain in spiritual ministry to soldiers. Ozyilmas was able to organize his own services, as depicted in a famous photograph of Muslim soldiers facing Mecca in prayer on the deck of a Navy ship bound for the war zone.

During the voyage, both chaplains also held joint social gatherings to promote good will among the Turkish and American men aboard the ship. Chaplain Dickinson later commented, *"This friendliness of ideas not only made for a pleasant voyage, but added greatly to the understanding and good neighborliness so essential for the world of today and tomorrow."*[224]

Unfortunately, in the present day, religious and political fanatics try to make it ever more difficult for men of good will to bridge the cultural divide that separates racial, ethnic, and religious groups from each other. It is more important than ever that religious leaders and lay people of all faiths do everything possible to see beyond this destructive agenda and keep reaching out to each other in peace.

To Read and Write

PVT. HERMAN NELSON landed at Pusan in August 1950. His eight-inch howitzer battery moved up the Korean peninsula as the Eighth Army advanced to the north. His battery provided fire support during the capture of Seoul and, as the weather got steadily colder, moved through Pyongyang and on toward the Yalu River.

One evening during a quiet moment a fellow soldier asked Nelson if he could talk to him. Nelson described an unusual conversation:

> *He showed me a stack of letters, and he asked me to read them to him because he had never learned to read or write. I agreed and found myself reading letters from his wife back home, most of them quite personal. I soon learned he also wanted me to write his wife, which I did. So I found myself with an extra duty, although one I eventually began to enjoy. Even though I was single, by the time I returned to the United States, about nine months later, I had acquired a lot of experience writing letters to "the wife."*[225]

It is difficult to imagine the helplessness of a soldier not being able to read or write. While in the physical presence of loved ones it may not have mattered, however, once removed to a far-off place, written letters became a lifeline.

Sometimes we find ourselves in the same predicament with our heavenly Father. For some reason we seem to have difficulty making contact. Either our words are inadequate or our listening skills are failing, as we sense remoteness from him.

Fortunately, there is a solution to this problem. To keep our lifeline intact, God has given his Holy Spirit to work within our hearts. The Holy Spirit guides and teaches us, and gives us the right words when we don't know what to say. He aids us in comprehending God's words to us written in Scripture. He is always there to help us read and write our letters to and from home.

> In the same way, the Spirit helps us in our weakness. We do not know what we ought to pray for, but the Spirit himself intercedes for us with groans that words cannot express.
> ~Romans 8:26

Soldiers or Farmers?

IN EARLY 1951, I Company, Fifth Cavalry, was given the job of clearing North Korean guerrilla fighters from an area behind the lines. These enemy soldiers had stayed in place when their larger units retreated and were ambushing supply trucks along the main supply route. The problem was distinguishing them from the local populace.

Going into an area hit frequently by attacks, the soldiers rounded up a group of fifty men, all in civilian clothing. As these people sat waiting in a field, they looked like a typical group of farmers. Soon a large, rough-looking Korean officer from the battalion staff arrived on the scene, and the soldiers explained their problem. Had they rounded up farmers or enemy soldiers? After a few minutes, the Korean walked over to the group and stood menacingly in front of them, as all eyes were glued on him. Suddenly, he snapped to attention and barked a command in Korean. All but one old man immediately jumped up and stood at attention. He then barked a few more commands, as the group faced right and then left. One of the soldiers present remarked, *"Then, one by one, you could see the 'I've been a sucker' light come on in their eyes. No longer would they be able to play the poor dumb farmer role."*[226] All but the old man were marched off and turned in to a prisoner collection point.

> For the message of the cross is foolishness to those who are perishing, but to us who are being saved it is the power of God. ~1 Corinthians 1:18

As Christians in an increasingly secular society, it is always encouraging to identify a fellow believer. Since we all look pretty much alike, we look for verbal cues, such as someone saying, *"Have a blessed day,"* or, *"I'll pray about that."* We, in turn, say these things for the same purpose, to identify ourselves and give encouragement to others. In this light, the little crosses we wear around our necks or display as pins take on added significance. They not only announce to the secular world who we are, they also serve as a unit insignia for fellow believers, telling them, *"We serve in the same army."*

Soldiers or farmers (Truman Library)

To Share

AS THE BATTLE approached, the prisoners were loaded into a train at Pyongyang, bound for a destination unknown to them. Looking out through a broken window in his crowded compartment, Larry Zellers could see lines of haggard soldiers filing by on the platform outside. It was a depressing scene. Many were wounded and could barely walk. They got no help from the North Korean guards.

> One man gives freely, yet gains even more; . . . A generous man will prosper; he who refreshes others will himself be refreshed.
> ~Proverbs 11:24, 25

Even after the train was loaded, it didn't move for a long time. Finally, after it was completely dark and a lot colder, the train jerked into motion. As it picked up speed, Zellers realized the broken window that had given him a view outside was now a curse. The frigid night air was flowing in and freezing him to the bone.

A young Catholic priest next to him saw his plight, unzipped the light yellow jacket he was wearing and handed it to Zellers. *"Here, put this on,"* he said.

"I can't take this," Zellers protested.

"Wear it for a while. We'll share it," the priest said.[227] It was decided that each man would wear the jacket for thirty minutes and then give it to the other. The agreement held, and so did their friendship.

Zeller later said, *"All my life I had heard talk of someone who would give you the shirt off his back. I had found such a person."*[228]

Almost thirty years later Larry Zellers and Philip Crosbie, the priest in this story, met again. Zellers mentioned the time when they shared the priest's jacket and asked if his friend remembered. *"No,"* Crosbie replied, he had no memory of it at all.

Zellers thought to himself, *Memory lapse is an admirable quality in people who know what it really means to share.*[229]

The poet William Wordsworth echoed this theme of unthinking selflessness, pointing out that the best parts of a good man's life are *"His little, nameless, unremembered, acts of kindness and of love."*[230]

No Greater Mission

CAPT. EDWARD B. HARP, JR. was promoted to the rank of rear admiral during the Korean War and appointed Chief of Navy Chaplains. He was well acquainted with wartime service, having served on the *USS Hornet* in the Battle of Midway during World War II. In 1953 he published a letter expressing his time-tested views on the mission of the Chaplain Corps at that time.

> It is generally conceded that the ultimate healing of our present erring and harassed world will come only through a rekindled religious faith. If this is true, then the need of a capable spiritual leadership has never been greater than it is today. Amid all the confusion and uncertainty that exists, men and women everywhere are seeking light and truth and whatever else that will give stability and meaning to their lives.
>
> In this respect, those who comprise the armed forces of our nation are no different. These young men and women whom we serve, both in the Navy and the Marine Corps, are looking to us for guidance, for encouragement, for enlightenment in all the things that make for character and a more fruitful life by faith in God. This is our mission. There is none greater.[231]

Chaplain Harp's words are as true today as they were during the Korean War. In fact, people today are more harassed by life's complications and more in search of understanding and meaning than ever. There has never been a greater need for the forgiveness, healing, and peace that can only come through faith in Jesus Christ. It is also true that now more than ever the task of bringing the light of Christ to those who need it is not just the job of our religious leaders. Sharing the gospel is the duty of every Christian. Most of us are not called to preach on street corners; however, all of us should be prepared to briefly share the story of what Jesus has done in our lives. This is the mission of every Christian. There is none greater.

> Therefore, since we have been justified through faith, we have peace with God through our Lord Jesus Christ, through whom we have gained access by faith into this grace in which we now stand. And we rejoice in the hope of the glory of God.
> ~Romans 5:1–2

Soldiers of God

DURING THE American Revolution the first military chaplains were ministers serving voluntarily with the militia from their own parishes. Eventually the Continental Congress authorized chaplains for regular duty with the Continental Army. Since that time chaplains have been integral to the American military establishment and have served in every war fought by this nation. In 1951, the Army Chief of Chaplains wrote about the latest episode in this illustrious history:

> You show that you are a letter from Christ, the result of our ministry, written not with ink but with the Spirit of the living God, not on tablets of stone but on tablets of human hearts ... Our competence comes from God. He has made us competent as ministers of a new covenant—not of the letter but of the Spirit.
> ~2 Corinthians 3:3, 5–6

When action in Korea began, the "Soldiers of God" were not found wanting and in the ensuing months the record of their daily duties has been one which merits "well done." Their citations are indicative of their activities:

"Noting evacuation was disorganized, immediately assumed charge of operation under intense enemy artillery and small arms fire . . . thereby saving lives of numerous American soldiers."

"Voluntarily remained behind to give his wounded comrades spiritual comfort and aid. When last seen . . . still administering to the wounded."

"He remained in the area to minister to the wounded until wounded and ordered to leave by a superior officer."

These "Soldiers of God" have given unstintingly of their strength, their wisdom, and their lives to bring God to men and men to God. In peace or in war, (they) serve Him faithfully in serving their fellowmen.[232]

Throughout the Korean War chaplains continued their heroic service with every branch of the military, ministering to soldiers, sailors, Marines, and airmen in need. As in other wars before and since, these men went to distant and dangerous lands, carrying God's comfort, compassion, and mercy to where they were needed most.

Chaplain holding service (US Army)

Star of Hope

HAROLD BERGER, chaplain to the Veterans Administration Hospital in Danville, Illinois, gave a special message of hope to both active duty servicemen and veterans of the Korean War:

I stood beneath a starless sky one night. There was darkness over all the town. And then I thought: "What if life were as dark and foreboding as the night; what if there were no light, no hope at the end of life's day!" And then I chanced to see the faint glimmer of a star. Oh, wonderful star of hope; oh, light that shineth in the darkness!

As one grows older he looks long and longingly towards the star of Bethlehem. The heart grows weary of the discordant sounds of the world. The trip-hammer crashing of industry's relentless iron jaws, the babbling voices of high-level politics, the dire warning of atomic destruction, the blatant stories of advertising, the brazen lies of polished diplomats, the hellish sounds of battle, the screams of the wounded, the mournful moaning of widows and the whimpering of orphaned children chill the soul.

Yes, the vast symphony of suffering composed by and under the direction of the prince of darkness leaves one with a feeling of nostalgia for the land that is fairer than day, for the Lily of the Valley, the fairest of ten thousand, the Prince of Peace, the Savior of the World.

The name of Jesus becomes sweeter as the years go by. The old, old story of His birth becomes nearer and dearer, His peace more blessed amid the accumulating needs of the soul—this poor, poor soul which He made so rich.

"Joy to the world, the Lord is come!"[233]

> After they had heard the king, they went on their way, and the star they had seen in the east went ahead of them until it stopped over the place where the child was. When they saw the star, they were overjoyed. On coming to the house, they saw the child with his mother Mary, and they bowed down and worshiped him.
> ~Matthew 2:9–11

Marine's Prayer

URING THE Korean War Lt. Col. R. D. Heinl proposed a prayer for the Marine Corps that began, *"Almighty God of battles, who rulest land, air, and sea, grant Thy blessings and Thy favor on the United States Marine Corps. Keep them always ready, always faithful, to do Thy work and to protect their country in its need."*[234] Years later *The Marine's Prayer* was formally adopted by the Navy Chief of Chaplains, echoing Heinl's words but written for use in prayer by individual Marines:

> And pray in the Spirit on all occasions with all kinds of prayers and requests. With this in mind, be alert and always keep on praying for all the saints.
> ~Ephesians 6:18

(USMC)

Almighty Father, whose command is over-all and whose love never fails, make me aware of Thy presence and obedient to Thy will. Keep me true to my best self, guarding me against dishonesty in purpose and deed and helping me to live so that I can face my fellow Marines, my loved ones and Thee without shame or fear. Protect my family. Give me the will to do the work of a Marine and to accept my share of responsibilities with vigor and enthusiasm. Grant me the courage to be proficient in my daily performance. Keep me loyal and faithful to my superiors and to the duties my country and the Marine Corps have entrusted to me. Make me considerate of those committed to my leadership. Help me to wear my uniform with dignity, and let it remind me daily of the traditions which I must uphold. If I am inclined to doubt, steady my faith; if I am tempted, make me strong to resist; if I should miss the mark, give me courage to try again. Guide me with the light of truth and grant me wisdom by which I may understand the answer to my prayer. Amen.[235]

Coming Home

HIS LAST letter was dated November 1, 1950. Sgt. William Brashear wrote home that his unit had gone about a hundred miles north of Pyongyang, North Korea, to a place called Unsan. A telegram soon followed announcing that he was missing in action. His unit, the Eighth Cavalry, fought a great battle against Chinese forces near Unsan, and there were hundreds of casualties. Brashear was presumed dead, but his body was not recovered. His family eventually reconciled to the likelihood that it never would be.

> But if Christ is in you, your body is dead because of sin, yet your spirit is alive because of righteousness. And if the Spirit of him who raised Jesus from the dead is living in you, he who raised Christ from the dead will also give life to your mortal bodies through his Spirit, who lives in you.
> —Romans 8:10–11

Sixty-one years and three days later, Brashear's niece, Helen Adkins, received a phone call that her uncle was coming home. Years before, a mass grave had been found near Unsan and remains were collected. However, the technology at the time did not permit identification of individual soldiers. Later a non-profit organization called the Korean War Project launched a program to identify these and other remains through DNA analysis, using DNA supplied by family members.

When she got the call that her uncle had been identified, Adkins said, *"All I could do was bawl. He was a wonderful uncle. I was eleven when we got the telegram that he was missing. All they found were a few bones and one tooth. I asked them to cremate him."*[236] Brashear was buried with full military honors in March 2012 beside his parents' graves at Elmwood Cemetery near Owensboro, Kentucky.

As Christians, we are better able than most to deal with the death of loved ones. Still, there are few things as upsetting and even depressing as having to make funeral arrangements during a time of grief. Making decisions about these details can be a gruesome task unless we remind ourselves constantly that the one we love is not in the casket or the urn—but is in a far better place where we will see him or her again in the presence of our Lord and Savior.

Hearing God

AS HE PONDERED one of the most important decisions of his life, Chaplain Robert Rayburn kept thinking of this passage from Isaiah setting forth God's promise to guide him. He had less than twenty-four hours to tell his commanding officer whether he would make a combat parachute jump with his unit. As a new man with absolutely no airborne training, he did not *have* to go on this operation, and he knew that he definitely did not *want* to go. As always, however, he wanted to be in God's will, and he knew that God would give him the guidance he needed even though time was short.

> Whether you turn to the right or to the left, your ears will hear a voice behind you, saying, "This is the way; walk in it."
> ~Isaiah 30:21

(National Archives)

The chaplain took his Bible and found a tent where he could be alone. He began praying earnestly, pouring out his heart to the Lord. He confessed the fear that gripped him for his own safety and the concern he felt for his family back home. As he continued to pray, he began to hear God speak to him. He explained that it was not an audible voice, but was as real as any he had ever heard: *"I know it was His voice, for the words were His Word. I could not think for a moment just where the verses were found. I had no remembrance of ever having consciously memorized them, but this is what He began to say to me:"*[237]

For he will command his angels concerning you to guard you in all your ways; they will lift you up in their hands, so that you will not strike your foot against a stone. ~Psalm 91:11–12

As soon as this passage entered his mind, Chaplain Rayburn knew he had heard God's voice giving him the perfect answer to his prayer—a perfect promise for a paratrooper going into battle. The Lord would see him through whatever lay ahead. He was almost overcome with the thrill of that precious moment and the realization that God had spoken to him with a clear and personal message.

Blessings for All

IN THE DARKNESS Chaplain Robert Rayburn became entangled with another jumper in midair. As the other soldier's chute collapsed, he had to cling to the chaplain's during their dangerous descent. They hit the ground hard, but fortunately landed in the soft earth of a rice paddy furrow. As they peered at each other through the darkness, the soldier finally recognized who he had shared a parachute with, exclaiming, *"Well, if I'd known whom I was riding down with I wouldn't have been half so scared!"*[238] They both laughed at this comment as they dragged the tangled mess of their parachutes off the drop zone.

Parachute Drop (National Archives)

Later, the chaplain thought a lot about this incident and thanked the Lord for protecting him during one of the most hazardous activities conceived by the army, a night parachute jump. He also came to realize God had a lesson for him in this incident. He had sought God's guidance before undertaking the role of airborne chaplain and had been assured of God's protection. The young soldier who parachuted with him had also benefitted from that protection. The chaplain concluded, *"We who belong to the Lord have a very great responsibility toward those who are round about us, whether they are believers or unbelievers."*[239]

God's amazing lesson for this chaplain is one every Christian should take to heart. It is up to believers to claim God's promises, not only to benefit themselves, but also to bring God's blessings to others in their families, communities, and nation. Even though the ungodly may oppose such spiritual appeals, when God sends his blessings, they fall like *"rain on the righteous and the unrighteous"* (Matthew 5:45). Even in an age when secularism seems to be advancing, believers have a responsibility to actively respond to God's promise given centuries ago:

If my people, who are called by my name, will humble themselves and pray and seek my face and turn from their wicked ways, then will I hear from heaven and will forgive their sin and will heal their land. ~2 Chronicles 7:14

Post-Traumatic Stress

DURING THE Korean War it was called *battle fatigue* or *shell shock*. Later, during the Vietnam War era, it became known as *post-traumatic stress disorder (PTSD)*. The phenomenon was the same. When soldiers bring death and destruction on others and witness it among friends, there are likely to be repercussions later. The same holds true for any person experiencing a severe accident or disaster. Men especially tend to compartmentalize their emotional reaction to traumatic events, causing problems later when these feelings start to surface. Since the person affected is usually the last to realize it, a Korean War veteran published the symptoms of combat fatigue, or PTSD, to help fellow veterans recognize the problem:

> *Recurrent, intrusive, and distressing thoughts about the event.*
> *Recurrent dreams, nightmares (sometimes called "night terrors") about the event.*
> *Flashbacks (a sense of reliving the event).*
> *Distress, caused by reminders of the event (sights, sounds, smells).*
> *Alienation, isolation and avoidance of people and places.*
> *Emotional numbing.*
> *Survivor guilt (for having survived when others did not, or for behavior required for survival).*
> *Difficulty falling asleep or staying asleep.*
> *Anger and rage.*
> *Difficulty concentrating or remembering certain facts about the event.*
> *Hyper-vigilance, or survivalist behavior even after you are away from the event.*
> *Exaggerated startle responses (usually to loud noises).*[240]

There are trained counselors available to help veterans and others bring these kinds of problems to the surface so they can be dealt with systematically. Those who need it should seek this kind of help. I believe, however, that the ultimate solution lies in the spiritual realm. I know many combat veterans who were only able to finally resolve their own issues of anxiety, guilt, anger, and depression through Jesus Christ. Only in him were they able to find the forgiveness and peace they so desperately needed to return to a normal and healthy life.

> Come to me, all you who are weary and burdened, and I will give you rest. Take my yoke upon you and learn from me, for I am gentle and humble in heart, and you will find rest for your souls. For my yoke is easy and my burden is light.
> ~Matthew 11:28–30

ROK troops march toward front (US Army)

US Troops advance past refugees (US Army)

To Listen

BIRCHARD KORTEGAARD was a brand new technical representative, or "tech rep," with the Philco Corporation when he was sent on an emergency mission to Korea to make repairs on a critical AN/CPS-5 Heavy Ground Radar system. When he arrived he found a group of senior officers assembled at the site, obviously upset about the loss of air control over most of North Korea for days.

> The fear of the LORD teaches a man wisdom, and humility comes before honor.
> ~Proverbs 15:33

Working with the sergeant in charge of the radar unit, Kortegaard spent hours exhaustively checking each component of the system until he isolated the problem to a cable called the modulator trigger wire. After rechecking his data, he told the sergeant to replace the cable and the problem would be fixed. After a long pause, the sergeant looked at him and said, *"Are you sure you want us to do that?"* Surprised at this apparent insolence, the tech rep snapped back, *"Sure? What do you think I'm doing, looking for Easter eggs? Of course I'm sure. Will you please just replace that wire?"*[241] The sergeant turned and left without saying anything else, leaving Kortegaard to regret his rude response.

It turned out there was a lot the young tech rep did not know about this particular radar installation. The faulty cable took hours to replace, but was only part of the problem. As he continued working with the sergeant, Kortegaard eventually learned that other modifications he had not noticed had been made to the system. With the sergeant's help he was finally able to get the vital radar installation up and running. After the crisis was over, he said,

> *I had committed the squadron to an excruciating delay, with absolute confidence. But in fact I had lacked crucial information, information available for the asking had I the humility and wit to invite criticism and suggestions before making a final decision.*[242]

The lesson learned by this young tech rep is useful for anyone in a position of authority. We usually get into trouble when we assume we have all the answers. Humility is a trait we can cultivate that makes us more prone to listen to others and heed good advice.

Friends Meet

DON COLTS was newly assigned to an infantry unit on the front line near Youngsan. As he was preparing for another long night in his foxhole, he noticed three bedraggled and unarmed men trudging up the hill toward him. As he gradually made out their features, he saw something strangely familiar about one of them. Suddenly, he recognized his best friend from childhood, Mikey Bevacqua.

He recalled, *"I couldn't believe my eyes when I noticed him coming up the hill."*[243] Bevacqua and his two buddies had been separated from their unit and lost for two days without food or water. They were very happy and relieved to make it back.

> Blessed are the poor in spirit, for theirs is the kingdom of heaven. Blessed are those who mourn, for they will be comforted.
> ~Matthew 5:3–4

Colts and Bevacqua had grown up in an orphanage in upstate New York, where they had become best friends. At age eleven, Bevacqua's father had taken him out of the orphanage. Soon after that, Colts had gone to live with a sister who happened to live across the street from Bevacqua's family. The two had remained close friends until each had joined the army separately, not to see each other again until a chance meeting on a hillside in Korea. On that occasion, they spent a night together in a foxhole, and Bevacqua left for his unit the next day.

Later in the war, Bevacqua went missing in action and did not return home. When Colts eventually got back, he went straight to Bevacqua's father to tell him about what had happened in Korea and how he and his friend had been reunited by fate in the midst of the war. For Colts this was one of those amazing coincidences without a logical explanation. For a grieving family, however, it was God's way of bringing comfort and some degree of closure to a tragedy with no real end. For a father with a son lost somewhere in a foreign land, it was comforting to know he had at least shared a moment with his closest friend.

Bedcheck Charlie

EVERYONE HAD a different opinion about Bedcheck Charlie. Some were amused. Some were highly irritated. North Korean pilots in pre-World War II Soviet-made biplanes made frequent nightly raids on US air-bases, dropping mortar rounds and hand grenades at random. Dubbed "Bedcheck Charlie," these North Korean pilots caused little damage other than interrupting the sleep of tired airmen. Some actually enjoyed the fireworks display as anti-aircraft fire boomed and arched across the night sky.

Bedcheck Charlie (Fantasy of Flight)

The various commanders on the scene felt that something had to be done about this nuisance. Radar tracking was practically impossible because the antique craft were made of wood, fabric, and paint. Anti-aircraft fire achieved few results. Since jet aircraft were too fast for these slow-moving targets, prop-driven planes were used with limited success. One Navy pilot flying an F4U Corsair managed to shoot down five and became the first "Charlie Ace." In spite of extensive bombing campaigns against North Korean airfields to disrupt this kind of attack, the Air Force was never able to completely solve the problem. All-in-all, Bedcheck Charlie caused a vast expenditure of resources to counter a mostly innocuous "threat."[244]

In modern times, it is somehow comforting that simple, old-fashioned methods still have a place. Personal computers, e-mail, and text messaging have given us amazing new ways to reach out to friends. We have to keep reminding ourselves, however, that a simple old-fashioned phone call or visit cannot be replaced. Seeing or hearing another's response to our comments makes our conversations infinitely more meaningful, and a human touch is often more important than words.

> She came up behind him and touched the edge of his cloak, and immediately her bleeding stopped . . . "Who touched me?" Jesus asked . . . "Someone touched me; I know that power has gone out from me." ~Luke 8:44–46

Meatball Surgery

RICHARD HORNBERGER was a surgeon with the 8055th Mobile Army Surgical Hospital (MASH) during the Korean War. Years later, under the pseudonym Richard Hooker, he published a novel titled *MASH*, which was acclaimed critically and made into a movie and long-running television series. Along with the humor and zany antics of its heroes, the story provides some real insight into surgical practice under combat conditions.

When a new doctor arrived at the fictional MASH, he showed a degree of disdain for the fast and, to his way of thinking, imprecise surgical practice that he saw, terming it "meatball surgery." When the new surgeon was stymied by a complex chest wound, the hero, Hawkeye Pierce, took over, saying, *"There will be times when you won't have the time to do it right. Lemme show you how to do it wrong."*[245] He later explained,

> *This is certainly meatball surgery we do around here, but I think you can see now that meatball surgery is a specialty in itself. We are concerned only with getting the kid out of here alive. Up to a point we are concerned with fingers, hands, arms, and legs, but sometimes we deliberately sacrifice a leg in order to save a life, if the other wounds are more important. In fact, now and then we may lose a leg because, if we spend an extra hour trying to save it, another guy in the preop ward could die from being operated on too late.*[246]

While practicing combat medicine, these doctors had to constantly focus on the issue of life or death, disregarding many rules taught in medical school. This story reminds me of the difficult passage in Mark's Gospel where Jesus says, *"If your hand causes you to sin, cut it off. It is better for you to enter life maimed than with two hands to go into hell, where the fire never goes out"* (Mark 9:43). The surgeon is concerned with life-or-death issues in the short run. Jesus is concerned with the same issues from an eternal perspective. If his words seem too harsh, we obviously haven't given due consideration to what eternity might be like without God.

> And if your eye causes you to sin, pluck it out. It is better for you to enter the kingdom of God with one eye than to have two eyes and be thrown into hell, where "their worm does not die, and the fire is not quenched."
> ~Mark 9:47–48

Standing Up

DURING THE Korean War the North Korean and Chinese euphemistically referred to their campaign to propagandize prisoners of war as "political education." The hungry, confused, and sick American servicemen were bombarded with political and atheistic lectures and slogans during long indoctrination sessions, usually twice a day. Objections to the points made were dealt with harshly, and one phrase was often repeated: *"Your life depends on your attitude."*[247]

> Because of the increase of wickedness, the love of most will grow cold, but he who stands firm to the end will be saved.
> ~Matthew 24:12–13

Chaplain Emil Kapaun listened to these lectures quietly with a calm resolve and respectfully asked questions of those giving the talks. On one occasion he was accused of spreading anti-Communist propaganda among the prisoners. He smiled and replied, *"No, it is not anti-Communist propaganda, it is Christian love, and I shall pray for your soul."* Another time, a guard said to the chaplain, *"Where is your God now? Let him come and take you from here. You cannot see or hear or feel your God, therefore, He does not exist."* Kapaun calmly replied that God was as real as the air they breathed, but could not see. He also said, *"One day the Good Lord will save the Chinese."*[248]

A fellow prisoner later wrote about the performance of the chaplain during these stressful confrontations:

> *Father Kapaun never backed down from the Chinese in discussing any subject of their choosing. He would never antagonize or engage them in debate, but when the opportunity came he was more intellectually armed than they were. He was always the gentleman and never displayed emotional strains. The Chinese seemed to both fear and respect him.*[249]

The great Christian hymn urges us to *"Stand up, stand up for Jesus, ye soldiers of the cross."*[250] Kapaun stood courageously for his Savior, setting an example for the ages in circumstances among the most difficult faced by any Christian in history.

A Shoelace

AN AMERICAN soldier in Korea finally received his orders home. He was hardly able to contain his joy as he wrote a last letter to his family:

> That little house is going to look like a palace to me. And, you people like Kings and Queens. Is it true some people eat three times a day, or more? And they sit on a chair, by a table. What's the matter, they can't dig a hole in the backyard like everybody else?
>
> I have spent 12 months over here. The longest 30 years of my life. A short time ago I was 18, and all I was worried about was cars, girls, and how much beer a real man could drink. Don't get me wrong, I will still want a hot car, a hot girl, and a cold beer, but there were times I would have traded them all for a warm blanket. A wool hat. A shoelace. A damned shoelace! There were times when I would have traded my soul for a cup of hot coffee. But I am coming home now.[251]

No one should have to go to war. Everyone, however, would benefit from some amount of physical deprivation. Hunger, exhaustion, and exposure to the elements tend to give anyone a new perspective. As shown in the soldier's letter, a certain amount of suffering gives an appreciation for the simple things we normally take for granted. I don't suggest anyone inflict such hardship upon himself unnecessarily, but many Christians have this kind of experience on mission trips to developing countries. It is often life changing to work with people in want of the things we have in such abundance at home, particularly when we experience that want firsthand. Jesus himself was led by the Holy Spirit into the desert to suffer hunger and temptation after his baptism in the Jordan River.

> Consider it pure joy, my brothers, whenever you face trials of many kinds, because you know that the testing of your faith develops perseverance. Perseverance must finish its work so that you may be mature and complete, not lacking anything. ~James 1:2–4

Our sufferings give us a new perspective on our lives, but are most valuable when they give us a new perspective on God. When we turn to him in difficulty, he becomes more real to us. This perspective is the greatest blessing we can find in this life and is worth more than anything we can give in exchange.

Opportunity in Danger

DURING THE Korean War, Dr. John Raley, president of Oklahoma Baptist University, wrote an article for college students facing the possibility of wartime military service, challenging them to look at the future positively:

> We do not glorify war, but neither do we suppose that "peace at any price" is a rational objective for men who expect to remain free. The judgment of men who have served and survived is that the war years are often the most intense of life, the constant adjustments a test of mettle, a fiery furnace in which character is utterly destroyed, or revealed in all its fullness. Your military service may actually prove to be a time for bringing into focus your sense of values. Men whose lives have had no purpose may suddenly be aroused to their destiny. Men who after years of easy, rudderless and foolish existence, are thrown into the most elemental struggle for survival, emerge in self-discovery.
>
> The future is a precious stone with many facets. One of those is uncertainty deepening into danger; another is opportunity dazzling into daring achievement. Because the one is present, youth must not overlook the fact of the other; for indeed, it supplies the power and technique for surmounting the difficulties of uncertainty.
>
> Around the ever widening horizon of danger in mankind's shadowland of today, there is a golden band of opportunity. Your job—your lifetime job—is to expand that circle of golden light until the frightening shadows flee away, and light covers the earth as the waters cover the seas. Faith in yourself, in your country, and in your God is a practical force, and a necessary one.[252]

Echoing Raley's theme, President John F. Kennedy once said, "The Chinese use two brush strokes to write the word crisis. One brush stroke stands for danger; the other for opportunity."[253] Linguists have objected to this interpretation, but the message is indisputable: In our life crises, there are always opportunities. For Christians, our most powerful witness to God's glory comes through the challenges we face and overcome as we lean on him for strength. Every crisis is an opportunity to grow closer to God and to become a more effective witness to his glory.

> Who shall separate us from the love of Christ? Shall trouble or hardship or persecution or famine or nakedness or danger or sword? . . . No, in all these things we are more than conquerors through him who loved us. ~Romans 8:35, 37

The Simple Things

I N THE VALLEY the thermometer read thirty degrees below zero. On the windswept ridgeline above it was even colder. Water in canteens had long since frozen, forcing men to eat snow to slake the thirst caused by their exertions. After a brief but savage fight, the men of A Company clung to a newly-won position on top of a knifelike ridge commanding the road below. The exhausted Marines dropped down into fighting positions recently occupied by the enemy. Suddenly, they faced a new danger—their own sweaty feet and the penetrating cold made frostbite imminent.

Before the attack, Captain Robert Barrow (a future Marine Corps Commandant) had made sure his men carried two extra pairs of socks. Under these conditions, however, changing socks was not a routine task. Barrow explained:

> *I learned that night that only leadership will save men under winter conditions. It's easy to say that men should change socks; getting it done is another matter. Boot laces become iced over during prolonged engagements in snowdrifts. It's a fight to get a boot off the foot. When a man removes his gloves to struggle with the laces, it seems to him that his hands are freezing. His impulse is all against it. So I found it necessary to do this by order, staying with the individuals until they had changed, then making them get up and move about to restore the circulation.*[254]

> For I have the desire to do what is good, but I cannot carry it out...
> Who will rescue me from this body of death?
> ~Romans 7:18, 24

A wise sergeant once told me, *"The things you have to do to succeed in combat are usually simple. Unfortunately, the simple things are always hard to do."* The apostle Paul seemed to have a similar difficulty doing the right thing as a Christian. Each of us has to struggle with our own human weaknesses. Only in Christ can we do the simple, but sometimes hard, things necessary to be a good husband, parent, or friend.

I Lift Up My Eyes

A YOUNG chaplain newly arrived in the Korean war zone was almost overcome by the desolate scenes around him. There was a nightmare-like quality to his surroundings that was only relieved when he finally looked up and turned his thoughts to the mountains towering over him:

> *You look for a building, and find only a mass of rubble. You look for a friend, an acquaintance of not so long ago . . . perhaps he is dead, perhaps a part of the shifting millstream. No one knows.*
>
> *But most of all the nightmare is in the faces of the people themselves. The Koreans, a puzzled and cowed people, caught in history's web of greed and lust. The soldiers, bitter, hard, with one obsession uppermost—to get out of this stinking hole as soon as possible. The homeless children, not understanding. There are things that no one can put into words.*
>
> *Killing . . . a fox-hole . . . the sudden, intense longing for a home, a glass of fresh milk, the touch of her hair, the quiet peace of your church on Sunday morning.*
>
> *This is the time for which the Psalmist could have written . . . the psalm written for all of us, Koreans, soldiers, children . . . the unchanging, constant love of God symbolized by the towering mountains all around. "I will lift up my eyes unto the hills, from whence cometh my help . . ."*[255]

The chaplain found respite in a dismal place by looking up and by remembering the words to one of our greatest Psalms:

I lift up my eyes to the hills—
     where does my help come from?
My help comes from the LORD,
     the Maker of heaven and earth.
He will not let your foot slip—
     he who watches over you will not slumber;
indeed, he who watches over Israel
     will neither slumber nor sleep.
The LORD watches over you—
     the LORD is your shade at your right hand;
the sun will not harm you by day,
     nor the moon by night.
The LORD will keep you from all harm—
     he will watch over your life;
the LORD will watch over your coming and
going both now and forevermore.
~Psalm 121

The Highest Calling

AS MORE AND more chaplains went to the Korean war zone, Chaplain Harold Berger wrote a moving article extolling the special nature of the chaplain's role in service to military men and women, and to God.

> If any man builds on this foundation using gold, silver, costly stones, wood, hay or straw, his work will be shown for what it is, because the Day will bring it to light. It will be revealed with fire, and the fire will test the quality of each man's work. If what he has built survives, he will receive his reward. If it is burned up, he will suffer loss; he himself will be saved, but only as one escaping through the flames.
> ~1 Corinthians 3:12–15

The ministry is the highest calling on earth. The minister is at home in every strata . . . and generally accepted by all. He is God's minister to the rich and the poor, the learned and the illiterate, the saints and the sinners alike.

Each day of his ministry presents a new challenge and opportunity of service for Almighty God. Each day can be a miraculous one wherein the darkness is turned to light, sorrow changed to joy, fear to trust, failure to victory. Each day can be one of bringing the lost to the cross of salvation, of causing the angelic chorus to soar with songs of joy before the heavenly throne. If the full meaning of our high calling is realized we shall want to cry out to God a personal magnificat for His great goodness.

Speaking from a personal viewpoint, I had rather be a minister, imperfect a vessel that I am, than to wear the crown of a king. I had rather preach the Gospel than to be a silver-tongued orator of political fame and influence. I had rather lay the hand of comfort upon the brow of the sick than to sign autographs for the fickle multitudes who worship earth's popular idols. I had rather be a worker in the vineyard, a builder of the Kingdom, than to build a skyscraper.

I thank God I am not earth-bound but heaven-bound, that I am building not only for today but also for the eternal day. I thank God that I am a minister.[256]

This chaplain's passionate expression of joy in his work should inspire every Christian, minister, and layperson alike. Whatever our daily task, we can bring to it an attitude either earth-bound or heaven-bound. The minister does indeed have a special calling. Every Christian, however, has his own unique opportunity to touch people where he lives and works. By word and deed, every Christian can bring the cross to someone who is lost and be counted among the ranks of God's faithful ministers.

Map 6.
Chinese Intervention
November 1950

CHINESE INTERVENTION

B Y LATE OCTOBER 1950, the war seemed largely won in Korea. UN forces had penetrated deep into North Korea and had captured the capital city of Pyongyang. The advance was continuing toward the Yalu River against scattered NKPA resistance. Gen. Douglas MacArthur was optimistic he would occupy all of North Korea by Thanksgiving. A gathering horde of Chinese Communist Force (CCF) armies, however, would radically alter this picture.

As darkness fell on November 1, bugles announced the attack on the Eighth Cavalry Regiment north of Unsan. Massed Chinese forces hit each of the regiment's three battalions, flowing between units and attacking from all sides. Roadblocks to the rear prevented withdrawal and reinforcement. As units were overrun, the survivors had to make their way out of the trap individually and in small groups. Over a third of the regiment was lost in the debacle. To the east, Chinese attacks similarly decimated several divisions of the ROK II Corps.

By November 6, the Eighth Army was consolidating forces along the Chongchon River, about half way between the 38th parallel and the Yalu River, when the Chinese offensive came to a sudden halt. CCF units seemed to melt away into the hills as a period of quiet settled over the battlefield. Once again, UN planners were thrust into confusion over the intentions of the Chinese. Although the field commanders were wary, Gen. MacArthur's staff still refused to believe that China would seriously intervene in the war. His intelligence section grossly underestimated CCF strength in North Korea by a factor of ten.[257]

In the lull created by the pullback of Chinese forces, Lt. Gen. Walton Walker prepared to renew the Eighth Army's drive to the Yalu. On November 24, all frontline units jumped off in the attack from their positions along the Chongchon River. Initial objectives were reached easily for the first two days against scattered resistance. The main concern of the Allied troops was keeping warm as temperatures began to plunge with the onset of winter. Unfortunately, some frontline units even resorted to campfires at night, needlessly exposing their positions.[258]

As darkness fell on November 25, the Chinese struck again in full force. Focusing on the Second Infantry Division in the center and on ROK units on the eastern flank, they again employed massive "human wave" attacks, pouring through gaps in the line and isolating units from each other. By noon on November 26, the ROK II Corps front folded, and Chinese forces poured through to the south, exposing the entire right flank of the Eighth Army. Most vulnerable of all was the Second Infantry Division deployed on either side of the Chongchon River north of Kunu-ri.

After four days of heavy fighting, the Second Division withdrew to Kunu-ri and was then ordered to withdraw directly to Sunchon, more than twenty miles to the south. After failing to dislodge Chinese troops from ridgelines on either side of the road, the division attempted to run the "gauntlet" and force their way through. The resulting disaster was among the worst ever experienced by the US Army. Heavy fire poured down from the hills, disabling vehicles and scattering troops along the congested road. Artillery pieces were abandoned as unit integrity was lost and small groups of soldiers tried to survive on their own. The division took almost 4,500 battle casualties, losing a third of its manpower and most of its equipment.[259]

With these defeats along the Chongchon River, UN hopes of reunifying Korea by force vanished for the time being. The Eighth Army consolidated a position on the Sunchon-Sukchon line, and then, even though not pressed, withdrew even further south to avoid further flanking maneuvers by the Chinese. Morale in the entire army sank to new lows with these retreats over previously-won territory, and the now-defunct promise of "home by Christmas."[260] General Walker decided his battered forces would have to withdraw south of the 38th parallel and the Imjin River to reach a line he could defend. This decision to abandon Pyongyang brought untold misfortune to Koreans in the capital who had welcomed and supported the UN occupation forces. Again, refugees flooded the roads and countryside as the war retraced its path. Meanwhile, the army and Marine units of X Corps on the east side of the peninsula had to face their own ordeal.

A New Perspective

AS THE UN advance moved north of the 38th parallel in October 1950 there was growing evidence of Chinese intervention. The First ROK Division, led by Gen. Paik Sun-yup, reached Unsan, less than one hundred miles from the Yalu River, when it came under attack from three sides. As the general was trying to reposition his units and deal with this crisis, he received an unexpected order. He was to leave First Division immediately and take command of ROK II Corps.

Although honored by this promotion, Gen. Paik found the situation at II Corps even more chaotic. He now commanded three divisions scattered over a wide area, with some elements almost at the Yalu River and under heavy attack. Traveling by jeep, he began meeting with his division commanders and assessing what they were up against.

> So from now on we regard no one from a worldly point of view. Though we once regarded Christ in this way, we do so no longer. Therefore, if anyone is in Christ, he is a new creation; the old has gone, the new has come!
> ~2 Corinthians 5:16–17

As he gathered his staff on October 27, events took another surprising turn. His old II Corps commander walked in and announced that all recent top level promotions had been rescinded, and officers were to return to their previous commands. Four days after becoming a corps commander Gen. Paik found himself on the way back to First Division. As was his nature, he looked on the bright side of this unusual sequence of events:

> I mulled the war over. In my absence, the 1st had been engaged in continuous, day-and-night combat with the Chinese Army. My stint as corps commander, however truncated, had allowed me to see the war from a much broader perspective, and this experience was to prove invaluable in subsequent operations.[261]

It is always good to understand the bigger picture. Anyone working in an organization should make the effort to appreciate what those in the hierarchy above are facing. By the same token, in our spiritual lives, we need to constantly seek the perspective of our ultimate Authority. God wants us to look beyond ourselves and our own interests. How are our actions contributing to *his* kingdom? What are we doing for *his* children? Even a small glimpse of his eternal nature puts our earthly activity in a completely new light.

A Fearsome Thing

EIGHTH ARMY liberated Pyongyang, the capital of North Korea, in October 1950. Two months later the Americans abandoned the city and all of North Korea to the overwhelming advance of Communist Chinese Forces. This turn of events caught countless North Koreans in a bitter dilemma. Many had openly celebrated the defeat of the Communists and had even helped the Allied forces in their occupation. They had to decide whether to flee to the south and face untold hardship in the open countryside or to stay and face probable arrest and death. Thousands chose to leave their homes with whatever they could carry and join the vast horde of refugees and retreating military units jamming a totally inadequate road system. Most of the bridges were commandeered by the army to avoid bottlenecks—sending civilian refugees into the frozen rivers and streams. Families became separated and many did not survive.

> In his hand is the life of every creature and the breath of all mankind . . . He makes nations great, and destroys them; he enlarges nations, and disperses them.
> ~Job 12:10, 23

Refugees in winter (National Archives)

An officer who was part of this tragic spectacle made a poignant and thought-provoking observation:

A great army in retreat is a fearsome thing. Its by-products are tragic. With all my being, I hope our people at home may never find themselves transformed into aimlessly wandering refugees searching for elusive simple safety.[262]

Fortunately, in modern America we have never witnessed our own population driven from their homes as in other war-torn countries around the world. When we consider we are no better or worse as human beings than those who do suffer in this way, our only appropriate response is the familiar and true saying, *"There, but for the grace of God, go I."* Although we pray we will never have to live out an Armageddon-like scenario, we have no guarantees against this or any other form of earthly pain and suffering. The only guarantee available to any human being is an eternal place with God. Not one of us has a greater priority in life than seeking this ultimate form of protection that can only come through his grace.

Call to Duty

DURING THE Korean War many reservists were recalled to active duty, disrupting homes, businesses, and congregations. One Lutheran pastor whose church was adversely affected made an appeal to the National Lutheran Council for help in obtaining his deferral. An official of the church wrote a moving letter in reply:

> I lost my own son, a captain in the 1st Marine Division on its fateful trek into North Korea last November, but it was comforting to know that a Lutheran chaplain had visited him shortly before he died of his wounds and that later he was given a Christian burial. I would not like to see any soldier, sailor, airman, or marine go to war or into battle feeling that the Church or its pastors would not go with them and share their dangers and hardships.[263]

The letter also made pointed reference to the fact that many others were equally affected by the recall to active duty:

> It is not only chaplains who are being recalled, but Reserve officers of all components . . . regardless of their vocation or profession. The fact that the recall comes at an inconvenient time to them personally or to their business, or, in the case of a pastor, his congregation, while regrettable, does not alter the validity of their obligation to their government in the hour of her need.[264]

This letter was a mild rebuke to the pastor seeking deferment from active duty. It ended, however, with some encouraging words: "I also have complete confidence in the promise of Holy Scripture that the 'steps of a good man are ordered by the LORD' (Psalms 37:23 KJV), and that the pastor will not be recalled save by God's will."[265]

Our call to duty from God will not always be convenient or without risk. When we prayerfully discern that call and faithfully respond to it, however, there is no safer or more satisfying place to be in this life.

> If the LORD delights in a man's way, he makes his steps firm; though he stumble, he will not fall, for the LORD upholds him with his hand . . . For the Lord loves the just and will not forsake his faithful ones.
> ~Psalm 37:23–24, 28

Falsely Accused

ZHOU BAOSHAN led his infantry company across the Yalu River during the night of October 21, 1950. A few days later the Chinese officer and his men went into action against ROK and American units defending Unsan. After midnight on November 1, he led his company in an assault on a heavily-defended hill, swept by machine gun and artillery fire. As he drove his men forward, he felt a blow to his leg, like someone had kicked him. Over half his men went down before he, and what was left of his command, struggled to the top. At that point, Zhou dropped down to examine his leg, now covered with blood. He had been seriously wounded and would go no farther.

Within days, Zhou was evacuated to a field hospital where he would spend three months in recovery. His leg never healed properly, and he was assigned to an engineering unit for the remainder of the war. After the war he continued to work as an engineer in Heilongjiang province in north China.

> Do not turn me over to the desire of my foes, for false witnesses rise up against me, breathing out violence. I am still confident of this: I will see the goodness of the LORD in the land of the living. ~Psalm 27:12–13

Many years later Zhou's combat service came into question by his fellow workers. During the so-called Cultural Revolution in the late 1960s, he was interrogated about his failure to gain promotion during the war and about his reassignment from an infantry unit to the engineers. He was accused of shirking his duty as a combat officer. Zhou described his reaction:

> I tried to defend myself by explaining that I was wounded in the first battle. Unfortunately, nobody believed me, and I was labeled a "deserter of the Korean War." I did not give any further explanation. I did not complain. Having thought so many times about my dead comrades, I considered myself lucky to be one of the survivors in the Korean War.[266]

Zhou was in every way a war hero. Nevertheless, he was a victim of one of the many Communist purges pitting citizens against each other to solidify the political power of a dictatorial government. The truth has been abused under every Communist regime, due to the fact that no higher authority or greater good is recognized than the state itself.

Soldiers call in Artillery Fire (US Army)

Soldier with captured equipment (Dept. of Defense)

Anger

A S THE CHINESE army poured hundreds of thousands of troops across the Yalu River into Korea, the United Nations forces reeled back from the onslaught. It was heartbreaking to the South Korean troops to abandon Seoul, their capital city, a second time. Once again they had to witness tens of thousands of their fellow countrymen flee to the south as refugees in the dead of winter.

> My dear brothers, take note of this: Everyone should be quick to listen, slow to speak and slow to become angry, for man's anger does not bring about the righteous life that God desires.
> ~James 1:19–20

As the armed forces withdrew further south, Gen. Paik Sun-yup had time to ponder the performance of his own unit, the ROK First Division. Even though they had fought well, they had been hit hard and forced to retreat. Gen. Paik himself had suffered a severe shock at this defeat and went into a temporary depression that almost rendered him ineffective. Somehow, he issued the necessary orders to pull his men back and to regroup in new positions.

In assessing these events, the Korean general assigned the responsibility to himself. He recalled an earlier attack of malaria and a weakened condition leading up to the battle. This impairment of his physical energy had caused him to be nervous and peevish. He knew he had directed outbursts of anger at his staff and subordinates. He concluded, *"If a commander allows himself to become testy, his subordinate commanders waste precious time and energy trying to read his mood and lose the edge they need to perform crisply in combat."*[267]

Anger can be destructive in any relationship. As in every marriage, my wife and I have had our arguments. Unfortunately, I sometimes allow myself to get angry to the point of saying something really hurtful. When this happens, my outburst becomes the focus of the argument, making the original problem practically insoluble. I do better when I remember the biblical advice given to help with this all-too-human tendency: *"A gentle answer turns away wrath, but a harsh word stirs up anger"* (Proverbs 15:1). *"A fool gives full vent to his anger, but a wise man keeps himself under control"* (Proverbs 29:11).

Healing

DEALING CONSTANTLY with the sick and wounded, Chaplain William Thierfelder thought a lot about the debilitating effect of fear and anxiety on the healing process. He observed that guilt was often a complicating factor, making it even more difficult to deal with the natural fear of death or disability:

> Fear and guilt, more frequently than not, go hand in hand. Guilt expects retribution. In the case of illness, retribution can only come in an equal measure to the degree of guilt one feels in one's conscience—thus reasons the anxious heart.[268]

The chaplain concluded he had a significant role to play in the healing process for many patients by bringing a message of forgiveness to them. By relieving the sick and wounded of their guilt, he could give them the ability to overcome their fear and better enable the normal healing process to work. He also knew that true forgiveness comes from one source: *"The small and great miracles of fear allayed are wrought through faith in the atoning blood of Christ."*[269]

Jesus Christ is the answer to our guilt.

If we confess our sins, he is faithful and just and will forgive us our sins and purify us from all unrighteousness. ~1 John 1:9

Jesus Christ is the answer to our fear.

Peace I leave with you; my peace I give you. I do not give to you as the world gives. Do not let your hearts be troubled and do not be afraid. ~John 14:27

Jesus Christ is the answer to our need for healing.

Just then a woman who had been bleeding for twelve years came up behind him and touched him and touched his cloak. Jesus turned and saw her. "Take heart, daughter," he said, "your faith has healed you." And the woman was healed from that moment. ~Matthew 9:20, 22

Leap of Faith

IN LATE OCTOBER 1950, a North Korean major took charge of a group of noncombatant captives in the town of Manpo near the Yalu River. The major informed the group they were to march under strict military discipline to the city of Chunggangjin, more than one hundred miles away. Various nationalities were represented in the group, including Americans, Englishmen, and Australians. Prominent among them were a number of Catholic priests and sisters, and Methodist missionaries. After becoming aware he had a contingent of church personnel present, the major made a point of expressing his views on religion:

> For although they knew God, they neither glorified him as God nor gave thanks to him, but their thinking became futile and their foolish hearts were darkened. Although they claimed to be wise, they became fools. ~Romans 1:21–22

Suppose you were an engineer on a train and the locomotive broke down. What would you do? Would you kneel down and pray that it would run? Or would you get an expert who knew about such things to repair it? In this country we know what we would do. We don't need you religious people anymore. You are parasites. There are things in this world that need repairing. We know what to do about that.[270]

It is not surprising to hear a North Korean official expound on the futility of religion. What is disturbing is the extent to which this line of reasoning resonates within our own culture today. Many of our scientists proclaim their atheism based on the belief that the findings of science leave no room for belief in God. Since they continue to find natural causes for more and more previously unexplained phenomena, they take their own "leap of faith" to believe that a natural cause will ultimately be found for everything, including the origins of the universe, life, and human consciousness. To most religious people, believing in a divine cause is a far less daunting leap of faith to explain these so-far-unexplained phenomena.

Propaganda

IN NOVEMBER 1950, the Chinese unexpectedly released a group of captured American soldiers in North Korea. Army officials debriefed these soldiers at length to determine the motive behind this unusual move. They learned the prisoners had been subjected to an endless series of repetitious lectures by English-speaking cadres along the following lines:

> Common people all over the world want peace. Millions of Chinese have signed the Stockholm appeal for peace. Wars are fostered for their own gain by capitalists, imperialists, and Wall Street millionaires, like your President Truman. However, we do not dislike the American masses; understand that. We think it is a shame that Americans have had to come here to die.[271]

Just before they were released, the soldiers were told, "*You are being freed and returned to your own people, now that you have been given 'understanding.'*"[272] The soldiers were told to go back and tell their comrades about the glories of Communism and how they were fighting on behalf of warmongers. The Chinese apparently believed these soldiers would do just that, since until that time Soviet and Chinese Communist cadres had successfully indoctrinated their own masses through such repetitive "reeducation" techniques.

These American soldiers were the first to be exposed to this kind of propaganda. This kind of "information" was a mixture of truth and falsehood, presented to further the Communist cause. It presumed a certain degree of ignorance on the part of the audience and for that reason had little success among American soldiers. We hope we are as immune to such rhetoric today, because we continue to hear radical, left-wing pronouncements eerily similar to what our soldiers heard in 1950.

> They are from the world and therefore speak from the viewpoint of the world, and the world listens to them. We are from God, and whoever knows God listens to us; but whoever is not from God does not listen to us. This is how we recognize the Spirit of truth and the spirit of falsehood. ~1 John 4:5–6

The continued existence of freedom is based on educated citizens who understand their own history, government, economics, and God-given values. Every day we have to sort out information from propaganda, due to the fact that the media of this world are full of "journalists" with a cause.

Minesweeping

THE THREE wooden-hulled minesweepers of Mine Division 54 plied their dangerous trade over the waters of Wonsan Bay clearing lanes for the amphibious landings to follow. Working under the covering fire of two battleships the little vessels worked ever closer to land and the North Korean shore batteries. One morning the *USS Heron* (AMS-18) was hit by a 75mm shell causing extensive damage, described by one of her officers:

> Her children arise and call her blessed; her husband also, and he praises her: "Many women do noble things, but you surpass them all." ~Proverbs 31:28–29

US Minesweepers (US Navy)

> *The bullet that hit the Heron entered the wooden hull on the forward starboard side, struck and exploded in the Handy Billy (an emergency gasoline powered pump that was stowed on the inside bulkhead). The explosion, above the water level, blew a huge gash in the side of the ship and the shell's detonator deflected through the bulkhead, into the galley and down through the galley deck, through the crew's quarters and deck below, and into the ship's magazine. It landed harmlessly on the deck of the magazine compartment.*[273]

After sustaining this hit, the *Heron* cut her minesweeping cables and retreated to the tender ship located outside the bay. There shipfitters patched the hull damage, caulked, repainted, and, within hours, sent the little ship back out onto the line. The dangerous work at hand had to be completed.

There is an old military axiom that says, *"Any ship can be a minesweeper. Once."* This saying implies that some tasks are best left to the true experts. The heroic minesweeper in my family has always been my wife, Lani. She is the true expert at clearing the emotional minefields that would sink the rest of her family if left undetected and unresolved. It is also true that she and most other mothers often suffer blows to their own morale, and, unfortunately, can find little time for repairs and refitting. There are always more mines out there threatening the safety of their families. God bless the amazing women who volunteer for the most important and demanding duty in this world—facing the hidden obstacles and uncharted waters of motherhood.

Cocky

DALE KING was an artilleryman with the Fifth Regimental Combat Team when his unit was cut off and surrounded by Chinese forces. As the circle tightened and ammunition supplies were exhausted, an officer finally surrendered King's unit. Chinese guards then marched the soldiers north, covering about twenty miles each night, to a prison camp somewhere in central North Korea. Ultimately King walked to the Yalu River, where his ordeal as a prisoner of war would last until he was repatriated more than two years later.

US POWs (Dept. of Defense)

King later recalled how confident he and his fellow soldiers had been when they were on the offensive during the furious advance into North Korea:

> *The units, when they marched north and went over the 38th parallel, we were quite cocky. For instance, the 5th Regimental Combat Team had a sign (on the road) that said, "You are now crossing the 38th parallel courtesy of the 5th R.C.T." When we marched back north as prisoners, that sign was on the same road we had to use. We were not so cocky.*[274]

Arrogance is a very human attitude we have to guard against. While most of us would never describe ourselves this way, we each nevertheless often harbor secret feelings of superiority over the bad habits or misbehavior of others—especially when they involve more egregious sins. When an acquaintance falls to alcoholism or adultery we think to ourselves, *"At least I'm not that bad,"* forgetting that all sin (yes, even our own) is abhorrent in God's eyes. As Christians we have absolutely no grounds for arrogance. In fact, an awareness of our sinfulness is the first and necessary step that allows Jesus to work in our hearts.

There is no one righteous, not even one; there is no one who understands, no one who seeks God . . . Therefore no one will be declared righteous in his sight by observing the law; rather, through the law we become conscious of sin.
~Romans 3:10–11, 20

God's Call

WALTER LEWIN served in both World War II and Korea as a Navy surgeon with Marine Corps units. He continued his surgical career after the war at Lutheran Hospital in Cleveland, Ohio, where he eventually became Chief of Surgery and team physician to the Cleveland Indians. His daughter Linda, herself a registered nurse, wrote a moving tribute to her dad including a poignant story about his work with an Irish nun at an orphanage in Korea. She opened with a passage of Scripture particularly relevant to the story:

> And we know that in all things God works for the good of those who love him, who have been called according to his purpose. ~Romans 8:28

While on shore leave from his hospital ship, the Repose, Lieutenant Lewin walked by a fenced area with young children playing outside of their orphanage, Star of the Sea, Inchon, Korea. He smiled and instantly was brought to mind of his own young children back home in Cleveland. Sister Philhelmena saw the medical insignia on his uniform and asked if he could help with health care. He stated that he wasn't a pediatrician but Sister persisted, stating that anyone with a medical background would be better than what they had. Most of the infants needed IV fluids because of dehydration related to their abandonment. Our dad would "liberate" IV fluids from the overstock of the ship. This action could have resulted in a court martial, but he couldn't ignore God's call to help those innocent babies.[275]

Linda described how countless babies survived due to her father's treatments for dehydration, pneumonia, parasites, malnutrition, and infections. During his time in Korea he worked long days performing trauma surgery on wounded Marines and then spent his off-duty hours doing acts of mercy for the orphanage. His greatest joy and most precious memories were providing medical treatment for, giving gifts to, and playing games with the children.

Lewin had responded to an unexpected call from God to serve in a unique way. He was forever thankful he did. His daughter remembered the stories of Sister Philhelmena and the Star of the Sea orphanage and recalled they were the only stories she heard him tell about the war. Thinking how her father and the sister came together to do God's work under these extremely difficult circumstances, she said, *"Their common call to Scripture is how they met and how they served."*[276]

Compartmentalizing

ONE DAY Lt. John Carrig received orders to send a squad to rescue three men pinned down by enemy fire during a foraging expedition. As the relief force was being organized, a new man stepped forward to volunteer. Harry Freeman had just joined the platoon and had not even been assigned to a squad. Just transferred from an administrative job, he was anxious to be an infantryman and to see combat. Two hours later, the young man was dead. He was tragically killed in his first combat action on November 11, 1950.

Later Carrig received a heart-wrenching letter from Freeman's mother asking for details about the events surrounding her son's death. As he read the words of the distraught woman he was almost overcome with feelings he usually kept carefully inside. The letter seemed to penetrate the protective shell he had so carefully built around his emotions to enable him to do his job and to survive the war. "Her letter moved me close to tears," he said. *"It opened my mind again to the reality that the horrors of war spread far beyond our small circle of riflemen."*[277]

In combat, soldiers have to compartmentalize their emotions. To function on the battlefield they have to put many feelings aside to carry on with the mission. Otherwise, they risk their effectiveness and even survival. Unfortunately, this practice is the root cause of post-traumatic stress disorder (PTSD), which can manifest itself later in feelings of anger, guilt, depression, and even suicide. Every combat veteran and family member of a combat veteran should be familiar with these symptoms and understand the danger. Help is available from counselors and treatment centers for veterans. The ultimate treatment for these emotional wounds, however, is offered by our Savior, Jesus Christ. When we turn to him for help with this kind of problem, he brings forgiveness and performs the spiritual healing that is the only way true peace can be restored to anyone's life.

> Be merciful to me, LORD, for I am faint; O LORD, heal me, for my bones are in agony. My soul is in anguish. How long, O LORD, how long? Turn, O LORD, and deliver me; save me because of your unfailing love . . . THE LORD has heard my cry for mercy; the LORD accepts my prayer.
> ~Psalm 6:2–4, 9

(US Army)

193

The Lord's Side

WILBUR S. "BIG FOOT" BROWN is a legendary figure in Marine Corps history due to an illustrious career spanning many decades. He fought in World War I as an enlisted man, attended and dropped out of the Naval Academy, and later reenlisted to earn a commission through the ranks. He spent years in Nicaragua during the 1920s campaigning against bandits, and during World War II commanded an artillery battalion and then a regiment during the Okinawa campaign. In the Korean War he commanded the First Marine Regiment in some of the most bitter fighting of the war. At one point, as casualties were mounting, he published a memorandum to the men of his regiment to give them a word of encouragement in their trials:

> If the LORD had not been on our side when men attacked us, when their anger flared against us, they would have swallowed us alive; the flood would have engulfed us, the torrent would have swept over us . . . Praise be to the LORD.
> ~Psalm 124:2–4, 6

A lot of comrades, officers and men, have died or been injured in this "police action." I fear that more, very probably, will be before it is over. But you are making traditions of valor and professional skill that will rank alongside of, or outrank, the achievements of Marines of the First World War, the Second World War and all our minor campaigns. And I urge you all to believe, whether or not you are, or have been, religiously inclined, that in this struggle for decency among men, we are fighting on the side of the Lord. The Communists who oppose us are fighting to deny His existence.[278]

During the Civil War, Abraham Lincoln was asked if God was on the side of the Union. He wisely replied, *"Sir, my concern is not whether God is on our side; my greatest concern is to be on God's side."*[279] I believe that Big Foot Brown was right to tell his men they were fighting for a just cause in the Korean War and a cause favored by God. These Marines were part of a decades-long struggle during which America fought gallantly to save many other nations from Communist domination.

The Calmest Person

CHAPLAIN JAMES CARROLL was with the Thirty-Eighth Regiment of the Second Infantry Division during the disastrous withdrawal from the Chongchon River on November 30, 1950. Trying to pass quickly through a narrow defile north of Sunchon the entire division was hit by Chinese units occupying the high ground on either side of the valley. Carroll's regiment suffered almost 50 percent casualties in one of the worst disasters of the war. Throughout the ordeal the chaplain went about his duties calmly, tending to the wounded and ministering to many scared and confused soldiers.

Twenty-three years after this battle, Chaplain Carroll was serving at Fort Hood, Texas, when he received an unexpected letter from a retired sergeant who remembered him from Korea. Although the sergeant's English wasn't perfect, the sentiments he expressed were:

> Now he who supplies seed to the sower and bread for food will also supply and increase your store of seed and you will enlarge the harvest of your righteousness. You will be made rich in every way so that you can be generous on every occasion.
> ~2 Corinthians 9:10–11

> Dear Sir:
> You are probably the only chaplin in the hold (sic) Army that I can remember his name . . . To let you know who I am, I was the one that jumped on you when we were ambushed at Conrea Pass . . .
> You sure did have a great influence on my life that day in Korea. I have never forgot how cool and collective you were when everybody was getting killed all around us. You said, "The Lord is with us and will get us out of this mess" which he did. You were the calmest person that I have every known.
> After Korea I started trying to find out in my own mind why you were so cool that day. Well I found it sometime late. I became a Christian. I am a Deacon and Sunday School Superintendant of my Church. Thanks very much.[280]

We never know what effect our actions will have on others. A kind word or deed for someone may be long remembered by them even though forgotten by us. When our actions show Jesus in our hearts, we plant long-lasting seeds that we may never see bloom, but that will always be there for God to water in his time.

Change of View

NORMAN STRICKBINE watched intently as the C-47 came in from the south and lined up on the valley below to drop supplies. From his hilltop position, he was actually higher than the airplane as it approached. Suddenly, the aircraft seemed to go out of control. It flipped upside down and dove into the ground with a tremendous explosion. In an instant, all Strickbine could see was flaming wreckage. Other GIs rushed to the scene, but there was nothing to be done. There were no survivors.

Strickbine thought about what he had seen and realized he and other soldiers in his unit often complained about the easy life of the "flyboys." They would talk about the warm beds and good food enjoyed by the airmen in contrast to their own rough living conditions. In the moment of that crash, however, they all had a huge attitude adjustment. Someone said, *"No sir, I'll take my chances on the ground."* Another commented, *"I'd rather die with a hole in me than be a piece of black toast."* Strickbine wrote later:

> Even though there were a lot of jobs that seemed to be more comfortable and safer in that frozen wasteland of North Korea, it became clear to me that we were all vulnerable and could "check out" at any time. From that time on, I don't think I ever begrudged another man's job or duty station.[281]

It is only human nature to feel some degree of envy at the apparent good fortune of others. There is always someone who seems to look better, have more, or worry less than we do. When I really get to know someone such as that, however, I invariably find that below the calm surface there is turmoil. I have gradually come to the firm conclusion that there is no such thing as a human being without problems. This simple truth is important to Christians in the realization that no one is unapproachable. There is no person who will not respond to a friendly gesture and genuine concern. Every person needs the love of Christ, and it is up to every Christian to share it.

All this is from God, who reconciled us to himself through Christ and gave us the ministry of reconciliation: . . . We are therefore Christ's ambassadors, as though God were making his appeal through us.
~2 Corinthians 5:18, 20

Letters Home

DURING THE months that William Dickson flew aerial observer missions in Korea he kept a brief, but daily, diary. Due to the demands of his job, his letter writing to his wife was somewhat irregular, and for security reasons he couldn't tell her much of what he was doing. Meanwhile, her letters were a constant morale boost to him. He wrote in his diary,

> She writes a letter a day and each one is like a little sparkling gem that brightens up this God forsaken place. Sometimes I get them a dozen at a time. Maybe the diary is my way of talking to her.[282]

The difficulties of a soldier writing home reminds me of a story told me by Gen. Mark Clark's wife, Renie. She was once helping him pack for one of his extended overseas deployments. Somewhere in his gear she discovered a packet of letters. Closer examination revealed they were all addressed to her and unsealed. When she confronted him, he confessed he had written ahead of time, knowing he would have difficulty writing later. Needless to say, Renie didn't let him get away with this little deception.

I think wives of soldiers generally appreciate the difficulty their husbands have communicating while away on dangerous assignments. During more "normal" times, however, when a man doesn't communicate so well, the woman's patience grows thin. Every husband can do a better job of sharing his thoughts with his wife and family, no matter the circumstance. Every wife, on the other hand, can better appreciate the fact that men tend to compartmentalize different areas of their lives. For better or for worse, most men have to deal with one thing at a time, and there are often good reasons why they sometimes seem removed. I think I speak for most husbands when I implore wives not to question our love just because we are being quiet.

> Love is patient, love is kind. It does not envy, it does not boast, it is not proud . . . It is not easily angered, it keeps no record of wrongs . . . It always protects, always trusts, always hopes, always perseveres.
> ~1 Corinthians 13:4–5, 7

Down to the Sea

NAVY CHAPLAINS have always had the difficult task of ministering to sailors scattered over wide areas in different ships. During the Korean War era, destroyers, minesweepers, and amphibious ships did not have individual chaplains, but were served by those assigned at the squadron or higher level. Consequently, lay leaders took on an important role in leading worship services, distributing religious material, and even providing counseling. Volunteers for

Burial service at sea (US Navy)

this kind of duty came from all ranks and specialties, as young sailors and officers of good character stepped forward to provide spiritual leadership under austere shipboard conditions. One officer observed:

> Here is evidence of real Christian action. God has revealed his mercy to man in Christ Jesus, and here are men reflecting his love by their Christian influence upon others.[283]

In our churches, the priests and ministers fulfill many vital roles, administering the sacraments, teaching, and encouraging. They deserve our support in every possible way. They also deserve a laity who will live up to their responsibilities in representing Christ to others within the environments where they work and play. There are circumstances when the lay person has more credibility and influence than even the most gifted preacher.

They that go down to the sea in ships, that do business in great waters; These see the works of the LORD, and his wonders in the deep. For he commandeth, and raiseth the stormy wind, which lifteth up the waves thereof. They mount up to the heaven, they go down again to the depths: their soul is melted because of trouble. They reel to and fro, and stagger like a drunken man, and are at their wits' end. Then they cry unto the LORD in their trouble, and he bringeth them out of their distresses. He maketh the storm a calm, so that the waves thereof are still. Then are they glad because they be quiet; so he bringeth them unto their desired haven. Oh that men would praise the LORD for his goodness, and for his wonderful works to the children of men! ~Psalm 107:23–31 (KJV)

Silent Night

A GROUP OF American soldiers were held prisoner in a little farming community named Sambakol, deep in the mountains of North Korea. The men called it simply "The Valley." Living conditions were harsh, as the poorly-constructed houses gave little protection from the forty-below temperatures typical of the bleak North Korean winters. The approach of Christmas offered little cheer to men struggling to stay alive.

> May the God of hope fill you with all joy and peace as you trust in him, so that you may overflow with hope by the power of the Holy Spirit. ~Romans 15:13

For some reason the prison staff decided that Christmas would be a good time to give the prisoners a demonstration of how well North Korean children had been indoctrinated into Communism. They brought a group of seven- to ten-year-olds from the local area into a small building to perform for the prisoners—not as a holiday gesture, but as a propaganda show. The children wore costumes, sang patriotic songs, and displayed the hammer and sickle—all to the glory of life under Communism.

During a pause in the performance, one of the prisoners began softly singing *Silent Night*. One after another, more voices around the room joined the chorus. Suddenly, the children started singing the song as well. The Americans were dumbstruck. These children knew the song, and they obviously knew about Christmas! As every voice in the room came together for the final words, *". . . sleep in heavenly peace,"* the guards realized their propaganda show had gone wrong. Whistles blew as the youngsters were herded out of the building, leaving a group of smiling American prisoners with a renewed sense of hope and the first stirring of the Christmas spirit.[284]

> Silent night, holy night,
> All is calm, all is bright
> Round yon Virgin Mother and Child.
> Holy infant so tender and mild,
> Sleep in heavenly peace,
> Sleep in heavenly peace.[285]

Ark of the Covenant

THE BOOK of Exodus tells the story of Moses receiving the Ten Commandments from God on Mount Sinai. He also received detailed instructions to build a tabernacle for worship and an ark to hold the tablets containing God's commandments.

Jewish Chaplain Samuel Sobel deployed to Korea with his own "ark," carefully constructed for him by Navy carpenters at Pearl Harbor.

> Have them make a chest of acacia wood—two and a half cubits long, a cubit and a half wide, and a cubit and a half high. [approximately 50x30x30 inches] Overlay it with pure gold, both inside and out, and make a gold molding around it . . . And make two cherubim out of hammered gold at the ends of the cover . . . The cherubim are to have their wings spread upward, overshadowing the cover with them . . . Place the cover on top of the ark and put in the ark the Testimony, which I will give you.
> ~Exodus 25:10–11, 18, 20–21

The entire oblong chest is of solid Philippine mahogany and, placed upright, has two doors opening from the middle. Superimposed upon the inside of each door is a hand-carved candelabrum which has been gilded to symbolize the golden candlestick in Sanctuary.

The veil, hanging inside the chest, is an intricacy of hand embroidery, including the crown in the lower portion and the Star of David above it. Also contained within the chest is a parchment scroll of the Torah, or manuscript of Law, from which a portion is read at every service.

Set on top of the Ark is a mahogany tablet of the Ten Commandments, or the Two Tables of the Law, and another small light fixture, symbolizing the Eternal Light.[286]

Chaplain Sobel was able to go to war with everything he needed to hold Jewish services. His attractive, intricately-made chest was suitable for use in permanent chapels or temporary rear-area facilities. It was also easily transported in its own canvas carrying case for use on the front lines. The chaplain may not have made a biblical Ark of the Covenant, but his vessel nevertheless carried the important symbols of his religion to places where they were most needed.

Forgive and Forget

ON A PITCH black Korean night, Pfc. Jerry Gill found himself alone in a foxhole with an M-1 rifle and a small supply of hand grenades, guarding a trail that Chinese infiltrators had been using to get behind the Marines' lines. Unable to see his hand in front of his face, his imagination began to run wild at every sound. Fearing he might not live to see the next day, he prayed fervently, *"God, get me out of this, and I will be your faithful follower forever."*[287]

Gill made it through that night and the rest of his tour of duty in Korea, but gave no thanks to God or further thought to the promises he made while fearing for his life. He returned to civilian life, married his sweetheart, Louise, and went to work in a Savannah, Georgia, paper mill. Unfortunately, a drinking habit gradually turned into a drinking problem that jeopardized his career and his family. When finally confronted by his wife, he reluctantly agreed to start attending church, more to pacify her than to help himself. After going through the motions for several years, an amazing thing happened.

One Sunday morning his pastor gave a sermon titled, *"Forgive and Forget."* During that brief twenty minutes, Gill's life changed forever. While he listened to the minister talk about the forgiveness embodied in Jesus Christ, his own life flashed before him, and he saw for the first time he needed forgiveness more than anyone he knew—from Louise, his children, and from Jesus. He remembered a promise made long before on a dark night in Korea. He asked Jesus into his heart and pledged that he would indeed be a faithful follower forever.

Today, Gill says, *"I still make mistakes, but I have no doubt that I am forgiven."*[288] He also quotes by heart the passage of Scripture that means most to him:

> Do not let your hearts be troubled. Trust in God; trust also in me. In my Father's house are many rooms; if it were not so, I would have told you. I am going there to prepare a place for you. And if I go and prepare a place for you, I will come back and take you to be with me that you also may be where I am. ~John 14:1–3

Nobody Called You

ON NOVEMBER 2, 1950, the Seventh Marine Regiment commenced the big push north from Wonsan, relieving Republic of Korea (ROK) units near Sudong on hilltop positions overlooking the main supply route. Higher headquarters continued to insist that Chinese intervention was unlikely, although the Marines on the ground knew better.

Cpl. Alphonso Burris, a native of Honolulu, was a mortar section leader with Baker Company as they moved into night defensive positions with the other frontline units. Sensing danger, he made sure his men were alert and mortars were well positioned.

> Suddenly an angel of the Lord appeared and a light shone in the cell. He struck Peter on the side and woke him up. "Quick, get up!" he said, and the chains fell off Peter's wrists. ~Acts 12:7

He found an abandoned ROK bunker, lined with rice sacks, which he claimed for his own use. Later, as work was completed and watch rotations were set, he went to sleep in his somewhat luxurious accommodation. After a while, however, he was rudely awakened by a loud voice commanding, *"Out of your hole, Burris! Out of that hole. On the double!"*

He immediately grabbed his weapon and scrambled out of his bunker. He then heard, *"And stay out of there!"* loud enough to rouse the whole company. To his surprise, no one else around him seemed to stir. He crawled over to his platoon sergeant and asked him what he wanted, but was told nothing had been said. Another man whispered to him, *"I didn't hear a d--- thing. Haven't heard a sound since I took the watch."*

"Hey, somebody called me out of my hole," Burris insisted. *"The lieutenant didn't call me, either?"*

"Nobody called you."[289]

Burris went back to his hole, but stayed outside, lying on the ground nearby. He didn't know who or what had called him, but he decided he would do what he was told. A few minutes later, the entire company was jarred awake as bugles blared and rockets ripped through Baker Company's line. One of the first rounds was a direct hit on the hole Burris had just abandoned.

Troops face advancing winter (US Army)

Turkish Troops move near Chongchon River (UPI)

Unit Integrity

ON NOVEMBER 30, 1950, the Second Infantry Division was ordered to move south as the massive Chinese invasion began to hit the Eighth Army. The division was already heavily engaged and faced the prospect of moving along a narrow dirt road dominated for six miles by ridgelines on each side and unknown enemy forces. When the effort to clear the ridgelines was repulsed, the division commander ordered an attack directly down the road.

> In Christ we who are many form one body, and each member belongs to all the others.
> ~Romans 12:5

The vanguard of the column was the Second Battalion, 38th Infantry, mounted on a dozen Sherman tanks. The troops were to dismount and, with tank support, punch through any resistance. Prior to jumping off, however, someone on the division staff had another idea, as described by the Army historian, S. L. A. Marshall:

> *It was felt that the armor should be distributed along the length of the column so that one tank would be covering a serial of about ten thin-skinned vehicles. In consequence, Second's companies were split apart, and before the move started, the battalion was scattered along the length of the column. The last chance for control passed from the hands of the men who led (the battalion).*[290]

As events unfolded, everything that day seemed to work against cohesive action. As the convoy came under fire, stopped, and started, the other units became separated and disorganized. Within hours practically every man of the Second Division was fighting on his own, leading to one of the gravest disasters in US Army history.

The importance of unit integrity has been understood by military commanders since antiquity. In biblical times, Nehemiah had to defend the walls of Jerusalem being rebuilt by the Israelites. When threatened by attack, he assigned defenders by family to the vulnerable points. He kept the trumpeter with him so all could be assembled at any critical point. He knew that men fighting alone would not be effective, regardless of their numbers.

Unit integrity is an important concept for Christians, as it highlights the importance of our churches. In our churches we are trained, organized, and empowered to do God's work in an ever more secular society. We each need the body of Christ, just as it needs each of us.

The Captain's Hit!

COMPANY L of the Ninth Regiment, led by Capt. Maxwell Vails, was defending an isolated hill west of the Chongchon River when the Chinese invasion struck on November 25, 1950. The main attack came unexpectedly from the rear of the company. As the assault closed on the American lines, rifle, machine-gun, and grenade fire grew in intensity. At some places the fighting was hand-to-hand. As ammunition ran low and the supply of grenades was exhausted, the American line began to waiver. At this climactic moment, a cry rang out from the vicinity of the command post, *"The Captain's hit!"* These words seemed to dissolve the fighting spirit of L Company. Men began moving off the hill despite the efforts of the other officers. Even shouts from their wounded company commander could not stem the tide. Individually and in small, isolated groups, what was left of L Company fled under cover of darkness.[291]

> Just as each of us has one body with many members, and these members do not all have the same function, so in Christ we who are many form one body, and each member belongs to all the others. We have different gifts, according to the grace given us.
> ~Romans 12:4–6

There were many things working against these soldiers on that fateful night. Poor intelligence, insufficient ammunition, and faulty judgment all played a role. However, the debilitating effect of losing the commander points to another problem. The fighting effectiveness of any unit cannot depend on one person.

Over time, I have witnessed several unfortunate church crises over the loss of one person—the pastor. When this occurs, it also indicates a bigger problem within the church. We have lost sight of the fact that the church is not one person. The church is the congregation, including every member. The church is the body of Christ under Christ's leadership and authority. If a pastor is lost, other leaders have to step forward, but more importantly, every member has to turn to Jesus and stand by his or her own post, carrying the load and supporting the rest of the body.

A Korean Boy

JOHN MCCURRY and a friend were in a rear area awaiting a new assignment. One morning as they walked to a nearby USO for coffee, they found a little Korean boy crying beside the road. McCurry sat down beside him and put an arm around him. He knew the boy couldn't understand his words, but he talked softly to him in a soothing voice to calm him down. At some point during this one-way conversation, his friend took a picture of McCurry and his young friend.

> Whoever heard me spoke well of me, and those who saw me commended me, because I rescued the poor who cried for help, and the fatherless who had none to assist him.
> ~Job 29:11–12

The two soldiers found an interpreter and learned that the boy's parents were dead. McCurry and his buddy took care of him for a while and then took him to a nearby temporary orphanage where the village women were taking care of other lost children. With a tearful farewell, McCurry gave his young friend a hug and explained that this was to be his new home.

McCurry never forgot that little boy and prayed for him many times over the years. He feels confident that God has watched over him as he has grown to adulthood. The picture shown on this page is one of McCurry's most prized possessions. Remembering this brief episode, he says, *"It sticks with me that this is the best summary of the Korean War I could ever come up with."*[292] Just as two soldiers went to the rescue of a small boy, so America held out a hand to a young nation in trouble, giving it a chance to survive and grow to maturity.

John McCurry with Korean orphan (Rudy Durcansky)

Not What, but Who

AS THE FIRST Marine Division moved ever deeper into North Korea, the casualties began to mount. At a forward aid station, Chaplain John Craven worked long hours giving assistance to the wounded. Over time he began to see more and more men shaken up by the heavy fighting, suffering from a condition known in previous wars as "combat fatigue." On one occasion he was actually attacked by a Marine wielding a knife, fortunately restrained by others before he could do any harm. Chaplain Craven described his best treatment for these shaken men:

> *The most effective help I found in working with these psychological casualties was to hold their hand or arm and say, "Let's pray The Lord's Prayer together." Sometimes this was difficult, but as they struggled with the words they quieted down and in many cases they were calmed down completely by the time we reached the "Amen." The majority of these Marines returned to the fighting with their units.*[293]

After fourteen days of constant combat the lead elements of the division reached friendly lines at Hamhung. Throughout this time the flow of casualties into Craven's constantly-moving aid station had been unremitting. With little food, water, or sleep all were in a state of exhaustion. At one point the regimental surgeon turned to Craven and said, *"Chaplain, I don't know what keeps you on your feet."* The chaplain replied, *"Doc, it's not 'what' but 'Who.'"*

Chaplain Craven's comment reminded me of a similar statement I heard years ago, soon after I became a Christian. During a Bible study discussion, a friend said to me, *"It's not what you know that counts, but who you know."* These words, like those of the chaplain, have helped me redirect my efforts from learning *about* God, to *knowing* God—the never-ending journey of every Christian.

> For who among men knows the thoughts of a man except the man's spirit within him? In the same way no one knows the thoughts of God except the Spirit of God. For who has known the mind of the Lord that he may instruct him? But we have the mind of Christ.
> ~1 Corinthians 2:11, 16

Amazing Grace

MOVING NORTH to the Chosin Reservoir, Fox Company, Second Battalion, Seventh Marines, stopped briefly in Hagaru-ri, a little Korean village that had taken on the appearance of a mining camp. Canvas tents had sprung up around the dilapidated houses, while vehicles and supplies were staged everywhere. On one end of the town Marine engineers were operating bulldozers around the clock to carve an airstrip out of the frozen ground. It wasn't much, but it was the most civilization these Marines had seen in weeks.

Before moving on, Pfc. Gray Davis and several members of his squad commandeered one of the village huts for a brief respite from the biting cold to clean their weapons and heat frozen C-rations. Inside they found a mother with two children in a typical Korean house where the chimney was ducted under

> So in Christ we who are many form one body, and each member belongs to all the others. ~Romans 12:5

the floor for radiant heat. As the Marines relaxed in the warmth and ate their food, one of them hummed a few bars of the old hymn, *Amazing Grace*.

Suddenly, Davis noticed that the woman and children standing nearby were smiling. The mother sent one of the children outside, and he returned soon with the father. As the man came in, he walked straight to a corner of the hut and reached into a sack of potatoes. Not knowing what to expect, the Marines stood up and leveled their weapons at him. What he pulled out of the sack, however, was an old and tattered hymnal, probably left ages before by a missionary. The entire family then lined up and sang "Amazing Grace" in Korean for the flabbergasted Marines.[294]

Davis and his comrades would never forget that moment when two cultures came together briefly in a dismal, war-torn setting in the words of an old Christian hymn:

Amazing grace! How sweet the sound that saved a wretch like me!
I once was lost, but now am found; was blind, but now I see.

Through many dangers, toils and snares, I have already come;
'Tis grace hath brought me safe thus far, and grace will lead me home.[295]

One Body

JOHN CRAVEN enlisted in the Marine Corps in 1933 and was discharged to attend college and Baptist seminary. During World War II he was commissioned in the Navy Chaplain Corps and served with the Marines in four Pacific campaigns.

> This mystery is that through the gospel the Gentiles are heirs together with Israel, members together of one body, and sharers together in the promise in Jesus Christ.
> ~Ephesians 3:6

In 1950, Craven was assigned to a Marine battalion on routine deployment in the Mediterranean when the Korean War started. His unit and assigned ships made their way through the Suez Canal and across the Indian Ocean, to eventually land at Inchon with the First Marine Division. During November and December with the Marines at the Chosin Reservoir, the chaplain endured the brutal winter and savage Chinese attacks. As was his custom, he spent most of his time in the aid stations, giving assistance to the wounded and dying. However, in the midst of the brutal campaign, he met a group of people he would never forget:

> The North Korean Christians looked upon the Marines as their heaven-sent deliverers from the communists. At Hagaru-ri we met an old Presbyterian minister and his saintly wife. They had been hiding in the caves and rocks for several months before our arrival. Their church had been destroyed but the parsonage was still standing—marked by a small cross on its highest peak.[296]

With Craven's help, the Korean minister held a church service for the first time in many months, using a bombed-out theater. The chaplain even found the church's bell, which had been confis- cated by the Communists for use as an alarm by the local police. When he returned the bell to its rightful owners, the tears flowed freely down the faces of the pastor and his small congregation. At their request, the chaplain then preached at their first service with the aid of an interpreter. In this remote, war-torn North Korean village, people who were literally worlds apart in culture and circumstance came together for one purpose—to wor- ship the Savior of all, Jesus Christ.

Chaplain John Craven with a Marine (US Navy)

Returning Home

SOLDIERS RETURNING from war have always had difficulty readjusting to family life. The Korean War was no exception. With separations of a year or more, the resulting strains on service families were severe. The soldiers themselves often came home with new attitudes toward life, or with problems associated with the stress of combat. They also found that their wives and children had changed in significant ways. One chaplain had some simple advice for servicemen about what to expect and what to do as they reclaimed their roles as husbands and fathers:

> Whoever wants to become great among you must be your servant, and whoever wants to be first must be slave to all. For even the Son of Man did not come to be served, but to serve, and to give his life as a ransom for many.
> ~Mark 10:43–45

The many months of worry will no doubt have added some age-lines to the wife, not to mention the fact that she has had to carry the full responsibility of the family during the husband's absence. Perhaps a child has been added which the father has not even met. The tiny tots that he left will probably be children with their own ideas, and will have changed greatly in appearance. He must remember that his children cannot be ordered around like soldiers he outranked. Their father will come back a hero and he must not disappoint them. Every word he speaks may be imitated by his children.

The returned veteran should not assume the attitude that since his wife was able to manage without him, she can continue to take upon herself the full responsibilities of running the household. Tasks which he may have considered too menial to do in military life may be a requirement for peace and harmony in the family. Although he may be a war hero in the eyes of his family, when he gets home he should keep in mind the words of Jesus: "Let him that would be great among you, be your servant."[297]

There could be no better advice for fathers and husbands of every age than these words spoken by our Savior. A man will be truly first in his home only when he puts his family before himself.

(National Archives)

Advent

IN THE CHRISTIAN church calendar, Advent is the season of preparation and expectant waiting for the celebration of Christ's birth and his return. It is a time of prayer and introspection, especially for military men and women in lonely and dangerous places far from home. During the Korean War the Chief of Navy Chaplains published a poignant Advent message to naval personnel serving in the Korean war zone, recalling past Christmases and other conflicts:

(US Army)

> *Cold casernes filled with lonely unpaid soldiers in 1917; tired and worn, yet happy, warriors recently released from combat in 1918; children's parties organized and paid for by shipboard Navymen and Marines; celebrations held in the tropics, both afloat and ashore on overseas duty where there was little to remind us of home; candlelight services in chapels in the open air, and in ships; carols sung when peace reigned, but none as moving as aboard a ship cruising under wartime conditions of danger; religious services and the sacrament of Holy Communion even in the darkest hours of war.*
>
> *All these and more come flooding into my memories. Through them all may be heard the message of Advent:*

For unto us a child is born, unto us a son is given: and the government shall be upon His shoulder: and His name shall be called Wonderful, Counsellor, The mighty God, The everlasting Father, The Prince of Peace.
~Isaiah 9:6 (KJV)[298]

The chaplain expressed confidence that the men and women of the navy and Marine Corps would welcome the Christ child during that Advent season and future ones as well, whether *"in beautiful chapels at home and abroad, in ships on the high seas and in hostile waters, or with Marines on the field of battle."* In the holiest of seasons, he offered a final prayer and hymn to the One who gives light in the darkness and hope to the world: *"O Holy Child of Bethlehem, descend on us we pray; cast out our sin and enter in; be born in us today."*[299]

Divide and Conquer

WITH THE First Marine Division strung out over a single road seventy miles long, the Chinese forces attempted to divide and conquer the Americans. Every effort was made to cut the lines of communication and to isolate individual units. They followed this strategy as a US relief force fought its way north from Koto-ri on November 29, 1950. The nine-hundred-man Task Force Drysdale was trying to reach Hagaru-ri to relieve the beleaguered garrison when the Chinese successfully destroyed one of the vehicles in the middle of the convoy. As the lead elements continued ahead, this effectively isolated the rear elements, enabling the Chinese to focus on these separate units, further cutting them up into small groups which they either overwhelmed or forced to surrender.

Fortunately, this Chinese strategy was ultimately unsuccessful on a larger scale. The small garrison at Hagaru-ri held until reinforcements arrived, enabling the isolated units at Yudam-ni to fight their way into the perimeter. The bulk of the division was then able to break out to the south, collecting the rest of its units along the way to Hungnam. The success of this campaign is attributed to the fighting spirit of the Marines and the brilliance of Gen. O. P. Smith, who, even before the surprise onslaught of two Chinese armies, recognized the vital importance of being able to consolidate his forces.

> I have given them the glory that you gave me, that they may be one as we are one: I in them and you in me. May they be brought to complete unity to let the world know that you sent me and have loved them even as you have loved me. ~John 17:22–23

Unfortunately, Satan often has more success in isolating those he wants to attack. Our separation from the body of Christ is usually not physical, but mental, as we distance ourselves from others. Whether due to the wiliness of the evil one or to our fallen nature as human beings, we seem programmed to turn inward in the face of discouragement or depression. In reality, at such times, we need our brothers and sisters in Christ more than ever. Satan or the world will never divide and conquer as long as we firmly plant ourselves in the body of Christ.

Korean Winter (National Archives)

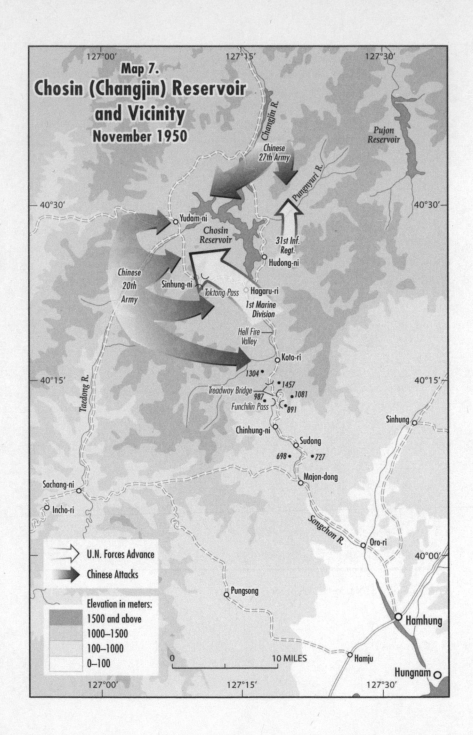

Map 7.
Chosin (Changjin) Reservoir and Vicinity
November 1950

127°00' 127°15' 127°30'

Changjin R.

Pujon Reservoir

Chinese 27th Army

Pungnyuri R.

40°30' 40°30'

Yudam-ni

Chosin Reservoir

31st Inf. Regt.

Hudong-ni

Chinese 20th Army

Sinhung-ni

Toktong Pass

Hagaru-ri

1st Marine Division

Hell Fire Valley

Koto-ri

40°15' 1304 •1457 40°15'

Treadway Bridge 987 •1081

Funchilin Pass •891

Sinhung

Chinhung-ni

Sudong

698• •727

Taedong R.

Majon-dong

Sachang-ni

Incho-ri

Songchon R.

Oro-ri

40°00'

→ U.N. Forces Advance

➤ Chinese Attacks

Pungsong

Hamhung

Elevation in meters:
1500 and above
1000–1500
100–1000
0–100

0 10 MILES

Hamju

Hungnam

127°00' 127°15' 127°30'

CHOSIN RESERVOIR

THE MARINES called it "Operation Yo-Yo." Packed tightly in amphibious ships, they sailed from Inchon on October 16, 1950, for a scheduled assault on Wonsan four days later. However, as they arrived off the east coast, they found the mine clearing operation in Wonsan harbor still incomplete. For seven more frustration-filled days they steamed back and forth in the Sea of Japan before finally landing for the big push to the Yalu.

At this stage of the war, First Marine Division, Seventh Infantry Division, and two ROK divisions composed X Corps under the command of Lt. Gen. Ned Almond, operating independently of the Eighth Army for the advance up the east coast of Korea. As the Marines went ashore at Wonsan, the Seventh Division landed one hundred miles to the north at Iwon, where they also found ROK units there ahead of them.

As soon as these forces were ashore, General Almond commenced pushing hard to the north. On the right, he sent the ROK divisions along the coast road toward Chongjin. From Iwon, the Seventh Division headed for the Yalu River at Hyesanjin. The First Marine Division attacked due north from Hamhung toward the Chosin Reservoir and beyond. The terrain and weather facing these units were formidable. The rugged Taebaek Mountains rose to more than 7,000 feet in elevation, and good roads were nonexistent. Narrow dirt trails wound through deep gorges and along cliffsides, presenting a severe challenge to the men and vehicles. Temperatures plunged below zero.

At midnight on November 3, the Seventh Marine Regiment, leading the way toward the Chosin Reservoir, was hit hard by a Chinese division near Sudong. After four days of hard fighting, the Chinese forces suddenly disappeared as they had on the western front. Confusion reigned in X Corps about what to expect next. Somehow, General MacArthur and General Almond continued to think the Communist Chinese Force (CCF) threat minimal, and so ordered the advance to continue at an even faster pace. However, instead of minimal forces opposing them, there were in fact twelve CCF divisions with more than one hundred thousand men.[300]

Maj. Gen. Oliver P. Smith, commanding the First Marine Division, complied with General Almond's orders while exercising extreme caution.

Aware of the increasing Chinese presence in his zone, he came into frequent conflict with his superior over this slow and deliberate advance. By November 27, the Seventh Marines and Fifth Marines reached Yudam-ni at the western end of the Chosin Reservoir. The battalions of the First Marine Regiment were defending the division's sixty-mile main supply route to Hamhung in positions at Chinhung-ni, Koto-ri, and Hagaru-ri.

Just after dark on November 27, the Chinese struck the scattered forces of X Corps in a coordinated attack designed to isolate and destroy the units piecemeal. Two divisions struck the Seventh and Fifth Marine Regiments at Yudam-ni with massed assaults. In bitter hand-to-hand fighting the Marines held their positions until General Smith ordered them to fight their way back to Hagaru-ri. In order to do this, the Marines had to take the high ground overlooking the fourteen-mile road to ensure safe passage of their vehicles, equipment, and wounded. The key feature along this route was Toktong Pass, which had already been outposted by Fox Company of the Seventh Marines. After five days of constant attack the company was reduced from 240 to 82 men, but held onto the critical pass until relieved.[301]

East of the Chosin Reservoir, elements of the Thirty-First Infantry Regiment of the Seventh Division were advancing to the north when they were also struck by massive Chinese attacks. Pulling back to Hagaru-ri, these units suffered devastating casualties, including the capture of Col. Allan MacLean, the regimental commander.[302] Remnants of these units joined the Marines' ranks at Hagaru-ri.

When a reporter asked General Smith about the dire situation, he made the classic and historic reply, "We are not retreating. We are just attacking in a different direction."[303] As the Marines consolidated their positions, supplies were brought in by air, and casualties evacuated from a hastily-built airstrip. Then, on December 7, the Seventh Marines led the way out of Hagaru-ri, attacking to the south. Every ridgeline and peak threatening the advance was taken, often with bitter hand-to-hand fighting. By December 11, eleven thousand Marines and one thousand soldiers from the Chosin Reservoir reached friendly lines at Hamhung after fighting their way through two Chinese armies.[304]

Out of Body

THE MARINES made first contact with Chinese forces on November 4, 1950, just south of a town called Sudong-ni fifty miles south of the Chosin Reservoir. A Company, First Battalion, Seventh Marines, had taken position on a horseshoe-shaped group of hills, dubbed "The Boomerang," just south of town, overlooking the main road north. During the night, every platoon was hit hard by Chinese attacks. Early that morning the company commander asked Lt. W. J. (Bill) Davis, his mortar section leader, to move up to his position to better coordinate mortar fire. Davis grabbed another Marine, some phones, communications wire, and a canteen of coffee and started up the hill. At that moment, he had some unusual thoughts:

> As Sieck and I started up the steep rear slope of Hill 727, an eerie feeling overtook me. It began with a question that would enter my mind many times in the next two months: What am I doing here? Am I really here? Is this actually happening to me? It was like I was outside my body looking over this Marine Corps environment, much like I had seen in movies of WWII battles, with John Wayne usually as the Great White fighter . . .[305]

I identify with this Marine's thoughts on several levels. First, John Wayne was an important figure in my youth, especially when he starred as a Marine sergeant in *Sands of Iwo Jima*. I also identify with Davis' "out-of-body" experience. There were many times in Vietnam when I was hot, tired, frustrated, or fearful, and suddenly seemed to look down on my plight from above. This distance seemed to give me a new perspective on where I was and what I was doing—and a better attitude about it.

> I pray also that the eyes of your heart may be enlightened in order that you may know the hope to which he has called you, the riches of his glorious inheritance in the saints, and his incomparably great power for us who believe.
> ~Ephesians 1:18–19

I now find this distance in my everyday life through prayer. We never know God's perspective on our lives and events fully, but when we try to see ourselves as he sees us, our troubles take on a different light. From an eternal perspective, there is more significance in *how* we solve our problems than in the actual solving. Through prayer, every difficulty presents an opportunity to distance ourselves from the world and come closer to God.

A Marine's Prayer

LT. BILL DAVIS was with A Company, Seventh Marines, during the Chosin Reservoir campaign. On Sunday, November 26, 1950, his unit conducted a patrol to the southwest of Yudam-ni to establish contact with enemy forces threatening the main supply line. Late that afternoon, the lead platoon came under intense fire. Davis' good friend, Frank Mitchell, known by officers and men alike as "Mitch," was at the point of attack. Even though wounded early in the firefight, he moved constantly among his men, directing fire and covering their withdrawal. While firing an automatic weapon and throwing grenades, he was mortally wounded. For his heroic actions that day, Mitch was later honored posthumously with the Medal of Honor.

> He came and preached peace to you who were far away and peace to those who were near. For through him we both have access to the Father by one Spirit.
> ~Ephesians 2:17–18

Davis and the men of A Company were crushed by the loss of this great Marine and friend. During a somber return from the patrol, a prayer learned long before suddenly came to the young officer's mind. He began saying it over and over, *to console, to remotivate, to perhaps assuage guilt over what more could have been done.*[306] He has said this prayer every day since, always remembering his friend Frank Mitchell:

Oh, God!
From whom all desire, right counsel, and just works proceed,
Give to thy servants that peace which the world cannot give,
So that our hearts, being inclined to obey thy commandments,
And the fear of our enemies being removed,
Our time, by thy merciful protection, may be peaceful
(Through Christ Our Lord).
Amen[307]

Davis commented further about the faith underlying this prayer: "The saying that there are no atheists in foxholes is so true, as comes to light in the Corps, when you've done all you can in a given tactical situation, and you have to turn it over to someone who will help, when all else fails."[308]

Medal of Honor

O N NOVEMBER 26, 1950, First Lt. Frank Mitchell was killed leading his platoon in a bitter battle near the Chosin Reservoir. He gave his life to save the lives of many others. News of his death was a blow to every other Marine of First Battalion, Seventh Marines. His Medal of Honor citation told the story:

Frank
Mitchell
(USMC)

Leading his platoon in point position during a patrol by his company through a thickly wooded and snow-covered area in the vicinity of Hansan-ni, First Lieutenant Mitchell acted immediately when the enemy suddenly opened fire at point-blank range, pinning down his forward elements and inflicting numerous casualties in his ranks. Boldly dashing to the front under blistering fire from automatic weapons and small arms, he seized an automatic rifle from one of the wounded men and effectively trained it against the attackers and, when his ammunition was expended, picked up and hurled grenades with deadly accuracy, at the same time directing and encouraging his men in driving the out-numbering enemy from his position. Maneuvering to set up a defense when the enemy furiously counterattacked to the front and left flank, First Lieutenant Mitchell, despite wounds sustained early in the action, reorganized his platoon under the devastating fire and spearheaded a fierce hand-to-hand struggle to repulse the onslaught. Asking for volunteers to assist in searching for and evacuating the wounded, he personally led a party of litter bearers through the hostile lines in growing darkness and, although suffering intense pain from multiple wounds, stormed ahead and waged a singlehanded battle against the enemy, successfully covering the withdrawal of his men before he was fatally struck down by a burst of small-arms fire. Stouthearted and indomitable in the face of tremendous odds, First Lieutenant Mitchell, by his fortitude, great personal valor and extraordinary heroism, saved the lives of several Marines and inflicted heavy casualties among the aggressors. His unyielding courage throughout reflects the highest credit upon himself and the United States Naval Service. He gallantly gave his life for his country.[309]

> My command is this: Love each other as I have loved you. Greater love has no one than this, that he lay down his life for his friends. ~John 15:12-13

On August 6, 1952, a ceremony was held at the Sixth Marine Corps Reserve District in Atlanta, Georgia. Mitchell's widow, Beverly, and their daughter were present to receive the nation's highest award on behalf of a heroic husband, father, and Marine.

A Cough

FIRST SGT. ROCCO ZULLO mounted the truck and took over the .50-caliber machine gun as the convoy of US and British Marines was being riddled by fire from Chinese troops blocking the road forward. For hours he poured fire on one enemy position after another, enabling the convoy to inch ahead toward the embattled garrison at Hagaru-ri. Already wounded several times from shrapnel, Zullo went down when a burst of rifle fire struck him in the abdomen. Several men placed him in one of the trucks and tried to administer first aid, but blood was gushing from the gaping wounds as his pulse steadily weakened. As the convoy cleared friendly lines, one of the Marines announced, *"I can't find a pulse."*[310]

In a state of shock, three Marines of George Company carefully lifted Zullo off the truck and took him to a tent set aside as a morgue. There, they added his body to others stacked in rows outside the tent and reported back to the rest of the company the sad news: the first sergeant was dead.

> I have set before you life and death, blessings and curses. Now choose life, so that you and your children may live and that you may love the Lord your God, listen to his voice, and hold fast to him.
> ~Deuteronomy 30:19–20

More than an hour later, a corpsman passing by heard the sound of a cough from the stacked bodies. Startled, he began searching for the source. After another cough, he found Zullo, in terrible shape, but alive. He got a stretcher team together and rushed the fallen Marine to the medical tent, where surgeons spent hours repairing his perforated abdomen and treating his other wounds. If he had lain much longer in the subzero cold, Zullo would have frozen to death or died of his wounds. Ironically, a cough saved his life.[311]

This story reminded me of a line from *Rubaiyat* of Omar Khayyam: *"A Hair perhaps divides the False and True—and upon what, prithee, may life depend?"*[312] This verse says to me we can't take life for granted, and conveys a simple, spiritual message: regardless of our circumstances, we have an ever-present urgency to ensure we are constantly ready to meet our Lord.

Faith of a Forgotten Soldier

NILE MARSH was a soft-spoken and unassuming man, a veteran of two wars. In Korea he was a member of the ill-fated Task Force Faith, decimated east of the Chosin Reservoir in December 1950. Wounded and unable to walk, he had to fight his way to safety. He later described his journey:

> I started my trip back in a ¾ ton truck, that lasted about five miles, next a four mile ride in a jeep, next a three mile drive in a 2 ½ ton truck . . . At one time I begged the boys to shoot me and roll me into the ditch but they only laughed. I crawled for 500 yards in open ground with a cross fire from all sides but did not even get one single slug. All we had to eat was snow for the last three days.[313]

Marsh described his ordeal as *"hell and death, both on the same plate."*[314] Fortunately, he made it to safety and eventually home for a long recuperation from his wounds. He passed away peacefully in 1981.

Gary Johnson and his family were not related to Marsh but were friends for many years before and after the war. To Johnson, it did not seem right someone like Marsh should be a forgotten figure from a forgotten war. Based on three letters saved over the years, he compiled a moving tribute to this man who gave so much for his country. He described Marsh's ordeal as *"Ten miles and a lifetime."* As the story is told in the words of the man himself, the faith of a young soldier shines through. Describing his miraculous odyssey to Hagaru-ri and air evacuation under fire, Marsh wrote, *"Don't worry, the Good Lord and some of his angels were behind me. I can only thank God for helping."*[315]

> You know that the testing of your faith develops perseverance. Perseverance must finish its work so that you may be mature and complete, not lacking anything.
> ~James 1:3–4

Thanks to a caring friend, this soldier of an almost forgotten war will not be forgotten himself. The perseverance and faith of a young man going through one of the worst ordeals imaginable continues to inspire others facing their own and often less severe trials in life.

Never Surrender

CECIL MCMORRIS was a member of the ill-fated Task Force MacLean attacking east of the Chosin Reservoir in December 1950. He was one of three men in his company to survive the Chinese onslaught. The overwhelming masses of enemy soldiers who attacked his unit over and over would be the subject of nightmares for much of his life. Early in the battle he suffered a gunshot wound to his hip and was left practically helpless. Someone put him into a truck with other wounded men for a desperate attempt to break out of the enemy encirclement.

> If only my anguish could be weighed and all my misery be placed on the scales! It would surely outweigh the sand of the seas ... Then I would still have this consolation—my joy in unrelenting pain—that I had not denied the words of the Holy One. ~Job 6:2–3, 10

Unfortunately, the trucks did not get far. Enemy troops swarmed over the convoy as those able to fight ran out of ammunition. When his vehicle stopped, McMorris somehow crawled out and dropped to the ground, almost breaking his neck in the process. He heard some men nearby surrender and at that point thought to himself, *I know what Custer felt like.*[316] With a few other soldiers, however, he crawled along a ditch to a culvert where he spent a long night. The next day he kept crawling until he reached the frozen-over Chosin Reservoir. There he found a small boat where he took refuge for several days, without food or water, wondering if he would ever make it out.

Amazingly, the wounded, half-frozen soldier was finally discovered by a Marine patrol who took him to Hagaru-ri, from which he was air-lifted to a hospital in Japan. He eventually made it home, but, unfortunately, lost both of his feet from frostbite. Just as he fought on the frozen wastes of Korea, however, he fought on through his recovery. He learned to walk on prosthetics and eventually made a career of making artificial limbs for others. He also shared his story with countless other wounded veterans, encouraging them in their fight to recover, always with a simple message: *"Never surrender to discouragement."*[317]

First Marine Division moves north (USMC)

Marines take the hills (USMC)

A Life of Faith

JOHN MCCURRY went to Korea with a New Testament in his uniform pocket and a sure faith in God. He had known Jesus Christ since his teenage years but would find his faith tested by combat. In November 1950, he was making a resupply run north of Wonsan through an area where enemy guerillas were active. As his jeep came to the top of an incline he discovered too late that a bridge had been partially destroyed. Unable to stop in time, he struck an abutment with a violent crash. McCurry immediately found himself in almost unbearable pain; he thought his back was broken. He pulled himself out of the wreckage and lay on his back for two hours, completely helpless, at the mercy of subzero weather and any enemy who might have found him. In spite of his pain he was able to pray throughout the ordeal. He knew Jesus was with him, and he had no fear of death.

> Now faith is being sure of what we hope for and certain of what we do not see. This is what the ancients were commended for.
> ~Hebrews 11:1–2

Later, two Marines found the injured soldier and evacuated him to a nearby hospital. Because of poor X-ray equipment, the extent of his injuries was not diagnosed, and within days he was bandaged up and sent back to his unit. It was months later, after returning to the United States, that he learned he had suffered a compression fracture of one vertebra, and a sliver of bone had almost severed his spinal cord. He had come within a hair of being a quadriplegic. Even then, he said of his ordeal, *"I felt peace in my mind and heart that is hard to describe, but I was certain that the Lord was with me. I was never without faith and that faith kept me alive."*[318]

John McCurry in North Korea

McCurry's faith was important during his time in war and has grown even deeper over the years since. During a busy career in engineering he dedicated himself to helping others, especially disabled veterans. I have known him as a loyal friend and energetic supporter of his church, always witnessing to the power of faith through his actions.

Walk or Die

DURING THE Chosin Reservoir campaign, E Company of the Thirty-First Infantry Regiment had to make a long and difficult march over a mountain range at night with enemy forces close at hand. There was no time to waste and no going back. The company commander knew that any man who fell out of the march could not be carried and would either die in the snow or be killed by the Chinese. It was either walk or die. Realizing the dire circumstance, he took a drastic measure: *"The first sergeant marched to the rear, and he was ordered to use his rifle sling as a whip. Any man who fell was lashed until he got up and kept going."*[319]

> Anyone who lives on milk, being still an infant, is not acquainted with the teaching about righteousness. But solid food is for the mature, who by constant use have trained themselves to distinguish good from evil. ~Hebrews 5:13–14

Surprisingly, in this test of endurance, one American seemed to think the Korean soldiers fared less well. He considered them tough fighters, but concluded, *"At a certain point, physical condition gives way to basic stamina. The Americans were going on a lifetime of beef and potatoes, while the Koreans were going on a lifetime of fish and rice."*[320]

Modern nutritionists would disagree with this soldier's observation. The Asian diet of rice with small amounts of meat is generally considered superior to the American fondness for heavier fare, based on concerns for cardiovascular health and longevity. Still, fitness experts continue to study the nutritional requirements of hard physical work, seeking the best way to build stamina to sustain performance at the limit of endurance.

The author of the book of Hebrews was concerned about the *spiritual* diet of believers and their stamina for God's work. Even though his fellow believers had received the gospel, he considered many of them still spiritual infants, sustained only by the milk of their elementary understanding. He encouraged them to seek the solid food mature Christians need. Only solid food will sustain those who have to "walk or die" for their Savior. Christian stamina is built on the spiritual food—a thorough knowledge of Scripture, which gives us the confidence to apply God's Word to our everyday lives.

A Sign

PVT. ED REEVES had been on his feet for several days and nights in the bitterest cold imaginable. He finally dropped down in his assigned spot on a hilltop overlooking the Chosin Reservoir. A rifleman with the Third Battalion, Thirty-First Infantry Regiment, he was ordered to get ready for an attack northward the next day. Neither he nor anyone else in the chain of command was aware Chinese troops *en masse* were about to alter the course of the war.

> The LORD said to Moses, "How long will these people treat me with contempt? How long will they refuse to believe in me, in spite of all the miraculous signs I have performed among them?" ~Numbers 14:11

Early in the morning of November 28, 1950, Reeves' position was attacked and overrun by an overwhelming enemy force. Making his way in darkness to a friendly perimeter in the valley below, he suffered painful wounds to his legs from an enemy grenade. He and other wounded soldiers were loaded into a truck convoy trying to link up with other units to the south. Unfortunately, the convoy reached a point where the trucks could not go on, and those who could walk or crawl were forced to continue on their own. This left helpless in the trucks Reeves and others who couldn't move on their own. Shortly thereafter, Chinese soldiers began crowding around the trucks, pilfering supplies and bayoneting many of the wounded.

Suddenly, a Chinese officer looked in Reeves' truck and made an amazing statement in perfect English: *"I stopped to say, God bless you, the Lord be with you."*[321] He then turned and walked away. All the American soldiers in the truck were astounded, and most became angry that the officer had not offered help of any kind. Not so for Reeves. He took this unusual encounter as assurance from God. He was convinced God was telling him, *"You're not alone. I know all about this."*[322]

Hope

LAYING WOUNDED and abandoned in a truck with other helpless GIs, Ed Reeves was almost overcome with despair. He reached into his pocket for the little New Testament he always carried and turned to the Twenty-Third Psalm. He read aloud, and his comrades listened quietly to the comforting words of hope.

Suddenly, the wounded soldiers began to see smoke and realized Chinese troops were setting the vehicles in the abandoned convoy on fire with the wounded inside. As they approached Reeves' truck, he was resigned that his time was up. He prayed for strength to face death like a man. He told Jesus he would be with him soon and watched in horror as the enemy troops gathered around his vehicle.

> The LORD is my shepherd, I shall not be in want. He makes me lie down in green pastures, he leads me beside quiet waters, he restores my soul. He guides me in paths of righteousness for his name's sake. Even though I walk through the valley of the shadow of death, I will fear no evil, for you are with me; your rod and your staff, they comfort me.
> ~Psalm 23:1–4

(National Archives)

Amazingly, Reeves' truck had sustained small-arms fire, and bullet holes had drained the gas tank. The Chinese soldiers could not set it on fire. Instead, they climbed into the vehicle and started killing the wounded with single shots to the head. One by one, the shots rang out. The man next to Reeves was killed, and then a rifle was pointed at his face. He said aloud, *"Jesus, here I come,"*[323] as the muzzle blast knocked him back. He lay dazed and confused, but somehow still alive. After the enemy soldiers left, he felt his head and found only a scalp wound. Reeves was now alone and practically helpless. Still, he continued to pray and to hope.

Crawl before You Walk

Lord, if the mortar didn't kill me, the shooting didn't kill me, and the beating didn't kill me, you must want me out of here. But I can't walk. How can I get outta here?[324]

AS PVT. ED REEVES lay helpless on the frozen ground beside the now abandoned and destroyed truck convoy, he continued to pray. Suddenly, God seemed to answer him as a thought came to his mind: *You must crawl before you can walk.*[325]

> Though I walk in the midst of trouble, you preserve my life; you stretch out your hand against the anger of my foes, with your right hand you save me. ~Psalm 138:7

Painfully lifting himself to his hands and wounded knees, Reeves started crawling over snow-covered fields in the direction he hoped would take him to friendly lines. He passed more Chinese troops who somehow made no effort to stop him. Darkness fell, and he continued his slow, painful journey. He began to sing over and over, *"Yes, Jesus loves me!"*[326] Finally, he felt the hardness of ice underneath him and knew he was on the Chosin Reservoir. His hands and feet slipped frequently, causing him to hit the ice painfully. Each time he fell it took a greater effort to straighten his arms and get back to his knees. Exhaustion and the mind-numbing cold were almost overwhelming. Amazingly, the song of his childhood faith kept coming back to him: *"Jesus loves me, this I know, for the Bible tells me so."*[327]

Finally, almost a week after first being wounded, Reeves was spotted on the ice by a Marine patrol. He was taken by jeep directly to an airstrip and loaded with other wounded men on a C-47. As the aircraft lifted off the rough runway, Reeves pondered how God never answered his prayers as he expected—but nevertheless, *"He answered. Every time I asked God, He answered."*[328]

Prepare a Place

AS I FIRST heard the story of Pvt. Ed Reeves crawling across the Chosin Reservoir, barely alive, singing *"Yes, Jesus loves me,"* I was taken back to my childhood in the Kingston Presbyterian Church of Conway, South Carolina. We often sang the same song in Sunday school:

Jesus loves me! This I know,
For the Bible tells me so.
Little ones to Him belong;
They are weak, but He is strong.[329]

I had no thought of this song for most of my adult life spent outside the church as a religious skeptic. When I became a Christian at age fifty-three, the first persons with whom I shared my new faith was a favorite cousin, Cookie Stogner, and her husband, Tab. At the time, Tab was in the hospital in very poor health. In spite of his illness, he was delighted at my news and encouraged me in my newfound faith.

> In my father's house are many rooms; if it were not so, I would have told you. I am going there to prepare a place for you.
> ~John 14:2

Shortly after this meeting Tab passed away. Unfortunately, I had to be out of town at the time of his funeral. On the Sunday he was buried in South Carolina, my wife and I were at a hotel in Washington, D.C. I awoke that morning singing the Sunday school song that I hadn't thought of for forty years: *"Yes, Jesus loves me!"* I commented to my wife that this little song pretty well summed up the gospel, and joyfully sang it to myself several times.

That evening I made a telephone call to Cookie to check on her and to ask about the funeral. She said all was well and that the funeral was beautiful. She then told me that, at Tab's request, they had sung his favorite Christian song, "Jesus Loves Me." At first I was astounded that such a "coincidence" could occur. Then I was seized with a firm assurance that God was speaking to me in my newfound faith: Tab was in the place he always knew he was going. I could have the same confidence in the fact that Jesus has prepared a place for my loved ones and me.

Divine Guidance

RAY CESARETTI and Don Auellar were close friends in the Seventh Marines during the Chosin Reservoir campaign. One day, they were given clean, dry socks after going days without taking their boots off. To their horror, they found their socks had become part of their feet, which were black and blistered from frostbite. Auellar groaned, *"What happened? These aren't my feet."*[330] They reported to the battalion aid station, where the doctor ordered Auellar to ride out on the convoy, while sending Cesaretti back to his unit. Each man was afraid the other would not survive—one from the danger of constant combat, the other from lying helpless in a truck. They said their goodbyes, not knowing if they would see each other again.

> A man of many companions may come to ruin, but there is a friend who sticks closer than a brother. ~Proverbs 18:24

Back in his unit, Cesaretti found no letup in the fighting. His company was part of the battalion sent cross-country to rescue the Fox Company Marines holding Toktong Pass. Totally exhausted and suffering even worse frostbite after another week of bitter fighting, he was finally airlifted out on one of the last flights from Hagaru-ri. He was taken to the Air Force Hospital in Fukuoka, Japan, and then to the Naval Hospital in Yokuska, where he was moved from place to place due to the overcrowded conditions. For a while his stretcher was in a hallway, then a warehouse, and then in a chapel laid across the tops of the pews. Finally, he was assigned to a bed in a ward. As he lay there, feeling miserable and sorry for himself, he looked over to the bed next to his. Looking back at him was his friend Auellar.

The two friends had a great celebration, rejoicing in each other's unlikely survival and their even more unlikely reunion. Cesaretti later recalled the moment:

> *With all the hospital ships at sea, and all the hospitals in Japan, what was the chance of us being in the same ward—and next to each other? Don and I both knew it was Divine Guidance; from God; nothing is impossible.*[331]

Take the High Ground

TO WITHDRAW from the Chosin Reservoir, the First Marine Division had to use a gravel road cut through mountainous and largely uninhabited terrain running from Yudam-ni to Hamhung, a distance of about fifty miles. This road, referred to as the MSR (main supply route), was needed for the vehicles moving the artillery, equipment, supplies, and wounded to safety. Passing often through the valleys and low ground, the road was dominated by ridges and peaks overlooking its winding course. The attacking Chinese forces sought to close the road by seizing those ridges and peaks.

> Small is the gate and narrow the road that leads to life, and only a few find it.
> ~Matthew 7:14

It was clear to the Marine commanders that the high ground along the MSR had to be taken and held to cover the movement of the vehicles on the road. This was one of the most difficult missions ever undertaken in wartime. The mountain slopes were steep and icy, and units often had to attack in almost single file along sharp ridge lines. As temperatures plunged to thirty below zero, just surviving on the windswept hills was a challenge. The Chinese also learned that if they fired low and wounded a Marine, four others would be forced to carry him down the mountain. The infantry units doing this deadly work were inexorably whittled down in size. Thankfully, they never wavered in getting this vital job done.

"Take the high ground" is a well-worn military axiom, and, even today, a sound tactical principle. The troops at Chosin, however, showed how difficult it is to put an obvious idea into practice. The fast and easy path lay along the valley floor, not in the peaks above. The hard road took time, effort, and unending courage.

Men typically face a choice of this kind in their relationships. In marriage, it often seems easier to take the path of silence, rather than confront the emotional issues that concern their wives. Taking this kind of high ground may never be easy for a man, but is the only way to build the kind of relationship that leads to a lasting marriage.

231

Warming Tent

DURING THE Chosin Reservoir campaign some of the units had small, pyramidal tents with stoves; these were designated as warming tents. When possible, troops were rotated from their exposed positions back to a warming tent for a brief period of thawing out. This was an almost heavenly respite for men fighting in thirty-below temperatures.

(Dept. of Defense)

One feature of these tents, however, was a buildup of humidity from sweat and water heating on the stove. Just as eyeglasses fog up going from an air-conditioned building into the humid outdoors, so anything brought from the outside cold into the warming tent received a coating of moisture. One man described the effect on a rifle:

> As soon as you go outside, wham! Those many droplets of water immediately become ice, in the receiver, in the slide mechanism, everywhere. And the next time you raise your rifle and fire, one round may go off but another doesn't enter the chamber. Your rifle jams and you must hand-feed every round, a frustrating and dangerous experience when they are coming at you by the dozens.[332]

The Marines and soldiers learned the hard way to keep their weapons bone-dry in winter conditions and to never take them into warm places. They had to recognize and overcome this hidden danger.

Unfortunately, many of the things we enjoy in our ordinary lives also have dangers not easy to discern. No one intends to become addicted to alcohol or other drugs when they start using them socially. No one intends infidelity when they start flirting with a co-worker. Many of our activities are innocent in themselves but have potential for abuse. Writing to the church in Corinth, the apostle Paul addressed this tendency and gave advice for the Corinthians and all Christians:

Everything is permissible—but not everything is beneficial. Everything is permissible—but not everything is constructive. Nobody should seek his own good, but the good of others. So whether you eat or drink or whatever you do, do it all for the glory of God. ~1 Corinthians 10:23–24, 31

Souvenir

HARRELL ROBERTS said, *"The only souvenir I brought home from Korea was a piece of shrapnel from a Chinese mortar."*[333] He then told the story of acquiring his "souvenir" while with Task Force Drysdale in its fight to relieve the garrison at Hagaru-ri in November 1950:

> And surely I am with you always, to the very end of the age. ~Matthew 28:20

> *The Brits took the first hill, and then we attacked the next—Hill 1182. We called it "Telegraph Hill" because there was a line of telegraph poles across it. The Chinese fell back at first as we neared the top but then counter-attacked. There was no cover and several men around me went down. I burrowed in the snow and began firing my M-1 as fast as I could. My platoon sergeant went down nearby. A mortar round went off beside me, almost jolting the rifle out of my hands. I looked up to see a shattered hand guard on my M-1 and a piece of white-hot metal smoldering in the snow. As I watched, it turned red and then black. I slipped it in my pocket and kept on fighting. That piece of shrapnel was the only thing I brought home from Korea.*[334]

Harrell Roberts

A few days later at Hagaru-ri, Roberts was wounded in the left wrist by a .50-caliber bullet. He spent six months in a hospital and was eventually discharged from the Marine Corps. He returned home to Savannah, Georgia, and a distinguished career with the US Army Corps of Engineers. I met him at a Marine Corps League dinner in 2012, where we talked about his wartime service. I asked him if his experience in combat had affected his faith in any way. He explained:

> *My family moved to Savannah and joined the First Baptist Church when I was eight years old. When I was sixteen I knew it was time. I accepted Jesus Christ as my Savior and was baptized. My experience in Korea only made my faith stronger. I worry about people who don't have Jesus in their lives. Who do they turn to when the chips are down?*[335]

Roberts' question is one we can all ponder. He has been to hell and back, and has his own "souvenir" to remind himself of it. When the chips were down for Roberts, Jesus Christ was with him and never left his side.

Every Marine

PHIL BAVARO enlisted in the Marine Corps in 1946 and attended the cooks and bakers course at Camp Lejeune, North Carolina. He was medically discharged due to an injury the next year, but came back into the Corps in time for the Korean War. When someone noted his prior training, he was assigned as a cook to a rifle company in the Seventh Marines, and, upon landing at Wonsan in October 1950, was issued a skillet and a coffee grinder to add to his gear. In the campaign to follow, however, it was hard to tell he was a cook. He was called on constantly to fill in as a stretcher bearer, runner, ammunition carrier, and rifleman. At Toktong Pass, he was in a foxhole on the front line for the entire battle, fighting alongside the rest of his company.[336]

> "You are my witnesses," declares the LORD, "and my servant whom I have chosen, so that you may know and believe me and understand that I am he." ~Isaiah 43:10

It has always been a basic philosophy of Marine Corps training that "Every Marine is a rifleman." This principle recognizes the fundamental mission of the Marine Corps and ensures that every Marine is first a warrior, regardless of his occupational duties. The effectiveness of this approach was demonstrated repeatedly in Korea. During the fighting at the Chosin Reservoir composite units were formed repeatedly of cooks, bakers, clerks, drivers, radio operators, and staff personnel to plug holes in the line or to reinforce depleted units. Before the end of the campaign every able-bodied man had had a rifle in his hands.

Christians could benefit from this mission-focused attitude as we do our work in service to God's kingdom. Within the church, we usher, sing, do altar guild, teach Sunday school, and perform other duties, while outside we do community service and charitable work. Although all this activity is important and pleasing to God, we need to remember that all of it is in support of a higher mission given us by Jesus himself: "*Therefore go and make disciples of all nations*" (Matthew 28:19). To carry out this mission, every Christian must at one time or another be an evangelist with a personal witness to share with someone in need when the time is right.

A Pledge

CPL. WALT HISKETT was a tough kid from Chicago. His father walked out on his family when he was six, and his mother died when he was fifteen. He found a home in the Marine Corps and was a fire team leader with Fox Company, Second Battalion, Seventh Marines, at Toktong Pass. He took a bullet in his shoulder during the night of November 28, 1950, and was evacuated to a medical tent in the center of the company perimeter. With the other wounded, he lay in helpless anxiety as the rest of Fox Company fought on against savage attacks that frequently broke the Marines' thin lines.

At one point, as enemy soldiers were heard shouting outside the medical tent, the wounded men expected the worst. At that moment Hiskett's mind went back to his childhood and an elementary school teacher who had made his class memorize the Twenty-Third Psalm. He also remembered a janitor who had given him a piece of candy whenever Hiskett came to a Bible study and said the Lord's Prayer with the group. He had not prayed since then, but the words of the psalm and prayer came to his mind as he lay on the ground in that tent fearing for his life. He also found himself uttering a prayer from deep in his own heart: "*I let God know that if I was able to get through this thing, that I would serve Him any way I could.*"[337]

> Moses said to the heads of the tribes of Israel: "This is what the LORD commands: When a man makes a vow to the LORD or takes an oath to obligate himself by a pledge, he must not break his word but must do everything he said."
> ~Numbers 30:1–2

Hiskett survived the battle at Toktong Pass and was evacuated to Japan, where he underwent surgery to remove the bullet from his shoulder. When he returned to Chicago, he went back to school and eventually attended Chicago Lutheran Seminary. He joined the Navy and served a twenty-four-year career as a Navy chaplain, serving often with the Marines. In 1968 he saw combat again in Vietnam with his old unit in the Seventh Marines.[338] Hiskett spent most of his life serving God and others, honoring the commitment he made on a barren Korean hilltop in 1950.

Marine Hymn

FOR ALMOST a week, two Marine regiments held their own at Yudam-ni against the onslaught of two Chinese divisions bent on their destruction. In the immortal words of the First Marine Division commander at that time, they then *"attacked in a different direction"*[339] back along the fourteen-mile main supply route to Hagaru-ri to link up with the rest of the division. After days and nights of hard fighting in bitter cold, the battered and exhausted Marines finally approached the perimeter. Lt. Col. Ray Davis, commanding the lead battalion, called a halt and shouted to his men, *"Shape up and look sharp. We are going in like United States Marines."* [340] The weary men picked up the cadence as they began *marching* into the friendly lines. Someone began singing the Marine Corps Hymn, and it was quickly picked up throughout the column and the surrounding hills, as the words rang out:

> From the Halls of Montezuma,
>   To the shores of Tripoli;
> We fight our country's battles
>   In the air, on land, and sea;
> First to fight for right and freedom
>   And to keep our honor clean:
> We are proud to claim the title
>   Of United States Marine.

What is man that you are mindful of him, the son of man that you care for him? You made him a little lower than the heavenly beings and crowned him with glory and honor. ~Psalm 8:4–5

One of my proudest moments came at a presidential state dinner honoring the Apollo 11 astronauts at the Century Plaza Hotel in Los Angeles on August 13, 1969. During the program the Marine Corps Band played a medley of service music, and each tune received a polite round of applause. When the first notes of the Marine Hymn sounded, however, all fourteen hundred guests rose in unison and cheered.

This was an amazing event and sincere tribute to the Marine Corps. However, this famous song has never had such meaning as when it was sung by battle-weary men on the road to Hagaru-ri. When it meant the most, these men voiced their courage and their faith—in each other, in their fallen comrades, and in fellow Marines of every generation. May God bless the memory of these great men who stood tall when it counted.

Psalms

CHAPLAIN WILLIAM HEARN was at Hagaru-ri in December 1950 ministering to the Marines under the worst possible conditions. Whenever he had a moment, he turned to his Bible for inspiration and consolation. He found that many of the old and familiar psalms seemed to come to life in new ways, prompting him to write a moving essay titled "Psalms at Hagaru:"[341]

The sun breaks through the morning clouds. It paints the snowy hills of Hagaru with a delicate shade of pink against blue skies. Another day, another place, this would be beautiful; but today there is no time for thoughts of beauty. There are 50,000 and more reasons why one cannot dwell on beauty this morning. Hidden someplace in these hills are the 50,000 and more reasons, each armed with rifle, mortar, or machine gun. And look yet again at the hills, at the snow, at the sun. Before the mountains were formed in the fiery fury of a young earth, before the snows, yes, before the sun cast forth its first light and flame, God was.

LORD, thou hast been our dwelling place in all generations. Before the mountains were brought forth, or ever thou hadst formed the earth and the world, even from everlasting to everlasting, thou art God. ~Psalm 90:1–2 (KJV)

Fear stalks above and pauses in each foxhole and leaves with each a part of itself; unwelcome visitor, intangible, but more real than gun or mountain. Time creeps by despite my assurances unto my soul. Fear creeps in and sits beside my prayers.

The LORD is the strength of my life; of whom shall I be afraid? ~Psalm 27:1 (KJV)

As we wait in the darkness for the morning, we watch the shadows and listen to the stillness. They move by night silently, so silently. Oh for the sun of the morning, the planes flying over in their dawn strike, light to send the quiet menace back beyond the hills.

My soul waiteth for the Lord more than they that watch for the morning: I say, more than they that watch for the morning. ~Psalm 130:6 (KJV)

The waves of hell subside and grow still with the morning. The lines have held. Yes, we have found the deliverance for which we waited through the dark and fearful night.

Wait on the LORD: be of good courage, and he shall strengthen thine heart: wait, I say, on the LORD. ~Psalm 27:14 (KJV)

Feelings of Doom

AFTER THE long ordeal from Yudam-ni to Koto-ri, the Marine column was stopped at the Funchilin Pass due to a blown-out bridge. While waiting for combat engineers to remedy the crisis, units of First Battalion, Seventh Marines, went into the surrounding hills to provide security for them. As the Marines waited hour after hour, a strong north wind brought the coldest temperatures and greatest misery they had endured so far. Along with the numbing cold, Lt. Bill Davis felt an unusual depression eating through his parka and into his bones:

> Listen to my words: When a prophet of the Lord is among you, I reveal myself to him in visions, I speak to him in dreams. ~Numbers 12:6

> *And then it hit me: the feeling of Doom. I had the distinct feeling that after all we had been through together, the world's greatest mortarmen and myself, that we were going to end up on this panoramic observation post FOREVER. This was Doom calling me, saying that I had been pretty lucky up until now, but everyone has to go sometime.*[342]

Davis fought his mental battle by praying fervently. Even then, he was left wondering if the "eternal peace" he so often prayed for was about to be granted. He was finally experiencing the mental state he had heard others describe but had never understood.

Blown Bridge (USMC)

I have never had feelings of impending doom but have known others who have. I don't discount the possibility that God *can* give foreknowledge to someone when it suits his purpose. He might want to prepare us or loved ones for what is to come, or there might be unfinished business he wants us to resolve. I pray now that if I do ever have "feelings of doom," God will give me the wisdom to react in a positive way and to take care of the business important to him. Beyond that, I only pray for strength to place the future where it belongs, in his hands, and to continue living with the positive purpose with which he has blessed my life so far.

Air Evacuation of wounded (National Archives)

Troops move to ships in Hungnam Harbor (US Army)

One Faith

SNOW BEGAN falling. It dropped to 35 degrees below zero at night. We were completely surrounded by the enemy much of the time. Our only supplies were parachuted in. There were no Marine replacements. We were it." Joe Quick continued describing what it was like with the First Marine Division at the Chosin Reservoir: *"We were on 100 percent alert, fighting day and night. We had very little sleep and nothing but frozen C-rations to eat. They would come at us like fire ants—wave, after wave of enemy soldiers."*[343]

In early December 1950, on a hilltop position near Hagaru-ri, Quick was wounded by a mortar blast that lifted him off his feet, inflicting shrapnel wounds to his back and legs. He didn't know how long he was unconscious, but he finally woke up in a blacked-out tent surrounded by dead, dying, and other wounded Marines. He couldn't see anything, but he could hear a Catholic chaplain administering last rites. Finally, the chaplain crawled over to him.

> Make every effort to keep the unity of the Spirit through the bond of peace. There is one body and one spirit—just as you were called to one hope when you were called—one Lord, one faith, one baptism; one God and Father of all, who is over all and through all and in all.
> ~Ephesians 4:3–6

"Father, I'm not a Catholic, I'm a Baptist," Quick said.

The chaplain asked, *"Son, do you believe in God?"*

"Yes, sir."

"Let's say a prayer together," he suggested.[344]

Sometimes denominational differences can seem pretty trivial. A warm-up tent for the wounded on a Korean hillside would definitely be one of those situations. Such dire circumstances shouldn't be necessary to bring Christians of different denominations together. Most of our differences have to do with governance and relatively little with our understanding of the gospel. We should take every opportunity to reach across these man-made lines to do God's work in the world—in Christian unity.

Was I Right?

DR. HENRY (HANK) LITVIN did all he could for the four wounded Marines. He told the battalion commander they would probably die unless they got additional medical treatment. The colonel took the doctor's advice and told him to put the men on a truck to go ahead of the slow-moving column of troops. What neither the doctor nor the colonel knew, however, was that they were already surrounded by Chinese units who had cut the road ahead. Unfortunately, the truck was ambushed and all were killed, including the four wounded men.

> The Lord is near. Do not be anxious about anything, but in everything, by prayer and petition, with thanksgiving, present your requests to God. And the peace of God, which transcends all understanding, will guard your hearts and your minds in Christ Jesus. ~Philippians 4:5–7

Litvin later came upon the gruesome scene of the burned-out truck. He hoped the men were not alive by the time it burned. He was bothered by the incident long after, wondering if those Marines would have made it if he had kept them with the main column. He tried to console himself:

> *With the information I had in hand, I certainly made the only decision possible. But still, was I right? I guess it's just one of those things that make war so loathsome.*[345]

It's human nature to second-guess ourselves when things turn out badly. This is all the more reason to carefully assess our motives and actions ahead of time. We should take our decisions, great and small, to God, in prayer. His answers come in many ways, but usually take the form of a quiet voice that has to be patiently discerned. His guidance often comes to me with a growing sense that a certain course of action is the right one. I try to make sure I am always open to his direction in whatever form he chooses to give it.

Mourning the fallen (National Archives)

God honors our efforts to align our actions with his plans. He wants us to live confidently in an ever-closer relationship with him, with no regret and no second-guessing.

Faith and a .45

D URING WORLD WAR II in July 1944, Lt. Carl Sitter pushed his
Marines forward in the attack to seize the island of Guam. He gave
orders, shouted encouragement, and ducked
under cover himself as the enemy fire intensified. In the midst of the confusion of battle
an amazing incident occurred:

> Therefore we are always
> confident and know that
> as long as we are at
> home in the body we are
> away from the Lord. We
> live by faith, not by sight.
> ~2 Corinthians 5:6–7

*Shouting orders, he rose from his position to
attack the enemy. As quickly as he had risen,
he was driven back to the ground by a hor-
rible blow to the chest. In that millisecond
between the moment the bullet arrives and
the conscious mind records its last impulse, he knew he had been shot
in the heart. There was a moment when all was numb . . . then the young
officer realized that he was still breathing . . . still conscious of the gunfire around him. Instinctively, he reached his hand to his chest, felt the
ragged edges of his uniform and the warm flow of blood. And cold, hard,
shattered steel.*

*Slowly (his) mind began to clear, and he came to an amazing real-
ization. The torn, cold steel he felt was the shattered remnants of the .45
caliber pistol holstered below his left shoulder. It had taken the direct
impact of the enemy round, and saved his life.*[346]

The young lieutenant continued directing his men in the attack and
was hit a second time. Refusing evacuation, he led his platoon until the
job was done, earning a Silver Star and Purple
Heart for his actions in one of the critical battles
of World War II.

Carl Sitter grew up in Pueblo, Colorado, the
son of a steelworker and the grandson of a Presbyterian minister. He was raised in the church
but never gave much thought to God and drifted
away as he grew older and entered the Marine
Corps. His attitude about spiritual matters
changed, however, on that island in the Pacific
Ocean. He said, *"That's when I started getting close to God."*[347] After
that, his faith—and his .45—saw him through the rest of World War II
and, six years later, the Korean War as well.

.45 cal. automatic

Hell Froze Over

Carl Sitter (USMC)

SIX YEARS after doing his time in "hell" on Guam, Carl Sitter went to Korea, where he said, "Hell froze over."[348] As a company commander he led his men through the Chosin Reservoir campaign and one of the coldest winters ever recorded. He took his faith in God with him and a .45 caliber pistol strapped over the left side of his chest.

On November 29, 1950, Sitter was ordered to take a heavily-defended hill in a strategic location. Urging his men forward, he took the hill with heavy casualties, and then defended it over thirty-six hours of continuous, bitter combat, often in hand-to-hand fighting. Wounded multiple times, Sitter continued to direct and encourage his men throughout the ordeal.

For his actions on that bleak Korean hillside, Sitter was awarded the Medal of Honor. His citation called attention to his superb qualities as a leader:

During the night when a vastly outnumbering enemy launched a sudden, vicious counterattack, setting the hill ablaze with mortar, machine gun, and automatic-weapons fire and taking a heavy toll in troops, Captain Sitter visited each foxhole and gun position, coolly deploying and integrating reinforcing units consisting of service personnel unfamiliar with infantry tactics into a coordinated combat team and instilling in every man the will and determination to hold his position at all costs. He fought gallantly with his men in repulsing and killing the fanatical attackers in each encounter. Painfully wounded in the face, arms, and chest by bursting grenades, he staunchly refused to be evacuated and continued to fight on until a successful defense of the area was assured.[349]

Sitter survived Korea and went on to a long and successful Marine Corps career. He was eventually buried in Arlington National Cemetery, where his grave marker displays the Scripture that sustained him through those dark hours on Guam and the Chosin Reservoir.

The LORD is my light and my salvation; whom shall I fear? The LORD is the stronghold of my life—of whom shall I be afraid?
~Psalm 27:1

I Panicked and Survived

AS THE MARINES fought their way out of the Chosin Reservoir, Dr. Hank Litvin did his best to save the countless wounded brought to his makeshift aid stations. He also had to be concerned with saving himself at times. Fortunately, he had a corpsman who had been in World War II and knew the ropes. When his corpsman ducked, he ducked. When the corpsman dug a foxhole, he dug a foxhole. It seemed to work well for most of the way. Things came apart suddenly, however, on the brutal fourteen-mile stretch between Yudam-ni and Hagaru-ri. As small-arms and mortar fire opened up on their convoy, the corpsman jumped into a ditch and Litvin followed. As they huddled there, hoping for help, the doctor was suddenly seized with a sense of panic. He got up, ran to his jeep, and dove under it. As he turned to yell to his corpsman, small-arms fire suddenly riddled the ditch, killing his assistant instantly. Litvin knew he had made a stupid move, but he was still alive. He knew they would both have been dead if he hadn't run to the jeep. After thinking about the incident, the doctor said, *"He made all the right moves, while I panicked and survived. I guess in the long run I was just lucky."*[350]

> You see, at just the right time, when we were still powerless, Christ died for the ungodly . . . God demonstrates his own love for us in this: While we were still sinners, Christ died for us.
> ~Romans 5:6, 8

As a religious skeptic during the time I was in combat I also felt I experienced extreme luck at times, and, in fact, had a foreboding sense I was using up my allotted share. In my own superficial way, I did pray in fearful moments but never thought about giving God credit for pulling me through. Later in life, when I became a believer, I was almost overcome with a sense that God had indeed protected me during these times. Even when I had no faith in him and in spite of my ungratefulness, he was faithful to me. Now, I live my life with gratitude for a God who not only watched over me during bad times, but continued to reach out to me until I was ready to come to him.

Highest Tradition

John Page (US Army)

L T. COL. JOHN PAGE was an artillery officer in the US Army during the Korean War. He had been assigned stateside duty during World War II and so, to his disappointment, missed

> Be on your guard; stand firm in the faith; be men of courage; be strong. Do everything in love.
> ~1 Corinthians 16:13

combat duty. He made up for this with a vengeance when given the chance at the Chosin Reservoir. After completing a special mission from the base in Hamhung to set up radio relay sites north along the main supply route, he voluntarily remained with the Marines at Koto-ri. There, he gathered individual soldiers who had made their way into the perimeter and formed a tactical unit to serve as a reserve force. Providing security to other troops building a vital airstrip, he constantly exposed himself to enemy fire and even manned a tank machine gun to disrupt enemy attacks. On one occasion, he flew from the airstrip in a small observation aircraft to scout enemy positions in the surrounding hills. Flying low over the ridgelines, he dropped grenades and directed rifle fire on enemy troops scurrying below.

During the night of December 10, 1950, the convoy of Marines and soldiers moving out of Koto-ri were held up by Chinese forces pouring small-arms fire on the road. Page's actions at that point are best described in his Medal of Honor citation:

> *Lt. Col. Page fought his way to the head of the column and plunged forward into the heart of the hostile position. His intrepid action so surprised the enemy that their ranks became disordered and suffered heavy casualties. Heedless of his safety, as he had been throughout the preceding 10 days, Lt. Col. Page remained forward, fiercely engaging the enemy single-handed until mortally wounded. By his valiant and aggressive spirit Lt. Col. Page enabled friendly forces to stand off the enemy. His outstanding courage, unswerving devotion to duty, and supreme self-sacrifice reflect great credit upon Lt. Col. Page and are in the highest tradition of the military service.*[351]

Page remains a revered figure in US Army history and in that of the US Marine Corps as well. In addition to the Medal of Honor, he received a Navy Cross for his heroic actions during the most bitter campaign of the war.

Well Done

AFTER SURVIVING combat and subzero cold for more than a month, the Seventh Marines reached Hamhung in mid-December, 1950, and embarked on transport ships waiting in the harbor. Lt. Bill Davis didn't know how long he slept, but it was a long time. When he woke up he got his first look at himself in a mirror and was appalled at the sight—long hair, beard, and filthy uniform. Someone put a new set of clothes in his hands and sent him to the shower. There he went through the long process of stripping off everything he had been in for the last month—underwear, long johns, sweater, utilities, etc. It took a lot of hot water and scrubbing to get down to clean flesh. Afterward, as he got dressed, he discovered his feet had swollen to the point he couldn't get his boots back on.

As Davis was shuffling gingerly down one of the ship's passageways headed for his room, he happened to see the Commanding Officer of Seventh Marines, Col. Homer Litzenberg, approaching. Davis thought he was probably about to be chewed out for not having his boots on. Instead, the colonel stopped and stared at the young lieutenant for a full thirty seconds and then put a hand on his shoulder. With a tear in his eye, he whispered hoarsely:

> Loo-ten-ant, I want to thank you for all the wonderful accomplishments you and your men have made for our Corps and the First Marine Division and the Seventh Marine Regiment. I'm sorry about your feet, but they have traveled the toughest miles in the ruggedest terrain that any Marine's ever did. Well done. Semper Fidelis.[352]

As the colonel moved on down the passage, Davis found himself alone and crying. He thought to himself this was like hearing the voice of God. And what more could any of us want in this life or the next than to feel we have done a good job and been recognized by our ultimate Authority? What more, than to hear our Savior say,

Well done, good and faithful servant! You have been faithful with a few things; I will put you in charge of many things. Come and share your master's happiness! ~Matthew 25:21

Sharing

DURING THE long days and nights in combat, Lt. Bill Davis lost track of how many times he said the little prayer he had learned in church, at times repeating it almost like a mantra: *"Give to thy servants that peace which the world cannot give . . ."* He especially liked the part, *". . . the fear of our enemies being removed,"* which reminded him of the Twenty-Third Psalm. The prayer was a constant reminder to him that there was a source of comfort to which he could cling.

There were times when the young officer felt he should share his prayer with the men in his unit, to give them something to help them through their ordeal. Instead, he kept it to himself:

> *I just didn't have the guts. Lots of good Marines have been brought up in different religions, and with their own prayers, so they don't want some Lieutenant who is paid to lead them in battle to also drive their dealing with God for them, so I kept my mouth shut. But when we are just plodding along like this, it is really great—for me, anyway.*[353]

This is the issue facing every Christian, every day. When do we share our faith? Like the lieutenant, we usually find reasons not to, and often these reasons are valid. We might have been turned off ourselves at some time by street evangelists or religious billboards. We don't want to turn someone else off to Jesus by being "inappropriate."

The answer to the question is not so difficult if we think in terms of *planting a seed.* It doesn't have to be all or nothing. In most cases, it is not up to us to convert another person, especially our casual acquaintances. A simple, *"God bless you," "I'll pray for you,"* or any other brief reference to our faith plants a seed of interest that God can use in his own time. For those we get to know better, there are always those moments when something more meaningful is appropriate. This is when we have to guard against our rationalizations. These are the moments when we can and should speak boldly about the power of the gospel in our lives. Our continuing mission for Christ is to reveal him to others with our words and with our deeds.

> The kingdom of heaven is like a mustard seed, which a man took and planted in his field. Though it is the smallest of all your seeds, yet when it grows, it is the largest of garden plants and becomes a tree.
> ~Matthew 13:31–32

Four Chaplains

ONE OF THE most famous and stirring examples of heroism ever recorded occurred on February 3, 1943, in the Atlantic Ocean near Greenland. On that night the troopship *SS Dorchester* was torpedoed and sunk. Amid the chaos, four chaplains from the units on board worked together to help others abandon ship. As the supply of lifejackets was exhausted, they gave away their own to men in need. As the ship went down, the chaplains were last seen with their arms linked together and heads bowed in prayer.

> It was he who gave some to be apostles, some to be prophets, some to be evangelists, and some to be pastors and teachers, to prepare God's people for works of service, so that the body of Christ may be built up until we all reach unity in the faith. ~Ephesians 4:11–13

Seven years later, the Alexander D. Goode Lodge (named for one of the four chaplains) of B'nai B'rith instituted the Four Chaplains Award to be given a chaplain in each service that best represented the spirit of brotherhood and cooperation exemplified in that famous incident. The first Navy recipient of the award was the chaplain of the First Marine Division who served throughout the Chosin Reservoir campaign. The citation was read at the Naval Gun Factory, Washington, DC, on March 31, 1951:

> *Commander Robert M. Schwyhart, Chaplain Corps, U. S. Navy has expressed his firm faith in God by exemplifying to the men whom he served, the 1st Marine Division, Fleet Marine Force, great steadfastness in the face of adversity; notable courage when circumstances tended to promote fear and discouragement; a broad charity which manifested itself in service to all his men regardless of their creed, rank, or position; the spirit of sacrifice which caused him to give of his strength with compassion and to suffer hardship and danger with equanimity; and faithfulness in his stewardship of the things of God which was consistent with that of the four chaplains in whose memory this award is presented.*[354]

Robert Schwyhart was true to his men and to God during one of the most difficult series of battles in Marine Corps history. He was a fitting recipient of an award honoring the memory of one of the finest examples of faithful service ever recorded.

Four Chaplains commemorative stamp (US Govt.)

The Architect

LT. GEN. ALPHA BOWSER was a hero of World War II and Korea. As a Marine colonel in 1950 he was the operations officer (G-3) for First Marine Division during the Inchon landing and was credited with being the man who designed the campaign to extricate the division from the Chosin Reservoir. Early during the X Corps' advance to the north he became concerned about the appearance of Chinese soldiers on the battlefield, realizing the full implications of this new threat. He began advising those above him to slow the attack and to take precautions by leaving units in defense of key points along the way. Well in advance of the full Chinese onslaught, he advised his staff to start drawing up plans to withdraw. His plans eventually resulted in official orders from Gen. Oliver P. Smith to attack *"in a different direction."*

Years later, at a reunion of The Chosin Few in Arlington, Virginia, General Bowser addressed the assembled veterans who had participated in the campaign:

> *The program for this reunion states that I was the "architect" of our withdrawal from Chosin. Maybe so, but architects don't build anything. They only draw the plans. It takes workers and builders to get things done, and you are the guys who did it.*[355]

In his simple humility General Bowser conveyed an important truth. The greatest plans, just like the best intentions, have to be put into practice by people willing to do the hard work. In the military it's called "boots on the ground." Troops must often be committed before lofty military or humanitarian missions can be brought to successful completion. In God's kingdom we might say "workers in the vineyard." God blesses us with the opportunity to be his workers and to help carry out his plan for the salvation of the world. He wants those who will do the hard work and are willing to put their boots on the ground where they are needed.

When he saw the crowds, he had compassion on them, because they were harassed and helpless, like sheep without a shepherd. Then he said to his disciples, "The harvest is plentiful but the workers are few." ~Matthew 9:36–37

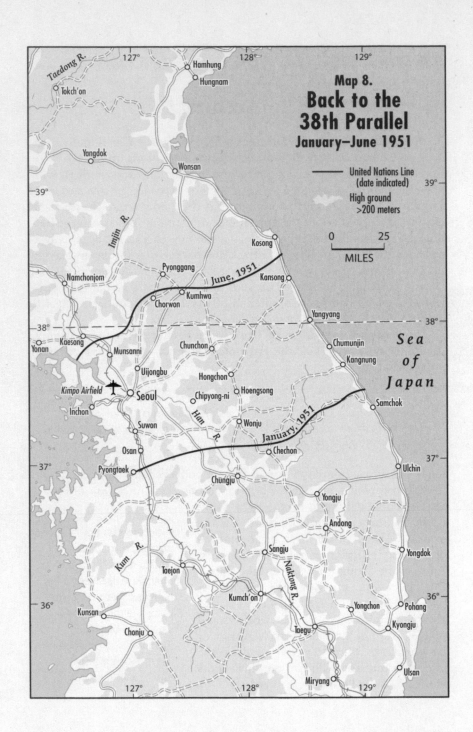

Map 8.
Back to the 38th Parallel
January–June 1951

—— United Nations Line
(date indicated)
High ground
>200 meters

0   25
MILES

BACK TO THE 38TH PARALLEL

THE EVACUATION of X Corps at Hamhung was complete by Christmas Eve 1950. About 105,000 Marine and army troops, eighteen thousand vehicles, and ninety-eight thousand refugees cleared the harbor on Navy vessels and merchant ships as demolition charges destroyed the remaining dock facilities.[356] Almost at the same time the last troops were boarding, a tragic accident occurred on the other side of the peninsula. Lt. Gen. "Johnnie" Walker was killed when his jeep hit another vehicle, forcing the Eighth Army to undergo a change of command while reeling on all fronts from Communist attacks. Within days, Lt. Gen. Matthew Ridgway, a famed World War II airborne commander, took charge of a retreating and demoralized army. There would be no respite from the Communist Chinese Forces' offensive.

On December 26, a major attack hit UN forces north of Seoul, forcing another thirty-mile pullback to the Han River. When attacks in the center of the country threatened to outflank Seoul, General Ridgway reluctantly had to abandon the capital. For the third time in the war Seoul changed hands. After intense fighting and further demoralizing withdrawals, the UN forces began to consolidate on a line thirty miles south of Seoul running from Pyongtaek on the west coast to Wonju in the center and ending at Samchok on the east coast.

By this time in the war the Eighth Army consisted of five corps, manned primarily by US and ROK troops, although contingents from the United Kingdom, Australia, France, India, the Netherlands, the Philippines, Sweden, Thailand, and Turkey made it a truly United Nations force.[357] Immediately opposing them were seven armies of Chinese and North Korean soldiers, battered and depleted during their offensive drive. They had no shortage of manpower, but they were suffering logistical problems as their lines became more and more extended. With shortages of supply and stiffening UN resistance, the advance finally slowed.

Taking advantage of the enemy's weakening effort, General Ridgway launched his own limited offensives, termed "Operations Thunderbolt and Roundup." Within each corps, one division was committed to the attack while larger forces were held in reserve.[358] Careful control of the advance was maintained by using terrain-based phase lines beyond which units could not move without orders. By February 11, UN forces had taken Inchon and Kimpo Airfield and a line generally extending to Hoengsong in the center of the peninsula. This offensive came to a stop, however, on the night of February 11–12 as five CCF armies launched a concentrated assault in the X Corps zone near Hoengsong.

Within a few days, most of X Corps had been pushed back to Wonju. On the left flank, however, the Twenty-Third Infantry Regiment of the Second Division still clung to Chipyong-ni, a key road junction controlling access to the Han River valley. The Twenty-Third Regiment, reinforced by a French battalion, gallantly held its position during three days of all-out attacks by massed Chinese forces, until an armored column punched through in relief.

Within a week the Chinese offensive was spent, enabling General Ridgway to regain lost ground and continue his own advance to the north. During Operations Killer, Ripper, Rugged, and Dauntless, UN forces recaptured Seoul for the second and last time and pushed the Communist forces north of the 38th parallel. A fifth and final Chinese offensive was contained during May, and again UN forces attacked to the north, occupying the so-called Kansas and Wyoming Lines north of the 38th parallel by June 15. There, Allied troops began constructing defensive positions as the US Secretary of State announced American willingness to accept a cease-fire along that line. Within a few weeks the Soviets, Chinese, and North Koreans agreed to open negotiations. There would be no more grand offensives by either side, as the front stabilized where it then existed.

During the spring of 1951, the UN and US war aims shifted from conquest of North Korea to a settlement that would guarantee the existence of South Korea. Gen. Douglas MacArthur fought against this change in policy, several times publicly. After a highly-critical letter written to a congressman was made public, President Truman relieved the venerable hero of World War II and Inchon, creating a firestorm of public outrage in the United States. Meanwhile, the war effort in Korea went on largely unaffected. General Ridgway was moved up to replace General MacArthur, and Lt. Gen. James van Fleet replaced General Ridgway as the Eighth Army commander. A lot of fighting still lay ahead as peace talks began.

What Are We Fighting For?

GEN. MATTHEW RIDGWAY stepped off his aircraft at Taegu in December 1950 to take over a demoralized army. His first priority was to assess just how bad things were. Traveling from unit to unit he quickly got the impression that the men were not mentally or spiritually ready for the kind of offensive operations he envisioned. The first MP he encountered seemed to be typical:

> He was correct in posture and in gesture—correct in every way, except in spirit. That extra snap to the salute, that quick aggressive tone and gesture, that confident grin that had always seemed to me the marks of the battle-seasoned American GI, all were missing.[359]

General Ridgway soon undertook to solve the myriad tactical and logistical problems confronting his new command; however, he remained focused on the troops—their lack of morale and purpose, poor discipline, and the general atmosphere of defeat. Within weeks he concluded they needed to hear a clear answer from their commanding general to the question, *"What are we fighting for?"* For him it was not complicated:

> The god of this age has blinded the minds of unbelievers, so that they cannot see the light of the gospel of the glory of Christ, who is the image of God. ~2 Corinthians 4:4

> The real issues are whether the power of Western civilization, as God has permitted it to flower in our own beloved lands, shall defy and defeat Communism; whether the rule of men who shoot their prisoners, enslave their citizens, and deride the dignity of man, shall displace the rule of those to whom the individual and his individual rights are sacred; whether we are to survive with God's hand to guide and lead us, or to perish in the dead existence of a Godless world.
> In the final analysis, the issue now joined right here in Korea is whether Communism or individual freedom shall prevail.[360]

With this message to the Eighth Army, dated January 21, 1951, General Ridgway articulated for his soldiers and for every American the meaning of the Korean War and America's worldwide conflict with Communism.

Hearing the Call

THE SOLDIER was among the last to reach Hungnam Harbor. The Marines had already been evacuated as his unit crowded onto the docks. The scene was one of mass confusion with vehicles, equipment, and thousands of men jammed together with no one apparently in charge. Totally exhausted from lack of sleep, he unrolled his sleeping bag, lay down amid the confusion, and went out like a light, oblivious to all around him.

> After the wind there was an earthquake, but the LORD was not in the earthquake. After the earthquake came a fire, but the LORD was not in the fire. And after the fire came a gentle whisper.
> ~1 Kings 19:11–12

Much later, Pvt. Paul Noll was rudely awakened from his very sound sleep by a bright light and deafening siren. He peered out of his sleeping bag to find himself alone on the dock. There was one freighter alongside, sounding its ship's siren, and shining a spotlight on him. It finally dawned on him he was supposed to be on that ship. As the freighter pulled away from the dock, he scrambled up a cargo net dropped from the side and barely avoided being left behind in North Korea.[361]

I have wondered at times why God's voice isn't as loud and clear as a ship's siren. Who would fail to respond if he issued unmistakable orders that couldn't be ignored or misinterpreted? I have come to the obvious conclusion he simply did not intend it to be that way. He didn't create men and women to be passive subjects, waiting for his commands. By creating us in his own image, he gave us the intelligence to make our own choices and reach our own decisions. He wants us to be in a relationship with him, but it would be a meaningless relationship if forced on us. Faith itself would be meaningless without the freedom to choose it or reject it. He does speak to us, but only after an effort on our part to hear. We have to pick up his Word and read it carefully. Sometimes we have to study it to find his "orders" for us. We also hear his voice in prayer when we patiently and quietly attend to it. In his love for us, God does not overpower us. Instead, he waits patiently for us to come to him.

Esprit de Corps

CHAPLAIN KEVIN KEARNEY served with the First Marine Division during the Chosin Reservoir campaign. On December 8, 1950, as his unit neared Hungnam and safety, he made an entry in his diary about the men around him:

> *Morale among the Marines is as high as if they were fresh from triumph.*
>
> *You should see the group that is about me as I write . . . dirty, bearded, their clothing food-spattered and filthy . . . they look like the castoffs of creation. Yet they have a sense of loyalty, generosity, even piety, greater than any men I've known.*
>
> *These rugged men have the simple piety of children. You can't help but loving them, in spite of their language and their loose sense of private property.*
>
> *You cannot exaggerate about the Marines. They are convinced to the point of arrogance that they are most ferocious fighters on earth. And the amusing thing is that they are.*[362]

Chaplain Kearney has given an amazing insight into the nature of Marine *esprit de corps*. This intense commitment of every Marine to the Corps and to each other has been the key to success in battle over many generations. It is a powerful force characterized by intense pride that at times may indeed border on arrogance.

Since leaving active duty as a Marine, I have been blessed to find a commitment of an even higher order. Those who follow Jesus Christ have a deep faith in him and strong love for each other. Christian *esprit de corps*, however, is characterized by humility, reflecting the nature of Jesus himself. Jesus was never arrogant. In his own life he replaced arrogance with supreme confidence in his relationship to his Father in heaven and sense of purpose in doing his will. He wants this same confidence to animate the lives of his followers and to infuse his church with a truly spiritual *esprit de corps*.

> Therefore, brothers, since we have confidence to enter the Most Holy Place by the blood of Jesus . . . let us draw near to God with a sincere heart in full assurance of faith, having our hearts sprinkled to cleanse us from a guilty conscience and having our bodies washed with pure water. Let us hold unswervingly to the hope we profess.
> ~Hebrews 10:19, 22–23

Time

L T. GEN. MATTHEW RIDGWAY took command of the Eighth Army in December 1950 under grim conditions. The unexpected and overwhelming invasion of Chinese forces had sent US units reeling in retreat. Also, for the first time in his career as a commander, he was completely on his own. Before, he had always been part of a larger force with additional resources. His higher authority was 700 miles away in Tokyo, with no other troops to commit to the conflict. The safety of every soldier in Korea was his sole responsibility.

This grace was given us in Christ Jesus before the beginning of time, but it has now been revealed through the appearing of our Savior, Jesus Christ, who has destroyed death and has brought life and immortality to light through the gospel. ~2 Timothy 1:9–10

General Ridgway knew he had to do many things quickly. To instill a renewed fighting spirit in the troops, he had to instill confidence in the soundness of his decisions. He knew the troops were skeptical of their commanders. They had the feeling those above them were drawing phase lines and arrows on maps, leaving it to them to do the impossible. Gaining their confidence would take all his energy and the one resource he had so little of—time.

> In truth, the larger the command, the more time must go into planning; the longer it will take to move troops into position, to reconnoiter, to accumulate ammunition and other supplies, and to coordinate other participating elements on the ground and in the air. By proper foresight and correct preliminary action, he knows he can conserve the most precious element he controls, the lives of his men. So he thinks as far ahead as he can. To a conscientious commander, time is the most vital factor.[363]

In his predicament, time meant everything to General Ridgway, and he had to use it judiciously. Just like every one of us, however, he could not control it. In fearful circumstances minutes can seem like hours, or, on more joyful occasions, days can pass in a flash. Fast or slow from our perspective, time inexorably ticks away, beyond our control. It is a quality of the universe and our lives beyond our comprehension. Only God knows the parameters of our time and its relationship to the timelessness of eternity. Time is his, and the small piece he gives each of us is all we have in this life. Our purpose is to live every minute of it to the fullest—and to his glory.

Give-up-itis

ON NOVEMBER 28, 1950, Len Maffi-oli's convoy was completely surrounded by the enemy. After fighting for twelve hours, he and those left alive in his unit were forced to surrender. Chinese soldiers then marched these men more than a hundred miles to a prison camp near the northwestern border of North Korea. Many were not able to complete the trek due to untreated wounds, malnutrition, and subzero weather. Conditions did not get much better in the camp. The diet there consisted of barely enough soybeans and sorghum seed to stay alive. Medical facilities were almost nonexistent, and many men continued to suffer from untreated wounds and frostbite.

> This is a trustworthy saying that deserves full acceptance (and for this we labor and strive), that we have put our hope in the living God, who is the Savior of all men, and especially of those who believe. ~1 Timothy 4:9–10

Many men died due to these terrible conditions, but Maffioli observed a number of his fellow prisoners succumbing to a different kind of malady:

> *There was something else . . . It was called "give-up-itis" for want of a better term. I had a young trooper in my squad. It seemed there was nothing we could do for him. When he was captured, he had been waiting to hear news about a serious operation his mother had to undergo back home. Now he didn't know if his mother was dead or alive, plus he had seen a lot of his buddies killed in action, so he just went into a state of depression. And unless you had somebody to keep an eye on you, you could just crawl into a corner, throw a blanket over your head, and be dead in a period of twenty-four hours.*[364]

These soldiers had ample reason to be depressed considering the situation they were in. Even though few of us ever encounter such dire circumstances, depression is a common condition affecting countless people leading ordinary lives. When hope fades, courage to wrestle with our problems and to move on in spite of them also fades, and those problems can seem overwhelming.

Although many with depression need medical attention and benefit from it, I believe the ultimate cure can only come with a renewal of hope. Our Savior taught us about a peace that passes all understanding. When we have Jesus in our hearts we have that peace and the cure for "give-up-itis." In him every person is able to rediscover hope for the future and courage to meet it head-on.

257

The Right to Worship

THERE WERE about three hundred civilians living in Hagaru-ri when the Marines arrived in the winter of 1950. They had never seen an American and had no idea what to expect. The local Communist chief had fled a few days before, but his pregnant wife and other party members remained behind. The Marines viewed them all suspiciously, not knowing who was friend or foe.

John Lee was a Korean interpreter with the First Marine Division and the only man who could communicate with the villagers. He told them the Marines would protect them unless they committed hostile acts. He tried to keep a close eye on them, not knowing if there were some who might sneak away to lead enemy units into the camp. This job was easy enough during the daytime, but more difficult at night. One evening as Lee was going from house to house in the village he observed a group of about twenty locals silently entering one of the huts. He waited in the shadows until all were inside and then carefully crept up to the door and peered in through a crack. He was surprised at what he saw:

> The LORD said, "I have indeed seen the misery of my people in Egypt. I have heard them crying out because of their slave drivers, and I am concerned about their suffering. So I have come down to rescue them." ~Exodus 3:7–8

In their hands I saw old Bibles and hymn books they must have brought from deep hiding places. They began to sing with low voices, then prayed together. I saw faces in torment for their souls, because they had suffered under communist domination, denied to worship God and tortured for their belief. When the Marines came, they regained their precious right to worship.[365]

Lee knew that these people had regained a long-denied right, but he worried, *For how long?* He knew the Marines would not stay there forever, and, sure enough, within a short time they began the long withdrawal to the coast. Amazingly, these Korean Christians went with them, even though often in the crossfire of vicious battles, to become part of the mass exodus of refugees at Hungnam. They were willing to risk everything for the freedom to worship.

Paratroopers waiting for the signal (National Archives)

Generals Ridgway and MacArthur at the front (National Archives)

Mercy Ship

THE *USS MEREDITH Victory* was a World War II cargo ship reactivated for service in the Korean War and manned by a US Merchant Marine crew. After the crew partially unloaded a cargo of jet fuel at Pusan, she received emergency orders to proceed to Hungnam to aid with the evacuation of US forces. The *Meredith* arrived on December 20, 1950, to a chaotic scene. Not only were American troops evacuating, but the docks were thronged with one-hundred-thousand terrified North Korean refugees, desperately fleeing the advancing Communist Chinese.

> Moses answered the people, "Do not be afraid. Stand firm and you will see the deliverance the LORD will bring you today."
> ~Exodus 14:13

Shortly after entering the harbor behind a minesweeper escort, the *Meredith Victory* was boarded by a party of senior army officers who asked her thirty-seven-year-old captain Leonard LaRue if he would be willing to take some refugees off the beach. Even though his ship had no accommodations for extra passengers and the request could have been refused, LaRue did not hesitate. He said he would take his ship in and load all the refugees possible.

By the time the *Meredith Victory* was alongside a dock on December 22, the First Marine Division and Seventh Army Infantry Division were already at sea. The Third Infantry Division, holding the perimeter against the advancing Chinese, was falling back to the beaches. Gunfire from the battleship *USS Missouri* and two heavy cruisers was crashing overhead. Realizing the dire situation he was in, LaRue kept the engines online and turned the ship around so her bow pointed out to sea.

USS Meredith Victory
(Moore-McCormack Lines)

At 9:30 that night, the flood gates were opened, and refugees began boarding. LaRue told his first mate, *"Let me know when the count reaches ten thousand."*[366] Through a long night, all five holds and all the other spaces on the ship were filled. By 11:00 a.m. the loading was complete, and the count had reached fourteen thousand. The ship's crewmen were aware they were witnessing a miracle in progress.

Exodus

The refugees were loaded like cargo. They were placed in every cargo hold and between decks. We had no food or water for them. No doctors. No interpreters. The temperature was well below freezing, but the holds were not heated or lighted. There were no sanitary facilities for them. They brought all their earthly possessions with them—children carried children, mothers breast-fed their babies with another child strapped to their backs, old men carried children together with whatever food they had saved. I saw terror in their faces.[367]

In your unfailing love you will lead the people you have redeemed. In your strength you will guide them to your holy dwelling. ~Exodus 15:13

THESE WERE the words of one officer describing the human cargo received on board the *USS Meredith Victory* during the night of December 22, 1950. In all, fourteen-thousand North Koreans were loaded onto the little ship. The captain said, *"It was impossible, and yet they were there. There couldn't be that much room—yet there was."*[368] With the sounds of battle moving closer and closer, the little ship carefully maneuvered out of the port of Hungnam the next day under a cold, wintry sky, ever conscious of the threat of enemy shelling and underwater mines.

Crowded deck on the *Meredith Victory* (Moore-McCormack Lines)

The *Meredith Victory* was one of the last ships to leave Hungnam and played a key role in one of the most amazing events of the war. In all, more than one hundred thousand refugees were saved from the beaches of Hungnam by navy and merchant marine seamen. These desperate people had left their homes all over North Korea in the face of the advancing Communists. They risked untold hardships traveling in winter conditions with whatever they could carry to an unknown destination. Once aboard ship, the uncertainty and deprivation did not abate. After days of uncomplaining suffering, they joyously debarked at Koje-Do to a safe, but uncertain, future.

It so happened the captain of the *Meredith Victory* was a religious man. Of their successful rescue mission and survival Leonard LaRue said, *"I believe God sailed with us those three days. I believe this because by all the laws of logic, the loss of life could have been enormous. Yet not a soul perished. Time after time, dangers that threatened to explode into disaster were miraculously averted."*[369]

God's Hand

Leonard LaRue
(Moore-
McCormack
Lines)

F OR HER heroic rescue operation during the evacuation of Hungnam, the South Korean government honored the *USS Meredith Victory* with a Korean Presidential Unit Citation, stating in part: *"This humanitarian mission . . . is remembered by the people of Korea as an inspiring example of Christian faith in action."*[370] The US Congress passed a special act, signed by President Eisenhower, designating the ship and crew a "Gallant Ship." A news release called this *"the greatest rescue operation by a single ship in the history of mankind."*[371] A large audience of congressmen, admirals, and other dignitaries gathered for the award ceremony August 24, 1960.

Among the ship's personnel gathered for the Gallant Ship award ceremony was a quiet and unassuming Benedictine monk named Brother Marinus. The monk was none other than the former Leonard LaRue, captain of the *USS Meredith Victory*. He had left the merchant marine after the war, dedicating himself to the religious life that had always been so important to him. In prepared remarks he told the audience why he made this choice. Quoting the simple and moving words of Father Raphael Simon, he said,

> To fall in love with God is the greatest of all romances.
> To seek him, the greatest adventure.
> To find Him, the greatest achievement.[372]

Of the rescue mission itself, he said:

> *I think often of that voyage. I think of how such a small vessel was able to hold so many persons and surmount endless perils without harm to a soul. And as I think, the clear, unmistakable message comes to me that on that Christmastide, in the bleak and bitter waters off the shores of Korea, God's own hand was at the helm of my ship.*[373]

> Humble yourselves, therefore, under God's mighty hand, that he may lift you up in due time. Cast all your anxiety on him because he cares for you. ~1 Peter 5:6–7

Thank God

BOB TATE was seventeen-years-old when he went to Korea. He came under sniper fire his first night and said later, *"I remember wondering to myself what the heck I was doing there and thinking I should be home in school instead of where I was."*[374]
The plunging temperatures added to his misery. One night he climbed into his sleeping bag with wet socks and found ice between his toes the next morning.

> Praise be to the LORD, to God our Savior, who daily bears our burdens. Selah Our God is a God who saves; from the Sovereign LORD comes escape from death.
> ~Psalms 68:19–20

Tate was with the Seventh Infantry Division advancing north from Wonsan toward the Yalu River when the massive Chinese attack came in November 1950. Somehow he became separated from his unit as it began pulling back to the south in a race against time. He was able to hitch a ride on a passing Air Force vehicle and made it out. He later said, *"We barely made it before they cut it off and closed the trap. I thank God for not being caught in that part of Hell."*[375] The young soldier was thankful to reach the safety of the harbor at Hungnam, even as thousands of other less fortunate soldiers and Marines were still fighting for their lives.

There are times when each of us can look back at moments in our lives and wonder how things might have turned out differently. One night my wife and I took a wrong exit on an interstate highway, delaying us on our trip by several minutes. Shortly after, we came on a terrible traffic accident in which several people were killed. We realized that we could easily have been part of that scene except for our unusual delay. Like the young soldier in this story, we thanked God for his protection, which in our case came from a wrong turn. We each have these fateful moments that cause us to wonder, *What might have happened? How might our lives have changed?* When we have these thoughts, it is comforting to remember that no matter what turns we take in our journey, God is in control and will be with us no matter what happens. He will get us to our final destination on time.

Perfect Peace

Stepping Out the Door

THE CHAPLAIN had never made a parachute jump, much less one into combat. Robert Rayburn joined the 187th Regimental Combat Team in March 1951 and learned he was to be part of a major airborne operation into enemy territory. Two days later he was seated uncomfortably in a C-119 Flying Boxcar with forty-three other men laden with parachutes, weapons, and equipment. As the airplane took off, he could see the tension in the faces of the soldiers around him, and he could feel himself beginning to shake with panic. How could he step out that open door into the void beyond? His few hours of instruction seemed totaliy inadequate. At that moment he bowed his head onto the reserve parachute on his chest and began praying earnestly, asking God to calm his fears:

Suddenly, as I prayed, the Lord spoke to me in words unmistakable and clear. This time it was just one comforting statement from the most familiar of Psalms: "I will fear no evil, for thou art with me!" What a promise! Could anything be better?[376]

In that moment, Rayburn knew that Jesus was beside him and would be with him as he jumped from the aircraft. Filled with peace, he fell into a sound sleep for the duration of the flight. Someone jarred him awake in time to stand up, hook up his static line, and exit the aircraft—for his first parachute jump. God had not only given Chaplain Rayburn the courage to do his job; he had given him the perfect testimony for a chaplain serving with paratroopers. His reputation spread quickly, as the new officer who slept peacefully through the most nerve-racking phase of the operation—the long, tense flight to the drop zone. He had countless opportunities to witness to other men about the source of this kind of inner strength. He told them about a Savior who is so real, whose promises are so sure, that he can give perfect peace in even the worst circumstances.

> Do not be anxious about anything, but in everything, by prayer and petition, with thanksgiving, present your requests to God. And the peace of God, which transcends all understanding, will guard your hearts and your minds in Christ Jesus. ~Philippians 4:6–7

The Leap

L T. DAVID HUGHES was leading K Company, Seventh Cavalry Regiment, in the attack on Hill 347. The Chinese defenders were in a four-foot-deep trench line near the crest of the hill and almost impervious to direct fire from below. From their covered position the enemy soldiers were able to rain hand grenades down on the advancing Americans. Three times the company attacked the hill, only to be repulsed with heavy losses.

> My message and my preaching were not with wise and persuasive words, but with a demonstration of the Spirit's power, so that your faith might not rest on men's wisdom, but on God's power.
> ~1 Corinthians 2:4–5

Hughes gathered what was left of his company and reorganized for a final attempt. He had about thirty men left, counting six riflemen and all his headquarters personnel and mortar crewmen. He decided that something different had to be done. He instructed his men to run through the grenade fire, leap the trench line, and continue up the hill. They would then turn and take the trenches from above. His plan was risky, but it worked. Once above the trenches the soldiers were able to systematically rout the enemy from the hill.[377]

As I read this story and envisioned a group of soldiers jumping over a trench line under fire, I thought about the spiritual equivalent to such an action. To become Christians, many have taken a "leap of faith." Skeptics (such as I was) perceive many obstacles to religious belief. They seek answers to an array of theological questions on an intellectual level. For me, taking a leap of faith meant temporarily putting those questions aside while accepting one very simple truth: *Jesus is who he said he was—the Son of God.*

When I accepted this truth and took this small step, Jesus came into my heart and changed my life completely. As his faithful follower, I have since been able to go back and deal with those theological questions that held up my spiritual advance for so long. A Christian friend has described this simple, yet profound, act as *"Letting go, and letting God."* It is as easy as it sounds.

Warnings

B Y EARLY 1951, the North Koreans could no longer venture into Wonsan Bay by boat to reset mines that had been removed by US forces. To continue trying to disrupt US operations, they instead attached mines to pieces of timber, bales of straw, and other types of flotsam. They set these adrift, hoping the tides and currents would take them into contact with vessels operating in the harbor.

> And we urge you, brothers, warn those who are idle, encourage the timid, help the weak, be patient with everyone.
> ~1 Thessalonians 5:14

Ens. Burl Gilliland, an officer on the *USS Heron*, described an incident that occurred one evening when his ship and two other minesweepers were anchored beside a small island in Wonsan Bay. As the crew was eating dinner, word came down that one of the other ships, the *USS Firecrest*, had spotted a floating bale of straw and was getting underway to check it out. The men on the *Heron* had already received numerous false alarms about this kind of threat and were not unduly concerned.

As the *Heron*'s crew watched from the deck, the suspicious object drifted by within a few feet. Gilliland could clearly see the pieces of straw. As it drifted away, the *Firecrest* was able to sight in her machine gun and, to the amusement of the *Heron*'s crew, opened fire on the apparently innocent bale of straw. The laughter stopped, however, when, with a WHOOM!, the bale erupted in a tremendous explosion, sending spray and black smoke upward for hundreds of feet. Gilliland said, *"We were embarrassed over our premature, ill-advised, risky, and immature behavior. We never again took for granted any item of flotsam that drifted in the currents of Wonsan Bay!"*[378]

Minesweeper hits a mine (US Navy)

As Christians, we also need warning when our spiritual well-being is in danger—and there are times when we need to warn others. God works to caution us and protect us in many ways, but his most direct and reliable means is the patient and loving counsel of brothers and sisters in Christ.

Sleeping

GLEN SCHROEDER stepped onto the dock at Pusan on March 26, 1951, after two weeks at sea en route to Korea. As a Navy corpsman, he was assigned immediately to an engineer company in First Marine Division, taken by bus to an airfield, and flown to an airstrip near Taegu. He was then trucked north to a camp where he was issued gear and treated to a hot meal. The food tasted good because he had been seasick for most of the voyage over and had not eaten for days.

When Schroeder was given two thirty-round magazines of ammunition and several hand grenades, he knew things were getting serious. Along with the cold weather gear, he was also given a short lecture he wouldn't forget. These were the survival tips he hadn't learned in corpsman school:

> Lesson One: The sleeping bag had a "panic" zipper. If pulled clear up, the bag would fall open.
> Lesson Two: Sleep in your clothes and field boots.
> Lesson Three: Sleep with your weapon loaded on safe.
> Lesson Four: Sleep with your K-bar (combat knife) or bayonet.[379]

Live ammunition was one thing, but this little talk really got the young corpsman's attention. He was in a combat zone and near enough to the front lines to be attacked at any time. Being prepared to fight would be a constant necessity, even when trying to sleep.

Jesus also warned his disciples about the dangers of sleeping during perilous times. Using sleep as a metaphor for spiritual apathy, he urged them to stay awake and alert. He wanted his followers then and now to be prepared for a time when they would see him again—a time known only to his Father in heaven:

Therefore keep watch, because you do not know on what day your Lord will come. But understand this: If the owner of the house had known at what time of night the thief was coming, he would have kept watch and would not have let his house be broken into. So you also must be ready, because the Son of Man will come at an hour when you do not expect him. ~Matthew 24:42–44

Sharpening the Senses

WE SPENT *a lot of time 'in front of the front,'*[380] Glen Schroeder explained. His combat engineer unit had to clear minefields and other obstacles to enable the tanks and infantry to advance. In this exposed position, he often came under fire. As the Marines advanced to the north, the valleys got narrower, the hills steeper, and the brush hiding the enemy denser. A few days after joining his unit, Schroeder saw what happened when they missed a mine. A nonmetallic device failed to alert the mine detectors, and no one saw the telltale indentation in the road. A tank struck the mine, blowing off its track.

> As iron sharpens iron, so one man sharpens another. ~Proverbs 27:17

Fortunately, the old-timers in the unit took an interest in their new corpsman and began to coach him along. They taught him to keep his weapon ready with plenty of ammunition on hand. He learned to keep his eyes moving to spot snipers in the brush and mine trip wires, and, especially, how to find cover quickly under fire. He was taught to keep a safe distance from the tanks since they were favorite targets of the North Korean gunners. Talking about his on-the-job training, Schroeder said,

> I was okay but scared to death! I certainly developed all of my sensory perceptions very quickly. My power of observation increased beyond my belief. I think I could see an ant move in the brush or a mine indentation or trip wire from twenty yards![381]

It is obvious that survival on the battlefield requires a sharpening of the senses. When Christians realize the dangers present on their own battlefields, they see the need to sharpen their spiritual senses as well. From my experience this is best accomplished in small groups. Maybe it's because I am a man, but I feel men especially need the camaraderie of other Christian men, beyond their business and sports acquaintances. We need to sharpen our spiritual senses through the prayer, study, and accountability that only a small, close-knit group of fellow Christians can provide.

On Edge

AS A NAVY corpsman with First Marine Division, Glen Schroeder could have been assigned to either an aid station or a line unit. Aid stations provided a considerably more comfortable existence, positioned behind the lines with more reliable access to supplies and food. During his entire tour of duty, however, he served with a line unit, very much in the action. He always felt he was in extreme personal danger and that just surviving the war was a deadly serious business. He treated dozens of wounded Marines and was himself wounded by shrapnel. Considering all he had to deal with during the war, it is surprising what bothered him most:

> For our struggle is not against flesh and blood, but against the rulers, against the authorities, against the powers of this dark world and against the spiritual forces of evil in the heavenly realms.
> ~Ephesians 6:12

I think the most disconcerting thing in Korea was the Chinese psychological warfare. We'd climb hills with the infantry, kick the Chinese off the ridge line, and dig in. Our job was to string concertina wire, plant anti-personnel mines, and tie some C-ration cans with rocks in them to the wire. All the time we'd be doing this, (the Chinese) would crank up a PA system and start screaming over it, "You Marines will die if you don't go home. Truman is sleeping with your wives and girlfriends," etc., etc. Or, "We will attack you when the bugles blow." In a few minutes, some bugles would blow. We'd jump into foxholes and aim rifles and BARs down the hill. It always put one's teeth on edge.[382]

One might argue that a modern-day version of this kind of mental harassment is cable television news. It is there every minute of every day with dire economic and political forecasts and up-to-the-minute details on every serious crime and disaster in progress on the planet. The more we watch, the more our teeth are set on edge. Sometimes it seems television and other media are waging a form of psychological warfare against our spiritual well-being.

The difference between television and an enemy PA system is, of course, we can turn the television off. With less television we would have a better chance of finding the solitude we need to read our Bibles, meditate on God's Word, and pray. We need time alone with God to distance ourselves from the spiritual warfare the world is constantly waging against us as believers.

Chain of Command

LT. BILL DAVIS stated a universal truth about combat that applies to other areas of human endeavor as well: *"There is an inverse ratio between your distance from the enemy and your sense of uneasiness about Who of the enemy can do What, When, Where, and How."*[383]

In other words, the more danger you are in, the more information you need. Unfortunately, frequently in combat, the more danger you are in, the *less* information you have . The man on the front line often knows the *least* about the so-called "big picture." Usually, what is known is passed successively down the chain of command from higher headquarters, to the division, regiment, battalion, company, platoon, and squad levels. On rare occasions the individual soldier might finally hear something useful to him personally.

In Old Testament times the Israelites were in somewhat the same situation in their relationship to God. There was an established chain of command through the Levitical priesthood. Only the priests were permitted to enter the inner sanctum of the temple, which was shielded by a curtain. Wiser men were needed to interpret and catalogue all of God's rules and regulations, considered too complex for most to comprehend on their own.

With the coming of Jesus Christ, there was a drastic reordering of this chain of command to God. At the moment of Jesus' death, *"The curtain of the temple was torn in two from top to bottom"* (Matthew 27:51). Through his Son, God gave every human being direct access to his heavenly throne. There is now one and only one priest who intercedes for us with God—and *is* God. He is the totality of our chain of command.

> Because Jesus lives forever, he has a permanent priesthood. Therefore he is able to save completely those who come to God through him, because he always lives to intercede for them. Such a priest meets our need—one who is holy, blameless, pure, set apart from sinners, exalted above the heavens. ~Hebrews 7:24–26

Survival

LIVING OUTSIDE in thirty-below-zero weather is hard to imagine. Exposed flesh freezes in seconds, bare hands stick to metal, and canteen water becomes solid ice. Troops in Korea learned to freeze dry their wet socks by attaching them to the outside of their packs and then shaking out the frozen moisture. Unable to heat their C-rations, many carried them under their clothes to thaw them out enough to eat. One senior army officer said, *"The cold in Korea was an order of magnitude more brutal. I do believe the conditions endured by the troops were the worst through which any American troops have ever suffered."*[384]

> We have peace with God through our Lord Jesus Christ, through whom we have gained access by faith into this grace in which we now stand. And we rejoice in the hope of the glory of God.
> ~Romans 5:1–2.

Under these conditions, the first order of business for the individual soldier and Marine was survival. Socks had to be changed, even though taking off boots to change them was one of the most difficult chores imaginable. Whenever possible troops would take turns going to a warming tent or spend a few minutes in their sleeping bags. They checked each other for signs of frostbite. Throughout the winter campaigns, the men had to fight to survive the cold before they could fight the enemy.

Enduring the Cold (National Archives)

Sometimes we have to look to our own survival needs before we can deal with other issues that demand our attention. Airline passengers are instructed to secure their own oxygen masks before attempting to assist someone else. You can't be of much help to anyone if *you* become unconscious first. In the same way, our first order of business spiritually is to nourish the all-important relationship we desperately need with God. If this relationship isn't as it should be, we're not going to be of much help to ourselves, our families, or our friends. Jesus told us clearly, *"Seek first his kingdom and his righteousness, and all these things will be given to you as well"* (Matthew 6:33).

The Cross

IN APRIL 1951, Capt. Bob Ward was shot down over enemy lines in Korea. As he ejected from his P-80 jet fighter, both his legs were broken when they struck the canopy. He was captured near the front lines and held in an enemy trench, suffering severe pain and diarrhea for days without medical attention. Thinking he wouldn't last much longer, he fashioned two sticks together with some string, making the form of a cross. He then did some serious praying. One of his captors noticed the cross and quietly asked, "Christian?" Ward nodded his head.[385]

Amazingly, this same soldier was assigned to take Ward by truck to a rear-area prison camp. During the nighttime trip, the North Korean stopped the truck and pulled off the road. He picked up the injured airman and carried him to the top of a nearby hill. He then went back and stripped the battery and a headlight off the truck. He had picked a location in the path of American bombers making night raids, and, as aircraft passed overhead, he flashed his makeshift light toward them. This went on for two long nights.

> For Christ did not send me to baptize, but to preach the gospel—not with words of human wisdom, lest the cross of Christ be emptied of its power. For the message of the cross is foolishness to those who are perishing, but to us who are being saved it is the power of God.
> ~1 Corinthians 1:17–18

Meanwhile, back at a US base, a young intelligence officer was diligently debriefing bomber crews about their missions when he heard several mention an unusual light flashing at a point along their flight path. Based on this sketchy information, a helicopter and fighter escort went out early the next morning to investigate. They soon spotted a Korean waving frantically from a hilltop with another man beside him on the ground. Within minutes, Ward was snatched from the hill with his new friend and savior. Both were flown to safety and a new life.

Bob Ward and Pancho Pasqualicchio, his fellow pilot who told me this story, have ever since considered this miracle of survival and redemption an amazing demonstration of the power of the cross.

The Children

DURING THE Korean War, Richard Mellinger served with the Seabees (derived from the initials "C. B." as in "Naval Construction Battalion"). His unit built airfields, roads, and bridges all over Korea, as well as a host of other construction projects of all types. He came under mortar, artillery, and sniper fire on numerous occasions but was not wounded. The most difficult part of the war for him was witnessing the endless flood of refugees moving through the countryside. He and his friends tried to give them all the aid they could, but had to be wary because North Korean soldiers sometimes camouflaged themselves as civilians.

> But if anyone causes one of these little ones who believe in me to sin, it would be better for him to have a large millstone hung around his neck and to be drowned in the depths of the sea.
> ~Matthew 18:6

Most heartbreaking of all were the children. Everywhere Mellinger looked he saw lost, abandoned, and orphaned kids. They were scared, bewildered, and sometimes wounded. He explained,

There were big families, and they couldn't take care of the kids. A lot of times you would see 20 or 30 abandoned children, all looking for something to eat and crying. That was really hard to imagine. Some kids, they were losing their entire families.[386]

Mellinger and his fellow Seabees gave the children all the food they could and even built orphanages for them. Still, many years later he continued to be haunted by the images. He said, *"I never want to see another war. There's got to be a better way."*[387]

How often children are lost in the wars of adults! They are always innocent victims of conflict not of their making. The physical deprivations of

(National Archives)

war are horrendous, but the mental trauma of family tension and breakup are just as devastating and long-lasting. Parents too often put the welfare of their children last as they hash out their adult problems. Truly, there's got to be a better way.

You'll Be Fine

THEY WERE angels. When a wounded man just off the front lines first saw a nurse looking over him, it was a heavenly apparition. The blood, dirt, and chaos of combat were gone. The smell of cordite was replaced by an antiseptic aroma. The warm touch and friendly smile of a woman in white brought humanity back into his life. It was a moment no soldier would forget.

Unfortunately, many of these wounded men never had a chance to express their heartfelt gratitude. In many cases they never even knew their nurse's name. Fifty-years later, many of these soldiers and Marines told their stories, hoping their words of thanks would be meaningful to every nurse who had served. A Marine lieutenant recalled,

> Praise be to the God and Father of our Lord Jesus Christ, the Father of compassion and the God of all comfort, who comforts us in all our troubles, so that we can comfort those in any trouble with the comfort we ourselves have received from God. For just as the sufferings of Christ flow over into our lives, so also through Christ our comfort overflows.
> ~2 Corinthians 1:3–5

I was naked on my back on the bed. It was a genuine bed, with sheets, but I couldn't enjoy the luxury of it because the pain chewed at me. When I tried to lift my head, it pounded fiercely. I had just a glimpse of my feet. They were elevated and covered with white netting. I didn't know what was wrong with them, but they wiggled when I tried to move them.

"Hi, Marine." I looked up into the beautiful brown eyes of a Navy nurse wearing a starched white uniform.

"Frostbite?" I asked. My raspy voice sounded like someone else. She nodded. This was the first I knew I had frostbite. Frostbite could mean amputation. That scared the hell out of me.

The Navy nurse bent down beside me and held my hand. Her voice was soft, yet firm, "You'll be fine. It will all work out."

I was safe. I fell asleep.[388]

Every person needs a comforting touch. Our greatest blessing as human beings is to know a God who comforts us in our pain, enabling us in turn to comfort others. Each of us can be an angel of mercy to someone.

Machine gunners support an attack (US Army)

Soldiers watch bombardment (National Archives)

Virtue Rewarded

COL. BILL MCCAFFREY was the youngest American regimental commander of the Korean War. He took command of the Thirty-First Infantry, Seventh Division, in March 1951, leading it heroically during the UN counteroffensive and operations in the Hwachon area. He earned two Silver Stars in addition to one awarded during World War II. He ultimately retired a three-star general, after service in three wars.

> I have labored to no purpose; I have spent my strength in vain and for nothing. Yet what is due me is in the LORD's hand, and my reward is with my God. ~Isaiah 49:4

One of his many assignments after Korea brought him to Charleston, South Carolina, where he became Commandant of Cadets at The Citadel. Part of his job was to guide me, an immature twenty-year-old, in the performance of my duties as regimental commander. His practical, mature outlook as an experienced combat commander often bumped up against my obstinate stand in favor of what I thought was Citadel "tradition." At that time, my horizon on these traditions was my three years' experience as a cadet. Colonel McCaffrey guided me through this relationship and my many trials with a patient and fatherly hand. He usually stood firm in his decisions, but he also listened and made many accommodations. He always worked at broadening my perspectives on leadership.

On the morning of my Graduation Day I was with him in his office, when he gave me a final bit of advice, telling me there was one lesson I had not learned. He said, "Larkin, you need to know that virtue is not always rewarded in this life." I didn't think much about these words at the time, but when I later had occasion to feel I was unjustly judged by others, I recalled his words and found comfort in them. Since becoming a Christian, I have become aware of God's perspective on my efforts, and I am able now to find even greater comfort in the knowledge that he knows my heart, no matter what others think. I know now that the only virtue that counts is my faith in his Son and the grace that flows from a relationship with him.

A Dirty Child

AS AN INFANTRY company commander, it was Logan Weston's practice to make an inspection of his lines every evening. Starting on his left flank, he walked by each position to check on the condition of his men, their weapons, and fields of fire. On his last night with the unit, he saw an unusual sight as he completed his inspection—in the valley below his lines he saw a small, red speck beside an abandoned pagoda.

> Let us draw near to God with a sincere heart in full assurance of faith, having our hearts sprinkled to cleanse us from a guilty conscience and having our bodies washed with pure water.
> ~Hebrews 10:22

Making his way down the steep slope, he approached the pagoda and found a small Korean girl wearing a dirty red coat, huddled in the brush and cowering in fear. He bent down to her cautiously and offered her a candy bar, which she took and ate greedily. He decided to take her to the battalion aid station where someone could look after her until she could be evacuated to a safer place. Talking quietly to gain her trust, he was able finally to pick her up. As he held her in his arms, he couldn't help noticing her dirty, matted hair and tear-streaked face, the lice in her clothing, and the terrible smell coming from sores on her body. In spite of the assault on his senses, he climbed the hill carrying the little girl and completed his self-assigned mission.

Weston thought about this incident later and came to the startling realization he had a lot in common with this dirty Korean girl:

An Abandoned Child
(National Archives)

> *Looking back on that experience, I realized that the Lord at one time felt the same way about me. I had wallowed in the dirt. I was contaminated and filthy, and altogether unlovely. I was without hope and very discouraged. But He came down to earth, picked me up, and gave me a purpose for living. He took me into the fold of the family of God, where things were brighter, purer, more beautiful. From that day to the present I have attempted to serve Him by serving others.*[389]

Founding Authority

Pres. Truman with
Cardinal Cushing
(Truman Library)

IN 1951 a group of Christian church leaders assembled in Washington, DC, to research the documents created during the nation's founding. President Harry Truman addressed the group and affirmed his views on the religious influences that shaped America:

You will see, as you make your rounds, that this Nation was established by men who believed in God. You will see that our Founding Fathers believed that God created this Nation. And I believe it, too. They believed that God was our strength in time of peril and the source of all our blessings.

You will see the evidence of this deep religious faith on every hand.

If we go back to the Declaration of Independence, we notice that it was drawn up by men who believed that God the Creator had made all men equal and had given them certain rights which no man could take away from them. In the beginning (of) their great enterprise, the signers of the Declaration of Independence entrusted themselves to the protection of divine providence.

To our forefathers it seemed something of a miracle that this Nation was able to go through the agonies of the American Revolution and emerge triumphant. They saw, in our successful struggle for independence, the working of God's hand. In his first inaugural address, George Washington said, "No people can be bound to acknowledge and adore the invisible hand, which conducts the affairs of men, more than the people of the United States."

> For there is no authority except that which God has established.
> ~Romans 13:1

Another fact which you will notice in the course of your pilgrimage is that the makers of our Constitution believed in religious toleration. Theirs was the highest type of religion, forbidding the use of coercion in matters of mind and spirit. Religious freedom was a part of their religious faith.[390]

Our Founding Fathers did not just *believe* in God. When they daringly cut the ties to British royal authority that had been in place for centuries, they very deliberately turned to God as the one true Source of authority in the universe. It was God who granted dignity and unalienable rights to human beings, and God who guaranteed them. The government founded under this principle places the individual citizen at the top of the political hierarchy, because it is the individual citizen who has a relationship with God, *not* with a king, a president, or any governing body.

Talking to Him

R ON ROSSER grew up in Columbus, Ohio, during the Depression, one of seventeen children. As the oldest boy he always considered it his duty to stick up for his siblings: *"We were a close knit family. When somebody bothered my family, I punched their lights out, so to speak. That's the way I grew up."*[391] From necessity, he went to work at an early age and left school in the tenth grade. He enlisted in the army in 1946, served in an airborne unit during peacetime, and returned to civilian life when his enlistment was up.

Rosser's younger brother, Richard, joined the army at age eighteen and was killed in Korea at the battle of Chipyong-ni

> For where two or three come together in my name, there am I with them. ~Matthew 18:20

in 1951. Figuring it was his duty to finish his brother's combat tour, Ron re-enlisted and went to Korea with the Thirty-Eighth Infantry Regiment. Serving as a forward observer for a 4.2-inch mortar company, he was constantly on the front lines with infantry units. As a corporal, he led the final assault on Hill 472 when all the officers in his company were either killed or wounded. For his actions, he was awarded the Medal of Honor by President Truman on June 27, 1952, as his entire family looked on.

Rosser remained on active duty and, as a Medal of Honor winner, became something of a celebrity inside and outside the army. During one of his many interviews, he was asked about his religious views and commented, *"If they've got any sense, I think everybody is religious. I spent a lot of time on the battlefield in as bad a stuff as a man could stand. I never saw God on the battlefield. Not once. But I heard a lot of people talking to him. Every once in a while I thought I heard my voice talking to him too."*[392]

In his own way, I believe Rosser articulated a significant truth. There aren't many of us who have "seen" God on the battlefield, or anywhere else. We know our heavenly Father through Scripture, prayers, and, perhaps most importantly, other Christians. When we worship together, we hear him in the voices and see him in the faces of our friends.

Personal Valor

RICHARD DE WERT was eighteen years old when he enlisted in the navy. After boot camp he volunteered for medical training and eventually went to Korea as a corpsman with First Marine Division. After participating in the Inchon landing and Chosin Reservoir campaign, he was with Seventh Marines near the 38th Parallel in April 1951. While advancing toward the enemy his company came under heavy automatic weapons fire, and he soon heard the inevitable cry from the front line: "Corpsman!" Like so many other young men in this difficult role, De Wert did not hesitate. His actions in the next few minutes are described in his Medal of Honor citation:

> Have I not commanded you? Be strong and courageous. Do not be terrified; do not be discouraged, for the LORD your God will be with you wherever you go.
> ~Joshua 1:9

Hospitalman De Wert rushed to the assistance of one of the more seriously wounded and, despite a painful leg wound sustained while dragging the stricken Marine to safety, steadfastly refused medical treatment for himself and immediately dashed back through the fire-swept area to carry a second wounded man out of the line of fire. Undaunted by the mounting hail of devastating enemy fire, he bravely moved forward a third time and received another serious wound in the shoulder after discovering that a wounded Marine had already died. Still persistent in his refusal to submit to first aid, he resolutely answered the call of a fourth stricken comrade and, while rendering medical assistance, was himself mortally wounded by a burst of enemy fire. By his courageous initiative, great personal valor, and heroic spirit of self-sacrifice in the face of overwhelming odds, Hospitalman De Wert reflected great credit upon himself and upheld the highest traditions of the United States Naval Service.[393]

On May 27, 1952, the Secretary of the Navy presented the Medal of Honor on behalf of De Wert to his mother, Evelyn. In 1982 the guided missile frigate *USS De Wert* (FFG 45) was named in honor of the heroic young corpsman.

USS De Wert (US Navy)

Piece of Cake

WHEN WORD came to saddle up, Sgt. Seymour Harris asked his platoon leader, *"What's the deal, lieutenant? How's it look?"* *"Nothing to it,"* the officer said. *"Seems they got a bulge in the line. We'll straighten it out. Piece of cake."* Soon, the soldiers were struggling up the steep slopes of a looming hill mass that would eventually earn the title Heartbreak Ridge. Harris explained:

> *Heartbreak Ridge was worse than any place I'd ever seen, as it seemed there was nowhere you could get where you weren't subject to enemy fire of some sort. No matter where you were you could be shot. Be it a sniper, or self-propelled artillery. And mortars. They came in like hail stones at times, especially during the day. They saved the rockets for night.*[394]

On September 13, 1951, the Twenty-Third Infantry Regiment led the attack on the heavily-fortified hill. A two-week battle followed that took on a familiar pattern. The infantrymen would struggle up the rocky slopes, destroying enemy bunkers by direct assault. When a much-depleted force reached the top of the hill, exhausted and low on ammunition, the North Koreans would counterattack with fresh troops to retake the hill. Thirty-seven hundred men were lost in this grim effort. As Harris and his men fought on, their rallying cry became, *"Piece of cake!"*

> Take my yoke upon you and learn from me, for I am gentle and humble in heart, and you will find rest for your souls. For my yoke is easy and my burden is light.
> ~Matthew 11:29–30

These soldiers continued with their mission in spite of serious miscalculations by higher headquarters. Without the benefit of the big picture, Harris and his men made the best of a bad situation, persevering in their assigned task.

This is, of course, all any of us can do as we struggle to live godly lives in a materialistic world. Even though we never fully understand God's perspective on what we're doing, we never have to worry about miscalculations on his part. We can always be confident he is in control. The ultimate victory belongs to him. It is up to us to persevere in the task we are assigned and to make our own contribution, big or small, to that victory. We can always be confident every hill we climb for him will truly be a "piece of cake."

Letter from a Foxhole

DURING THE first ten days of June 1951, the First Marine Division experienced its highest casualties of the war attacking the Hwachon Reservoir in the Punchbowl area. The mountains were steep and rugged, and the enemy troops were well entrenched in heavily-fortified positions with mortar and artillery support. There was little room to maneuver, as each hill had to be taken in turn by frontal assault. Chaplain Henry Austin was with the First Marine Regiment during this campaign and wrote a moving letter home after one of the most bitter battles:

> Praise the LORD, all you servants of the LORD who minister by night in the house of the LORD. Lift up your hands in the sanctuary and praise the LORD. May the LORD, the Maker of heaven and earth, bless you from Zion. ~Psalm 134

> *The Chinese and North Koreans were really dug in and poured murderous concussion grenades, machine gun and burp-gun fire, plus mortars down our throats, literally, so in the Marine tradition our battalion took the objective on "blood and guts" alone. In the face of what looked like annihilation, our men stormed up "676" and secured the same at 2115 Sunday, 10 June.*

> *At the moment, I have my foxhole dug right on top of "676" which we paid for with many men wounded and several men killed. Last night was our roughest night since I joined the 2ⁿᵈ Battalion, so I stayed up all night and helped the doctors. It was 4 am before we could evacuate the last wounded, because we had to carry them over 2 ½ miles along a mountain ridge under enemy fire in the drizzly dark. I helped as stretcher bearer, prayed with the seriously wounded and dying, gave out cigarettes and water, and tried to give some comfort to the men.*

> *I never prayed more sincerely in my life and God blessed us, because most of the wounds of our men were clean and I think the majority of the wounded will live. The view from my foxhole is beautiful, and one thing is sure—I'll never forget this mountain. We expect to hold a special Thanksgiving service tomorrow. You'll be interested to note "The Secret Place" (a daily devotional) reading for 10 June was titled "A Mountain to Climb"—coincidence, isn't it?*

> *Keep praying—God is blessing us. Over 200 men have accepted Christ out here, and to date I have baptized 97 of our fighting Marines.*[395]

Every Christian strives to put his faith into action. There could be no better example than that of a young minister, working for God's kingdom in the midst of the toil and tears of combat on a remote hilltop in a difficult and unpopular war.

Sharing

IN JULY 1952, the Seventh Regiment of the Third Infantry Division was moving north at night through the Chorwon Valley. The sound of distant artillery fire echoed off the surrounding hills. Cpl. Paul Tardiff and his fellow soldiers were near exhaustion when the orders came to set up camp for the night. Unexpectedly, hot food soon arrived by truck in thermal cans and was served to the weary soldiers on their aluminum mess kits. Afterward, large amounts of leftovers were disposed of near the camp. Later that evening, Tardiff was awakened when he heard a group of Korean women and children digging excitedly through the remains of the soldiers' meal. After seeing this, the young soldier was unable to sleep the rest of the night.

> Through Jesus, therefore, let us continually offer to God a sacrifice of praise—the fruit of lips that confess his name. And do not forget to do good and to share with others, for with such sacrifices God is pleased.
> ~Hebrews 13:15–16

When Tardiff found out his unit would remain in place the next day, he sought out his unit's Korean interpreter. He asked him to find the women who had come the previous night and have them come back at 4 o'clock that afternoon. At that time, the trucks arrived on schedule with food for the soldiers. As they began to line up with their mess kits they could see the women, children, and babies watching from a distance. Tardiff told what happened:

> I walked to one of the mothers who had a baby on her back and placed my mess kit in her hands. (The interpreter) told her it was a gift, and that she should take it. She did, and she began to eat. One by one, other soldiers followed me, until each one of the women and children had food to eat. They spoke to us in Korean, each expressing thanks. We were gone the next day, but the memories of those displaced war refugees haunt me to this day.[396]

We often wonder what we can do to please God. This story illustrates the simple answer he has already given us: "*And what does the LORD require of you? To act justly and to love mercy and to walk humbly with your God*" (Micah 6:8).

Duty, Honor, Country

Gen. Douglas MacArthur (US Navy)

AFTER ALMOST fifty years of military service, Gen. Douglas MacArthur was relieved of command by President Truman in April 1951 to return to civilian life. In 1964 he gave a farewell address to the cadets at the US Military Academy with an eloquent tribute to the ideals that inspired his own illustrious career:

Duty, honor, country: Those three hallowed words reverently dictate what you ought to be, what you can be, what you will be. They are your rallying point to build courage when courage seems to fail, to regain faith when there seems to be little cause for faith, to create hope when hope becomes forlorn.

They build your basic character. They mold you for your future roles as custodians of the Nation's defense. They make you strong enough to know when you are weak, and brave enough to face yourself when you are afraid.

They teach you to be proud and unbending in honest failure, but humble and gentle in success; not to substitute words for action, not to seek the path of comfort, but to face the stress and spur of difficulty and challenge; to learn to stand up in the storm, but to have compassion on those who fail; to master yourself before you seek to master others; to have a heart that is clean, a goal that is high; to learn to laugh, yet never forget how to weep; to reach into the future, yet never neglect the past; to be serious, yet never to take yourself too seriously; to be modest so that you will remember the simplicity of true greatness, the open mind of true wisdom, the meekness of true strength.

The code which those words perpetuate embraces the highest moral law and will stand the test of any ethics or philosophies ever promulgated for the things that are right and its restraints from the things that are wrong. The soldier, above all other men, is required to practice the greatest act of religious training—sacrifice. In battle, and in the face of danger and death, he discloses those divine attributes which his Maker gave when He created man in His own image. No physical courage and no greater strength can take the place of the divine help which alone can sustain him. However hard the incidents of war may be, the soldier who is called upon to offer and to give his life for his country is the noblest development of mankind.[397]

> These are the words of the Son of God, whose eyes are like blazing fire and whose feet are like burnished bronze. I know your deeds, your love and faith, your service and perseverance.
> ~Revelation 2:18–19

The Soldiers

A S HE CONTINUED his farewell address to the cadets of West Point, Gen. Douglas MacArthur gave a moving portrait of the men these officers would lead into future battles.

(US Navy)

And what sort of soldiers are those you are to lead? Are they reliable? Are they brave? Are they capable of victory?

Their story is known to all of you. It is the story of the American man-at-arms. My estimate of him was formed on the battlefield many, many years ago and has never changed. I regarded him then, as I regard him now, as one of the world's noblest figures; not only as one of the finest military characters, but also as one of the most stainless.

His name and fame are the birthright of every American citizen. In his youth and strength, his love and loyalty, he gave all that mortality can give. He needs no eulogy from me; or from any other man. He has written his own history and written it in red on his enemy's breast.

But when I think of his patience in adversity, of his courage under fire and of his modesty in victory, I am filled with an emotion of admiration I cannot put into words. He belongs to history as furnishing one of the greatest examples of successful patriotism. He belongs to posterity as the instructor of future generations in the principles of liberty and freedom. He belongs to the present, to us, by his virtues and by his achievements.

In twenty campaigns, on a hundred battlefields, around a thousand camp fires, I have witnessed that enduring fortitude, that patriotic self-abnegation, and that invincible determination which have carved his statue in the hearts of his people.[398]

Not possessing the eloquence of General MacArthur, I can only echo his sentiments of respect and affection for the American fighting men I have been fortunate to serve with and to know. They carried on this long and honorable tradition and heroically bore the burden of an unpopular war without complaint. God bless the soldiers of every era who have stood ready to serve their nation and to give themselves in service to others.

> Therefore, I urge you, brothers, in view of God's mercy, to offer your bodies as living sacrifices, holy and pleasing to God—this is your spiritual act of worship.
> ~Romans 12:1

Jeepside Religious Service (US Army)

Marine praying (USMC)

AIR WAR

US AIR OPERATIONS started in Korea within days of the North Korean invasion. As transport aircraft were airlifting civilians from Kimpo Airfield on June 27, 1950, Lt. William Hudson, flying an F-82 twin Mustang, shot down a propeller-driven Yak fighter threatening the airlift. By the end of the day, seven North Korean aircraft were destroyed in the air over Kimpo in the first aerial encounters of the war.[399] A few days later B-26 medium bombers flying out of Japan struck North Korean airfields, destroying large numbers of aircraft on the ground. Within the first month the North Korean air force was largely eliminated as a threat to UN operations.

The first Allied aircraft to deploy to Korea was the famous fighter of World War II, the F-51 Mustang. Considered obsolete at the time due to the introduction of jet aircraft, the F-51 was recalled to duty because of its range and firepower. The first to arrive in Korea were hastily refitted tow planes from Japan that went into immediate service attacking North Korean convoys and troops advancing south of Seoul. An Australian squadron with twenty-six F-51s arrived on June 29, and a month later the USS Boxer delivered 145 F-51s and 70 pilots.[400]

Air Force aviation assets in Korea came from the Far East Air Force (FEAF) commanded by Lt. Gen. George Stratemeyer. The Fifth Air Force, based in Japan, had an authorized strength of more than one thousand aircraft, of which only about six hundred were operational at the beginning of the war, including five wings of fighters, bombers, and troop carrier/cargo aircraft. The relatively new F-80 jet fighters were on hand but were of limited use for some time due to their short range.[401]

On July 3 naval Task Force 77 reached position in the Yellow Sea off the west coast of Korea, where the USS Valley Forge launched F4U Corsairs and F9F Panther jets on strikes against targets around Pyongyang. The Corsairs were World War II-era propeller aircraft, especially well-suited for attacking ground targets. Task Force 77 was able to position itself anywhere off the Korean coast and proved a potent striking force throughout the war.

US air superiority was threatened for the first time in November 1950 when Soviet-built MiG-15 fighters entered the conflict. Based in airfields north of the Yalu River in Manchuria they were immediately successful in curtailing Allied bombing raids over North Korea. The only US aircraft that could match the MiG-15 was the new F-86 Sabre, which began to arrive in small numbers in December. Soon the first all-jet aerial combat actions began over North Korea in what became known as "MiG Alley." Fortunately, the US pilots were generally more skilled than the Chinese and North Koreans, enabling the Sabres to keep tenuous control of the air. Even when Soviet pilots entered the war, the United States achieved a ratio of ten MiGs to one Sabre shot down during the war.[402]

At the start of the Korean War, the Marine Corps introduced a new concept of close air support. In August 1950, the ground elements of the First Provisional Marine Brigade arrived at Pusan, while three Marine air attack squadrons were positioned on aircraft carriers at sea under direct command of the brigade commander. Forward air control parties with each infantry battalion were able to precisely coordinate air strikes in support of tactical maneuvers by units on the ground. This kind of cooperative effort continued throughout the war and contributed to the effectiveness of all Marine operations.

The first helicopters to see duty in Korea also arrived with the Marines. Sikorsky HO3S helicopters of Marine Observation Squadron 6 (VMO-6) began flight operations on August 3 carrying supplies and evacuating wounded from units engaged on the Pusan Perimeter. The same aircraft would be used throughout the war by the US Air Force and Navy in supply, rescue, and observation missions. Army Bell H-13 helicopters of *M*A*S*H* movie and television fame arrived in Korea in December 1950, and, with their external stretchers, evacuated more than five hundred casualties in their first month of operation. They became the US Army's workhorse throughout the war. Later, the Marines introduced the Sikorsky HRS, a troop transport helicopter capable of lifting eight combat-equipped Marines. These were used for the tactical movement of units in combat for the first time in so-called "vertical envelopment" operations.

Calm under Stress

PRIOR TO becoming a student pilot in the Air Force, Robert Pomeroy attended Peekskill Military Academy and the US Military Academy at West Point. He had always wanted a military career and seemed to thrive on the discipline. He also learned to tolerate a certain amount of harassment, a trait that would be especially beneficial in flight school.

> And the peace of God, which transcends all understanding, will guard your hearts and your minds in Christ Jesus. ~Philippians 4:7

Primary flight training during the Korean War era was conducted in the single engine, prop-driven AT-6 Texan. This aircraft had two seats and dual controls so an instructor could routinely fly with the student. At the time, the overall washout rate in flight training was 36 percent. Since early dropouts saved time and money, primary flight instructors were given wide latitude to pressure candidates and to drop those who didn't measure up. One student pilot said, *"The instructor was not your friend: they were trying to wash you out the entire time."*[403]

Pomeroy had an exceptionally overbearing instructor who would yell at him constantly during each flight. Even during the stress of flying "under the hood" on instruments, his instructor would constantly berate him for small errors, making a difficult task almost impossible. This one instructor washed out five students in the class, and Pomeroy always felt he would have been one of them had it not been for his West Point training: *"You have to have rocks in your head to enjoy the Academy, but it did give you an emotional reserve and teach you to let verbal abuse roll off your back!"*[404]

Having experienced the high-tempo training of The Citadel's "fourth-class system" I can attest to the benefits of learning to deal with mental pressure. This kind of training gives anyone a degree of physical and emotional calmness in stressful situations.

There is another and more important calmness, however, that can only come in the spiritual realm and from one Source. When Jesus Christ enters a person's heart, he freely gives the gift that is his alone to give—a calm soul.

Feel

SOME PILOTS flunked out of flight training for academic reasons, failing to get passing grades on written tests. Most, however, failed flying itself, which was a difficult skill to judge. Evaluations were of necessity subjective and at times arbitrary. Some criteria involved specific procedures, but most often students were judged on their ability to control the aircraft. This required a feel for flying that each man had to find for himself, as one pilot explained:

> As the plane climbed, he (the instructor) explained about coordinating rudder and aileron pressures in turns, about how too much rudder without aileron control made the airplane skid to the outside of the turn and too much aileron control without rudder made it slip to the inside. Demonstrating, he told me how to feel it in the seat of my pants when we slipped or skidded. Hanging on grimly, with increasing queasiness, I tried to feel what I should.[405]

Before Jesus came into the world, mankind was in somewhat the same predicament as the student pilot, trying to get a feel for God and ways to appease him. Even after he gave the Israelites the Ten Commandments and other specific rules to follow, Jewish priests and scholars devoted whole careers to elaborating on and interpreting God's law, trying to provide a rule for every conceivable eventuality. Try as they might, the Israelites were never able to live up to these expectations. The Old Testament is the story of man's futile effort to live in obedience to the law. The prophet Jeremiah foretold God's solution to this problem, looking forward to the day when mankind would finally understand how to please God without reference to a rulebook. By sending his Son into the world, he would give those who receive him an intuitive understanding, or "feel," for what is right and wrong that transcends the written law.

> This is the covenant I will make with them after that time, says the Lord. I will put my laws in their hearts, and I will write them on their minds . . . Their sins and lawless acts I will remember no more. And where these have been forgiven, there is no longer any sacrifice for sin.
> ~Hebrews 10:16–18

Sebille

Louis Sebille (US Air Force)

AS THE Pusan Perimeter continued to shrink in August 1950, air support became more and more critical. On August 5, Maj. Lou Sebille led a flight of F-51 Mustangs out of Ashiya, Japan, in response to a call from ground forces near Namchang. During his first run on a group of North Korean troops and tanks he dropped one five-hundred-pound bomb with devastating effect. On his second run he encountered a wall of anti-aircraft fire and pulled up, announcing over the radio that he was hit. His wingman told him to head south for the nearest friendly airfield, only five minutes away.

Instead, the other pilots watched in fascination as Sebille turned back into another dive. He launched all his rockets and fired his machine guns as he passed the danger level of two thousand feet. He kept diving and firing below one thousand feet, and then five hundred feet. With his remaining five-hundred-pound bomb still under the wing, he flew his aircraft into the ground, obliterating the target.[406]

His squadron mates could only speculate about the motives behind this action. Sebille knew the critical nature of his mission and that ground troops were depending on him for survival. Yet, they also knew that no armored convoy was worth the life of one of their own. Suicide missions have never been an acceptable practice within the American military. They concluded that the gallant aviator had been so badly wounded he knew he would not make it back to a safe landing.

> I eagerly expect and hope that I will in no way be ashamed, but will have sufficient courage so that now as always Christ will be exalted in my body, whether by life or by death. ~Philippians 1:20

Instead, he used the last moments of his life to do all he could for the forces on the ground. For his heroic actions, his wife, Jane, and their five-year-old son accepted the Medal of Honor for Sebille on August 24, 1951.

Tension

WALTER BRYAN was an F-51 pilot with the Fortieth Fighter Squadron when the Korean War started. For months he flew almost daily missions from his base in Japan. His flight would land first at Taegu to arm and refuel, and then continue over enemy territory to bomb or strafe assigned targets. Finally, he had to make the return trip to Japan over one hundred miles of open ocean. At this point, a rough-running engine was not unusual in the aged aircraft. Also, the weather was often bad, the ceilings low, and the necessary electronic systems for instrument landings not in existence. As he described it, all this made for "heart-stopping moments." After months of this kind of flying, the young pilot began to complain of very uncomfortable back problems. A knot formed between his shoulder blades that would not go away.

On February 16, 1951, Bryan flew his last combat mission north of Seoul. It was, fortunately, uneventful. When he landed at Pusan and climbed out of the cockpit, the first thing he noticed was that the knot between his shoulders was gone. For the first time in months he was able to relax. His war was over.[407]

It is well known that some illnesses stem from unrelieved anxiety. There is an obvious correlation between tension, high blood pressure, and many diseases. Unfortunately, we cannot just wish away many of the internal and external knots that plague us. As with a combat pilot, there are real problems in our lives that are forced on us or that we bring on ourselves. Fortunately, there is a way to relieve whatever tension is building in our lives. Our Savior gave very specific instructions for every person focused on his or her own tribulations:

> Seek first his kingdom and his righteousness, and all these things will be given to you as well. Therefore do not worry about tomorrow, for tomorrow will worry about itself. ~Matthew 6:33–34

Elation to Anger

LT. RICHARD GRUBER was flying a search-and-destroy mission over enemy territory, when he spotted people in an open field. Dropping down to take a closer look, he flew his F-51 Mustang at about twenty feet directly over a number of old men and children doing farm work. As he started to pull up, however, he saw the red flashes of machine gun fire coming at him from a group of soldiers on a hillside directly in his flight path. He pulled back harder on the stick but was totally exposed for more than ten seconds. He tried to shrink himself in the cockpit as he waited for something to break loose on his aircraft. When he reached a safe altitude unharmed, he was filled with elation that he had made it. Looking down, though, he saw the machine gun still firing at him. For some reason, at that moment he was seized with rage at these soldiers who had given him such a scare. Nosing back over he dove directly at the still-firing gun and obliterated it with the fire of his own six .50-caliber machine guns.[408]

> In your anger do not sin: Do not let the sun go down while you are still angry, and do not give the devil a foothold.
> ~Ephesians 4:26–27

Gruber eventually flew 331 combat missions in two wars. However, this incident in Korea always stood out in his mind, as he had so quickly gone through a range of emotions, from fear to elation, and then an all-consuming anger. He knew this was not a good state of mind for effective flying or decision making. He was fortunate his anger did not lead to a serious error of judgment.

Most of us know it is seldom wise to act in anger. When we feel our temperature rising, we try to step back and cool down before saying or doing something we will later regret. To my disappointment, however, even though I know better, there are still those moments when my anger comes out. Angry outbursts are inevitable when we are in the wrong state of mind and consumed with ourselves. This is not where God wants us to be. He wants us to stay close to him and pray to him before we speak or react to our irritating situations. He is always ready to dissolve our anger with his calming presence.

Air Rescue

CAPT. JOHN SHUMATE was an army pharmacist who transferred to the Air Force to join the newly-created Air Rescue Service early in the Korean War. On October 10, 1950, he was flying as a para-doctor on an H-5 helicopter called to rescue a downed British pilot deep in enemy territory north of Seoul. At the scene of the crash Shumate risked his life to save the seriously injured pilot, earning a Silver Star for his heroic action. The citation for his medal tells the story of his selfless deed:

> Each one should use whatever gift he has received to serve others, faithfully administering God's grace in its various forms . . . If anyone serves, he should do it with the strength God provides, so that in all things God may be praised through Jesus Christ. ~1 Peter 4:10–11

Capt. Shumate left the helicopter upon landing near the crashed aircraft, and rushed to the aid of the pilot. Enemy forces from a nearby farm house opened fire with small arms in an attempt to prevent any aid by Captain Shumate. At the risk of his life, (he) leaped to the wing of the aircraft and attempted to lift the pilot out of the cockpit. The pilot, paralyzed from the waist down and unable to help, was pinned to the wreckage by his flying suit. Still under enemy small arms fire, Captain Shumate lifted and held the pilot with one arm and with his free hand cut away the pilot's flight suit, freeing the pilot. Practically exhausted, Captain Shumate managed to carry and drag the pilot to safety from the small arms fire. Assisted by the helicopter pilot, the injured British fighter pilot was placed aboard the helicopter and flown to a hospital.[409]

H-5 helicopter (US Navy)

After performing this daring rescue on the ground, Shumate performed a first in aviation history once in the air. He administered blood plasma to the injured man during the helicopter flight.[410] For his heroism and skill he was also awarded the British Military Cross. His gallantry and devotion to duty were truly *"in keeping with the highest tradition of the military service."*

Bailing Out

A COMBAT PILOT in the Korean War could sometimes be detached from the reality of war. Enemy fire appeared as tracers passing by or as silent puffs of smoke, sometimes followed by a quick jolt. Ground targets were ant-like figures moving on the ground or toy trucks in convoys. An upturned face seen at low altitude was only a blur. There were often moments of stark fear, when the tracers or flak got too close or hit the aircraft, but usually within half an hour the pilot would be on the ground joking with his crew and counting the holes in his aircraft.

> Salvation is found in no one else, for there is no other name under heaven given to men by which we must be saved. ~Acts 4:12

There were countless ways, however, things might not go so well. If a shell causing one of those holes were to strike a fuel line, sending fuel over a red hot engine, the resulting catastrophe would be immediate. An engine fire in an F-51 aircraft would burn inches from the pilots' legs, as oil cascading over the windshield blocked all visibility.[411]

When a pilot had to leave his aircraft, his life in the cocoon of his cockpit ended suddenly:

> *In that instant the entire war for a pilot changed. Now he would see the world as those condemned to fight on the ground saw it. If he survived hitting the ground he'd suddenly be aware of all the elements outside of a cockpit.*[412]

I have experienced this kind of dramatic reorientation, but in reverse. I have left behind the dirt, smell, and fear of a Vietnam landing zone and been lifted by helicopter into the cool, safe air high above. Either of these experiences could be a good metaphor for the dying process. We go from one state to another instantly, in one case to something better, in the other to something worse. When the time comes we go to the place that has been prepared for us, and, for better or worse, there is no reversing the outcome. Religious skeptics should at least consider the possibility that there is a way to be certain of where they are going when that moment comes—the way countless others, including many of their own ancestors, have found, by putting their faith in Jesus Christ.

The Narrow Gate

JESSE BROWN aspired to be the first black naval aviator. It would not be easy. He was from a small Mississippi town and grew up in a home without electricity or running water. At that time segregation was strictly enforced and served to limit the dreams of many young black persons. Even though most successful black high school students applied to black colleges, Brown gained admission to The Ohio State University, where he found the rest of the student body 99 percent white.

> Enter through the narrow gate. For wide is the gate and broad is the road that leads to destruction, and many enter through it. But small is the gate and narrow the road that leads to life, and only a few find it.
> ~Matthew 7:13–14

Brown had always had an interest in flying and applied for a naval aviation program at the university. He was discouraged from doing this since no black man had ever been admitted. Nevertheless, he forged ahead. In 1947, he entered the Naval Air Training School, the only black cadet in a class of six hundred. During a grueling training program, he was the victim of continuing prejudice and harassment, even among his flight instructors. On many occasions, he heard or read the message, *"Go home, nigger boy."*[413] Unfortunately, he never felt there was anyone to whom he could complain.

Naval flight training also had its non-racial challenges. The difficult process of learning to fly and navigate washed out half the class. The final and greatest hurdle was taking off and landing on the deck of an aircraft carrier. He made it on the first try, and then completed five more attempts. On October 21, 1948, Jesse Brown's commanding officer pinned his wings on his chest. The occasion was noted in an official press release titled, "First Negro Naval Aviator," followed by

Jesse Brown (US Navy)

an Associated Press article and photograph in *Life* magazine.[414] In spite of many obstacles, Jesse Brown had kept his focus on his goal and what he had to do to achieve it.

F4U Corsair Landing on USS Philippine Sea (US Navy)

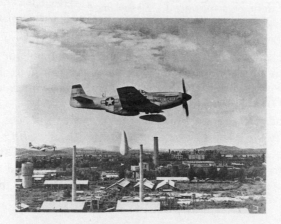

F-51 Mustang dropping napalm over North Korea (US Air Force)

I'm Going In

LT. (J.G.) THOMAS HUDNER joined Fighter Squadron 32 in 1949. He soon met the black aviator, Jesse Brown, who by then was one of the old hands, with seven months' seniority. The two men could not have had more different backgrounds. In contrast to Brown's humble beginnings, Hudner came from a well-to-do Massachusetts family and had attended the Naval Academy. In spite of their differences, the two men developed a close friendship.

On December 4, 1950, Brown and Hudner flew together on a mission bombing targets over enemy territory in Korea. After his first bomb run Brown announced over the radio, "I think I may have been hit,"[415] and his Corsair began descending toward the hostile mountains below. His fellow pilots watched anxiously as his aircraft hit hard on the side of a steep hill and broke up. They could see Brown in the cockpit, waving to them, but not getting out of the wreckage.

After surveying this situation for a few minutes, Hudner made a decision. Without anyone's authorization and, with no regard for his own safety, he announced, *"I'm going in."* Wheels up, he crash-landed his own Corsair a short distance away and made his way to his friend. He found him barely alive, pinned inside his cockpit. Despite all his efforts, he could not free the injured airman who gradually succumbed to his wounds. With his last breath, Brown asked Hudner to tell his wife, Daisy, he loved her.

> I tell you, use worldly wealth to gain friends for yourselves, so that when it is gone, you will be welcomed into eternal dwellings. ~Luke 16:9

For his actions that day, Hudner was awarded the Medal of Honor. He commented, *"One of the worst things . . . is feeling that you're alone. Just being with him . . . was worth the effort."*[416] At the time of his death Brown was a famous man. However, Hudner did not crash-land his Corsair and risk his life for the purpose of saving the first black naval aviator—he did it to help a friend in trouble.

Above and Beyond

ON APRIL 13, 1951, Navy Lt. Thomas Hudner, his family, and a large crowd of dignitaries gathered at the White House for a Rose Garden ceremony. President Harry Truman placed the first Medal of Honor of the Korean War around Hudner's neck and read the citation:

Thomas Hudner
with Pres. Truman
and Daisy Brown
(US Navy)

For conspicuous gallantry and intrepidity at the risk of his life above and beyond the call of duty. . . Lt. (j.g.) Hudner risked his life to save the injured flier who was trapped alive in the burning wreckage. Fully aware of the extreme danger in landing on the rough mountainous terrain and the scant hope of escape or survival in subzero temperature, he put his plane down skillfully in a deliberate wheels-up landing in the presence of enemy troops. With his bare hands, he packed the fuselage with snow to keep the flames away from the pilot and struggled to pull him free. Unsuccessful in this, he returned to his crashed aircraft and radioed other airborne planes, requesting that a helicopter be dispatched with an ax and fire extinguisher. He then remained on the spot despite the continuing danger from enemy action and, with the assistance of the rescue pilot, renewed a desperate but unavailing battle against time, cold, and flames.[417]

A shy, young black woman was also present at the Rose Garden that day. The Navy had arranged for Daisy Brown, the widow of Jesse Brown, to be flown to Washington to attend the ceremony. President Truman quietly expressed his condolences. Through tearful eyes she smiled and shook hands with Hudner as he delivered Brown's last words and message for his wife: *"Tell Daisy I love her."*[418]

> Religion that God our Father accepts as pure and faultless is this: to look after orphans and widows in their distress and to keep oneself from being polluted by the world. ~James 1:27

Trolling

IN SEPTEMBER 1951, Lt. Robert "Pancho" Pasqualicchio was leading a two-ship flight of F-51 Mustangs on an interdiction mission over North Korea when he heard a radioed call for help. Another pilot had crash landed in enemy territory, and a helicopter had been shot down attempting a rescue. There were five men on the ground in trouble and one aircraft flying air cover low on fuel.

> So then, just as you received Christ Jesus as Lord, continue to live in him, rooted and built up in him, strengthened in the faith as you were taught, and overflowing with thankfulness.
> ~Colossians 2:6–7

When Pancho arrived over the scene he saw the wreckage of the two aircraft on the ground in a valley with hills rising sharply on either side. However, he could not spot the enemy gun positions that had shot down the helicopter. To do that, he decided he would have to use himself as bait. Leaving his wingman at altitude, he dove down and flew a low pass down the valley. He described it as *"trolling"* for enemy activity. Sure enough, after several passes, he drew fire from one of the hillsides, enabling him to get a firm fix on the gun positions. As a second helicopter made its approach into the valley, he and his wingman strafed the hill and silenced the enemy guns. All five men were successfully rescued.

For his heroic actions during this mission, Pasqualicchio was awarded the Distinguished Flying Cross. When he returned to the States a month later, he was invited to the White House to meet President Harry Truman, who had read of his daring exploit.

In addition to being a career fighter pilot, Pancho has also been a devout Catholic since early childhood. When asked if he prayed during this mission, he

Pancho Pasqualicchio

said, *"I don't remember whether I prayed at that exact moment or not, but I do know I was wearing the St. Christopher medal my wife Patty gave me, and I have since thanked God many times for being with me on that mission and many others."*[419]

Direct Line

PANCHO PASQUALICCHIO released his bomb and pulled back on the controls of his F-51. In that instant he felt a thump under his left heel and knew that his aircraft had been hit. As he gained altitude, his wingman told him the bomb had hit the target but, unfortunately, coolant was streaming out from the underside of his fuselage.

As he watched his temperature gauge start to rise, Pancho knew his minutes in the air were numbered. He turned due south toward friendly lines, never giving a thought to bailing out of his fatally-wounded aircraft. He would ride it down as far as it would go toward home. He finally came down in a rice paddy north of the Han River, still behind enemy lines. The landing was rough as the air scoop projecting underneath his fuselage hit a dike and nosed him over abruptly, leaving him with a fractured skull. Fortunately, there was no fire, and, best of all, his radio was still working.

With a direct line to his wingman above, he was able to give him and other pilots arriving on the scene details about what was happening on the ground. As a group of Koreans approached him, he told his fellow pilots they were farmers, not soldiers, thus saving them from destruction. When the rescue helicopter arrived, he was able to talk to the pilot and coordinate his own rescue. Based on this experience, Pasqualicchio was instrumental in seeing that future pilots always carried portable radios on their missions, giving them the same advantage even if their aircraft were destroyed.[420]

In the present age of cell phones we can hardly imagine being without communications. We need that direct line to our loved ones, and miss it when it is not there. How much more important to maintain an open line to the one who loves *us*—our Father in heaven. Our direct line to him is through prayer, which requires expressing our thoughts and, more importantly, listening for his. The apostle Paul told us how:

Do not be anxious about anything, but in everything, by prayer and petition, with thanksgiving, present your requests to God. ~Philippians 4:6

Be joyful always; pray continually; give thanks in all circumstances, for this is God's will for you in Christ Jesus. ~1 Thessalonians 5:16–18

Gear

FOR US NAVY pilots flying off aircraft carriers in the Sea of Japan in winter, the task of getting into their airplanes was often the hardest part of the mission. They had to walk, penguin-like, under the load of almost forty pounds of extra weight. The gear meant for their protection in the air made it almost impossible to move on the ground.

The base layer was the G-suit, designed to maintain consciousness during tight maneuvers. Next came woolen underwear plus a wool shirt and trousers. A quilted blue jumpsuit was then added as the inner liner for the Mark III exposure suit, affectionately referred to as the "poopy suit." As one writer put it, "The poopy suit was at once the pilots' most vital and most loathed piece of gear. A neck-to-toe, one-size-fits-all galvanized-rubber affair, the suit had the smell, inflexibility, and texture of an inner tube."[421]

> For our struggle is not against flesh and blood, but against the rulers, against the authorities, against the powers of this dark world and against the spiritual forces of evil in the heavenly realms. Therefore put on the full armor of God.
> ~Ephesians 6:12–13

Finally, the outer layer of gear included a land survival vest, "Mae West" life preserver, knife, .38-caliber pistol, gloves, helmet, goggles, oxygen connection, dye markers, shark repellent, flashlight, and whistle. Amazingly, these pilots got used to the procedure for donning this cumbersome gear and, once airborne, gave it little thought. It was there for the duration of every flight giving them protection from the frigid air, freezing water, and the enemy.

Christians also have protective gear, referred to in the book of Ephesians as the "full armor of God." "The belt of truth," "the breastplate of righteousness," and "the shield of faith" are necessary equipment to enable us to stand against evil. There is also one other item of special importance meant for both defensive and offensive action: "the sword of the Spirit," or God's Word. For this item in our arsenal to be effective, however, we must have an understanding of it. Disciplined study may seem burdensome at times, but knowledge of Scripture is our key to survival in an ever more secular world.

I'm Blind

I'M BLIND! *For God's sake, help me; I'm blind!"*

Howard Thayer heard the cry for help over his radio. Searching the sky for some sign of an aircraft in distress, he saw another A-1 Skyraider from his squadron in a steep climb toward a cloud layer above. Thayer called urgently, *"Put your nose down. Put your nose down."* Slowly, it began to level off.

> I will lead the blind by ways they have not known, along unfamiliar paths I will guide them; I will turn the darkness into light before them and make the rough places smooth. ~Isaiah 42:16

As Thayer moved into position beside the other aircraft, he could see Ken Schechter was the pilot. The cockpit of the Skyraider was almost shot away, and his friend was slumping forward. Surveying the damage, Thayer wondered how Schechter was still alive. He kept talking to him, making small adjustments, and reassuring him he was level. Then he heard through his headphones, "Get me down, Howie."

Thayer positioned himself a few feet from Schechter's left wing and kept talking. They turned south, jettisoned bombs, and gradually started to descend. Soon after clearing friendly lines, Thayer spotted a short, dirt airstrip. He talked the other pilot through every maneuver, until the damaged Skyraider hit the ground hard, slid along the gravel runway, and came to rest in one piece. From above, Thayer saw his friend climb from the cockpit as several soldiers in a jeep came to his aid. One of the great dramas of US naval aviation had ended in success.[422]

Howard Thayer (US Navy)

A Calm Voice

KEN SCHECHTER was totally confused and disoriented. He remembered the bombing run and explosion in his cockpit. He touched his face, and realized it was a mess. The engine noise and air blast were deafening. Worst of all, he couldn't see. He knew he was pulling out of a dive when he was hit, but had no idea after that. His call for help over the radio brought the voice of a friend, Howard Thayer, urging him, *"Put your nose down. Put your nose down."* With no idea what he was doing, he pushed the stick forward.

> The sheep listen to his voice. He calls his own sheep by name and leads them out . . . he goes on ahead of them, and his sheep follow him because they know his voice. ~John 10:3, 4

Schechter's world was now reduced to a black void and a faint voice on the radio. He fought to keep his focus as he listened and responded to that voice: *"Left wing down slowly. Nose over easy. Little more. Drop your ordnance."* Schechter slipped in and out of consciousness, and he seemed to lose track of time, until he heard, *"Ken, we're going down. Push your nose over."* All he could do was try to keep responding to the voice: *"Flaps down. Hundred yards to the runway. Pull back a little. Easy. Easy. That's good. You're level. You're OK. You're over the runway. Twenty feet. Kill it a little. You're settling down. OK, OK, OK. Cut."*[423]

Schechter's ordeal is difficult to imagine—flying an aircraft over enemy territory, blind. Of all the physical requirements to be a fighter pilot, the most important is perfect vision. How could anyone fly an airplane without it?

The plight of this aviator is worth considering when we realize how blind *we* are in reality. Our perspectives are narrow and our vision of the future dim to nonexistent. Unforeseen events buffet us about and force us to realize we are not in control. Fortunately, we know there is a calm, quiet voice waiting to guide us home. When we listen to it and trust it, we know we will always land safely.

We Created a Miracle

AFTER SEEING his friend safely land on an abandoned airstrip, Howard Thayer turned toward home base, the *USS Valley Forge.* He landed to a hero's welcome and got to hear the entire episode replayed later over the ship's PA system. Thayer became a career pilot, staying in the Navy after Korea. Tragically, he was killed in 1961 flying an A-4 Skyhawk over the Mediterranean Sea.

> You say, "I am rich; I have acquired wealth and do not need a thing." But you do not realize that you are wretched, pitiful, poor, blind and naked. ~Revelation 3:17

Ken Schechter was evacuated to the hospital ship *Constellation* where he underwent surgery to remove shell fragments from his face and both eyes. Although he remained permanently blind in his right eye, he was thankful and optimistic for the future. Of his experience that day, he said,

> *My career as a Navy carrier pilot was over. My life was not—because although I was blind that day over North Korea, I was not really alone. Howard Thayer had been my eyes. Together we created a miracle. Today, still living on "borrowed time," I am thankful for every moment of every day.*[424]

In 1995, Schechter was belatedly awarded the Distinguished Flying Cross in a ceremony in San Diego, California. Thayer's widow and three grown children attended. In a short, emotion-filled speech, Schechter spoke to them from his heart. He gave thanks for *"God, country, and family,"* and told Thayer's children about the exploits of a father they had hardly known.[425]

Howard Thayer and Ken Schechter (US Navy)

One Run Only

AS A NEW pilot in Korea, John Glenn got good advice from his fellow flyers. They warned him repeatedly not to make a second run at a target, due to the fact that North Korean anti-aircraft gunners were getting more and more proficient. He was warned specifically about the danger of going after an anti-aircraft battery spotted on a bomb run. There would undoubtedly be other guns nearby in support.

This advice went out the window one day as Glenn was on a steep dive-bombing run. He caught the flash of anti-aircraft guns as he dropped his bombs, and, instead of pulling out, he circled back at low altitude. He felt a sense of solid satisfaction as he raked the enemy gun position with twenty-millimeter cannon fire. Then, however, he felt a jolt and his F9F Panther, flying at five hundred miles per hour, nosed down sharply. Fighting the controls, he narrowly avoided hitting the ground and fought the controls all the way back to base. There he discovered a hole in the tail of his aircraft big enough for his head and shoulders to fit into. He said later, *"That was the last time I went back in for a second run."*[426]

There is an old military axiom that advises, *"Never eject over an area you just bombed."* This and Glenn's story seem to be about exposing yourself to the same risk twice. When Jesus sent his disciples out into the countryside he had some surprising advice along similar lines:

> And if any place will not welcome you or listen to you, shake the dust off your feet when you leave, as a testimony against them. ~Mark 6:11

These instructions may seem unlike the patient and forgiving Jesus we know. I believe, however, he is telling us there is important work to be done for God's kingdom, and sometimes we need to focus our effort on places where there is more chance of success. In some cases we have already done the job meant for us by planting a seed someone else is meant to water. Before moving on, however, we should prayerfully seek God's guidance about how many "runs" to make on any target for his kingdom.

Just Go Home

JOHN GLENN was flying wingman for Lt. Col. John Giraudo on a strafing run against a North Korean truck convoy when Giraudo's F-86 Sabre was hit by anti-aircraft fire. Unable to control the aircraft he had to eject over enemy territory. After calling for a rescue helicopter, Glenn and the other pilots in the flight watched the parachute descend and flew tight circles around the landing spot to protect the downed pilot.

> Now we see but a poor reflection as in a mirror; then we shall see face to face. Now I know in part; then I shall know fully, even as I am fully known.
> – 1 Corinthians 13:12

Soon, the circling aircraft began to reach the critical point on fuel. Glenn ordered the others to return to base, choosing to remain on station until either a helicopter arrived or his fuel ran out. Unfortunately, the latter happened first. With no rescue helicopter in sight, Glenn climbed to forty thousand feet as his engine flamed out. Somehow, he guided his powerless aircraft back to base, leaving his friend alone. Giraudo was not rescued and was listed as missing in action.

Months later, after the cease-fire, Glenn finally saw his friend's name on a prisoner of war list and went to Freedom Village at Panmunjom to greet him as he was released. When Giraudo saw Glenn, he cursed at him, laughed, and then told him the story. After landing, he was painfully wounded in the shoulder and then captured by a North Korean patrol. Every time Glenn flew over, the soldiers would throw Giraudo in a ditch and jump on top of him. In his agony, he kept thinking, *John Glenn, would you please just go home?*[427]

Glenn's act of extreme heroism turned out to be futile and paradoxically even counterproductive—as sometimes happens in war. Military officers are trained to make decisions even when complete information is lacking, under the assumption that decisive action is usually better than aimless confusion. Glenn made a selfless and heroic decision with the best information available—which is all anyone can ever do.

It is an unfortunate fact that we seldom, if ever, have all the information we need. We can only trust that God will help us find the right way when we prayerfully seek his guidance. Thankfully, he can even redeem our bad decisions.

L-5 Rescue

MANY DOWNED pilots were picked up successfully by helicopter during the Korean War. Rescues by fixed-wing aircraft, however, were extremely rare. On December 11, 1950, an unusual mission was performed by Lt. Donald Michaelis flying a light airplane known as an L-5 Sentinel. While in the air that day he heard a distress call from an F-80 pilot who had bailed out behind enemy lines. Since it was late in the day and darkness was approaching, Michaelis knew a helicopter could not reach the pilot in time. On his own, he proceeded to the scene where jets circling overhead directed him to the downed pilot. Selecting a frozen rice paddy for a landing strip, he put his L-5 down on his third try under enemy fire. As the fighters flew strafing runs to suppress the fire, the downed pilot made a dash for the L-5. Michaelis then took off, still under enemy fire, and successfully completed the daring rescue. For his heroic actions, he was awarded the Silver Star a month later. His citation read in part:

> He reached down from on high and took hold of me; he drew me out of deep waters. He rescued me from my powerful enemy, from my foes, who were too strong for me. ~Psalm 18:16–17

L-5 (US Army)

> *Realizing that the interval of time necessary to alert and dispatch a helicopter would necessitate (a possible) unsuccessful evacuation after darkness, Lt. Michaelis proceeded without hesitation to the reported position. Locating the pilot, this officer displayed superior airmanship and profound courage by landing his light reconnaissance aircraft on a frozen rice field five miles south of the city of Pyongyang, Korea. Under fire from enemy snipers, Lt. Michaelis at great personal risk succeeded in locating and evacuating the downed pilot, again demonstrating great skill and courage in making a successful take-off under adverse conditions.*[428]

This event is an amazing example of courage and initiative combined. No one ordered this young airman to fly into enemy territory. No one ordered him or even expected him to land his small, vulnerable aircraft under fire. His heroic actions show what can be accomplished by one person who sees something to be done and, in spite of the obstacles, has the courage and the initiative to do it.

LSO

DURING THE Korean War, US Navy pilots routinely flew from aircraft carriers operating at sea. They faced many risks, including one of the most difficult and dangerous feats performed by anyone in military service—landing an airplane on a moving ship. Nothing looks so small from the air as an aircraft carrier flight deck. Rough seas and nighttime conditions made the operation even more hazardous.

LSO (US Navy)

As the pilot approached the carrier deck, he had to judge the distance, set up the proper rate of descent, and maintain the proper interval behind the next aircraft. Then, during the final approach, a landing signal officer (LSO) positioned on a platform at the left rear of the flight deck would take over supervision of the landing. The pilot still had the controls, but he reacted to signals from the LSO waving reflective paddles: bank right, bank left, pull up, let down. About ten seconds to touchdown, the final call would come from the LSO—land or go around. He had to know the condition of the pilot and aircraft and what to expect from each. For his part the pilot had to put his complete trust in the skill and knowledge of this one person. For a safe landing, the pilot, in this brief but intense moment, had to relinquish control and put his fate in someone else's hands.

Most of us would make poor carrier pilots for a lot of reasons. Among them, we would have difficulty giving up control in such a tense moment, just as we have difficulty giving up control at most other times in our lives. We pray, ask God's advice, and then often do what we wanted to do in the first place. We neglect the process of discerning God's answer to our prayer, often found by patiently studying Scripture, listening to Christian friends, and searching deeply within our own hearts. An important part of this process is giving up control of the outcome by putting our trust in the Lord. As a fellow church member puts it, we have to *"Let go, and let God."*

> Trust in the LORD with all your heart and lean not on your own understanding; in all ways acknowledge him, and he will make your paths straight. ~Proverbs 3:5–6

I Got You

ENS. ED JACKSON was an F9F Panther pilot flying off the *USS Philippine Sea*. On September 17, 1950, he was leading a flight in search of targets of opportunity near Seoul. Flying low along the Han River he spotted a string of about seventy enemy boats and dropped to fifty feet for his strafing run. He could see soldiers diving into the water as his 20mm cannon churned the river and splintered boat after boat. The returning small-arms fire seemed to do no damage. However, as he passed over the last boat, he caught a glimpse of something ahead. Suddenly, there was a jolt, a loud bang, and oblivion.

Jackson's Panther had been clotheslined by a cable stretched across the river as an aerial booby trap. The cable was snapped but not before it had split the aircraft's nose and shattered the cockpit. Jackson himself was knocked unconscious as glass shards lacerated his face. Fortunately, the aircraft was climbing during the next half minute, when he was not in control. As his mind began to clear, he had trouble seeing or hearing while the wind blasted through the cockpit. He could hear his wingman over the radio. They climbed to two thousand feet, leveled off, and headed for their aircraft carrier.

> Man, despite his riches, does not endure; he is like the beasts that perish. This is the fate of those who trust in themselves, and of their followers, who approve their sayings. Selah
> ~Psalm 49:12–13

The wingman talked Jackson through their approach. As they began their descent toward the carrier deck, other pilots in the air and crewmen on the ship listened intently over the radio as the tension built. Finally, to everyone's relief, the voice of the ship's landing signal officer, Lt. (j.g.) Les Bruestle, came on the air, stating calmly, *"Ed, this is Les. I got you."*[429]

The confident and familiar voice talked the dazed pilot onto the carrier deck. The damaged aircraft caught the last arresting cable stretched across the carrier deck and jerked to a stop.[430] Jackson and his Panther Phantom would miraculously live to fight another day—thanks to relying on the voice of an unseen friend.

Pray at the Same Time

CAPT. WILLIAM DICKSON volunteered for duty as an aerial observer (AO) as a way to get home faster. AO missions were extremely hazardous and earned points for early rotation out of the war. There were many days he questioned the wisdom of his decision.

L-19 Birddog (US Air Force)

Typically, Dickson would fly low over enemy territory, seeking out enemy troop and weapons positions for engagement by artillery or air strikes. Flying in a single engine Cessna L-19, he was a slow-moving target for anti-aircraft and small-arms fire, both of which came his way frequently. He prayed often during these missions but had to learn to do it while a lot of other things were happening. In his diary, he recorded these thoughts:

> We ran into flak up over Pyongyang—in Flak Alley—I was scared that day, I mean really scared. I prayed without knowing what I was doing. I spotted the guns though. I guess that training is what enables you to sit in the plane during the slipping and sliding of evasive action, hold your glasses, spot your map, see the terrain, check the time, plot the position, and pray, all at the same time.[431]

An army chaplain once encouraged his men to use "bullet prayers" every day to stay close to God. He felt it was not necessary to wait for a quiet time or a church setting to connect with his heavenly Father. I believe we in fact build a stronger relationship with God when we share our needs and concerns at the time they arise. Any time of the day is a good time to seek his presence and the comfort we always find in it. It is not that difficult to work or play, and pray, at the same time.

> Be joyful always; pray continually; give thanks in all circumstances, for this is God's will for you in Christ Jesus.
> ~1 Thessalonians 5:16–18

Guardian Angel

WILLIAM CHATFIELD was bombardier and navigator on a medium bomber flying interdiction missions over enemy territory in North and South Korea. In spite of this dangerous work, he always felt that God's hand was protecting him from harm on each of his fifty-five missions. His most memorable "guardian angel" moment, as he called it, came during a low-level bombing attack on a truck convoy moving through a narrow valley. At that time the North Koreans were using cables stretched across certain valleys to disrupt air attacks. These were taken down and moved often, making them difficult to spot.

> Are not all angels ministering spirits sent to serve those who will inherit salvation?
> ~Hebrews 1:14

As the bomber reached the target and released bombs, a large volume of anti-aircraft fire erupted. Chatfield knew the pilot was about to pull up, but something caused him to yell out, *"Down!"* The pilot responded, and within an instant they felt a jolt. The aircraft kept flying but didn't handle properly on the way back to base. Once on the ground the crew found part of the rudder sheared off by a cable they never saw. They realized that if the pilot had pulled up at the moment Chatfield called out, they would have hit the cable head-on. In recalling the incident, the airman knew that the urge that came to him was no accident. He said, *"I'm a believer in guardian angels, I really am."*[432]

The Bible tells us God created angels to fulfill many tasks. They guide, encourage, and protect human beings as God directs. We learn from the Psalms that, *"The angel of the LORD encamps around those who fear him"* (Psalm 34:7), and *"He will command his angels concerning you to guard you in all your ways"* (Psalm 91:11). I haven't seen them physically, but I know my own guardian angels have been on the job often. Many of my fellow believers share the same conviction. We thank God for sending his angels and his protection when we need them most.

F-86 Sabres over Korea (US Air Force)

F-84 Thunderjets carrying bombs (National Archives)

Loyalty

BAILING OUT of an aircraft over enemy territory has been traumatic in every war, and especially in Korea. The summers are hot and the rice paddies foul places to land. In winter, pilots might experience a one-hundred-degree temperature change from cockpit to outside air. Once on the ground they were trained to hide their parachutes, seek cover, and evade the enemy when necessary. This was often nearly impossible due to wounds from enemy fire or injuries from the parachute jump itself. The shock and pain of this sudden trauma were often disorienting.

The saving grace for a downed pilot was the fierce loyalty and protectiveness of his fellow aviators. Within minutes of going down, other aircraft would be circling overhead and laying down a curtain of fire to stop approaching ground forces. Someone would determine the best approach and exit for a rescue helicopter and try to keep that corridor open. For a pilot lying numbly on the ground after a crash landing, the psychological impact of having friends aloft was crucial. The sight of comrades circling at treetop level gave many downed pilots the mental strength to carry on. One pilot described this scene as *a mother eagle hovering over a fallen chick.*[433]

> Yet this I call to mind and therefore I have hope: Because of the Lord's great love we are not consumed, for his compassions never fail. They are new every morning; great is your faithfulness.
> ~Lamentations 3:21–23

The motto of the US Marine Corps is *Semper Fidelis*, or "always faithful." Nothing could epitomize this more than the attitude of these pilots toward a comrade in trouble. There were actual instances where pilots exhausted their own fuel staying on station to protect a fellow flyer on the ground.

Loyalty and faithfulness are attributes important to our survival in peace as well as war. We need friends with character who will stand beside us in difficult times, just as they need us to stand with them. This kind of loyalty is modeled perfectly by the One who created us. Our saving grace, literally, is the amazing fact that we have a heavenly Father who is always faithful to us.

Ted Williams

TED WILLIAMS was one of the greatest baseball players of all time. During his career with the Boston Red Sox from 1939 to 1960, he hit 521 home runs and was league batting champion three times. He was the last man in baseball history to achieve a batting average over the seemingly insurmountable .400 barrier. Displaying an unusual humility about his achievements, he said, *"Baseball is the only field of endeavor where a man can succeed three times out of ten and be considered a good performer."*[434]

> Humility and the fear of the LORD bring wealth and honor and life.
> ~Proverbs 22:4

As marvelous as his baseball career was, it would have been even greater except for his service as a Marine aviator in two wars. He entered service too late to actually see action in World War II but was recalled to duty during the Korean War and flew thirty-seven combat missions with Marine fighter squadron VMF-311. One of his squadron mates was future astronaut John Glenn. Glenn admired Williams as a fellow Marine aviator and commented, *"He gave flying the same perfectionist's attention he gave to his hitting."*[435]

Ted Williams (USMC)

Williams did not volunteer for combat duty; however, he went when he was called, even though there were ways he could have avoided military service. He simply did his duty. President George W. Bush said of Williams' career at the time of his passing away:

> *Whether serving the country in the Armed Forces or excelling on the baseball diamond, Ted Williams demonstrated unique talent and love of country. He inspired young ballplayers across the Nation for decades, and we will always remember his persistence on the field and his courage off the field. Ted gave baseball some of its best seasons—and he gave his own best seasons to his country.*[436]

Williams did his duty at the expense of the career he loved. Above and beyond his fame as a baseball player, his fellow veterans will always remember him as a combat fighter pilot, American patriot, and hero.

A Wing and a Prayer

JIM SERVICE flew more than seventy combat missions in an F9F Panther from the deck of the *USS Valley Forge*. He encountered a lot of anti-aircraft fire and was constantly under threat of attack by enemy aircraft. Like most young men in their twenties, however, he considered himself bulletproof. Everything was an adventure. He always felt that landing on the moving deck of an aircraft carrier was his greatest risk.

He came closest to disaster on one landing when he got a late call from the landing signal officer (LSO) on his final approach to the flight deck. His instinct was to go around, but since the LSO signals were mandatory, when he was told to cut power, he cut. Even as he did so, he knew the consequences of missing the arresting wires. If he overshot the flight deck, he would wind up in the ocean with only minutes to live before freezing to death. He recounted his thoughts at that moment:

> For in the gospel a righteousness from God is revealed, a righteousness that is by faith from first to last, just as it is written: "The righteous will live by faith."
> ~Romans 1:17

Ever hear the expression, "flying on a wing and a prayer"? That's the feeling I had coming in. I took the late signal, came in, touched down well forward, and although I succeeded in collapsing the nose gear on my airplane, it stayed on the deck. It was a heart stopping moment for me.[437]

Everyone has had his or her share of heart-stopping experiences. Although some of mine have been in combat, one in particular came in peacetime, during a very quiet moment—the moment I took the first step of faith toward Jesus Christ. My prior life as a religious skeptic was characterized by intellectual objections over many theological issues. When, at age fifty-three, I suddenly became convinced Jesus Christ was who he said he was—the son of God sent to reconcile mankind to God—I had to put on hold many of those intellectual questions that had been stumbling blocks for most of my adult life. Accepting the simple truth of the gospel message, I took my first step of faith and let go of the controls, on "a wing and a prayer." It was literally a heart-stopping moment, as I died to my former self and was born again into a new and glorious life of the Spirit.

Not to Worry

A MISSION over MiG Alley required a lot of preparation. Three hours before a dawn takeoff, pilots would get up, have breakfast, and assemble for briefings. One staff officer after another would cover the ground war, enemy situation, weather, rescue procedures, and, finally, the mission itself. There was always an emphasis on escape and evasion, which only highlighted more the danger ahead. All knew that some might not return.

As part of his gear, each pilot was issued a standard survival kit containing food, first-aid kit, and .45-caliber pistol. Every pilot, however, had his own ideas about survival in enemy territory. One pilot was particularly thorough:

> Then you will go on your way in safety, and your foot will not stumble; when you lie down, you will not be afraid; when you lie down, your sleep will be sweet . . . for the LORD will be your confidence and will keep your foot from being snared.
> ~Proverbs 3:23–24, 26

He also carried dried milk, berries, nuts, oatmeal, ten pounds of rice, sterno, a pot, a fold-up camp stove, a monocular, maps, shaving equipment, a sleeping-bag vacuum packed in a picnic-ham can, a shelter-half, and enough sulfa to cure pneumonia three times. In addition, he packed a radio, three batteries, and a special SAC issue .22 caliber Hornet rifle.[438]

Survival Gear (National Archives)

When asked about his obsessive precautions, the pilot made the rather profound observation that this was his way of managing fear—that it *"helped him not to worry."*[439]

I can identify with this strategy for handling anxiety through preparation. Before combat operations in Vietnam, I also paid careful attention to my own gear and that of my men, and tended to overstudy the maps and information available on the mission. In my present life I am most often anxious about upcoming speaking engagements, which I handle invariably by over-rehearsing. If I am successful, the nervousness dissipates. When fear motivates us to more thoroughly prepare ourselves for a difficult task, it is not necessarily a bad thing.

We always need to remember, however, that there is an ultimate source of stress relief—the knowledge that God has the ultimate control over events and our lives. This is the only assurance we need to enable us to face any difficult or dangerous task with peace in our hearts.

Brothers

LOW ON fuel after an uneventful patrol, the two F-86 Sabres turned south from the Sinuiju area. Frederick Blesse was on his 121st mission and ready to finish this one, when suddenly a flight of MiG-15s appeared. Sending his less-experienced wingman on to safety, Blesse engaged the MiGs and, after several passes, made his own narrow escape. Now critically low on fuel, he set a course for the island of Pen Yang Do where he thought he could be reached by Air-Sea Rescue. After flying through a lot of flak during his descent, he finally ran out of fuel and crossed the coastline in a glide at about three thousand feet.

As the plight of this pilot unfolded, his squadron mates on the ground at Tienpo airfield gathered in the ready room to listen to the radio transmissions back and forth. They heard Blesse make contact with an Air-Sea Rescue seaplane that had arrived on the scene. They listened as Blesse announced he wasn't going to be able to reach the island and was going to eject. In the few remaining seconds, several men in the ready room grabbed the mike. One said, *"You get back here. You owe me ten bucks!"* Another, *"Good luck, buddy, we'll see you at supper."* Others chimed in with their own encouraging words. Blesse later commented on his thoughts at that moment:

> This is how we know what love is: Jesus Christ laid down his life for us. And we ought to lay down our lives for our brothers. ~1 John 3:16

> I'll tell you, it sent chills up and down my spine. I was about to pull the handles here, and the only thought in my mind was, "God, what a marvelous bunch of guys."[440]

Blesse would never forget the support of comrades when he was in trouble. Friends in time of need are indeed one of life's greatest blessings, in time of war or peace. That is why we are not meant to go it alone as Christians. When our faith or courage falters and we need help, God most often comes to us through our brothers and sisters in Christ. The relationships we build in good times are what see us through the bad.

Target Fixation

Lt. Richard Spivey

THE MISSION of Luke Air Force Base in 1953 was to provide combat-ready pilots for duty in Korea. At that time the Arizona air base had the worst accident rate of any in the Air Force, reflected in the commanding officer's stated view, *"It's cheaper to kill a pilot in training than in combat."*[441]

My brother, Lt. Richard Spivey, reported to the base early in 1953 to learn to fly the F-84 Thunderjet and master the difficult art of low-level bombing and strafing. Strafing was especially complex with a flight of four aircraft orbiting a spot on the ground, maintaining separation, making tight, high-banked turns, and lining up on the target. Diving at 400 miles per hour, the ground rose quickly, giving the pilot only seconds to bring his six .50-caliber machine guns to bear. The closer to the target, the more accurate the fire and better the gunnery score.

One day after a strafing exercise, my brother landed to find a bullet hole in the underside of his fuselage. He had flown so close to the target that a ricochet from one of his own bullets had struck his aircraft. That night, at the Officers' Club, he discussed this event with his roommate and expressed his resolve to quit worrying about gunnery scores and to focus more on flying. Even though his friend heartily agreed, the next day that same friend was unfortunately killed when he flew his F-84 into the ground on the same kind of strafing run.

These pilots were dealing with a phenomenon now known as "target fixation," a term denoting the tendency to concentrate on a target while losing awareness of the surrounding situation. Christians can evidence this same tendency when they become fixated on the works they do for God's kingdom, while neglecting their relationship with God himself. Writing to the church in Ephesus, the apostle John, the author of Revelation, warned Christians then and now,

I know your deeds, your hard work and your perseverance . . . Yet I hold this against you: You have forsaken your first love. ~Revelation 2:2, 4

Simple Things

WITH THE development of air-to-air missiles after the Korean War most weapons experts concluded that guns mounted on aircraft were a thing of the past. With radar-guided and heat-seeking missiles, targets could be engaged and destroyed at great range, making close-in combat seemingly obsolete. Col. Frederick Blesse, an F-86 pilot and ace from aerial combat over Korea went to the Pentagon to argue against this policy. He used a simple analogy:

> Jews demand miraculous signs and Greeks look for wisdom, but we preach Christ crucified: . . . Christ the power of God and the wisdom of God.
> ~1 Corinthians 1:22–23, 24

This reminds me of two guys in a phone booth. One guy has a short blade knife, and the other guy has a rifle. Now, the rifle is obviously a better piece of equipment, but not in a phone booth.[442]

Blesse pointed out the obvious. If two aircraft are still closing in after firing their missiles, there is going to be a close-in fight. A short-range weapon in aerial combat would not be obsolete.

This story is about simple solutions. Sometimes we make it too complicated as we overlook the obvious. As a religious skeptic for most of my adult life, I entertained many complex objections to Christianity. Like other skeptics, I challenged the validity of the Bible and wondered about the existence of so many other religions in the world. I sought answers to the questions I had about life in philosophy and science. I was amazed at how simple the answers turned out to be when Jesus Christ came into my heart.

When we consider the awesome task of sharing the gospel with unbelievers, we need to rely on Jesus and remember the simplicity of his message. Theological argument and biblical expertise are seldom needed. A brief statement of what we were like before and after Jesus is more powerful than the most brilliant discourse on religion. When a believer tells his or her own story, there is no room for argument as the power of the gospel comes alive for someone else.

Troops board H-19 helicopter (US Army)

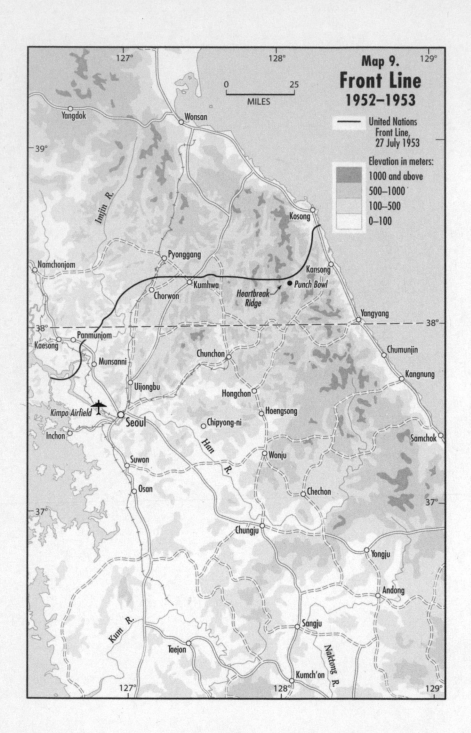

Map 9.
Front Line
1952–1953

United Nations
Front Line,
27 July 1953

Elevation in meters:
1000 and above
500–1000
100–500
0–100

0   25
MILES

Yangdok

Wonsan

Imjin R.

Namchonjom

Pyonggang

Kosong

Kansong

Kumhwa

Chorwon

Punch Bowl

Heartbreak
Ridge

Yangyang

Panmunjom

Kaesong

Chunchon

Chumunjin

Munsanni

Kangnung

Uijongbu

Hongchon

Kimpo Airfield

Hoengsong

Chipyong-ni

Seoul

Inchon

Han R.

Wonju

Samchok

Suwon

Osan

Chechon

Chungju

Yongju

Andong

Kum R.

Naktong R.

Sangju

Taejon

Kumch'on

322

OCTOBER

STALEMATE

A S PEACE negotiations started in the village of Kaesong on July 10, 1951, the opposing forces were arrayed along a line angled diagonally across the Korean peninsula from the northeast to the southwest. Starting from a point just south of Kosong on the east coast, the line ran to the Punchbowl area, Kumhwa, and Chorwon in the center, and then angled south through the Imjin River valley to the Yellow Sea at a point about twenty miles north of Seoul. Each side had roughly half a million troops facing the other across the line. The Communist forces were about half Chinese and half North Korean. The UN forces were also evenly split between US and South Korean units, with an additional 28,000 troops from United Nations countries, including Australia, Belgium, Canada, Colombia, Ethiopia, France, Great Britain, Greece, Luxembourg, Netherlands, New Zealand, Philippines, Thailand, Turkey, and the Union of South Africa.[443]

During the summer of 1951, the peace talks made little progress over the first and foremost issue: location of the demarcation line. Earlier in the summer, Dean Acheson, the American Secretary of State and Trygve Lie, the Secretary-General of the United Nations, had both publicly mentioned the possibility of a truce "at or near" the 38th parallel.[444] However, the latest UN offensive had carried well north of that line to terrain that offered better defensive positions. The UN negotiators held out for the actual line on the ground against bitter and prolonged argument on the Communist side. Finally, on August 23, the Chinese and North Koreans broke off negotiations.

Rather than succumbing to the Communists' demands, Gen. Matthew Ridgway planned a new offensive to occupy terrain that would improve his defenses and negotiating position. On September 5, the Second Division launched an attack on a hill complex in the Punchbowl area that soon became known as Heartbreak Ridge. In some of the bitterest fighting of the war, the 23rd Infantry Regiment was almost shattered in repeated assaults up the heavily defended slopes. Finally, after a month of almost continuous combat and heavy casualties on both sides, the hill was taken. On October 25, peace talks resumed in a small village called Panmunjom.

After some initial sparring and concessions on both sides, the Communists finally agreed to the UN proposed cease-fire line. As the negotiators worked their way down the remaining agenda, however, they came to an issue not considered noteworthy up until that time—the exchange of prisoners. If the Geneva Convention were strictly adhered to, both sides would have agreed to immediately repatriate all prisoners. However, UN prison camps held more than forty-thousand South Koreans who had been impressed into service by the Communists. There were also thousands of North Korean and Chinese prisoners who did not want repatriation.[445] The Communist negotiators were unwilling to concede that any troops would not be returned, while President Truman stood firmly behind the issue of individual choice on moral principle.

This second standoff would last for more than a year as hostilities continued along the front. Each side continued artillery bombardment, patrolling, raids, and limited attacks against the other. For the troops involved, the war was not over and was just as dangerous as ever. Every day, thousands of artillery projectiles from each side struck the other, and few days passed without troops clashing somewhere along the line. The struggle continued into the winter months of 1952–53, when the weather again became the foremost enemy of every man in the field.

In early 1953 outside events came to bear on the Korean battlefield and negotiating table. In January, Gen. Dwight Eisenhower, the architect of Allied victory in World War II, was inaugurated President of the United States. A few months later the Soviet leader, Joseph Stalin, died. In April the negotiators returned to Panmunjom after a six-month hiatus with indications that the Communists were ready to relent on the repatriation issue. Unfortunately, as this and countless other details were being ironed out over the next two months, Communist forces undertook a series of violent offensives along the front. UN commanders at this point were unwilling to trade more lives for this disputed terrain. A final line and armistice agreement were reached on July 27, 1953, and the guns finally fell silent on the Korean peninsula.

First Chapel

IN THE FALL of 1951 a large group of Marines, soldiers, sailors, and Koreans gathered to dedicate the First Marine Division's first permanent chapel in Korea, located near the division headquarters. The low and unimposing Quonset hut, with seating for two hundred, was distinguished only by a large white wooden cross mounted over the entrance, visible over a wide area. Col. John Cook spoke to the gathering:

> The temple I am going to build will be great, because our God is greater than all other gods. But who is able to build a temple for him, since the heavens, even the highest heavens, cannot contain him? Who then am I to build a temple for him"
> ~2 Chronicles 2:5–6

Today we dedicate a new and beautiful chapel in this command. One of the finest traditions of American military life is the desire of men to build a House of God wherever duty calls them. Many of you know how during World War II, men in arms built chapels of thatch and bamboo, of concrete and steel, taking materials at hand to fashion some kind of a suitable place for prayer.[446]

Kim Chang Ho, a Korean Methodist minister, echoed the colonel's theme:

With one hand you fight against the wicked enemy of humanity, while with the other hand you build a chapel and dedicate it to God. I have learned that this is the way your ancestors did. They built a church first of all. They taught their children the Bible first of all. They did everything for Christ first of all. These are three most valuable traditions. Church, Bible, Christ— these are the foundations of your nation.[447]

The words of a Korean minister spoken in 1951 are a timely reminder today about our heritage as Americans. At the very beginning, our Founding Fathers turned to God as the source of their authority. They recognized they were endowed by God, not by men or governments, with their sacred rights, and that their first and most important right as citizens was the freedom to worship God according to the conscience of each individual. Americans built their houses of worship throughout the land and continue to do so on foreign shores wherever our men and women in uniform are called to serve.

Gave All He Had!

William
Thompson
(US Army)

PFC. WILLIAM THOMPSON was a machine gunner with the Twenty-Fourth Infantry Regiment. His platoon came under attack near Haman, Korea, in August 1951. When the platoon's other machine gun was knocked out, Thompson was left to provide the automatic firepower needed to stop the enemy assault. His Medal of Honor citation reveals that he did not back down from the task:

While his platoon was reorganizing under cover of darkness, fanatical enemy forces in overwhelming strength launched a surprise attack on the unit. PFC Thompson set up his machine gun in the path of the onslaught and swept the enemy with withering fire, pinning them down momentarily thus permitting the remainder of his platoon to withdraw to a more tenable position. Although hit repeatedly by grenade fragments and small arms fire, he resisted all efforts of his comrades to induce him to withdraw, steadfastly remained at his machine gun and continued to deliver deadly accurate fire until mortally wounded by an enemy grenade.[448]

At the time of his enlistment Thompson lived in the Home for Homeless Boys in the Bronx. He had left a broken home years before and was living on the street when the director of the home found him shivering on a park bench and took him in. He became a cheerful member of the little community but surprised everyone by enlisting in the army at age eighteen. No one expected the scrawny young boy to succeed as a soldier. After basic training, he returned to the orphanage to proudly show off his uniform.

> There is one body and one Spirit—just as you were called to one hope when you were called—one Lord, one faith, one baptism; one God and Father of all.
> ~Ephesians 4:4–6

Thompson did find a home in the army. He never aspired to rank or responsibility, but took great pride in his uniform, his equipment, and himself. He was a good soldier. At his funeral in Brooklyn, the pastor recalled the young man's early life at the orphanage and said, *"He was not a West Point man or a college graduate, but at the hour of need, heard the cry of his country and gave all he had!"*[449] William Thompson was the first African-American soldier to receive the Medal of Honor in the Korean War.

Too Easy

HILL 339 was a key terrain feature forward of the front lines near Yonchon. It had been fought over for weeks, as US and Chinese forces took it in succession, only to be beaten back by the other side within days. On September 21, 1951, K Company of the 7th Cavalry Regiment got the unenviable mission of taking it again. Lt. David Hughes prepared for the worst as he led his men up the hill under cover of an artillery barrage. Anticipating a deadly hail of small arms, he was surprised instead to see a red flare go off over the hill, followed by the sight of Chinese troops abandoning their positions.

Unopposed and counting their blessings, the men of K Company moved to the top of Hill 339 and started organizing their defense. Within five minutes, however, they learned the reason for their easy success. The Chinese had the hilltop registered for pinpoint artillery and mortar fire, and began raining destruction on the US troops. Hughes said,

> For we are God's workmanship, created in Christ Jesus to do good works, which God prepared in advance for us to do. ~Ephesians 2:10

"*I thought the roof was going to come off the hill.*"[450] This was to be their fate for the next week, enduring incessant incoming fire and suffering more than thirty casualties.

There is an old military axiom that says, "*If your attack is going too well, you're probably walking into an ambush.*" It definitely applied on this Korean hilltop. I interpret this little saying to mean we should beware of easy solutions to our problems.

This may be good advice some of the time, but, paradoxically, the opposite is true in our work for God's kingdom. We usually make it too hard on ourselves, as we try to do too many things and, even then, feel guilty about what we don't do. Amazingly, when we are doing the good work God intends for each of us, it is not hard. Our joy and sense of purpose in doing what he wants us to do should make our work for him almost effortless. A Christian axiom might be: "*If your work for God is going well, you are probably where you need to be—in his will.*" This truth makes it very important that we carefully discern what talents we have and what role they should play to further God's kingdom.

Footprints

AS A CORPSMAN with Fifth Marines, Joe Brown survived a lot of combat and had a lot to be thankful for. He was especially thankful to live through the attack on Hill 812 in September 1951. Under heavy fire all day he was hit once by shrapnel from an exploding artillery shell that would have been fatal a few feet closer. A little later he walked down a trail where he also could have been killed. He said, *"The next morning a Marine engineer removed several shoe box land mines from the same trail."*[451]

> He who sits on the throne will spread his tent over them.
> ~Revelation 7:15

Later in his life Brown read a little story about footsteps that seemed to give meaning to his traumatic experiences in combat and close calls with death:

Footprints in the Sand

One night I dreamed I was walking along the beach with the Lord. Many scenes from my life flashed across the sky.

In each scene I noticed footprints in the sand. Sometimes there were two sets of footprints, other times there was one only.

This bothered me because I noticed that during the low periods of my life, when I was suffering from anguish, sorrow or defeat, I could see only one set of footprints, so I said to the Lord,

"You promised me Lord, that if I followed you, you would walk with me always. But I have noticed that during the most trying periods of my life there has only been one set of footprints in the sand. Why, when I needed you most, have you not been there for me?"

The Lord replied, "The years when you have seen only one set of footprints, my child, is when I carried you."[452]

The simple truth conveyed in this story is that we often have to look back to see God's footprints—to understand how he has been involved in our lives. Only in retrospect can we see how he has changed us and how he has used events to guide us. This understanding of the past is where we gain great confidence to live in the present, knowing he is with us every step, no matter what trials we face.

Guilt

DURING THE battle for Hill 812 Joe Brown treated a Marine who had suffered a severe shoulder wound with a lot of blood and bone fragments. He had to make a quick decision about how much cleaning to do around the wound. Deciding he might cause more bleeding by cutting away the matted clothing, he applied a battle dressing over the area and gave the Marine morphine. He then went on to respond to the next call for help.

> If we claim to be without sin, we deceive ourselves and the truth is not in us. If we confess our sins, he is faithful and just and will forgive us our sins and purify us from all unrighteousness. ~1 John 1:8–9

Soon after the battle for Hill 812, Brown was rotated back to the field hospital where many of the wounded were treated during the battle. He made inquiries about the man with a major left shoulder shrapnel wound. Amazingly, he found the surgeon who had treated him. When Brown told the doctor he was the corpsman who had dressed the wound, he was astounded at the doctor's remark: *"He looked me square in the eye and said I didn't do my job. He said I should have cut more material away from the wound."*[453]

Right or wrong, this remark devastated the young corpsman. He said, *"I was ashamed, embarrassed, and didn't have a high regard for myself after that. I started drinking."*[454] Heavy drinking then led to a prolonged struggle with alcoholism after the war and the question that would not go away: *"Did I do enough?"* Decades later, he still wondered, *"Did I do the right thing, or did I screw up?"*[455]

This man's guilt may seem unreasonable from our present perspective. Like so many in war, he did the best he could with what he had at the time. However, his story should give us pause to think about our own shortcomings, real and imagined. Biblically, we know that, *"All have sinned and fall short of the glory of God"* (Romans 3:23). Each of us has done something or failed to do something we are not proud of. Each of us has guilt that needs to be addressed and a pressing need for someone greater than ourselves to help address it.

Be Still

SGT. LEONARD WALZ was a squad leader with G Company, Second Battalion, Seventh Cavalry Regiment, when he was killed in action near Chorwon on October 3, 1951. Months later, the Rev. Albert Gierke spoke at a funeral service for the deceased soldier, bringing a thoughtful and heartfelt message of comfort to a grieving family.

> Come to me, all you who are weary and burdened, and I will give you rest. Take my yoke upon you and learn from me, for I am gentle and humble in heart, and you will find rest for your souls. For my yoke is easy and my burden is light.
> ~Matthew 11:28–30

When the disciples, tossed in their ship by a great storm, came to Jesus for help, He helped them, saying to the raging sea: "Be still!" And there was a great calm. May the Lord's Word produce a great calm in your hearts today, as I speak to you on the 10th verse of the 46th Psalm: "Be still and know that I am God."

In all stillness let us learn that God is personified wisdom, that our puny wisdom is not at all comparable to the wisdom of the All-knowing. Let us also learn that God has in all things His divine purposes, divinely counseled, divinely planned.

God says to all of us: "Be still and carefully lay on your heart My message of mercy and love coming down from high heaven: Be thou faithful unto death, and I will give you a crown of life." Leonard was faithful to his Savior unto death. By the grace of God, Christ was his everything. Leonard has been crowned with the crown of life.[456]

Be still. What better advice could we hear in our own time of grief? Only in stillness can we open our hearts to Jesus and allow him to fill us with the perfect peace only he can give. Even in the worst of times our hearts will be quieted by his gentle hand. Be still. Rest in him. He will heal the wounds that seem unbearable in the present moment and reveal God's purpose in the events that devastate us now but eventually work according to his purpose. In stillness, we are filled with the love, mercy, grace, and constant presence of our heavenly Father—and the assurance that he has prepared a place for our loved ones and for us.

Soldiers advance toward Heartbreak Ridge (US Army)

Religious services on a Korean hillside (US Navy)

Faith of a POW

RICHARD BASSETT was captured on October 6, 1951, when his platoon was ambushed near Kumhwa. During twenty-one months of captivity in a camp near Pyokdong he and his fellow POWs had to endure hunger, frostbite, dysentery, brutal mistreatment, and mental breakdown. Fortunately, he went into this ordeal with a strong faith and God's Word:

When I was captured I had the New Testament in my fatigue pocket. It had been my daily habit to read it, and now I found myself reading more and more each day. I also was spending much of my time meditating on what I had just read. In those troubled times, it greatly helped to have faith in God and to believe that everything would be all right as long as we kept our faith.[457]

Bassett not only had faith himself, but he shared it freely with others. Throughout his ordeal he held regular worship services with his fellow prisoners and even preached to them on occasion.

> I waited patiently for the LORD; he turned to me and heard my cry.
> He lifted me out of the slimy pit, out of the mud and mire; he set my feet on a rock and gave me a firm place to stand.
> He put a new song in my mouth, a hymn of praise to our God.
> Many will see and fear and put their trust in the LORD. ~Psalm 40:1–3

During my time as a prisoner, some of us would get together and study the scriptures, sing a few hymns, and pray. Prayer and religious fellowship brought me considerable comfort during my long months of captivity; in fact, I believe that the prayers of the folks back home and my faith in God played a tremendous role in my getting home.[458]

The power of one man's faith during supremely desperate times is encouraging to all of us as we deal with our own problems in life. God does not shelter us from every hardship and disaster, but he is never far away during our trials. He is always there when we turn to him and lean on him for support, and we have his assurance that any crisis will eventually be a blessing if it draws us closer to him.

Shield of Faith

THE GATES of hell seemed to open up as incoming artillery fire pounded the Marine lines. As the earth shook and shrapnel whined through the air, Pfc. Bob Durham lay huddled in the bottom of his trench praying and holding on to his Bible. Suddenly, over the din, he heard his name called. His sergeant told him to get his gear; they were moving out to help an observation post in trouble, Outpost Reno. Leaving the safety of his position was one of the hardest things he ever had to do.

To get to the beleaguered outpost, the Marines had to cross over a mile of no-man's land on a winding trail through barbed wire and mine fields, all the while under enemy fire. Their own casualties began to mount. It became worse as they fought their way up the hill closer to their comrades. Enemy troops were now swarming over the outpost and pouring small-arms fire on the Marines below. The rescue party was practically decimated on the hill and unable to reach the top. Word finally came to pull back.

As Durham turned to move down the hill, he discovered a group of wounded men huddled together. One of them reached out

> Stand firm then, with the belt of truth buckled around your waist, with the breastplate of righteousness in place, and with your feet fitted with the readiness that comes from the gospel of peace. In addition to all this, take up the shield of faith, with which you can extinguish all the flaming arrows of the evil one.
> ~Ephesians 6:14–16

and grabbed his leg, saying, *"Please don't leave us! We'll all be killed."*[459] The young man wanted to ignore the plea. He had orders to go, and that's exactly what he wanted to do. He didn't want to die or be seriously wounded in that God-forsaken place. Amazingly, at that moment he felt the power of the Holy Spirit within him—the source of strength who had helped him conquer his fears since childhood. With the Holy Spirit and the shield of faith around him he knew he would be all right. He would stay where he was with his wounded brothers and help them get to safety. He didn't stop praying.

Faith under Fire

OVERCOMING his fear, Bob Durham stayed with the wounded Marines on the slope of Outpost Reno. He sent word back requesting a Browning Automatic Rifle (BAR) and all the ammunition that could be spared. He then faced the advancing enemy, taking it on himself to cover the withdrawal of his unit and to protect those down around him. At that moment God's Word came to him and seemed to lift him up:

> The LORD is my light and my salvation—whom shall I fear? The LORD is the stronghold of my life—of whom shall I be afraid? When evil men advance against me to devour my flesh, when my enemies and my foes attack me, they will stumble and fall. ~Psalm 27:1–2

As Durham rose to a standing position with the BAR, he was the only American left able to resist the attack. Smoke and darkness made visibility difficult, and he could only see silhouettes of figures coming toward him. Unable to take careful aim, he fired from the hip at fleeting targets. He fired the heavy weapon, reloaded, and fired again for what seemed an eternity. Somehow, the enemy attack stalled before him.

Eventually, other Marines returned to assist the valiant Marine and continue the advance up the hill. The wounded men were evacuated to safety. Of the twenty-seven men who had gone to relieve Outpost Reno, twenty were killed and six wounded. Durham was the only man untouched. He was sure God's angels had surrounded him and protected him during this harrowing experience. He knew that his family and church back home were praying for him. He also knew that God had answered his own fervent prayers and had honored his faith under fire.[460]

(US Navy)

On the Eve of Battle

James Patterson

JAMES PATTERSON lied about his age when he joined the Marine Corps as a seventeen-year-old. In 1952 he was a sergeant on the front lines in Korea when another Marine, not much younger than he, came to him to talk. A major enemy attack was expected within hours, and the young man had a premonition. He said, *"Sarge, will you pray for me? I think I'm going to be killed tonight."* Patterson responded with a question: *"Do you know Jesus as your personal Savior?"* After a slight hesitation, the boy said, *"No."* Patterson then talked with him quietly about the gospel and what it means to be saved. He quoted two verses of Scripture:

For God so loved the world that he gave his one and only Son, that whoever believes in him shall not perish but have eternal life. ~John 3:16

Whoever is thirsty, let him come; and whoever wishes, let him take the free gift of the water of life. ~Revelation 22:17

The Marine listened intently as Patterson explained the power of the blood of Jesus. The two men prayed together, and the young man gave his heart to the Lord that night.

Patterson did not see this man again and to this day does not know whether he survived the battle that took place over the next few days. Regardless, he has always had a supreme sense of peace about the young Marine who came to Christ with him on the eve of battle. He said:

I don't know whether he was killed or not. If he was, he just barely made it on home before me—because heaven is my home and the kingdom of heaven is my country. That's where I'm going.[461]

Revenge

Ronald Rosser
(US Army)

AFTER HIS brother was killed in Korea, Ronald Rosser re-enlisted in the army and volunteered for combat duty. He said, *"I made up my mind that my brother didn't get a chance to finish his tour, so I was going to finish his tour for him as a combat soldier. I wanted to get even for him."*[462] He had his chance on January 12, 1952, when his unit attacked Hill 472. Due to withering fire from well-entrenched Chinese forces, the attack stalled near the crest of the hill. Rosser single-handedly continued the assault, silencing a machine gun bunker and fighting his way through the enemy trenches. When he ran out of ammunition, he withdrew briefly to replenish his supply and then went back again.

For his actions that day Rosser was awarded the Medal of Honor. The citation for his award describes the rest of his exploits on Hill 472:

> *Cpl. Rosser once again exhausted his ammunition, obtained a new supply, and returning to the hilltop a third time hurled grenades into the enemy positions. During this heroic action Cpl. Rosser single-handedly killed at least thirteen of the enemy. After exhausting his ammunition he accompanied the withdrawing platoon, and though himself wounded, made several trips across open terrain still under enemy fire to help remove other men injured more seriously than himself.*[463]

Later, reflecting on the actions that earned him the nation's highest award for heroism, Rosser realized his motives had changed during his time in combat:

> *At first, thoughts of my brother Richard who had been KIA was my guiding light, so to speak. That's what got me to Korea. But after I got there, I did it because it was my responsibility to do it. Thoughts of my brother were always there and I remembered, but I had all those other kids too. For the most part I was older than them. I felt responsibility for them.*[464]

This soldier went to a better place mentally when he was able to focus on the positive reasons for enduring the hardships of combat. The apostle Paul also had very specific guidance for Christians on the pitfalls of revenge:

Do not repay anyone evil for evil . . . Do not take revenge, my friends, but leave room for God's wrath, for it is written: "It is mine to avenge; I will repay," says the Lord. Do not be overcome by evil, but overcome evil with good. ~Romans 12:17, 19, 21

God Fixed It

IN EARLY 1952 a nineteen-year-old Marine was brought into the First Medical Battalion field hospital with a severe wound that had damaged the main artery in his upper leg. He had lost a lot of blood and was in shock. A young surgeon, not much older than the Marine, assessed the situation and knew he faced a difficult decision. He could perform a simple, straightforward amputation of the man's leg and save his life, or he could attempt a much riskier operation to repair the artery and possibly save the leg. The operation would be extremely delicate and would require great skill. He had seen it done but had never done it himself.

> I sought the LORD, and he answered me; he delivered me from all my fears. Those who look to him are radiant; their faces are never covered with shame.
> ~Psalm 34:4–5

At that moment the surgeon turned his head and looked at the man standing nearby. As was often the case, Chaplain Robert Schneck, the Seventh Marines regimental chaplain, was in the hospital giving aid and comfort to the wounded. Meeting the surgeon's gaze, he bowed his head in silent prayer, as the other man followed suit. After a few moments, the young surgeon turned his attention back to the operating table and began a long and tedious procedure with an uncertain outcome. The chaplain later reported:

Two days "post-op" I happened to be in the surgical ward tent at the same time our surgeon friend was making his rounds. I was behind him when he reached the cot of our young Marine . . . He began to talk to the patient and, while talking, almost hesitatingly touched the foot of the shattered leg. A smile appeared. Turning around, the surgeon saw me. "It's warm," he said. Those two words meant that the arterial repair had been successful since blood was reaching the foot. I congratulated the surgeon with great warmth and respect. He looked at me momentarily and then remarked, "Thanks for the prayers, padre. God fixed that one."[465]

The Pocket Bible

OUTPOST EERIE was well named. Sitting on a small hill in the middle of no-man's land, it was supposed to give early warning of enemy attack. Only two squads manned the exposed position a mile from friendly lines. On the night of March 21, 1952, Cpl. Herman Godwin was a medic with the small force at the outpost when it was attacked. As enemy automatic weapon fire swept the trenches, casualties began to mount, and he was called repeatedly to go to the wounded. He helped several who were hurt seriously get back to the relative safety of a bunker.

> All Scripture is God-breathed and is useful for teaching, rebuking, correcting and training in righteousness, so that the man of God may be thoroughly equipped for every good work
> ~2 Timothy 3:16–17

At about 1 a.m. Chinese troops breached the wire and began pouring over the outpost. Godwin threw all the grenades he could find and fired his rifle until he was out of ammunition. He finally dropped down into the bunker with the wounded men just as an enemy soldier threw a grenade into the bunker from another entrance. The force of the explosion knocked the medic unconscious.

As the Chinese troops swarmed over the hill, higher command decided to bring artillery fire directly onto the outpost. This was a desperate measure, taken in hopes that the friendly troops in their positions would be somewhat safer than the attackers out in the open. Soon proximity-fuzed shells began exploding overhead, showering the hilltop with shrapnel. Within minutes bugles sounded calling the enemy troops off the hill.

Pocket Bible

When Godwin regained consciousness he was amazed to be alive. The metal cover of the little pocket Bible he carried in his left breast pocket was dented. He could see his bunker had been searched as weapons and his own knife were missing. Fortunately, the search was cut short by the incoming artillery fire. Godwin survived the attack on Outpost Eerie thanks to proximity-fuzed shells and his little pocket Bible.[466]

Password

AS THE FRONT lines became more or less static during the Korean War, patrolling took on an important role. The enemy usually moved at night, and it was vital to get early warning of impending attacks. Fully camouflaged squads and platoon-sized patrols would go out through the wire and minefields into no-man's land following an assigned route. Any movement or noise had to be checked out.

The patrols would return in the dark, making sure to be within friendly lines by first light. This final phase was tricky.

Troops in frontline positions are always nervous, and dark figures emerging out of the night are cause for alarm. To enable positive identification, a password was used. For example, "Yankee clipper" would be given to troops all along the line as the password for the day. Any unknown figure would be challenged with *"Yankee,"* and would have to answer *"clipper."* It was not a perfect system, but it helped men approach each other in the dark.

Christians know that God has a password for those who would approach him—the name Jesus Christ. It is the only name by

> It is by the name of Jesus Christ of Nazareth, whom you crucified but whom God raised from the dead, that this man stands before you healed. He is the stone you builders rejected, which has become the capstone. Salvation is found in no one else, for there is no other name under heaven given to men by which we must be saved. ~Acts 4:10–12

which we are saved. This claim to exclusivity is one of the foremost stumbling blocks to Christianity for religious skeptics. Why is there only one way? What about the good Hindus and Muslims? This is a question of theology that I can't definitively answer. I don't know what provision God has made for the rest of humanity who have not heard Jesus' message. I do know that, unlike all other religious figures, Jesus does not require that we work our way to God. He offers forgiveness and acceptance purely as gifts. I can only definitively share my own witness: that my life changed on the day I asked Jesus into my heart. When I used God's only password, I felt his presence in my life for the first time and have had peace in my life and hope for the eternal future ever since.

Guilt

RALPH FLY arrived in Korea late in November 1952 and was soon on the front lines with First Battalion, Fifth Marines. As a brand new corpsman in a dangerous environment, he knew he had a lot to learn. Fortunately, he found a mentor. Sgt. Don Lupo took him under his wing to show him how to survive on the battlefield. Over several months the two became fast friends.

> Let us draw near to God with a sincere heart in full assurance of faith, having our hearts sprinkled to cleanse us from a guilty conscience and having our bodies washed with pure water.
> ~Hebrews 10:22

Whenever mortar or artillery fire hit their frontline position, it was Fly's duty to check the lines for wounded. He would never forget the one time Lupo told him to stay in the bunker while he went to check on the men. Within seconds he heard another explosion, followed by, *"Doc, I'm hit."* Fly soon found his friend riddled with shrapnel. Applying bandages and tourniquets he did all he could to stem the bleeding. As he placed the wounded Marine on a helicopter, Lupo said to him unexpectedly, *"I love you."*[467]

When Fly learned a few days later his friend had died, he became an emotional wreck. He said, *"I felt that I had failed so miserably. To me, it was a failure of cosmic proportions."*[468] The guilt was almost overwhelming and would stay with him for decades. He would never forget that his friend had gone out in his place and, when it counted most, his first aid had not been enough to save him.

Giving aid to the wounded (National Archives)

Decades later, Fly and several other veterans began a search for Lupo's family. They eventually contacted his niece, a young woman named Christine Vetter. She told them she had always been very close to her uncle and still felt his presence. She also told them she was greatly comforted by the knowledge he was so loved by good friends. Fly may never have completely overcome his guilt. He did, however, do something constructive about it. Turning guilt into positive action is the best step we can take toward healing. When we bring peace to others we have a chance of finding it ourselves.

Getting There

AS THE CHINESE tunneled deeper along the 38th parallel their bunkers became almost impregnable to US tank and artillery fire. The men of the 780th Field Artillery Battalion came up with a unique plan. They removed a 155mm howitzer from its carriage and replaced it with a larger eight-inch howitzer. Instead of firing overhead deep into enemy territory, they would take the weapon into the front lines and fire directly into the enemy positions. The plan was good, but the problem was getting there.

In what became known among the troops as "Operation Mountain Goat," engineers undertook the job of turning a ten-mile jeep trail into a road to the top of a mountain 3,800 feet high. This took almost three weeks. Then for three days the engineers and artillerymen pushed and pulled the weapon up the snow- and ice-covered track. Using a bulldozer to push and ropes to keep from backsliding, they doggedly worked their way up the hill.

> Each one should use whatever gift he has received to serve others, faithfully administering God's grace in its various forms. ~1 Peter 4:10

Once in position, the results were devastating. The weapon was immediately brought to bear firing its two-hundred-pound projectiles at targets only 1,800 yards away, destroying thirty-two bunkers in the first day. This work became more and more dangerous as the enemy reacted to the threat. However, they were not able to stop the destructive rain of fire. One US soldier said, *"We were blessed to have that huge cannon blasting out enemy positions . . . it not only destroyed their positions, but hampered their ability to launch attacks because they were very busy rebuilding."*[469]

We've heard the expression, *"Getting there is half the battle."* In this case it was more like the total battle. Once the physical obstacles of terrain and weather were overcome, the howitzer's effectiveness was a forgone conclusion.

A friend of mine once told me, *"Eighty percent of Christian service is showing up."* He was telling me that the hard part is getting there. Once we overcome our inertia and the many obstacles of time and distance, the actual work of serving our Lord with fellow believers is usually fun and always rewarding.

I Made Myself Move

AFTER MONTHS on the front line, Corpsman Ralph Fly was transferred to the relative safety of a battalion aid station. Working in a rear area, he felt removed from the immediate fear of enemy action. However, in March 1953, a major Chinese night attack struck his area, and enemy artillery fire began exploding in and around the lightly-defended battalion aid station. Everyone scattered to nearby foxholes or whatever protection was available. Ironically, at this point, the troops on the front lines in bunkers were better off than these men in open foxholes in a supposedly safe rear area.

> How can they hear without someone preaching to them? . . . As it is written, "How beautiful are the feet of those who bring good news!"
> ~Romans 10:14–15

As ear-splitting explosions went off around him, Fly lay paralyzed in his foxhole. The barrage continued until the inevitable happened. From the darkness came a moan and the cry *"Doc!"* Suddenly, it was up to him to leave his place of relative safety to help a wounded man, even while everyone else clawed themselves deeper into the ground. He described his thoughts at that moment:

> *I was completely terrified and shaking uncontrollably—but I made myself move out of the hole until I was belly-crawling foot by foot across the ground where I found my first wounded. Missiles were landing nearby as I was attending to this wounded man.*[470]

This young navy corpsman gives a magnificent example of physical courage under fire. He had to make a hard choice between staying safe or doing his duty. This kind of example should inspire us to be more courageous as Christians. Our risks are not physical but seem no less intimidating. Many of us fear embarrassment or ridicule for being too forward about our beliefs. Fortunately, few of us are called to preach on street corners; however, there are many moments in our lives when we are called to "make ourselves move." These are the moments we each experience when, with a little courage and effort, we can share the lifesaving news of the gospel.

Keeping Watch

IN ARMY RANGER School, would-be Rangers are taught to function on little sleep. After a long, exhausting training exercise, the troops usually clean up, eat, and then go to bed. Often, an hour or two later they are rudely awakened with a new mission. Most of the patrols are at night when all anyone can see is a small piece of luminous tape on the back of the man's cap in front, bobbing through the darkness. After several nights of this, I once fell asleep while walking, dreaming about the luminous tape. I woke up when I fell down after tripping on a dead tree branch.

On watch (National Archives)

Actually, such training is well designed to prepare soldiers for combat. Lack of sleep and physical exhaustion are ever present. As one soldier in Korea said about that war:

> One thing never changed—we were always dead tired. If we weren't on guard duty, we were repairing bunkers or doing some other damn detail. There were times when I think I would have given six months' pay for one night in a soft, warm bed. Once, when I was totally exhausted and afraid I would fall asleep on guard duty, I actually pulled the pin on a grenade and held it in my hand. I don't really recommend it, but I didn't fall asleep.[471]

I don't recommend this method, either. Any officer would be extremely upset to find one of his men holding a live grenade to stay awake. Nevertheless, in a combat zone, being alert while on duty is a life-or-death matter.

Being spiritually awake is equally a life-or-death matter, but *eternal* life or death. Our Savior gave some very pointed advice on this subject. While talking about the time of his return, he told about a man who left his house and put his servant in charge while he was away:

Therefore keep watch because you do not know when the owner of the house will come back—whether in the evening, or at midnight, or when the rooster crows, or at dawn. If he comes suddenly, do not let him find you sleeping. What I say to you, I say to everyone: "Watch!" ~Mark 13:35–37

Famous Last Words

THIRTY BELOW zero temperatures sapped the strength of every infantry-man fighting in Korea. Not considering weapons, ammunition, and sleeping bags, just the clothes they wore made every movement exhausting: long johns, utilities, sweater, field jacket, parka, etc. Faces, feet, hands, and ears were particularly prone to frostbite. Ears were only protected when parka hoods were worn up. This made hearing difficult, but many kept their

Marines fight the cold (USMC)

hoods up anyway, justifying to themselves, *"What you HAVE to hear, you will hear!"*

At the end of a long day on the march or in the attack, the mind-numbing cold also took its toll on the initiative of many small unit leaders. They needed to take great care in deploying their men and weapons for an effective nighttime defense. This took time and energy, and, sometimes, an exercise of iron willpower. As one officer described:

> *When that cold seeps inside your parka hood, the old brain slows down, along with the rest of your body, and it is just too easy to say to yourself, "Tomorrow morning we'll move further out and up with listening posts, but I'm sure that we can hear them from here without any trouble." These are known as "famous last words," both figuratively and literally.*[472]

Even under less stressful conditions, we often have our inner justifiers working over-time to make us feel better when we detour from the right course of action. In his little masterpiece *The Screwtape Letters*, C. S. Lewis has a senior devil instruct a subordinate, his nephew, to make sure his human subject looks at every small, sinful action as insignificant at the time committed, and reversible later. This is of course the path of ultimate capitulation to the Enemy. Every person should constantly examine his or her own conscience before accepting an *easy* solution to a problem. Is it also the *right* solution? Are our rationalizations becoming our own "famous last words"?

> Let us throw off every-thing that hinders and the sin that so easily entangles, and let us run with perseverance the race marked out for us. Let us fix our eyes on Jesus, the author and perfecter of our faith.
> ~Hebrews 12:1–2

Lost Child

IN 1953 Dave Chambers was a chaplain with First Marine Division. At the time of the cease-fire a sentry brought a Korean woman to him who had come to his compound from a nearby village. She told him about an accident that had occurred two years before when a military truck had struck her neighbor's eighteen-month-old daughter. The driver had stopped, picked up

> But we had to celebrate and be glad, because this brother of yours was dead and is alive again; he was lost and is found.
> ~Luke 15:32

the girl, and taken her away. The family never saw her again after that. The woman asked the chaplain if he could find the little girl.

Faced with a seemingly impossible task, Chambers prayed for God's guidance. He spent a lot of time on the telephone looking for leads but could find nothing specific. Too much time had passed. With little to go on, he made a trip to Inchon to visit the hospital ship stationed there. He learned that one of the earlier ships had treated some wounded Korean children. When the ship returned to the United States the children had been sent to orphanages ashore in Korea. Still with nothing specific to go on, Chambers began going from orphanage to orphanage with the story of a three-and-a half-year-old girl with a probable head injury.

After a long search, Chambers finally came to the Star of the Sea Orphanage, where Sister Theresa told him she did have a child that

(US Army)

seemed to fit his description. A young girl with a head injury had been brought from a hospital ship, but nothing else was known about her. He arranged for the woman who had first contacted him and the sister of the missing girl to come to the orphanage, where they were able to make a positive identification.

Finally and miraculously, a lost child was restored to her family. Chambers recalled the moment:

> *I cannot describe the mother's joy. I am still amazed that, with the myriad of possibilities as to what might have happened to the little girl and to where she might have been sent, we were led to Inchon and then to the Star of the Sea Orphanage.*[473]

What It Feels Like to Die

GENE SALAY was twenty-one years old when he arrived in Korea and was assigned to the Korean Military Assistance Group (KMAG) as a radio operator. He wound up with a South Korean unit defending a barren hillside near the North Korean border. The war at this point had become static along well-defended lines.

July 13, 1953, seemed like a routine day, with the occasional boom of outgoing artillery rounds passing overhead and men trying to stay dry in a steady rain. At about 7:30 p.m., however, enemy artillery fire began falling along the forward positions and grew steadily in intensity. At about 10 p.m., flares lit up the sky. Looking down, Salay saw what looked like a giant ant pile. Thousands of Chinese troops were in the valley below and moving up the hill at a steady trot. The sound of bugles seemed to come from every direction.

The enemy attack poured over Salay's position. He fired his M-1 rifle until he was out of ammunition, and then fought hand to hand. He was swinging his rifle like a club when something struck the back of his head that felt like a mule's kick. Lying on the ground, he realized he had been hit in the head with a gun butt and shot in the chest. He could not feel his left side. He could feel his own blood soaking his clothes, and thought to himself, *So this is what it feels like to die.*[474]

> Salvation is found in no one else, for there is no other name under heaven given to men by which we must be saved. ~Acts 4:12

Fortunately, this young soldier did not die on the battlefield. He was captured, spent the remainder of the war in a POW camp, and eventually returned home.

Most of us have had our own close calls where we had to at least consider the possibility of death. Just having that thought should give anyone pause. Would this be a moment of extreme panic or one of calm assurance about the future? Jesus Christ is the only source of a confident answer to this question.

Friendship

BRUCE WAREING was a twelve-year-old living in Manitoba, Canada, when he saw a movie about Gen. George Custer's last stand at the Battle of the Little Big Horn. He was so inspired by the film that he eventually joined a Canadian armored cavalry regiment during the Korean War. Combat duty was, however, far different from what he had imagined as a boy. His unit was in a static position on the front line with tanks dug into "hull-down" emplacements with only the gun turret above ground. The main danger was incoming enemy artillery fire. The shock and concussion of near misses *made one think you were in a bell.*"[475]

> I no longer call you servants, because a servant does not know his master's business. Instead, I have called you friends, for everything that I learned from my Father I have made known to you. ~John 15:15

Time spent outside the tanks in nearby bunkers was no better:

> *Bunker life was not very pleasant with water dripping from the roof, dropping on our candles. We only took our boots off, crawled into our sleeping bags with our wet clothes on, and covered ourselves with our ponchos. We woke in the morning, put our wet boots on, and stepped onto a wet dirt floor that had about two inches of water on it. No hand-to-hand fighting in the armored. Just a grunt's misery.*[476]

Wareing said later that the redeeming feature of his experience in Korea was the friendships forged under these harsh conditions. Unfortunately, one of his good friends was killed in action, but he always remembered their time together sharing a poncho. Wareing's father was from Australia, and he made many friends among the Australian troops who served with his unit. He often made tea and carried it to their bunker during idle moments. Many bonds of friendship sustained him and others during the worst ordeal of their lives. Wareing said,

> *I was 21 years old in combat and learned fast how to stay alive and still do my duty to my mates. I feel guilty about those that died. The war and fear brought out the friendship of us all. I realized that I was with a big band of brothers—all those great people I met, lived, and served with. God bless all those in the fight.*[477]

Korean trenchline (US Navy)

Subordination

AS THE Revolutionary War came to an end in 1783, George Washington was the most revered man in America. Many implored him to assume political authority over the new nation as a dictator or even king. Instead, he journeyed to Annapolis, Maryland, through cheering throngs to appear before the Continental Congress. There, he resigned his commission, saying, *"I consider it an indispensable duty to close this last solemn act of my official life by commending the interests of our dearest country to the protection of Almighty God."*[478] The most powerful man in America showed his lack of ambition for power and his own devotion to the subordination of military to civil authority, setting America firmly on the course of democratic government that recognized the Creator's protection.

> They brought the coin, and he asked them, "Whose portrait is this? And whose inscription?" "Caesar's," they replied. Then Jesus said to them, "Give to Caesar what is Caesar's and to God what is God's." And they were amazed at him.
> ~Mark 12:16–17

In 1953 another great military leader and one of the most respected generals in American history stepped down from power. Even after his own disputes with civilian authority, General of the Army Douglas MacArthur addressed the cadets of West Point on the proper role of the American soldier:

> *Your mission remains fixed, determined, inviolable. It is to win our wars. Everything else in your professional career is but corollary to this vital dedication. All other public purposes, all other public projects, all other public needs, great or small, will find others for their accomplishment; but you are the ones who are trained to fight. Yours is the profession of arms.*
>
> *Others will debate the controversial issues, national and international, which divide men's minds. These great national problems are not for your professional participation or military solution. Your guidepost stands out like a ten-fold beacon in the night: Duty, honor, country.*[479]

God has blessed America with great leaders dedicated to this tradition of military subordination to civil authority. We can only pray for civilian leaders in turn who have just as clear an understanding of their own subordination to an ultimate Authority greater than themselves.

Chinese Soldiers stand guard near site of peace talks (US Navy)

Memorial service for fallen comrades (National Archives)

R & R

LIFE IN the frontline trenches of Korea was dangerous and difficult. Incoming artillery and ground attacks were constant threats. Food was inconsistent—either rations in cans or a trek down a mountain trail in shifts to a mess tent far below. Everything was covered with dirt. It was often three to four weeks between trips to a shower unit more than ten miles behind the lines. A full night's sleep was unheard of due to guard duty and patrols every night. The only respite to this deadly routine was an infrequent event called "rest and relaxation" (or "rest and recuperation"), or "R & R." One soldier described it:

> At the end of six months, they would send us to Japan for five days. That was utter happiness. It did us good. It allowed us to recharge our batteries. But on the fifth day, we took a vehicle in the morning, crossed over on a plane into Korea, got back on the truck and we were there for another six months. When we would go to Japan in the plane, people would talk, they would sing. But when we got back on the truck, silence. And it was like that until we got back to the line of fire.[480]

Most of us are a lot better off than those soldiers. Even so, life is still difficult enough—work to do, children to raise, bills to pay. Sometimes, it can even be overwhelming. An occasional R & R from our daily routine helps us regain some perspective on our lives.

Even though vacations are a very good thing, we should appreciate the fact that our problems are usually wrapped up in our blessings. We struggle with our finances because we love our families. Our children drive us crazy but are the source of our greatest joy. We may long for a respite, but we should realize there is no magic point in the future when all our problems will be over. Whether on R & R or in the trenches, we can stop and count our blessings where we are every day.

> Praise be to the God and Father of our Lord Jesus Christ, who has blessed us in the heavenly realms with every spiritual blessing in Christ. For he chose us in him before the creation of the world to be holy and blameless in his sight.
> ~Ephesians 1:3–4

Waste Not

THE LOCAL newspaper of my youth was the *Horry Herald*, published weekly to inform the community about every good and bad thing happening in and around Conway, South Carolina. In 1953 my brother, Dick, was flying F-84s in Korea, and my mother sent the paper to him regularly to keep him apprised of the local news. In one of his infrequent letters home he advised, *"Keep the Horry Herald coming. We never have enough toilet paper."*

This problem was not uncommon among the troops serving in Korea. One Marine noted this deficiency and described another unusual solution:

> *Toilet paper was always in short supply. A few sheets came with our C rations, but generally not enough to meet our needs. One guy must have said something to his wife about the shortage, because he started receiving letters written on toilet paper. Very practical. If he carried his letters around with him, they could serve a very useful purpose.*[481]

This kind of ingenuity and frugality can be traced to the generation who lived through the Great Depression. My mother reminded me often to *"Waste not, want not."* This kind of attitude almost flies in the face of our consumer culture today. Shopping has become an activity. When economic downturns occur, our politicians actually tell us our patriotic duty is to borrow and consume more. A proverb for our time might be, *"Save not, want not."*

One blessing of hard times might be a return to tried and true values. We realize through necessity the value of thrift. We rediscover the biblical advice urging us to use our resources wisely: *"In the house of the wise are stores of choice food and oil, but a foolish man devours all he has"* (Proverbs 21:20).

Even though the industrious ant is a creature of little strength with no overseer, *". . . yet it stores its provisions in summer and gathers its food at harvest"* (Proverbs 6:7–8). After miraculously feeding the multitude, Jesus voiced a similar concern over the need to conserve what we have and to plan ahead for future needs:

When they had all had enough to eat, he said to his disciples, "Gather the pieces that are left over. Let nothing be wasted." ~John 6:12

Going Home

AFTER AN extended tour as a forward observer at a patrol base, Sgt. Bobby Martin was preparing to move back to the main line with his unit. As he was loading weapons and ammunition into a jeep, his platoon leader came up to him and said, *"Martin, you're going home. You are on the rotation list this morning."*[482] It was a moment he would never forget. He immediately gathered up his gear and caught a ride to Inchon Harbor where he boarded a ship. When he reached Sasebo, Japan, he had his first good meal in months—steak and ice cream. After he took several showers, put on new clothes, and turned in his weapon, he felt like a new person. He described the journey from there:

> I saw the Holy City, the new Jerusalem, coming down out of heaven from God, prepared as a bride beautifully dressed for her husband. And I heard a loud voice from the throne saying, "Now the dwelling of God is with men, and he will live with them. They will be his people, and God himself will be with them and be their God."
> ~Revelation 21:2–3

After a few days at Sasebo, we loaded on a ship and set out for home. After about two weeks on the ocean, we approached San Francisco Bay early on a foggy morning. "Look up there," someone shouted. We looked up and there it was, the Golden Gate Bridge just ahead of us. What a sight; this was an experience I would never forget. Someone on the bridge waved at us, and everyone on deck started waving back and yelling and laughing. It was truly a happy moment.[483]

I went to and from the Vietnam War on a PanAm charter jet. I always thought going to war that way was a cruel twist. My warrior ancestors had the benefit of long sea voyages to prepare for what lay ahead. I must say I didn't mind coming home in an airplane even though I missed the thrill described by Martin of seeing the Golden Gate Bridge appear through the fog. No matter how you do it, however, there is no thrill like returning home after a long separation.

If we could only imagine what awaits us at the time of our *heavenly* homecoming!

Golden Gate Bridge

Medals

AN ARMY officer who fought at Heartbreak Ridge voiced an opinion about medals shared by many who have been in combat: *"For every man who gets a medal, there are probably five or six who also deserve one but never get written up. As I watched the battle for Heartbreak, I knew there were a lot of men out there who were earning medals they would never get."*[484]

As a company commander in combat, I shared the frustration of this officer. I tried hard to make sure acts of heroism were recognized within my unit, but I know many were either not reported or that witnesses were wounded or transferred before incidents could be documented. There were times when paper-

Silver Star medal (US Govt.)

work of any kind was simply not feasible. To the countless heroes of our wars who have gone unrecognized, those of us who survived thank you for your unrecorded deeds and hope your own satisfaction has been a significant reward.

For good or bad, there are many areas of life where our achievements are not recognized by others, and we have to look within ourselves for reward. In fact, the true test of character is doing the right thing when we know no one will notice or applaud our actions.

There are also some things we do for God's kingdom that we should not seek praise for at all. Jesus specifically mentioned charitable work, prayer, and fasting, which he admonished us to do in private, avoiding the public displays so common to many religions. We may not get our medals in this lifetime, but we can only guess at the heavenly rewards that await us for the deeds we accomplish that only he sees.

> So when you give to the needy, do not announce it with trumpets, as the hypocrites do in the synagogues and on the streets, to be honored by men. I tell you the truth, they have received their reward in full. But when you give to the needy, do not let your left hand know what your right hand is doing, so that your giving may be in secret. Then your Father, who sees what is done in secret, will reward you. ~ Matthew 6:2–4

Out with a Bang

A S THE PEACE talks dragged on at Panmunjom, soldiers on both sides of the line lived in uncertainty. Even though rumors were constant that the war was about to end, men were being killed and wounded every day. Finally, at 11 a.m. Korea time on July 27, 1953, the men of Third Infantry Division were called together to hear the announcement—a cease-fire had been signed and would take effect at 10 p.m. that night. Everyone was surprised that the long-awaited event had finally happened.

Norman Parsons was with the 3rd Infantry Division and was one of the men on the front line that night waiting for the final moment. An hour before the cease-fire, however, all hell broke loose, as they say. Each side rained high explosives on the other as fast as the guns could be fired. No one knows who started it, but each side seemed bent on throwing a final punch. He described the scene:

> At 9 p.m. the sky lit up like you have never seen . . . I was next to a big gun that fired every minute during that last fight. The earth would rumble and sparks would fly when it fired. The war ended with a final blast.[485]

Such a concentration of deadly firepower within minutes of the war ending seems somewhat perverse. It is hard to imagine the built-up frustration that might have triggered it. "Out with a bang" is an expression we all know well, however, and it seems many soldiers wanted the war to end that way. Many also use the expression to describe how they want to leave this life—hoping they won't go peacefully. Most will be disappointed in this, however, as the vast majority of us are likely to die quietly. We will have to wait for the fireworks on the other side. We don't know what heavenly celebration awaits us, but we do know that it will be more spectacular than anything we have seen or can imagine.

But you have come to Mount Zion, to the heavenly Jerusalem, the city of the living God. You have come to thousands upon thousands of angels in joyful assembly, to the church of the firstborn, whose names are written in heaven. You have come to God, the judge of all men, to the spirits of righteous men made perfect.
~Hebrews 12:22–23

Charity for All

THE HOURS ticked by slowly on Sunday, July 26, 1953, as the White House staff waited for news from Panmunjom. An armistice was expected, but, as had been the case for many months, no one could be certain of the final outcome to the frustrating negotiations. President Dwight Eisenhower spent a long day waiting and even turned to his paint brushes and easel in the afternoon to take his mind off the tension. Finally, at 9:38 p.m. an aide brought a flash message announcing the formal truce agreement in Korea. At 10 p.m. the President went on the air to announce the news to the American people. His heartfelt address incorporated the words of a previous president in similar circumstances:

> Therefore let us keep the Festival, not with the old yeast, the yeast of malice and wickedness, but with bread without yeast, the bread of sincerity and truth.
> ~1 Corinthians 5:8

My fellow citizens:
Tonight we greet, with prayers of thanksgiving, the official news that an armistice was signed almost an hour ago in Korea. It will quickly bring to an end the fighting between the United Nations forces and the Communist armies. For this Nation the cost of repelling aggression has been high. In thousands of homes it has been incalculable. It has been paid in terms of tragedy.

With special feelings of sorrow—and of solemn gratitude—we think of those who were called upon to lay down their lives in that far-off land to prove once again that only courage and sacrifice can keep freedom alive upon the earth . . .

On this Sabbath evening each of us devoutly prays that all nations may come to see the wisdom of composing differences in this fashion before, rather than after, there is resort to brutal and futile battle . . .

My friends, almost 90 years ago, Abraham Lincoln at the end of a war delivered his second Inaugural Address. At the end of that speech he spoke some words that I think more nearly express the true feelings of America tonight than would any other words ever spoken or written. You will recall them:

"With malice toward none; with charity for all; with firmness in the right as God gives us to see the right, let us strive on to finish the work we are in . . . to do all which may achieve and cherish a just and a lasting peace, among ourselves, and with all nations."

This is our resolve and our dedication.[486]

Cease-Fire

I N JULY 1953, Mike Schack was an artillery forward observer assigned to a frontline position called Outpost Harry. For most of the month a lot of fighting was still going on. Artillery fire fell frequently on his position and the Chinese continued to probe the lines with limited attacks. Nearby, the battle for Pork Chop Hill raged for five days as both sides tried to occupy strategic terrain before the end of hostilities.

Just before the cease-fire finally went into effect on July 27, both sides fired all their ammunition with a great uproar. Then, at ten o'clock an eerie silence announced the end of the war. The next morning Schack was cleaning up and packing his belongings when something happened he would never forget: *"I looked over at the Chinese-occupied hills and saw the people waving at us. We waved back. Everyone was happy the war was over and we would be going home."*[487]

We struggle through life, as in war, fighting to be successful and to survive. We instinctively resist the idea of death, driven by a powerful urge to cling to the life we know, doing everything possible to protect ourselves and our loved ones. This instinct for survival is integral to our human nature. In reality, however, the end of life is only our own cease-fire from the hostilities of this world. When the time comes to lay down our arms and return to our true home, we anticipate a heavenly celebration and eternal joy we can barely comprehend in this world.

> Now we know that if the earthly tent we live in is destroyed, we have a building from God, an eternal house in heaven, not built by human hands. Meanwhile we groan, longing to be clothed with our heavenly dwelling, because when we are clothed, we will not be found naked. For while we are in this tent, we groan and are burdened, because we do not wish to be unclothed but to be clothed with our heavenly dwelling, so that what is mortal may be swallowed up by life. Now it is God who has made us for this very purpose and has given us the Spirit as a deposit, guaranteeing what is to come.
> ~2 Corinthians 5:1–5

Home at Last

SGT. LOUIS HORYZA, bound for home after serving his tour of duty in Korea, left Sasebo, Japan, on March 15, 1953, on the troopship *Gen. R. L. Howze*. The passage was not easy:

> Five days out of port we hit a terrific storm during which 90 percent of the troops were sick. The able bodied troops had to help run the ship. After the third day of being sick in my cabin, I went up on deck to get fresh air and to hit the railing to relieve my stomach. To get Dramamine to relieve the seasickness, we had to report to sick bay at the medical center. Sadly, not many could make it that far.[488]

The *Howze* arrived in Puget Sound during the evening of March 24 and anchored in the harbor while waiting for the tide and a berth at the pier. Looking out over the lights of Seattle, Horyza was filled with many different emotions. As he recalled, *"Many of the troops were crying and/or on their knees praying, thanking the Almighty for our safe returns home. I don't think anyone slept that night."*[489]

The next day, after the ship docked at Fort Lawton, everyone debarked, most to process out of the army. Horyza was discharged a few days later and boarded a train with some of his friends, bound for home. Almost two years to the day, he arrived back where he started, in Spokane.

> Homecoming was rather bittersweet. All the gang that we ran with was gone, with a number being killed in Korea. Others had married, so we had to start over making new friends. Going back to work was not easy, either. Fellows asked what it was like over there. We could not answer, because we knew they couldn't comprehend it. We simply responded, "It was pretty bad."
>
> That was it. You were home . . . HOME . . . at last.[490]

As we read about a soldier's homecoming, we think about our own joyful moments of returning after a long absence. We also contemplate the idea of our ultimate home, remembering the words of the apostle Paul:

Therefore we are always confident and know that as long as we are at home in the body we are away from the Lord. We live by faith, not by sight. We are confident, I say, and would prefer to be away from the body and at home with the Lord. So we make it our goal to please him. ~2 Corinthians 5:6–9

Gen. Mark Clark signs the cease fire agreement (US Navy)

AFTER THE CEASE-FIRE

I N ACCORDANCE with the final armistice agreement, prisoners were exchanged at Panmunjom between August and December 1953. More than seventy-five thousand Communist and twelve thousand UN personnel returned to their respective sides. Prisoners who had decided against repatriation were sent to a temporary camp administered by a five-member Neutral Nations Repatriation Commission. There, representatives from each prisoner's government were allowed to conduct interviews. After this process, more than twenty-one thousand Chinese and North Koreans elected to remain in non-Communist countries. The Koreans were allowed to resettle in South Korea, while the Chinese were sent to Taiwan. Three hundred forty-seven UN personnel, including twenty-one Americans, remained on the Communist side.[491] This freedom of choice for repatriated prisoners was an important statement of principle by the free world but was unfortunately paid for dearly with an extra year of fighting.

As the American POWs returned home, stories of Communist atrocities began to surface. The US Congress was flooded with correspondence from servicemen and their families describing the abuse of prisoners on the battlefield and in prison camps. A special Senate subcommittee was convened to hear testimony from servicemen and field commanders with firsthand knowledge. Evidence was documented of mass slayings by North Korean and Chinese officers, especially during UN offensives. Other war crimes were documented, including aggravated assaults, torture, deliberate starvation, and bayoneting.[492] Details of a death march also came to light. In November 1950, a group of seven hundred US soldiers and eighty-seven civilians were force-marched more than one hundred miles in winter weather to Chunggang-jin on the Yalu River. Included among the civilians were Catholic priests, nuns, Protestant missionaries, and Salvation Army officials. More than a hundred died from exposure or were executed during the ordeal.[493]

Since the end of the war, border incidents and clashes have occurred frequently and continue to this day. North Korean infiltrators have crossed the demilitarized zone (DMZ) on numerous occasions individually and in small units, firing on South Korean troops. From 1974 to 1990 four tunnels were discovered under the DMZ for use in planned North Korean invasions.[494] North Korean patrol boats have also provoked clashes at sea. In March 2010, the South Korean ship *Cheonan* exploded and sank, killing forty-five sailors. Evidence points to a torpedo launched from a North Korean submarine.[495] On November 23, 2010, North Koreans fired 175 artillery shells at the South Korean island of Yeonpyeong, killing four people and wounding fifteen others. Most ominously, against all international opposition, North Korea has continued to build nuclear weapons and rocket delivery systems while supposedly under a denuclearization agreement with South Korea. Nuclear devices were detonated in actual tests during 2006 and 2009, resulting in United Nations resolutions condemning the tests and imposing increased sanctions on North Korea.[496]

Veterans returning home from the Korean War found a nation largely indifferent to the conflict. The post-World War II economy was booming, and even enhanced by massive defense expenditures supporting the effort in Korea. Other than the servicemen themselves and their families, most Americans were generally unaffected by events in this far-off and little-understood part of the world. The relief of Gen. Douglas MacArthur by an unpopular president created considerable negative public opinion toward the war. Many agreed with the great military hero that a war ending in stalemate was a failure. In this atmosphere, many veterans came home content to forget about the war and to resume their normal lives.

It would not be until 1985 that scattered groups of veterans would coalesce into a national organization called the Korean War Veterans Association. Bill Norris, a former soldier with the Twenty-Fifth Division, led this effort and chartered the new organization to "maintain and foster the comradeship between the men and women who served . . . and to perpetuate the memory and reason which required our service during the Korean War."[497] In 1995, the Korean War Veterans Memorial was dedicated in Washington, DC. Its main feature is a group of nineteen statues depicting a squad on patrol with representatives from each service. A granite wall bears the simple and poignant message, "Freedom is not free."

Deceivers

PFC. GENE SALAY was wounded and captured when his unit on the front lines was overrun in July 1953. Chinese guards marched him and fifty other prisoners for more than a week into North Korea. One night they stopped at a man-made cave with a high ceiling and a dirt floor covered with several inches of water. The group got little sleep as they huddled together for warmth. Salay described what happened next:

> *In the morning, we were called out of the cave one at a time to be inter-rogated in a tent. After the first one of us was taken out, roughly 20 min-utes passed, and we heard gunfire. He didn't return. Another was taken by the arm, and 20 minutes later, more gunshots. He didn't return. This went on. When it was my turn, I made the sign of the cross and prepared to die.*[498]

Salay was taken into the interrogation tent where he sat before an English-speaking Chinese officer. The interrogator gave him a cigarette, spread out a map, and began asking about the location of US units. To every question Salay responded with his name, rank, and serial number. After this continued for a while, another officer began asking him questions about his home life. The weary soldier answered these questions with a mixture of lies and the truth. Finally, another guard grabbed him again and led him out of the tent. He said,

> *I thought my time was up and made the sign of the cross again. We went around a corner, away from the others still waiting to be queried, and I was surprised to see the guys who had preceded me standing there. As I neared them, a Chinese soldier fired his burp gun into a dirt bank. The interrogation was all a game.*[499]

This may have been a game to those doing the interrogating, but it was deadly serious to the men subjected to it. Sometimes Satan plays games with us, entering our thoughts to rationalize and trivialize our sins. His favorite ploy seems to be convincing us wrongful acts can be corrected later. Satan delights in these games, but they are deadly serious to us. Scripture gives us a clear warning of what to expect:

> Everyone who wants to live a godly life in Christ Jesus will be persecuted, while evil men and impostors will go from bad to worse, deceiving and being deceived. ~2 Timothy 3:12–13

Atonement

(Dept. of Defense)

RAY BAUMBACH could not erase the images of the dead from his memory. While in a North Korean prison camp he witnessed the death of more than three hundred fellow soldiers. When he returned home he was unable to put the experience behind him and turned to alcohol. He was on a downward spiral to self-destruction when God intervened to turn his life around. One day, as he prayed, he became convinced God had a plan for his life. He realized his experience in Korea qualified him uniquely to work with prison inmates. As he put it, *"They see that I am not a phony, but someone who has also been a prisoner."* He also said,

> I guess I'm trying to pay the Lord back for those three hundred prisoners I had to watch being buried when I was captured. So far I have talked to at least three hundred men in prison who have turned their lives around. So I think what I am doing is substituting the men in prison for those American soldiers I saw buried in Korea. I guess I haven't yet completed my obligation.[500]

This man's story reminds us of a word used often in the Bible. *Atonement* means the "covering over" of sin. In Old Testament times the blood of animals was offered in sacrifice to make amends, or atone, for wrongdoing. These sacrifices, however, never took all the sins away or brought permanent forgiveness and so had to be repeated endlessly.

Fortunately, through his Son, Jesus Christ, God has given us a way to not only cover over our sins but to wipe them clean, once and for all.

Day after day every priest stands and performs his religious duties; again and again he offers the same sacrifices, which can never take away sins. But when this priest had offered for all time one sacrifice for sins, he sat down at the right hand of God . . . By one sacrifice he has made perfect forever those who are being made holy. The Holy Spirit also testifies to us about this. First he says: "This is the covenant I will make with them after that time," says the Lord. "I will put my laws in their hearts, and I will write them on their minds." Then he adds: "Their sins and lawless acts I will remember no more." And where these have been forgiven, there is no longer any sacrifice for sin.
~Hebrews 10:11–12, 14–18

Germ Warfare

PFC. JACK CHAPMAN had been wounded and captured near the Chosin Reservoir on November 30, 1950, and held for thirty-two months in North Korean and Chinese prisoner of war camps. In addition to the physical ordeal, the young soldier suffered the mental torment of an unrelenting "education" program. The "lectures" would often go on for six to eight hours and would include readings from Communist newspapers about US war crimes. He wouldn't forget one phrase used over and over, even on posters: *"Your money mad bosses, the Capitalist Warmongers of Wall Street."*[501] Another irritating and oft-repeated accusation was that the Americans were using biological agents, or "germ warfare."

> This is the message we have heard from him and declare to you: God is light; in him there is no darkness at all. If we claim to have fellowship with him yet walk in the darkness, we lie and do not live by the truth.
> ~1 John 1:5–6

To inject a little grim humor into their lives and to agitate their captors, several men took up the germ warfare theme. They made a tiny parachute and drew the US Air Force insignia on it. They attached a dead mouse to the shroud lines and hung it in a tree for the Chinese to find. When a guard did find it, he screamed so loudly the whole camp came out. One guard retrieved the mouse with tongs and placed it in a glass jar that was placed on exhibit. This new evidence of US "germ warfare" was never revealed as an elaborate joke.[502]

The reaction of the Chinese officers to this little scheme reveals an important fact: they believed the propaganda they were putting forth. They were convinced these accusations of germ warfare and warmongering Wall Street capitalists were true. They had been well "educated" themselves and had never heard contradictory views.

The ability to hear all sides of an issue is the essence of the freedom we enjoy as Americans. Thanks to a free press, we do hear contradictory views. We also have the benefit of a standard of truth that no human being can manipulate—God's Word revealed in Scripture. Using this standard, we are able to discern right and wrong and to evaluate our own behavior and our nation's actions in the world.

Being a Friend

ROBERT FLETCHER and Elliott Sortillo were together in a North Korean prisoner of war camp. One was black and one white, but in that place race made no difference. In addition to their shared misery, they were sixteen and seventeen years old, giving them the common bond of youth. Sortillo was shunned by the older soldiers with wives and children back home who seemed to resent his youth and happy-go-lucky attitude. He felt fortunate to strike up one friendship. He and Fletcher would laugh and talk about basketball, football, high school, and girls.

> So neither he who plants nor he who waters is anything, but only God, who makes things grow. The man who plants and the man who waters have one purpose, and each will be rewarded according to his own labor.
> ~1 Corinthians 3:7–8

Many years later the two ex-soldiers met again at a reunion of POWs in Louisville, Kentucky. It was a poignant moment as they hugged each other and realized the depth of their bond. Fletcher described what happened then:

> His (Sortillo's) wife comes over and gives me a kiss and says, "I've been knowing you all my life and I thank you."
> I asked, "For what?"
> She says, "You saved my husband's life."
> I said, "Huh?"
> And Sortillo says, "Yeah, Fletch, I never told you. Before you and I started talking, I was thinking about committing suicide. Those guys didn't want me; they wouldn't talk to me."[503]

Sometimes we don't see the impact of our actions until much later. This story is a great reminder for Christians about the importance of patience and persistence. When we share the gospel, we often don't see the results. It is not normally our job to convert another into a believer at a particular moment. Our role more often is to plant a seed that God will bring to fruition. In God's time we will see the results of our planting and his nurturing. In the present moment we simply need to be the best friend we can be—with patience and persistence.

The Less Fortunate

PVT. SUSUMU SHINAGAWA was among the first prisoners of war released in April 1953. A native of Hawaii, he had also been one of the first American soldiers to see combat in Korea and was wounded twice before his capture in July 1950. Due to the virtual absence of medical treatment, his wounds never completely healed. When guards took him from POW Camp 3 near Chongson, North Korea, with fourteen other men, he found it difficult to

> What good is it, my brothers, if a man claims to have faith but has no deeds? Can such a faith save him? . . . Show me your faith without deeds, and I will show you my faith by what I do.
> ~James 2:14, 18

believe what was happening. Over several days he was given new clothes, good food, and the money taken from him when captured. His growing elation was only tinged by sadness at being separated from his buddies. He never even had a chance to say goodbye to them.

Tears flowed down his cheeks as he walked across the "Bridge of No Return" at Panmunjom and saw the American flag for the first time. He said later, *"It seemed so unreal, yet it was real. I was in a daze and couldn't comprehend the fact that I was no longer a prisoner of war—after thirty-three months and sixteen days."*[504] Soon after, Shinagawa found himself at Hickam Air Force Base in Hawaii, with conflicting thoughts:

> *I'm home. Only a few days before I was in some forsaken place in North Korea. My mind wandered and images of the men still in North Korea floated through my mind. I could see what they were doing. They were going about their hopeless daily routines. It seemed unfair.*[505]

This soldier's compassion for friends so recently left behind in misery is a poignant reminder for us who live comfortable lives. We often find it difficult to identify with the plight of the less fortunate. This is why the charitable work we do is as much for ourselves as it is for them. We leave our self-centeredness behind only when we focus on the needs of others.

Through Christian service we become more Christ-like as we emulate the compassion that characterized the life and death of our Savior.

US POWs released
(National Archives)

Restored to Honor

Cornelius Charlton (US Army)

THE ATTACK on Hill 543 was not going well. A devastating mortar barrage badly wounded the platoon leader and several other men as the rest sought cover. Sgt. Cornelius Charlton sensed the attack was stalling halfway up the hill. Taking command, he sent the casualties back and reorganized the remaining men. Against a hail of small-arms fire and grenades he led the platoon forward into the enemy positions. Wounded painfully in the chest, he refused aid and kept going until he personally destroyed the last key enemy defensive position on the summit. As his men secured the hilltop, a medic finally tried to help him. Unfortunately, it was too late, and the young sergeant died of his wounds.

On March 12, 1952, Van and Esther Charlton accepted the Medal of Honor on behalf of their son, a native of the Bronx. Shortly thereafter, the city of New York named a park for him in his Bronx neighborhood.

Over fifty years later a Vietnam veteran named Robert Gumbs noticed a weed-choked area covered with litter on East 164th Street in the Bronx named Charlton Gardens. He researched the park's history and was amazed to learn about its namesake: *"It was very emotional to find out about him. We found out he was one of two black men to be awarded the highest military honor in Korea."*[506] Gumbs and another veteran, Leroy Archible, worked with city officials to restore the park to its original condition, giving it back its lost dignity. In the process they returned an important American hero to his rightful place of honor.

> The LORD sends poverty and wealth; he humbles and he exalts. He raises the poor from the dust and lifts the needy from the ash heap; he seats them with princes and has them inherit a throne of honor.
> ~1 Samuel 2:7–8

Dulce et Decorum Est

THE ROMAN poet Horace wrote the famous line glorifying war: *"Dulce et decorum est pro patria mori."* Translated, "It is sweet and fitting to die for one's country," and continuing, *"Yet death chases after the soldier who runs, and it won't spare the cowardly back or the limbs, of peace-loving young men."*[507] Horace was a government clerk and part-time poet under Augustus Caesar when he wrote his *Odes*, a classic of Latin literature.

> On this mountain he will destroy the shroud that enfolds all peoples, the sheet that covers all nations; he will swallow up death forever. The Sovereign Lord will wipe away the tears from all faces; he will remove the disgrace of his people from all the earth.
> ~Isaiah 25:7–8

Ironically, Horace's poem served as the basis for one of the most famous anti-war pieces ever written. During World War I the Englishman Wilfred Owen wrote a now-classic poem with the same title as this story. In it he depicted the horrors of trench and gas warfare in vivid detail and closed with the lines:

> *My friend, you would not tell with such high zest*
> *To children ardent for some desperate glory,*
> *The old Lie; Dulce et Decorum est*
> *Pro patria mori.*[508]

Writing about his experience in the Korean War, a Marine officer also reflected on Horace and his own experience with the "glory" of war:

> *Memories grow dim. Even the places where they fought—the Pusan Perimeter, Inchon, Frozen Chosin, the Punch Bowl, Pork Chop Hill and Heartbreak Ridge—are all but forgotten. They were there because their country had ordered them to go there. By the act of their going and the shared tempering in the crucible of war, they were bonded. Remembering the faces of their dead, they carved in their fugitive hearts a secret place where no stranger could intrude.*
> *DULCE ET DECORUM EST PRO PATRIA MORI, as old Horace used to say. But it is not recorded that he did much time on Heartbreak Ridge when the shrapnel hummed like a swarm of bees, and the wounded cried for water.*[509]

As a veteran of another conflict, I also honor my fallen comrades and the cause they fought for—even while understanding fully the high price and ultimate futility of armed conflict. Every combat veteran prays that God will guide us to better ways of solving our disputes.

Duty

WHEN HE was released from captivity in North Korea, Herbert Lord knew his survival and eventual freedom were the result of answered prayer—not only his own, but that of many others. He had stayed in Korea when the North Koreans invaded hoping he would be able to continue the work he had started and somehow help the horde of refugees flooding the countryside. He was asked if he had done the right thing electing to stay even after the fall of Seoul. Lord's thoughtful reply:

> *Comrades of ours had been cut off from the international family of Salvationists for seven years during the war (World War II) until links were re-established in 1946. The reorganization of the work then made wonderful progress, corps were resurrected, homes were again meeting a great need, faith was high for advance and victory . . . When war came again I could not desert the friends who put so much faith in our leadership. There is no alternative to duty.*[510]

My father's favorite quotation was from Robert E. Lee: *"Duty is the sublimest word in the English language." Sublime* used this way means "exalted and awe inspiring." Lee used this word to denote the transcendent nature of our moral obligations or those things we are called to do by virtue of our positions in life. We know what they are. Our duties as a husband, father, employee, and church member are usually clear. It is seldom difficult to know the right thing to do.

Unfortunately, the right thing we are supposed to do is not always the easiest. The apostle Paul wrestled with the dilemma of knowing what to do and not being able to do it. He described a war within himself: *"When I want to do good, evil is right there with me. For in my inner being I delight in God's law; but I see another law at work in the members of my body, waging war against the law of my mind"* (Romans 7:21–23). Realizing his human weakness and inability to do what he knew he should on his own, Paul sought a higher and greater strength:

What a wretched man I am! Who will rescue me from this body of death? Thanks be to God—through Jesus Christ our Lord! ~Romans 7:24–25

Communist soldiers choose freedom (National Archives)

To Look after Orphans

JIM LANDRUM was a minister when he joined the Air Force to serve during the Korean War as a chaplain. As often happens, the Air Force had other plans, assigning him to intelligence duties with a strategic reconnaissance squadron based at Yokota Air Force Base near Tokyo. During his off-duty hours the young airman/minister found many ways to do God's work, involving himself in activities reaching out to the local people. He spoke at a local church, taught English at the high school, and often visited with the students in their homes, sharing meals and getting to know their families.

Jim and Betty Landrum

Every week he also spent time at the Hino Orphanage located high in the mountains near Tokyo. There he found a group of eighty African-American-Japanese orphans who had been abandoned during the post-World War II occupation. A small Japanese staff faithfully attended to the children but were chronically short of every necessity.

Landrum was touched seeing these children running through the snow in bare feet and eating in a room where the windows had no glass to keep out the cold. He and his friends started taking shoes, clothing, and food up the mountain. They bought a wood-burning stove and installed windows in the building. They spent all the time they could with the children. He taught them Scripture and even how to sing "Jesus Loves Me" in Japanese.[511]

After returning to the States, Landrum resumed his career in the ministry and continued to do what he could for the orphans at Hino and elsewhere, speaking frequently to civic and fundraising groups. He continued to collect money for food, clothing, building supplies, and medical care. To this day he is involved with a group that supports more than ten thousand orphans in different Asian countries. Landrum has lived a life energized by a simple but pointed Bible verse:

Religion that God our Father accepts as pure and faultless is this: to look after orphans and widows in their distress and to keep oneself from being polluted by the world. ~James 1:27

Go Home

FOR HIS heroic actions standing by wounded comrades on the night of March 27, 1953, Marine Pfc. Bob Durham was awarded the Silver Star medal. His citation read in part:

> With the action becoming more intense, he fearlessly continued to expose himself to the hostile fire, delivering accurate fire and hurling grenades and, when ordered to withdraw, took up a position at the rear of his unit to cover the evacuation of the many casualties. By his gallant fighting spirit, daring initiative and unswerving devotion to duty, Private First Class Durham served to inspire all who observed him and upheld the highest traditions of the United States Naval Service.[512]

Durham was honored to receive this award, but he knew that his actions were not the result of courage on his part. Without the certain knowledge of the Holy Spirit's presence, he would have run from that deadly scene. He knew in his heart that God had stood with him and preserved him throughout the ordeal. This knowledge filled him with wonder. Why would God have spared him when so many others died? He spent long hours praying about this question and reading his Bible. He finally came to a passage that seemed to be God's answer:

> As Jesus was getting into the boat, the man who had been demon-possessed begged to go with him. Jesus did not let him, but said, "Go home to your family and tell them how much the Lord has done for you, and how he has had mercy on you." ~Mark 5:18–19

"*Yes!*" Durham said as he read this passage. "*Yes, Lord, I will tell them how wonderful You are. How merciful and good You are. I know it wasn't Bob who stood up to the enemy; I know it was You.*"[513] Durham did go home, and he received a hero's welcome. He devoted himself, however, to sharing his witness with all who would listen. He made it his mission to tell family, friends, churches, and civic groups about God's grace on the battlefield.

Regrets

DON CHILDS spent a miserable night in November 1951 shivering in an unheated truck for hours as it crawled slowly over twisted Korean mountain roads. His unit was dropped off in the dark to trek for two more days over rugged terrain before reaching the base of Hill 355. Early the next morning, he and other soldiers made the torturous climb up the hill to reinforce a position that had been hit by a major Chinese attack. At the summit he found a scene he would never forget:

Winter in Korea (USMC)

> *There were dead G.I.s and Chinese soldiers strewn here and there all over the area. To my left was (a dead soldier) sitting with his head bowed, against the hill, in a destroyed bunker. In his jacket pocket was a letter from his mother. His mom was hoping he would soon be home. Oh, how I wish I'd kept that letter!*[514]

When Childs returned to the United States he said his thoughts were continually on that soldier. *"I wanted to get in touch with his parents, to let them know that he did not suffer, as he had died instantly; however, my mind was in no condition to do any research. As the years went by, my condition didn't improve."*[515] Finally, more than fifty years later, a friend in the Veterans Administration helped Childs track down the soldier he had never forgotten. Unfortunately, by that time the parents had passed away, and he was only able to talk to a sister who thanked him for calling.

Each one of us has regrets over lost opportunities. We should have said something, made a phone call, written a letter, or paid a visit. Who knows why we let time go by without doing the things we know we should do? These are the kinds of lapses we pray God will forgive, and he does forgive when we ask. However, a guilty conscience often serves a purpose. Maybe some amount of guilt will motivate us to do better. Or maybe it's still not too late to do what we've neglected for so long. God does forgive us for our sins of omission, but he also expects better of us the next time.

> Let us throw off everything that hinders and the sin that so easily entangles, and let us run with perseverance the race marked out for us. Let us fix our eyes on Jesus, the author and perfecter of our faith.
> ~Hebrews 12:1–2

Sole Survivor

P FC. BOB HAMMOND was with the Seventh Infantry Division when his artillery battery was overrun by Chinese forces east of the Chosin Reservoir and separated from other friendly units. Due to the almost unbearable cold he took his boots off at one point to massage his frostbitten feet. To his frustration, he couldn't get his boots back on and had to fashion shoes from a C-ration box. When it came time to abandon the position in an attempt to reach safety, a sergeant insisted he ride in one of the unit's vehicles. The young soldier protested this order, not wanting to leave his friends. However, the sergeant was adamant that he would only slow down the movement. At that point he was separated from his squad and, unfortunately, would never see them again.

> I pray also for those who will believe in me through their message, that all of them may be one, Father, just as you are in me and I am in you . . . I have given them the glory that you gave me, that they may be one as we are one.
> ~John 17:20–22

Eighteen years later Hammond was in Hawaii on vacation with his wife. They visited the National Memorial Cemetery of the Pacific, referred to locally as the "Punchbowl." They reverently viewed the many gravesites and more than fifty unit monuments. At one point he discovered a section dedicated to those who gave their lives in battle, but *whose final resting place is known only to God.* There he found the names of every man in his squad. He realized their bodies remained where they died, on that frozen battlefield of long ago. He said of that moment, *"I was the sole survivor. My wife patted my back as I leaned against the wall and sobbed. It is never over."*[516]

The idea of losing so many friends at one time is truly heart wrenching. None of us would ever forget such an experience. In thinking about this soldier and his loss, it occurs to me that I know several older people who, due to their longevity, have also lost most of their friends. In their circumstance, they are also becoming sole survivors. Considering this bleak prospect for them and for all of us eventually, I realize more than ever there is only one true comfort and hope: the eternal perspective of God and our place in his heavenly kingdom—where there are no sole survivors—where we will all be one with him.

The Names

JOHNNIE JOHNSON was eighteen-years-old and in Korea only nine days when he was captured near Chochiwon on July 11, 1950. With about six hundred other Twenty-Fourth Division soldiers he began a long forced-march to the rear. When several of the group died from their wounds, he realized most of these soldiers were from different units and didn't know each other. He thought that someone would want to know who they were and when they died. He started a list.

I had a little stub of a pencil, and I wrote these first names down on a piece of paper that I had ripped off the wall. I thought that would be the end of it, and that when we were freed in a month or so I would have this information for their families. I didn't know that I would be a prisoner for another three years and that I would add almost five hundred names.[517]

As Johnson's list grew he had the foresight to make a duplicate copy and to hide it separately. One of his lists was discovered during an inspection, and he was beaten severely for apparently trying to document war crimes. He was warned that he would never be released if he were caught recording names again. When he was finally repatriated in 1953, he courageously smuggled his remaining list out in a toothpaste tube.

Johnson's list of names eventually became the only definitive source of information about the fate of 496 American soldiers, bringing closure to many families who would not have found it otherwise. For his actions he was awarded the Silver Star.

I am the LORD; that is my name! I will not give my glory to another or my praise to idols. ~Isaiah 42:8

Fear not, for I have redeemed you; I have summoned you by name; you are mine. ~Isaiah 43:1

The sheep listen to his voice. He calls his own sheep by name and leads them out. ~John 10:3

Intuitively, this young soldier knew that names are important and should not be forgotten. This concern stems from a very human trait instilled in us by our Creator and emphasized in Scripture. Through his Word God revealed his name and declared to us the importance of our own. He not only created us in his image, but he knows each of us by name.

Old Wounds

Shell hitting bunker (USMC)

JOSEPH ALAIMO fought in Korea during the bitterly cold winter of 1951–52. He never forgot his worst day when an enemy mortar shell collapsed his bunker and buried him under a pile of timbers and sandbags. Recalling his feeling of helplessness, he said, *"I just cried, 'God don't let me die.'"*[518] God answered his prayer as fellow soldiers dug him out of the debris and got him to a hospital.

Many years later, Alaimo still suffered the effects of his wounds. He could feel the sting of frostbite in his feet and loss of hearing from too many explosions. Worst of all were back problems from the attack that collapsed his bunker and nearly killed him. Weeks in a hospital did not cure a nagging discomfort. He said, *"It stays with you all the time."*[519] Although God answered this young soldier's prayer, and he survived to return home, in a sense he never left Korea. His wounds ensured he would not forget.

The apostle Paul was also plagued with a wound that constantly irritated him. We don't know what it was, but we know he pleaded with God to take it away. He finally had to accept the fact that his discomfort had a purpose.

When our wounds remind us of our weakness and our complete dependence on our Savior, they are in fact a blessing. Illness, injury, aches, and pains are not pleasant, but they can serve a transcendent purpose. They can take us to a higher spiritual level—to a life centered on God's grace and the peace that comes when we finally get outside ourselves.

> To keep me from becoming conceited because of these surpassingly great revelations, there was given me a thorn in my flesh, a messenger of Satan, to torment me. Three times I pleaded with the Lord to take it away from me. But he said to me, "My grace is sufficient for you, for my power is made perfect in weakness." Therefore I will boast all the more gladly about my weaknesses, so that Christ's power may rest on me.
> ~2 Corinthians 12:7–9

Father Saves Son

RANDOLPH RABENOLD landed in the second wave at Inchon and fought with the First Marine Division in the advance to Seoul. His unit reached Kimpo Airfield in late September 1950, where he was awakened one night by another Marine who said to him, *"Wake up, Corporal. Your father has died, and you're going back to the States."*[520]

By the time the young Marine made his way home to Pennsylvania, with stops in Midway, Hawaii, and San Diego, he arrived too late for his father's funeral. All he could do at that point was spend time with his family and friends. Too soon, the cable arrived ordering him to report to San Diego for further transport by ship back to the war.

> Now we see but a poor reflection as in a mirror; then we shall see face to face. Now I know in part; then I shall know fully, even as I am fully known.
> ~1 Corinthians 13:12

While at sea, Rabenold learned that First Division was fighting near the Chosin Reservoir and was surrounded by Chinese forces. Before reaching Korea, however, he learned that the Marines had fought their way out. When he eventually rejoined his unit, Rabenold realized he had missed the most brutal combat of the war. His emergency leave had coincided exactly with the Chosin Reservoir campaign.

At the time, his father's death was a tragedy to this young man and his family. Later, however, he came to see this event from a different perspective. After he returned home he attended college. He married, had five children, and served a long and distinguished career as a teacher. Rabenold gradually became convinced his father had saved his life.

It is not always easy to understand God's purpose or his role in our lives. Often it becomes clear only when we look back. In retrospect, we can see how we have changed and what has happened to bring about that change. In my own life, I look back and see God's hand in every important decision and event. I am convinced he has indeed saved my life and shaped it according to his own purpose—just as he did that of a young soldier who missed a battle and survived the Korean War.

The World Is Waiting

DR. CHARLES MALIK was a famous philosopher and diplomat who served as Lebanese ambassador to the United States during the Korean War and later as the President of the General Assembly of the United Nations. He studied under Alfred North Whitehead and Martin Heidegger, earning his Ph.D. in philosophy from Harvard University. He was also a dedicated Christian who described his own conversion by saying, "*I came to know Christ directly in my life, forgiving my sins, strengthening me in trials when everything was dark and repulsive and when terrible loneliness and deep darkness were all around.*"[521]

> Therefore God exalted him to the highest place and gave him the name that is above every name, that at the name of Jesus every knee should bow, in heaven and on earth and under the earth, and every tongue confess that Jesus Christ is Lord.
> ~Philippians 2:9–11

In 1953, Dr. Malik gave an address to students at Boston University that was published in the *Navy Chaplains Bulletin* to stimulate thought and discussion within the military community:

> *The world is waiting to be told authoritatively—not by words only but by incarnate being—that there is real objective truth; that this truth is absolutely certain and dependable; that there is no cosmic joke played upon us, but that we are by nature perfectly able to know and abide by this truth.*
>
> *The world is waiting to be told authoritatively—not by words only but by incarnate being—that over and above every determinism the mind can still say "no" to error and tyranny; that in this act of freedom of thought and decision lies man's highest dignity.*
>
> *The world is waiting to be told authoritatively—not by words only but by incarnate being—that through love, fellowship, and faith the humblest tasks can be transfigured into a sacrament; that there is no joy and no peace which can compare with the joy and peace of him who is understood and forgiven; that evil, darkness, rebellion can be overcome with good.*[522]

Dr. Malik was telling his audience simply that the world is waiting for the gospel of Jesus Christ. Jesus is the Incarnation of God's authority, truth, and love in the world, bringing an eternal blessing to those who hear him and receive him into their hearts.

America's Challenge

IN JANUARY 1953, Brig. Gen. Wilbur Brown spoke prophetically to a group of Navy chaplains about the challenge of international Communism and the spiritual state of America:

President Truman made a true statement when he said that communism could only flourish where there is hunger, privation and despair. We have very little material hunger, privation and despair in America, and almost none in the Marine Corps. But we do have spiritual and psychological hunger, privation and despair throughout America, and the enemy within our gates are trading heavily upon it.

Marxist communism, as professed by the Russians and the International Commintern, categorically denies the existence of a Deity, either Christian, Jewish, Buddhist or Moslem. It is the arch enemy and implacable foe of Christianity. Karl Marx has stated the following which I quote from Das Kapital, "The democratic concept of man is false because it is Christian. The democratic system holds that each man is a sovereign being. This is a delusion, the dream of Christianity." It is all very clear. Communism wants to bring all men down to one level by class warfare. Christianity means to lift all men up to a higher level by brotherhood.

For the past hundred years of history, the so-called Christian nations have been undermining their own faith to their infinite harm. Atheism, agnosticism, materialism, cynicism, and good-natured or caustic contempt for all religion have created throughout Europe and America a spiritual slough of despond in which we are wallowing.[523]

> Those who are led by the Spirit of God are sons of God . . . Now if we are children, then we are heirs—heirs of God and co-heirs with Christ, if indeed we share in his sufferings in order that we may also share in his glory. ~Romans 8:14, 17

Today the overt threat of Communism has waned. Nevertheless, the same forces seem still at work in our nation. The progressive movement in our politics urges Americans toward ever more all-caring and all-powerful government, and a small, but growing, corps of atheists challenges every public expression of religious belief. These forces combine to erode the foundation of our spiritual heritage based on the God-given dignity of the individual human being as articulated in our Declaration of Independence. Our nation is founded on the bedrock belief that human beings' rights come from our Creator, not from government officials.

Similar to Me

LOU HARMIN went to Korea in April 1953 at age nineteen and was assigned to the Twenty-Fourth Infantry Division as a personnel clerk. Three months later, just before the end of the war, his unit was shipped to Cheju Island (Cheju-do) to guard a prisoner of war camp where mostly anti-Communist Chinese soldiers were being held. These prisoners had indicated a preference for release to Taiwan when the war

> If you greet only your brothers, what are you doing more than others? Do not even pagans do that? Be perfect, therefore, as your heavenly Father is perfect.
> ~Matthew 5:47–48

ended, and many had tattooed themselves with anti-Communist slogans and free-China flags. Harmin had some interesting observations about these men:

North Korean and Chinese prisoners (National Archives)

Each morning, a detail of two Americans would go to the camps and escort ten prisoners back to the American camp. There, the prisoners served as workers during the day. I did several escorts. Two of us would take the bullets out of our rifles and then walk the ten prisoners to our camp. We then put the rifles against the tents, and the prisoners worked as cleaners, cooks, or in some other job where they were needed. One fellow would set up his barber shop, and I had many a haircut from him. The prisoners were nice young men, very similar to me.[524]

It was unusual that a soldier in a war zone would develop such amicable relationships with enemy prisoners. His experience, however, should inspire us to reconsider some of our own animosities. There are people we dislike, either for good reason or no reason at all. They may have been rude to us in the past, or they may have mannerisms that irritate us. When circumstances put us together with these people, and we get to know them better, we usually find to our surprise they are very likeable. Christians shouldn't wait for this to happen accidentally; it should instead be an intentional process. Getting along with friends takes little effort. It does take effort to reach out to those we don't like. There is a saying often used by Christians, reminding us that we are each called to, *"Make a friend, be a friend, and bring a friend to Christ."*

PTSD

RALPH FLY saw a lot during his time as a Navy corpsman with combat Marines in Korea, and returned a different person. Even though being at home should have been the happiest time in his life, he suffered recurring periods of extreme sadness. Gradually, he was able to outwardly adjust to his new life as he successfully started a family and career. He developed ways to cope with his mood swings and to control his emotions. On rare occasions, however, angry outbursts occurred to hurt the ones he loved. He had a problem that would not go away, and it would take almost twenty years to discover the cause.

In the early 1970s the Vietnam War was in progress, and the term Post Traumatic Stress Disorder (PTSD) began appearing in newspaper and television stories. Fly was amazed when he listened to the symptoms of returning Vietnam veterans and realized they were the same as his. He finally understood that he had many suppressed emotions trying to surface. Over time, as he dealt with these emotions, he considered the loss of his best friend in Korea:

> I think that is one reason why it took me so long to find inner peace. I lost the person I needed the most at that time, and I blamed myself. I felt that I didn't try hard enough to save his life when, in fact, I was powerless. There were just many serious wounds. It took so long to find peace because I was not ready to forgive myself.[525]

PTSD continues to be a problem for many veterans. It seems to be similar to alcoholism in that the person suffering from it is the last to know. Combat veterans with symptoms of anger, guilt, or depression should seek help in dealing with feelings suppressed during stressful times. This kind of emotional help can be lifesaving.

There is also a source of spiritual help for anyone so afflicted. Reconciliation to God through his Son, Jesus Christ, is the one sure way to truly purge repressed emotions, find forgiveness, and restore lasting peace to a troubled heart.

> For God was pleased to have all his fullness dwell in him, and through him to reconcile to himself all things, whether things on earth or things in heaven, by making peace through his blood, shed on the cross.
> ~Colossians 1:19–20

A Man of God

CARL SITTER retired to Richmond, Virginia, in 1970 as one of the most decorated Marines in history, with a Medal of Honor, Silver Star, and four Purple Hearts earned in two wars. He started a second career with the Virginia Department of Social Services and served part time as a lay minister in his Methodist Church, striving to continue a life of service to God and his fellow man. He never took himself or his "hero" status too seriously and concerned himself instead with the needs of others.

> To the weak I became weak, to win the weak. I have become all things to all men so that by all possible means I might save some. I do all this for the sake of the gospel, that I may share in its blessings.
> ~1 Corinthians 9:22–23

In 1998, at age seventy-five, Sitter resolved to turn a lifelong interest into a total commitment—and entered Union Theological Seminary to prepare himself for full-time ministry. He said, *"I guess that's why I'm going back to school, to learn more about the Lord and to use that knowledge to help all people. God says we're to love everybody."*[526] Seeing him in class with younger students, a friend wrote:

> *A closer look at the aspiring minister reflects many differences between the man and his fellow students. The wrinkles in his face reflect the character of a man who has been to Hell and back. The hair is grayer, the posture stooped, the demeanor more that of a kindly old grandfather than a giddy, young college student. But one look in his eyes reveals the soul of the man, a man who deeply loves God, cares about others, and desires with all that is within him to serve others. Thus one can finally conclude, this man really ISN'T any different than the idealistic young people with whom he attends class.*[527]

People also wondered how a man could change to such an extent—from a man of war to a man of peace, from a leader of Marines to a gentle shepherd. Those who knew him knew he had not changed at all. In both roles he was the same great man—a man with a powerful sense of duty toward other people and God. Sitter passed away in April 2000, one month before graduating seminary. Up to the very end he was striving toward his third career and new opportunities to serve. Few have given such an example of faith and courage in one lifetime.

The Parade

Eisenhower Inaugural Parade (Truman Library)

ON JANUARY 12, 1953, President-elect Dwight Eisenhower met with his future cabinet and White House advisors at the Hotel Commodore in New York City. The group assembled there to discuss many of the weighty issues that would soon be their responsibility. The Korean War was in its thirty-first month with peace negotiations stalled. A large budget deficit loomed for the fiscal year. When the discussion turned to Inauguration Day itself, the new president showed a particular interest in one event, which he returned to several times—the Inaugural Parade. Concerned that a delayed start might cause hardship on participants, he said:

> *Speaking as one who has marched in one of the blankety–blank things and had to wait an hour on Pennsylvania Avenue while someone went up to lunch, I would very much like to help out several thousand people who will be waiting in the cold. If that Congressional Committee can seat us quickly, I don't see why we can't have a bite to eat in fifteen minutes, because the poor devils who march in that parade are going to have nothing to eat at all.*[528]

Reading President Eisenhower's comments has stirred my memories of another parade that took place eight years later. In 1961, I marched with a contingent from The Citadel in honor of John F. Kennedy's inauguration. It was a windy and bitterly cold day with freshly-plowed snow banks lining the streets. We stood in the cold and waited and waited. It was dark when we finally passed in review before the President's pavilion at the White House. All told, it was one of those great experiences made more vivid by the suffering that went with it.

There is probably no way to alleviate all the suffering that goes with this event. Still, it is gratifying to see a great general and president remembering his own experience and showing compassion for those literally following in his footsteps. This kind of thoughtfulness has always been the hallmark of a great leader.

Jesus called them together and said, "You know that the rulers of the Gentiles lord it over them, and their high officials exercise authority over them. Not so with you. Instead, whoever wants to become great among you must be your servant."

~Matthew 20:25–26

Inaugural Prayer

Pres. Eisenhower
(National
Archives)

PRESIDENT-ELECT Dwight Eisenhower and his family began the day of his inauguration by attending church services at the National Presbyterian Church in Washington, where many previous presidents had worshipped. The cabinet and their families were also in attendance. After the service he gave some thought to the upcoming swearing-in ceremony and his inaugural address, which he and his advisors had already given a lot of polishing. Then, in a quiet moment on a couch in his hotel suite he attended to one final task he wanted to do personally. He composed a simple but memorable prayer to go before his formal address:

My friends before I begin the expression of those thoughts that I deem appropriate to this moment, would you permit me the privilege of uttering a little private prayer of my own. And I ask that you bow your heads.

Almighty God, as we stand here at this moment my future associates in the executive branch of government join me in beseeching that Thou will make full and complete our dedication to the service of the people in this throng, and their fellow citizens everywhere.

Give us, we pray, the power to discern clearly right from wrong, and allow all our words and actions to be governed thereby, and by the laws of this land. Especially we pray that our concern shall be for all the people regardless of station, race or calling.

May cooperation be permitted and be the mutual aim of those who, under the concepts of our Constitution, hold differing political faiths; so that all may work for the good of our beloved country and Thy glory. Amen.[529]

Eisenhower's First Inaugural Address was a well-polished expression of America's ideals and hopes for the future. It is best remembered, however, for a plain-spoken expression of faith by a humble and God-fearing man.

> Surely this great nation is a wise and understanding people. What other nation is so great as to have their gods near them the way the Lord our God is near us whenever we pray to him?
> ~Deuteronomy 4:6–7

Oath of Office

JANUARY 20, 1953, was a cloudy day in Washington, DC, with a high of forty-nine degrees. Shortly before 12:30 p.m., when President-elect Dwight Eisenhower would step forward to be sworn in, the clouds receded and the sun came out. As Eisenhower stood on the left side of the podium, Chief Justice Fred Vinson faced him from the right to administer the Oath of Office prescribed in Article II, Section 1, of the Constitution. The voices of both men rang out over the public address system, as the oath was stated and repeated:

Swearing In (Library of Congress)

> *I, Dwight D. Eisenhower, do solemnly swear . . .*
> *That I will faithfully execute the office of President of the United States . . .*
> *And will, to the best of my ability, preserve, protect, and defend the Constitution of the United States . . .*
> *So help me God.*

The final words of the oath are not prescribed by the Constitution, but are said to have been added by George Washington.

As Eisenhower repeated the oath, he laid his left hand on two Bibles.[530] One was the historic Washington Inaugural Bible, used by George Washington in his inauguration, opened to a psalm:

> Except the LORD build the house, they labor in vain that build it: except the LORD keep the city, the watchman waketh but in vain. ~Psalm 127:1 (KJV)

The other Bible belonged to the President and was given him by his mother when he graduated West Point. It was opened to a passage from Second Chronicles:

> If my people, which are called by my name, shall humble themselves, and pray, and seek my face, and turn from their wicked ways; then will I hear from heaven, and will forgive their sin, and will heal their land.
> ~2 Chronicles 7:14 (KJV)

Watering the Seed

CPL. WALT HISKETT was recovering in Japan after his evacuation from Hagaru-ri on December 7, 1950. Only a few days before, when his situation at Toktong Pass seemed hopeless, he had prayed fervently for God's protection and had made a promise about what he would do if God answered him. Already, that promise seemed to fade with his return to safety and comfort. However, he went to a church service one day held by a chaplain named Jim Reeves, who delivered a pointed message, amazingly appropriate for Hiskett to hear:

> *You know, you guys, when the chips are down and the going is rough and everything looks like it's pretty bleak, you have a tendency to make a lot of promises to God. You get back here and you're on clean sheets, eating hot food, your wounds are healing—you have a tendency to forget about those promises.*[531]

Hiskett later described the effect of this message: *"That kind of set the hook in me."*[532] He returned home to Chicago, and, with the help of others, finished high school, college, and seminary—embarking on a lifetime career as a Navy chaplain.

When we share God's Word with someone, we shouldn't necessarily expect to see an immediate result. It is usually our job to plant a seed, which others or God himself will water and bring to fruition in due course. Sometimes, our words will water the seed someone else has planted. Reeves' little homily spoken in a wartime chapel may have fallen on many deaf ears, but for one man it was the key to a life-changing decision. Never be discouraged that words spoken to someone else in faith will be wasted. They may be the key that God wants to use in unlocking a closed door. Our only reward may be a future glimpse of his completed handiwork.

> I planted the seed, Apollos watered it, but God made it grow. So neither he who plants nor he who waters is anything, but only God, who makes things grow. The man who plants and the man who waters have one purpose, and each will be rewarded according to his own labor. For we are God's fellow workers. ~1 Corinthians 3:6–9

Reunion

IN 2006, the men of Fox Company, Second Battalion, Seventh Marines, held a reunion in Quantico, Virginia, in conjunction with the dedication of the Marine Corps Museum. There they were able to see a featured exhibit depicting their own heroic stand at Toktong Pass during the Korean War. A year later, the group assembled again in Orlando, Florida, for a memorial service honoring comrades who fell during the epic battle. The service was led by one of their own, the Reverend Walt Hiskett. Following through on a pledge made during that same battle, Hiskett had returned home from the Korean War and become a minister—continuing his military career as a navy chaplain.

> He humbled himself and became obedient to death—even death on a cross! Therefore God exalted him to the highest place and gave him the name that is above every name.
> ~Philippians 2:8–9

Speaking to the survivors and their wives, the chaplain related the Old Testament story of Gideon and his three hundred soldiers as they prepared to do battle against overwhelming odds:

> *Gideon was tasked by God to organize an army to rout the Midianites and Amalekites in order to restore peace to the people of Israel. Not unlike the task given to the Marine Corps when the North Koreans swooped down across the 38th Parallel in June of 1950—we were tasked to restore peace.*
>
> *We are here today because when we were faced with overwhelming odds, we fought, and many died, not just for self-survival, but for our Corps and for one another. We commemorate the memory of our heroic dead. They were the life, the spirit, and soul of our Corps. We will not, nor can we ever, forget the lessons they taught us about honor and faithfulness.*
>
> *We are the Marine Corps, and Semper Fidelis is our motto. Always faithful. That was the spirit of the Marines we honor here today. We are here today because they made the sacrifice then. They will live on forever in our hearts and minds because we are part of them and they are a part of us.*[533]

Hiskett was speaking for the survivors of every war who remember comrades who didn't come home. May these heroes rest in peace in the presence of a Savior who understands sacrifice more fully than any man who ever lived.

Korean War Memorial (National Archives)

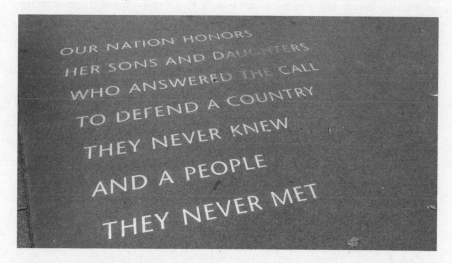

OUR NATION HONORS
HER SONS AND DAUGHTERS
WHO ANSWERED THE CALL
TO DEFEND A COUNTRY
THEY NEVER KNEW
AND A PEOPLE
THEY NEVER MET

Inscription at Korean War Memorial

Building Bridges

EARLY IN HIS career Chris Vaia did three tours in the Vietnam War, in which he earned the Silver Star, Bronze Star, and Purple Heart. Later he was assigned to an infantry regiment on the demilitarized zone in Korea, where he met and married Su Y. He was a sergeant major when he retired from the army with thirty years' service. After retiring, he and Su Y. moved back to Korea to live.

> For if, when we were God's enemies, we were reconciled to him through the death of his Son, how much more, having been reconciled, shall we be saved through his life!
> ~Romans 5:10

In 1991 the Vaias' thirteen-year-old daughter Jeni died tragically in Japan from a fatal asthma attack. The young girl was so well loved that her school built an International Friendship Bridge in her memory. Using the bridge as a symbol to honor the life of his daughter, Vaia founded an organization in Korea called "Bridgebuilders 46." His aim was to build relationship "bridges" among the Korean, American, and Japanese communities. His organization develops friendships through service projects in nursing homes, orphanages, and veterans' hospitals. He has a simple message: *"Any group or individual that feels they are up against hopelessness, fear, maybe even anger and despair, there is hope."*[534] Concerning the name of his organization, he said, *"I use the symbol of a bridge, which highlights the importance of its supports to build up relationships and its arch to restore broken or strained relationships."*[535]

The image of a bridge spanning a gap became an important symbol in Vaia's life and work. This image is also a perfect metaphor for the human condition. There is a chasm between us and God we would never be able to cross on our own. As fallen and imperfect human beings, we could never make ourselves good enough to be acceptable to him. The only way across that chasm is the bridge he himself has provided: his Son, our Savior, Jesus Christ.

Freedom

LORAN STUTZ served with the Seventh Infantry Division during the Korean War and saw combat on Pork Chop Hill and other, unnamed battlefields. In 2010, he returned to Korea with a group of other veterans and his son, Doug, a West Point graduate. Loran described the event as *"a most memorable and mind-altering trip."* He added, *"It's a great way to really understand the Korean culture."*[536]

Doug learned a lot about the nation his father fought for, but, more importantly to him, he learned something about his father as well:

Korean War Memorial
Poster (National Archives)

> As I watched [the veterans], you could tell this trip was a validation that their sacrifice and the sacrifice of their buddies who did not come back was worth it.
>
> They had done one of the best things anyone could do for another— put your life on the line to give another human being a chance to be free. These men and women were heroes and finally received the recognition they deserved.
>
> I went to Korea with my dad. I came home with a hero. This trip was a reminder to all that freedom is not free.[537]

Jesus replied, "I tell you the truth, everyone who sins is a slave to sin. Now a slave has no permanent place in the family, but a son belongs to it forever. So if the Son sets you free, you will be free indeed." ~John 8:34–36

Combat

STUDENTS OF history generally concede that the Korean War was a success from the viewpoint of South Korea and the nations who fought for its defense. A small, third-world nation was given a chance to determine its own future, to eventually choose democracy, and to become a shining light of progress to the rest of the world. The soldiers who did the fighting, however, seldom had this perspective at the time or such an exalted view of the combat they experienced. A veteran eloquently described the soldier's perspective:

> *I have memories. I remember long beastly cold nights on watch fighting to stay awake, so cold you thought you would never be warm again. I remember during the monsoon season being constantly soaked, of being ankle deep in mud, being so tired you fall asleep on your feet. I remember being lost on patrol and not being able to find your way back to your line until daylight. Of being pinned down by automatic weapons fire when it is just you and your God. Or being pinned in your foxhole during a mortar barrage, wondering if one is going to come in the hole with you, and you pray and curse at the same time. I remember the screams of the wounded and dying.*[538]

Any soldier's outlook on combat is obviously going to be vastly different from that of a historian. Similarly, as we live our daily lives, we also lack the historian's perspective on the long-range consequences of our actions. If we could see our lives and those of our family members in their entirety, our actions in the present might be very different. A wise man has pointed out that, looking back, very few people wish they had worked harder or longer at their careers. Most wish they had spent more time and built stronger relationships with their children. Many would treat their spouses in a totally different way if they could see the effects that arguments and abuse would eventually have on their families and future generations. When we are in the trenches of everyday life, it is important to occasionally take a historian's view of what we are doing. What are the long-range consequences? What is God's perspective?

> I consider that our present sufferings are not worth comparing with the glory that will be revealed in us. The creation waits in eager expectation for the sons of God to be revealed.
> ~Romans 8:18–19

Gratitude

Ernie Ardente

ERNIE ARDENTE was drafted in 1952 and served in Korea with the 780th Field Artillery Battalion. Before his tour was complete he rose to the rank of staff sergeant and earned the Bronze Star for his combat service. In 1954, he was discharged, returned to his home in Providence, Rhode Island, and married his childhood sweetheart, Marilyn. Together, they ran a successful supply business and raised four children.

Fifty years later, as a veteran of the "Forgotten War," Ernie received a touching letter from the president of the Republic of Korea:

On the occasion of the 50th anniversary of the outbreak of the Korean War, I would like to offer you my deepest gratitude for your noble contribution to the efforts to safeguard the Republic of Korea and uphold liberal democracy around the world. At the same time, I remember with endless respect and affection those who sacrificed their lives for that cause.

We Koreans hold dear in our hearts the conviction, courage and spirit of sacrifice shown to us by such selfless friends as you, who enabled us to remain a free democratic nation.

Half a century after the Korean War, we honor you and reaffirm our friendship, which helped to forge the blood alliance between our two countries. And we resolve once again to work with all friendly nations for the good of humankind and peace in the world.

I thank you once again for your noble sacrifice, and pray for your health and happiness.

Sincerely yours,
Kim Doe-jung
President of the Republic of Korea[539]

Ardente and thousands of other veterans served honorably in Korea and then went on with their lives. They and their loved ones were touched by this reminder from the past and message of gratitude from a nation that owed its survival to their sacrifice.

> Be strong and courageous. Do not be afraid or terrified because of them, for the LORD your God goes with you; he will never leave you nor forsake you.
> ~Deuteronomy 31:6

An Advent Message

IN THE PAPERS of Korean War Chaplain Emil Kapaun, there is an Advent message he prepared in anticipation of the Christmas season. It was his purpose to explain why Christmas is not just the celebration of a historical event. We do remember Jesus' birth, but we are also called to anticipate his coming again. Although he will come in the end with power and majesty to judge the world, we also look forward at Christmas to a much more imminent return. In this season we can strengthen and renew our relationship with Jesus by opening our hearts to him now. Kapaun's message stressed this personal coming of Christ and how we are to prepare for it:

> A voice of one calling: "In the desert prepare the way for the LORD; make straight in the wilderness a highway for our God. Every valley shall be raised up, every mountain and hill made low; the rough ground shall become level, the rugged places a plain. And the glory of the LORD will be revealed, and all mankind together will see it. For the mouth of the LORD has spoken."
> ~Isaiah 40:3–5

It is clear that besides the first historical coming of Christ there is a second coming that takes place every year in the Christmas mysteries. In what does this second coming consist? Obviously Christ cannot be born again in the flesh. This second coming we experience at Christmas is one in which Christ is reborn in our souls through grace. And this coming of Christ through grace is just as real, just as actual as his birth in flesh centuries ago. It is a new birth of Christ in us in the sense that . . . we are more closely united to him and become more and more like unto him.

Our task during Advent, therefore, is to prepare our souls for this second coming of Christ at Christmas so that it may produce abundant fruit in our spiritual life. Our best guide is none other than St. John the Baptist, the precursor of the Savior's first coming. "Prepare ye the way of the Lord, make straight his paths" (Matthew 3:3).

If we have prepared the way as best we can, Christ will enter our souls at Christmas as a mighty Redeemer and King. The Orientals prepared for the coming of their king by leveling hills, straightening roads, beautifying the route of his journey. Christ the King is coming into the kingdom of our soul. We prepare for this coming by prayer, almsgiving and penance. Thus we straighten our lives, we level the hills of sin and attachment thereto which have risen in the past and which mar the original beauty of our soul received at Baptism.

With expectancy and deep humility we await him who is to come.[540]

Korean War Veterans (National Archives)

Skyline of present day Seoul

MODERN KOREA

THE END of the Korean War was not the end of difficulty for either of the Koreas. North Korea began a downward economic spiral under the dictatorial rule of Kim Il Sung and his heirs that has not abated. Even though the hydroelectric power and natural resources of North Korea made it the industrial center of Korea before the war, decades of Communist control have led to stagnation and decline. As precious resources have been poured into military hardware and nuclear programs, the country has become more and more impoverished and isolated.

As a free society, South Korea has experienced a different problem: Political turmoil has plagued the rapidly developing nation. Syngman Rhee's popularly-elected government became more and more repressive until widespread demonstrations brought it down in 1960. Gen. Park Chung-hee seized power in 1961, beginning a period of military rule that lasted almost sixteen years. Finally, democratic government returned to South Korea in 1987 with the election of Roh Tae-woo to the presidency, and, since then, a series of popularly elected governments have kept the nation on the path of liberal democracy and growing prosperity.

South Korea's impressive economic gains have placed it among the world's most developed industrial countries, ranking third in Eastern Asia after Japan and China, and eleventh in the world.[541] Automobile, electronics, shipbuilding, and other manufacturing make up more than 40 percent of the gross domestic product. Its growth in per capita output since the early 1960s has been exceeded by few other countries.[542] Ever-larger portions of the population have benefitted from this rising prosperity.

The growth of Christianity in modern South Korea has been equally rapid and to many even miraculous. From modest beginnings, the Christian community in the Republic of Korea has grown to more than twelve million, or one-third of the population. The capital, Seoul, boasts ten of the eleven largest Christian congregations in the world.[543] In fifty years, the Yoido Full Gospel Church has grown from five people to a membership of 750,000. On a typical Sunday, more than two hundred thousand worshippers attend seven services in the stadium-sized church. The minister vows, "Sooner or later Christianity will be the major religion in Korea."[544]

This phenomenon traces its origins to the early twentieth century and Japanese colonialism. During those years the early missionaries and Christians identified strongly with the Korean independence movement and worked with the resistance. The gospel message struck a chord from the beginning with downtrodden people seeking freedom from oppression. The early missionaries also focused much of their effort on education, building schools, and improving the literacy rate throughout the country. Since the earliest Christians in the country were Korean themselves, indigenous leadership and self-reliance have also been important aspects of spiritual growth.

An amazing by-product of the growth of Christianity within Korea has been the upsurge in missionary activity outside the country. In 1980 there were fewer than one hundred South Korean missionaries worldwide—there are now an estimated twenty thousand, more than from any other nation except the United States.[545] As of 2006, South Korea was sending 1,100 new missionaries abroad annually, more than any nation.[546] Korean missionaries have gained acceptance in many areas of Asia and the Middle East resistant to western influence. More than 40 percent are now working throughout Asia, many in Muslim countries.[547] The Korean World Mission Association has an even more ambitious long-range plan of sending one hundred thousand missionaries abroad by 2030.[548]

South Korea's amazing story since the end of the Korean War should be a source of great pride for the servicemen and women who made it possible. The so-called "Forgotten War" ended in frustration and controversy as America's first war "not won." Reunification of North and South Korea and complete victory were not attained. However, the freedom of South Korea was restored and guaranteed for the future. On the fiftieth anniversary of the outbreak of the war, Kim Doe-jung, the President of the Republic of Korea wrote to all veterans of the conflict:

> We Koreans hold dear in our hearts the conviction, courage and spirit of sacrifice shown to us by such selfless friends as you, who enabled us to remain a free democratic nation. I thank you . . . for your noble sacrifice, and pray for your health and happiness.[549]

Balloon Offensive

SENDING BALLOONS over North Korea might seem whimsical to some but is a matter of life and death to a small group of South Korean Christians. Faced with a totally closed society that bars their entrance, this is one way they have found to share the lifesaving gospel with their brothers and sisters to the north. They call it Operation Dandelion after the little plant that spreads its seeds with the help of the wind.

Since 1991, an elderly woman named Oh Mo Duk and others living in Seoul have been carrying out their balloon ministry as often as the winds are right. They work in their homes printing biblical messages in Korean on bright orange balloons. Then, travelling by van as close as possible to the demilitarized zone, they fill the balloons with helium and prayerfully send them north. One of the activist South Korean believers said,

By sending these balloons, we let our North Korean brothers and sisters know that we are praying for them, and the scriptures on the balloons are meant to encourage them. This is not the most sophisticated or high-tech method, but when you are dealing with a country that is restricted, very secretive, and punishes its citizens, we have to try something to get hope to them.[550]

Placing his hands on Saul, he said, "Brother Saul, the Lord—Jesus, who appeared to you on the road as you were coming here—has sent me so that you may see again and be filled with the Holy Spirit."
~Acts 9:17

These balloons are a novel but practical means of sharing the gospel, but they are also very symbolic of the gospel message itself. I recently heard J. D. Greear, pastor of the Summit Church in Durham, North Carolina, contrast the difference between air-filled and helium-filled balloons. Those filled with air go up only if constantly pushed, which he compared to our lives when focused on obeying God's law—lives filled with constant effort to make ourselves worthy in his sight. With Jesus, however, our lives are like the balloons filled with helium—lifted weightlessly by a power greater than ourselves. Jesus makes us worthy before God with no effort on our part and fills our hearts with the desire to do good works for him—even sending balloons aloft for others.

Crossing the River

UPON HER release after six years in a North Korean prison, Soon Ok Lee was a totally disillusioned person. Her son had been dropped from school and her husband imprisoned because of her "crimes." She began to secretly listen to radio broadcasts from South Korea, where she heard Christian programs explaining God's love and providence, and how true freedom could be found only in him. She could feel a spiritual awakening within herself as she planned her escape from North Korea.

> Moses answered the people, "Do not be afraid. Stand firm and you will see the deliverance the LORD will bring you today . . . The LORD will fight for you."
> ~Exodus 14:13–14

In February 1994, Soon Ok Lee and her son walked all night across barren terrain, crossing the frozen Tumen River into China. A two-year odyssey took them through China to Hong Kong and, finally, to South Korea. Along the way they were helped by many people, especially one Christian couple in Heilongjiang Province, China, who not only gave them food and clothing but prayed every day for their safe journey to South Korea. They also prayed fervently that Soon Ok and her son would become children of God themselves. A powerful feeling began to come over Soon Ok that God had delivered her from prison and was protecting her during the long ordeal of their journey.

In 1995, Soon Ok and her son finally arrived in South Korea, where she was debriefed by a friendly government official who told her about his church and gave her a book she had never seen before—the Bible. As she began reading this new book she came to the story in Exodus of the Israelites fleeing oppression in Egypt. She was overcome with the conviction that God had brought her to freedom as well. She said, *"Every time I read, I knew it wasn't me who brought me this far but some other Power who allowed me to escape from prison and North Korea."*[551]

Freedom in Christ

WITHIN A week of arriving in South Korea, Soon Ok Lee attended church services for the first time. When she heard the hymn "Amazing Grace," she was astounded that she knew the words. As other familiar hymns were sung, she suddenly had a flood of long-forgotten memories of her mother and grandmother in North Korea. There had been times late at night when they and neighbors had gathered secretly to sing these hymns. She remembered her grandmother telling her, "*When you ask heaven, you will be given what you ask.*"[552]

Soon Ok had never understood these words before, but she now realized her family had been trying to tell her about God in a nation where it was a crime to mention his name. If a child mentions God's name in a North Korean school, the parents are arrested. Therefore, parents are careful what they say. In the safest way they could, Soon Ok's parents had tried to give her a religious message.

During one memorable service in her new South Korean church, Soon Ok felt the minister was speaking directly to her when he said, "*You must read the Bible to have a good life.*"[553] She had read passages from her new Bible, but now she began to study it more diligently. At first, she hoped the book would give her a better life in a material sense. She had been deprived of so much. However, as she continued to attend church and study more deeply, she discovered the pastor's true meaning. All her life, Soon Ok Lee had known bondage—in both a physical and a spiritual sense. Just as she had escaped bodily imprisonment, she also found release for her soul. She finally discovered the true meaning of a good life. In her favorite Bible verse, she found the freedom promised by Jesus Christ:

Jesus said, "If you hold to my teaching, you are really my disciples. Then you will know the truth, and the truth will set you free." ~John 8:31–32

Called on God

SO-YOUNG was sixteen years old when she escaped North Korea with a small group of friends. Crossing into China in February 2000, she was less than five feet tall, malnourished, and desperate. She and her friends were easy prey when a group of men offered them jobs and good salaries. The young women eagerly accepted this offer, not realizing they were placing themselves in the hands of sex traffickers. She explained:

> They transported us in the dark, so we didn't know where we were going. We didn't know they were going to sell us. We really didn't suspect anything at first. But even when we began suspecting something, we dismissed it, thinking we were too young and small to be sold. But the next morning, they took my friend. She's much taller than I am. They told us that they found a place for her to work, so she happily went with them. But later, I found out that she had been sold.[554]

So-Young soon learned she was being held captive at the mercy of these men. She was raped by them and then sold to a fifty-year-old Chinese man who raped her as well. Her life went from bad to much worse. Having grown up in North Korea, she knew nothing about God and had hardly even heard God's name mentioned. Nevertheless, in one of her bleak moments, she found herself looking upward. *"At that time, I only had a slight conception of a heavenly place. I was so disgusted, and I just called on God with tears, crying out, 'God in heaven. Help me!' It was just that one time that I cried out to him."*[555]

> The LORD is a refuge for the oppressed, a stronghold in times of trouble. Those who know your name will trust in you, for you, LORD, have never forsaken those who seek you. ~Psalm 9:9–10

Soon after this, So-Young was sold again, this time to a man who happened to live next to a house church. There she met a deacon of the church who befriended her and eventually helped her escape. Forever after she accepted this as God's answer to her prayer. She learned that God hears us in our dark moments and desolate places and is faithful when we call his name.

To Tell the Truth

KIM HYUN HEE boarded Korean Air Flight 858 in Baghdad, Iraq, on November 28, 1987. After planting a bomb disguised as a transistor radio in an overhead compartment, she deplaned in Abu Dhabi. Flight 858 continued on its way to Seoul, exploding in a fireball off the coast of Myanmar and killing all 115 passengers on board.

> Do not suppose that I have come to bring peace to the earth. I did not come to bring peace, but a sword.
> ~Matthew 10:34

Kim Hyun Hee was apprehended a few days later in Bahrain after unsuccessfully attempting suicide with a cyanide-laced cigarette. She was transferred to South Korea, where she was interrogated and confessed to her crime. As a North Korean agent, she was part of a well-orchestrated plot to disrupt the upcoming South Korean elections and 1988 Olympics. A South Korean court found her guilty of murder and sentenced her to death. Later, she was pardoned by the president of South Korea, who reasoned, *"The persons who ought to be on trial here are the leaders of North Korea."*[556]

Since these events, Kim Hyun Hee has lived in isolation, fearing reprisals from the North Korean government. She fears for her family most of all, telling an interviewer, *"Every day I pray to God they have survived. I have to keep thinking they are alive."*[557] Since her ordeal, she has become a devout Christian, thankful for having survived two near encounters with death, one from a poisoned cigarette and the other from a South Korean court. She poignantly states, *"From time to time I wish I were dead. Dying would have been easier. But God has a plan—and that's why I'm here."*[558]

This young woman took a difficult road, confessing her crimes and endangering her family. Her testimony is a witness to other Christians facing difficult life choices. Jesus never promised it would be easy to stand for truth and the gospel.

Two Worlds

IN 1999, a German doctor named Norbert
Vollertsen went to North Korea as part of
a medical humanitarian mission. Not long
after arriving he was treating a workman with
extensive burns and volunteered himself to
give skin grafts. For this unusual gesture he
was acclaimed in the North Korean media and
awarded the Friendship Medal by the national
government. Due to his elevated status he was
given a VIP passport and driver's license,
allowing him to travel to places in the country
never seen by foreigners or even many North
Koreans. He was particularly interested in children's medical treatment and
travelled outside the capital to see what was being done in the provinces:

> They conspire, they lurk,
> they watch my steps,
> eager to take my life . . .
> Record my lament; list
> my tears on your scroll—
> are they not in your
> record? . . . in God I trust;
> I will not be afraid. What
> can man do to me?
> ~Psalm 56: 6, 8, 11

> *In every hospital I visited I found unbelievable deprivation; there were
> no bandages, no scalpels, no antibiotics, no operation facilities—only
> broken wooden beds supporting starving children waiting to die. The
> condition of the children was deplorable, emaciated, stunted, mute, emo-
> tionally depleted.*[559]

While in North Korea, Vollertsen also had occasion to visit a high-
ranking member of the military, who was undergoing treatment in a
Pyongyang hospital, where he found different conditions:

> *Unlike any other hospital I visited, this hospital looked as modern as any
> German hospital and was equipped with the latest medical apparatus
> such as MRI, ultrasound, EKG, and X-ray machines. It was obvious to
> me that there are two worlds in North Korea, one for the senior military
> and the country's elite—for the rest of society, a world of Hell.*[560]

When Vollertsen began trying to track down how foreign medical and
food aid were being distributed by the North Korean government, he was
expelled from the country. He has since campaigned to expose what he con-
siders an evil regime. He believes the outside world has to intervene: *"To
improve human rights in North Korea the world has to speak out against
the current regime. The North Korean people cannot help themselves. They
are brainwashed and suffer from terror and pressure. They are afraid."*[561]

If anyone questions the power or even the existence of evil in this
world, they need only consider the dark forces that literally enslave the
beleaguered people of North Korea.

Yoido Full Gospel Church, Seoul (P. Chung)

Modern and ancient Seoul

Breakthrough

WHEN LEE PHILMON went to war in Korea, his daughter Karen was six weeks old. He returned almost two years later a complete stranger. When her mother announced, *"Daddy's home!"* Karen hid and cried. When he tried to come closer, she cried harder. This went on for two days. On the third morning he came into the kitchen for breakfast, and Karen started crying again. He told his wife not to scold her and picked her up. He took her outside, put her in the car, and drove away. After driving around for some time, Karen was still crying, and the nervous father did not know what to do next. Finally, he stopped at a country store and bought two Cokes. He gave one to her and went back into the store by himself. After a while he noticed she had stopped crying, and he hurried back to the car. She was staring intently into the Coke bottle as he approached.

> Love is patient, love is kind. It does not envy, it does not boast, it is not proud. It is not rude, it is not self-seeking, it is not easily angered, it keeps no record of wrongs.
> ~1 Corinthians 13:4–5

When he got into the car, she looked up and said, *"It's dirty, Daddy!"* He smiled and said, *"Here, take mine."*

He went back into the store and bought another drink. When he got back into the car, Karen moved over next to him and said, *"I like Coke, Daddy."* She cuddled closer and started talking a mile a minute. Philmon later said, *"From that time on, she was my little girl, and we were never far apart again."*[562]

When a relationship becomes strained, everything we do can seem wrong. After an argument with a spouse there is usually a period of difficult silence. At times we even forget what the original argument was about as we try to deal with the bruised feelings. At times like this we find some helpful advice in Scripture: *"The end of a matter is better than its beginning, and patience is better than pride"* (Ecclesiastes 7:8). As we search for the breakthrough to restore a relationship, the best thing we can do is focus on the love that brought us together in the first place.

Indifference

IN 2003, Steve Bousquet interviewed people who had lived in Florida fifty years before, during the last year of the Korean War. He got an interesting picture of the culture of that time. Forty-five rpm records were in vogue. Kids danced to Rosemary Clooney, Patti Page, Les Paul, and Mary Ford. Esther Williams drew crowds to the movie theater, if for no other reason, because it was air conditioned. Girls wore Peter Pan collars and crinoline skirts, while boys were in dress shirts and khakis. Black people and white people still drank from separate water fountains.

> I know your deeds, that you are neither cold nor hot. I wish you were either one or the other! So, because you are lukewarm—neither hot nor cold—I am about to spit you out of my mouth.
> ~Revelation 3:15–16

It was a different time and far removed from the war. One woman told of graduating high school that year, saying, *"There wasn't a great concern about war. It was going on. But we weren't really attuned to it."*[563] A navy veteran was struck by the indifference when he came home: *"I came back and nobody paid any attention. People were interested in other things . . . building houses, raising families."*[564]

The Korean War stands in sharp contrast to our previous wars. There was no sense of national emergency or shared sacrifice during this so-called "police action." Unfortunately, this set the pattern for later conflicts. Today life goes on at home while our men and women in uniform and their families bear the burden. If our young people have to go into harm's way for their country, they deserve more from their countrymen than indifference. Those of us on the home front may not be able to share the burden directly, but we can show our support in many ways. A Google search for "support our troops" reveals many purposeful ways to help.

Indifference in attitudes or relationships is a dangerous condition. We know that our heavenly Father has no patience with those who are indifferent to him.

Korean Soldier

WHEN WAR broke out Hee Sung Lee was living in Seoul and working as an interpreter with the US Korean Military Advisory Group (KMAG). After the North Koreans captured the city, they arrested and imprisoned him because of his association with the Americans. He escaped three months later, made his way to US lines and joined the South Korean army. His unit was hit hard during the Chinese invasion in the winter of 1951, and he was medically evacuated due to malnutrition and the effects of the extreme cold.

Lee became a patient in the 629th Medical Clearing Company in Wonju, and, while he was recuperating, the senior doctor recruited him to remain with the medical unit to work with South Korean patients and North Korean prisoners. It was his job to strip their weapons, interview them, and take their medical histories. One of the American soldiers said, *"His expertise with the languages was essential in explaining to those who did not speak English just where they were being sent, and what would happen to them when they were well."*[565]

> Therefore, since we are receiving a kingdom that cannot be shaken, let us be thankful, and so worship God acceptably with reverence and awe. For our God is a consuming fire.
> ~Hebrews 12:28–29

For the duration of the war Lee served with US medical units, doing all he could to help the wounded and save lives. After the cease-fire in 1953, he relinquished his military rank to work on the final prisoner exchange.

Fifty years later, Lee tried to express his gratitude to "the young men who had forsaken their homes and families to help a far-away nation, with a foreign culture and language, whose people desperately needed their help." He said:

> *Who knows the miserable circumstances we saw, and who knows what is a war? To all the soldiers who fought in Korea, God will congratulate that. And from the bottom of my heart, thank you for all your distinguished military services. The Korean people will never forget what you did for them. Remember—tell America—"Freedom is not free." You are good men and soldiers. God bless you all. God bless America.*[566]

Note to a Son

DEWEY AND Faye Arnold met at Ft. Dix, New Jersey, and were married in 1950. The next year, a month after their son, Don, was born, Dewey received orders to Korea. Within days of his departure Fay started receiving letters from her husband, cataloging his journey across the country and overseas. From Korea he sent sketches of where he was stationed and descriptions of his training. He wasn't happy being away from his family, writing: *"Sherman aptly described war. It is hell. But now I know what the hellish part is. Being away from the ones you love more than anything in the world."*[567]

Because Arnold always wanted his wife to know the truth about what he was doing, he didn't gloss over the dangers he faced. The tone was different, however, in his letter dated October 2, 1951. He told her his platoon had to lead an attack the next day, and he asked her to pray for him and his forty-six men. He also did something else very unusual. He tore the First Cavalry Division patch off his uniform, wrapped it in a piece of paper, and wrote a message for his son: *"As my 1st Sgt., you take good care of our Mom. She's the most wonderful person you or I will ever know. Dad."*[568]

When Jesus saw his mother there, and the disciple whom he loved standing nearby, he said to his mother, "Dear woman, here is your son," and to the disciple, "Here is your mother." From that time on, this disciple took her into his home. ~John 19:26–27

Tragically, the young soldier did not return from that battle, leaving his son to carry out his last poignant orders. Fifty years later, Don Arnold was able to reflect on the legacy of his heroic father, and felt some confidence he had lived up to his charge. Married, with two children of his own, he had his mother living with him in his home, still taking good care of her. In spite of his difficult family history, he was able to say, *"I don't know a family that doesn't have some sort of tragedy. The tragedy would have been if he had no one, if he had left no one."*[569]

This story is for every father. Don Arnold did not have an easy life, but, thanks to the courage and foresight of his dad, he had a life with purpose and a heroic example to follow.

Suffering for Him

I N SPITE of the North Korean government's efforts to suppress religion, evidence continues to leak of underground church activity. In his book, *Escaping North Korea,* Mike Kim told the story of Pastor Jun, a Korean-Chinese man who made a trip to Pyongyang, where he met an elderly woman working in his hotel. In a quiet moment when they were alone, he said to her, *"Believe in Jesus. If you don't know about him, I'll tell you about him."* The woman stared at him, but did not respond. Pastor Jun repeated his words, but the woman continued to stand in front of

> I want to know Christ and the power of his resurrection and the fellowship of sharing in his sufferings, becoming like him in his death.
> ~Philippians 3:10

him as if frozen. After a third time, the woman suddenly turned and ran to the door. She closed it and came back to the pastor with her hand on her heart, exclaiming, *"Oh! I believe in Jesus. I believe in Jesus. Thank you. Thank you."* The woman then said she knew several hymns by heart and began singing "God's Great Grace" in a low voice. As she sang, tears rolled down her face, and the pastor cried with her. Afterward, she said, *"I can't sing that song out loud, but every day I sing it quietly in my heart. A day doesn't pass by when I don't sing that song and pray to Jesus."*[570]

The apostle Paul wrote about what happens when we suffer for Jesus. He stated, *We are heirs—heirs of God and co-heirs with Christ, if indeed we share in his sufferings in order that we may also share in his glory* (Romans 8:17). Considered in this light, the North Korean Christians such as the woman in this story have a blessing hidden in their difficult circumstances. In their suffering, they can more strongly identify with Jesus than can most of us who live with the freedom to worship openly.

When the time does come that we have to experience a life crisis and the pain that goes with it, we should recognize this as our own opportunity. This will be the time to approach our Savior in a more intimate and urgent way. Our time of suffering is also our opportunity to witness powerfully for him in a way no one else can.

Mustard Seeds

IN 2009, the International Christian University in Mitaka, Japan, celebrated its sixtieth anniversary. This unique institution has grown from humble beginnings during the Korean War era to its present status with three campuses and more than three thousand students from Japan and other nations around the world pursuing undergraduate, masters, and doctoral degrees in a wide range of liberal arts majors. The mission from the beginning has been, *"The establishment of an academic tradition of freedom and reverence based on Christian ideals, and the education of individuals of conscience."*[571]

> The kingdom of heaven is like a mustard seed, which a man took and planted in his field. Though it is the smallest of all your seeds, yet when it grows, it is the largest of garden plants and becomes a tree, so that the birds of the air come and perch in its branches.
> ~Matthew 13:31–32

In 1951, the *USS Bryce Canyon* was on a seven-month deployment to the Western Pacific, operating in Korean waters out of Japan. During one port visit in Japan, a group of interested Navy personnel from the ship visited the newly formed school. One officer described the scene:

> *The 350 acres of land and the partially built buildings looked strange at first sight for they had formerly been under construction to become the model industrial plant for the Nakajima Aeronautical Corporation which built military airplanes.*
>
> *After going through these buildings, now designed to house students, classrooms, offices, gymnasium, and library, the men were entertained at a tea party. Here, they met the leaders of this new Christian university and heard them express their Christian faith and vision concerning the vital role I. C. U. would play in developing new leaders for a new Japan. For many of the group, this was "the most worthwhile and inspiring experience we've had in Japan."*[572]

After this visit, the officers and men of the *Bryce Canyon*, representing twenty-nine states and eleven denominations, were inspired to contribute their own money to a scholarship fund for students attending the university. They also encouraged untold donations from churches back home. This story of international goodwill is a modern illustration of Jesus' parable of the mustard seed. From small seeds, planted in faith, a mighty Christian institution has flourished.

The Little Ones

NO ONE knows how many Christians there are in North Korea. Estimates range from twelve thousand to one hundred thousand worshipping secretly in underground house churches.[573] In *Escaping North Korea*, Mike Kim tells the story of an elderly Korean-Chinese woman who serves as a missionary to North Korea, where she leads a network of 116 Christian families. Describing her visits, she says, *"I write down for them the Apostle's Creed, the Lord's Prayer, and hymns . . . We sing together all night in fellowship . . . When I go to North Korea I just cry and cry as I see the situation they're living in."* When asked about the police, she said, *"We sing late at night. We gather with one or two other people and sing very quietly. When we sing or pray we have to make sure the kids are sleeping, or if we meet during the day we send them outside."*[574]

> But if anyone cause one of these little ones who believe in me to sin, it would be better for him to have a large millstone hung around his neck and to be drowned in the depths of the sea.
> ~Matthew 18:6

The Koreans have to go to such lengths to insulate their children because the children are all interrogated at school about unusual activity at home. Their innocence and honesty has become the government's first line of defense against every possible subversion—whether political or spiritual. Instead of sharing their faith with their children, parents have to quarantine them from worship to prevent their unwitting betrayal. Such perversity is difficult to comprehend. Parents are forced to relate to their children not as protégés, but as potential informants. Christ was very specific in condemning actions that lead children astray. One can only imagine his attitude toward a system of government that not only segregates children from faith, but *uses them* to undermine the faith of others—even their own parents.

Putting the Pieces Together

Korean War Memorial, Washington, DC

CPL. DONALD JEETER went missing in action in December 1950. Other than a notification in 1953 that he was presumed dead, his family never learned what happened to him. In 2010, a relative finally decided someone should try to find out. Cypert Whitfill was Jeeter's younger cousin and remembered him fondly from their days together as boys in Wichita Falls, Texas. His quest would take him on many twists and turns, through books, historical and military websites, and personal accounts.

Whitfill's first breakthrough came when he identified his cousin in casualty lists on a Korean veterans' site and learned he was with the Medical Company of the Thirty-First Regiment. The regiment's history placed it at the Chosin Reservoir in December 1950 and gave details of the battle. He eventually found his way to the *Changjin* (the Korean name for *Chosin*) *Journal,* where he found two personal accounts mentioning his cousin by name. He learned that Corporal Jeeter was driving a jeep for his company commander when both were wounded and cut off from friendly lines. Another witness saw him placed in an ambulance that was hit and destroyed by enemy mortar fire. It was not a happy story, but it did finally have an ending.

The details of this young soldier's death were undoubtedly painful for his mother and the rest of the family. However, there was at least a conclusion to his story that had been missing for too many years. Sadly, Whitfill explained, *"We never had an opportunity to hear Donnie recount any of his experiences of the war."*[575] By painstakingly unearthing the details of Jeeter's last days, Whitfill filled in those blanks and, in the process, honored his cousin's life and service. He ensured that another casualty of the "Forgotten War" would not be forgotten.

> As a father has compassion on his children, so the LORD has compassion on those who fear him; for he knows how we are formed, he remembers that we are dust.
> ~Psalm 103:13–14

Opportunities to Witness

James Patterson

L T. COL. JAMES PATTERSON retired from the US Army in 1982 after a distinguished career highlighted by combat duty in Korea and Vietnam. He was a Christian from an early age, growing up in a small church in Iberia, Missouri, where he developed a lifelong relationship with Jesus Christ. Throughout his life he was active in whatever church he belonged to, holding services, teaching, and raising funds. After retiring from the army, he served as administrator for a large church in North Carolina and as vice president of Crossroads Christian Communications, a major Canadian television network.

Patterson was always eager to share the gospel with others and in 1985 went on Crossroads Television to reach an even wider audience. During his talk, he made this statement: *"The Lord will give you opportunities to witness for him no matter where you are—if you will stay sensitive to the leading of the Holy Spirit."*[576] He then described how he brought another soldier to Christ on the eve of a great battle of the Korean War.

Patterson died in 2000 and was buried with full military honors. At the funeral service the Rev. David Mainse spoke about this great Christian man and showed the video of the talk described above. At Patterson's prior insistence, Rev. Mainse then gave an invitation to those in attendance to receive Jesus as their Lord and Savior. Several stepped forward for the first time, including three members of the honor guard. Even at his own funeral, the Lord gave Patterson another opportunity to witness for him.

> I am not ashamed of the gospel, because it is the power of God for the salvation of everyone who believes. ~Romans 1:16

Today this great Christian continues to share the gospel each time someone watches his amazing video online at the following Internet address: http://100huntley.com/video.php?id=VoYMSLbr48g

Third-Grade Teacher

MARY KAY PARK'S father was befriended by an American soldier during the Korean War. The soldier arranged for the young Korean to go to America where he received an education, became a minister, and started his own family. Since Korean was spoken at home, Mary Kay had some problems in elementary school. She would always remember her third-grade teacher, Mrs. Sanders, and a special moment in her class.

> Each one should use whatever gift he has received to serve others, faithfully administering God's grace in its various forms. ~1 Peter 4:10

One day Mrs. Sanders was having her students read aloud from a second-grade reader. Mary Kay waited her turn nervously, knowing she would have difficulty. When finally called on, she stammered through the assigned passage. She was completely mortified when a boy behind her muttered, *"What a dummy. She can't even read from a second-grade book."*[577] At that point, Mrs. Sanders stepped in and asked Mary Kay if she could write something on the blackboard in Korean.

The young girl went to the board and began writing furiously. After a few minutes, one of the other children asked her to write his name in Korean, and then all the others did, too. She described her feelings at that moment: *"I was instantly transformed from a dummy who couldn't read English to a smart new kid who could read and write in another language. I felt like a star."*[578]

Mary Kay always considered that moment in third grade the point where her life was infused with purpose and direction. She came to see that Mrs. Sanders was the true star, providing her students a blueprint for later life. Having learned the lesson well, Mary Kay would say, *"How many good intentions of serving others die prematurely when discouraged by the task that seems too large? What if we focus on helping just one person?"*[579] Helping one person at a time is a blueprint that has worked for Mary Kay Park and should serve as a model for every Christian facing the awesome task of doing God's work in a complex world.

413

A Comma in Eternity

IN DECEMBER 1952, based on this Scripture from the book of John, the Rev. Frederick Proehl from Milwaukee, Wisconsin, sent an eloquent statement of the Christmas message to military men and women serving in Korea and other locations around the world:

> In the beginning was the Word, and the Word was with God, and the Word was God. He was with God in the beginning. Through him all things were made; without him nothing was made that has been made. In him was life, and that life was the light of men.
> ~John 1:1–4

A singular thing strikes us as we read the opening verses of John's gospel. He begins with eternity while the others begin with time. He gives us a glimpse of the eternal past and shows us the Word as He existed beyond the genesis. In Him was the life in its fullest sense, life eternal, the blessed life of God. He speaks of life in contrast to life as we see it in all living being created by the Word. Creatures receive life as a gift from the Source of Life and must surrender it in the hour of death. Life is perpetual in the Logos, incapable of change and never subject to deterioration, while human life is but a comma in the great sentence of eternity.

In Him was life reaching back into eternity, where all works of grace have their inception and lose themselves in the mystery of God's all-embracing love. Christ, the eternal One, the same yesterday, today and forever, entered into the eternal plan of salvation. Wonderful and beyond human understanding is the revealed truth. In Him, who is the Source of Life, we find the only hope of eternal life.

This is the only reason for celebrating Christmas. It is the age-old message of hope and redemption which we preach from our pulpits, words of life for a dying world.[580]

Our short lives on earth are truly commas, not only in the sentence or even the book, but in the great library of God's work throughout eternity. Only in his Son, God's true Word, do our commas find any purpose or meaning.

> Yet to all who received him, to those who believed in his name, he gave the right to become children of God—children born not of natural descent, nor of human decision or a husband's will, but born of God.
> ~John 1:12–13

Light of Christmas

THE CREW of *USS Consolation* would not forget Christmas 1950. While lying alongside a pier at Hungnam harbor, they had taken aboard Marine casualties from the Chosin Reservoir until the ship was filled to capacity. With not an inch of space left, the ship got underway at about midnight on Christmas Eve. The battleship Missouri was firing sixteen-inch projectiles overhead to cover the withdrawal. Enemy forces were closing on the harbor, and the anxiety level was high.

In spite of the tense situation and extreme workload, the crew of the ship did what they could to display a little Christmas cheer—for the benefit of the patients and themselves. One officer described the efforts to construct a Christmas tree with scant resources:

> *The corpsmen did a great job decorating the ship. They were certainly imaginative . . . given the resources they had. I remember the Christmas tree outside of the operating room that kept falling down. The trunk was made of a swab handle. Branches were coat hangers with strips of green dyed sterile wrapping paper. They filled light bulbs with colored water. Cotton balls were strung like popcorn. Icicles were fringed foil wrap. And the poor little tree kept falling down.*[581]

The story is reminiscent of the comic strip *Peanuts* and Charlie Brown's meager little Christmas tree. The *Peanuts* story was about the over-commercialism of Christmas and a reminder of what Christmas is actually about—the birth of Jesus Christ. Whatever its shape or size, the decorative lights on our Christmas trees depict the light that came into the world on that day more than two thousand years ago. Whether grandiose or meager, the Christmas tree points to what we are celebrating—the arrival on Earth of God's redemption for mankind.

> In him was life, and that life was the light of men . . . The true light that gives light to every man was coming into the world. ~John 1:4, 9

Pyongyang Church

JOHN CALDWELL was a State Department official in Korea when the war began. He told one of the great stories to come out of the Korean War. Refugee congregations of Christians from several North Korean cities had made their way to the safety of the Pusan Perimeter, where they banded together to form the Pyongyang Church. By December 1951 the church had been in existence for only a little over a year when the congregation made an amazing decision. An astonishingly large Christmas offering was taken to help other refugees, including non-Christians.

When the congregation met to consider the Christmas offering, the minister reminded everyone that they had fled their homes and arrived in South Korea, *"by the grace of God, with no possessions except what could be carried."*[582] Since these people had arrived in their new home with practically nothing and God had provided for them, they were able to rely on their faith to start again from scratch. Each gave everything he or she had saved, rendering themselves practically penniless and as destitute as they had been when they were refugees.

This story brings a sobering thought and a tear to the eye of any Christian wrestling with the decision of what to pledge to the church. How much can I afford to give this year? These Korean men and women in the midst of their own horrendous hardship gave all they had. This is of course a sensitive issue and a matter for each to work out with God and his or her own conscience. As part of this process we should also ponder the words of Jesus when he saw a destitute widow give her two small coins to the temple:

> "I tell you the truth," he said, "this poor widow has put in more than all the others. All these people gave their gifts out of their wealth; but she out of her poverty put in all she had to live on." ~Luke 21:3–4

A Christmas Story

IN MID-DECEMBER 1950, as the Chinese invasion forced the Eighth Army to retreat, some units moved south by Korean freight train. A group of officers and enlisted men were tightly packed into a bare, unheated boxcar with all their gear. One of the enlisted men was called "Yorick" by his fellow soldiers. During a start-and-stop journey, the young soldier voiced an unusual complaint several times. Christmas was coming, and he had no Christmas cards to send home. He said, *"It's just not right not sending cards this time of year. Gosh darn!"*583

> All who heard it were amazed at what the shepherds said to them. But Mary treasured up all these things and pondered them in her heart.
> ~Luke 2:18–19

As the train moved haltingly to the south, Korean refugees climbed on and filled the top of the boxcars, clinging precariously to their possessions and each other. Each time the train stopped, some would drop stiffly to the ground and move about in search of food. Probably for the first time the soldiers on the train got an up-close look at starving men, women, and children. Yorick decided to do what he could to help. At one stop he gave away his morning ration to a family of three. At succeeding stops, he began seeking out food peddlers. With his own money he bought apples, peanuts, dried fish, bread, and rice cakes, giving it all away to the cold and hungry cartop riders. He received smiles, tears, and graceful little bows in return. He did all he could with the money he had.

At one stop late in the day, the soldier was approached by a mild-mannered, bearded Korean man, who pressed an oblong package into his hands and said, "I have watched you, sir. I thank you, and on behalf of my people here I want you to accept this from all of us."584 Later, the soldier opened the package to find twenty sheets of soft white paper, each with a brightly colored hand-painted picture. Below each picture was hand-painted in bold English letters: "MERRY CHRISTMAS!" He would never learn how an unknown Korean man happened to have and to give him his one wish: Christmas cards for home.

Christmas Tree

SGT. BOBBY MARTIN arrived in Korea in mid-November and joined the First Cavalry Division just in time for the great withdrawal to the south. His unit leapfrogged others, each taking turns providing rear security. Food was scarce due to chaotic supply lines, and the subzero weather brought untold misery to everyone. Martin's unit continued its long retreat, reaching the outskirts of Seoul by mid-December.

Despite the deprivation and anxiety that were a part of their ordeal, the soldiers resolved to celebrate the approach of Christmas as best they could. This would require a Christmas tree. Martin and his friends found one on a nearby hillside and brought it back to their temporary camp. After that, some typical GI ingenuity was required:

> *We discovered we didn't have anything to make a stand for the tree, so we took a pickax and dug a hole over a foot deep in the frozen ground. Next, we set the tree in the hole, held it upright, and poured water into the hole. It took only about thirty minutes for the water to freeze, and our Christmas tree was firmly locked in the hole. To decorate the tree, we took the cans from our beer rations and Cokes and cut them into stars and moons, or whatever, and then hung them on the tree with communications wire. One of our artistic guys cut out the letters for "Merry Christmas" and "Happy New Year," and we tied them together and wrapped them around the tree.[585]*

We all have our holiday traditions, and many of them are centered around the family Christmas tree. From obscure origins in fifteenth-century Germany, the custom of having a tree in the home at Christmas spread to England and then to America, where the symbol has taken on more and more commercial and secular overtones. In addition to the lights, however, one part of the tree retains its original purpose in acknowledging the birth of Jesus Christ. On the very top we place either a star or an angel, representing the star of the Magi or the heavenly host who announced to the shepherds our Savior's birth.

> They went on their way, and the star they had seen in the east went ahead of them until it stopped over the place where the child was. When they saw the star, they were overjoyed.
> ~Matthew 2:9–10

The Christmas Event

HISTORY IS an important part of Marine *esprit de corps*. Every new recruit is well educated on the great battles of the past. At any ceremony Marines may hear mention of Belleau Woods, Iwo Jima, Khe Sanh, or Fallujah. The Chosin Reservoir campaign may have occurred more than half a century ago, but every Marine today knows that in December 1950 the First Marine Division fought its way through ten Chinese divisions in thirty-below-zero weather. Marine Corps *esprit de corps* is not based on a nebulous faith in past glory—it is based on knowledge of specific events performed by real men and known units.

At Christmas time, Christians should proclaim the same confidence in the nature of their faith. On the occasion of our Savior's birth, we reaffirm that Christianity is not based on theological concepts or brilliantly-reasoned philosophy. Our faith does not come from belief in a vague mythology or religion. Christianity is based on a historical event. As predicted by generations of Hebrew prophets, a child was born in the town of Bethlehem in Palestine in the first year of the calendar by which all western civilization dates time. As confirmed by Roman and Jewish historians Jesus Christ was born and lived in this small but known corner of the Roman Empire. Our faith is not based on an idea—it is based on this fact of history.[586]

In those days Caesar Augustus issued a decree that a census should be taken of the entire Roman world. (This was the first census that took place while Quirinius was governor of Syria.) And everyone went to his own town to register. So Joseph also went up from the town of Nazareth in Galilee to Judea, to Bethlehem the town of David, because he belonged to the house and line of David. He went there to register with Mary, who was pledged to be married to him and was expecting a child. While they were there, the time came for the baby to be born, and she gave birth to her firstborn, a son. She wrapped him in cloths and placed him in a manger, because there was no room for them in the inn. ~Luke 2:1–7

Suddenly a great company of the heavenly host appeared with the angel, praising God and saying, "Glory to God in the highest, and on earth peace to men on whom his favor rests." ~Luke 2:13–14

All Is Calm

IT HAD BEEN a hard, cold winter for Bob Mills and the other Marines in camp near Masan, South Korea. After surviving the hardships of the Chosin Reservoir fighting, an unusually warm Christmas Eve in a safe place was an almost heavenly respite. Mills and a small group of friends gathered in a tent to have a beer and a quiet celebration. Early in the evening a delegation of eight Korean children appeared outside their tent carrying homemade paper lanterns of different colors, lit by flickering candles. The scene became totally quiet as the children began to sing:

> Silent night, holy night!
> All is calm, all is bright.
> Round yon Virgin, Mother and Child.
> Holy infant so tender and mild,
> Sleep in heavenly peace,
> Sleep in heavenly peace.
>
> Silent night, holy night!
> Shepherds quake at the sight.
> Glories stream from heaven afar
> Heavenly hosts sing Alleluia,
> Christ the Savior is born!
> Christ the Savior is born.[587]

> An angel of the Lord appeared to them, and the glory of the Lord shone around them, and they were terrified. But the angel said to them, "Do not be afraid. I bring you good news of great joy that will be for all the people. Today in the town of David a Savior has been born to you; he is Christ the Lord."
> ~Luke 2:9–11

When the children finished singing, the Marines thanked them, and they quietly moved on to another tent. Mills said later, *"It was very touching. We were in Korea on Christmas Eve, away from home, and of course this brought a touch of home, even for tough Marines."*[588] The most famous Christmas carol of all time still has the amazing power to bring us home, no matter where we are. For a moment it takes us back to the Christmases of our childhood and refocuses our thoughts on the true meaning of the day—Christ the Savior is born.

Christmas Eve

ROBERT REICHARD was with the Eighty-Eighth Military Police Company during the evacuation at Hungnam. He was part of the force guarding the harbor and keeping the main supply route open for the troops entering the perimeter. By mid-December 1950 the Marines were embarked and out to sea. As other units and refugees continued boarding ships, the perimeter kept shrinking toward the port. Throughout this time Reichard was working twenty-hour days in the bitter cold of the North Korean winter to keep the evacuation route open.

Troops embark at Hungnam (US Navy)

On Christmas Eve, the exhausted young soldier was finally relieved of his post and sent to a landing craft. As he wearily walked on board his thoughts turned to the season:

> Christmas would soon be with us, but any thoughts of "silent nights" were a thing of the past, because it was anything but silent. Our artillery was set up along the shore, and the battleship Missouri, the cruiser Rochester and numerous destroyers were throwing a stream of shells over us into the enemy.[589]

As his ship maneuvered out of Hungnam harbor, someone nearby had a radio tuned to Armed Forces Radio in Japan. The announcer was describing the Christmas menu for the troops in Korea, starting with tom turkey and then listing all the trimmings. Reichard commented poignantly, "I was eating a can of spaghetti, just thankful to be alive."[590]

It is the season to be thankful, even if our problems are large and our circumstances difficult. It is a time to think more of others and less of ourselves. Our men and women in uniform in lonely outposts around the world deserve our thoughts and prayers—and even more visible signs of support. Somewhere tonight other soldiers are far away from home and family in dangerous places, eating cold food, and thanking God for being alive.

> Let the peace of Christ rule in your hearts, since as members of one body you were called to peace. And be thankful.
> ~Colossians 3:15

Christmas Gift

ON CHRISTMAS Day 1951 thousands of lonely GIs in Korea assembled in small groups on the front lines and rear areas to celebrate Christmas. Many were tired, hungry, and fearful, while almost all were preoccupied with thoughts of home as they remembered loved ones and their own Christmas traditions—usually involving special food, Christmas trees, and presents. A few heard a message that day on the theme of gift giving based on what the apostle Paul called God's "indescribable" gift to mankind: *For you know the grace of our Lord Jesus Christ, that though he was rich, yet for your sakes he became poor, so that you through his poverty might become rich* (2 Corinthians 8:9). These soldiers heard that the appropriate response to a gift of this magnitude had to be thankfulness:

> This service that you perform is not only supplying the needs of God's people but is also overflowing in many expressions of thanks to God . . . Thanks be to God for his indescribable gift!
> ~2 Corinthians 9:12, 15

(National Archives)

God is right here with us today, but how can we look Him in the eye and say, "Thank you"? It's interesting to note that St. Paul originally talked about this unspeakable gift of Christ, and this grace of Jesus Christ who became poor that we might be rich, in connection with a very real and practical piece of thanksgiving. St. Paul gathered a collection of gifts for some Christians who were in terrible need. He wanted them to give their gifts prompted not just by kindness in general but by God's love in Christ Jesus. He was very happy about some Christians who gave to his collection, "but first gave their own selves to the Lord and unto us by the will of God."

It's your blueprint for thanksgiving! First give yourself to the Lord. Realize that He has bought and paid for you. His Christmas gift is really a purchase price, a claim check, which has taken your whole self into custody and has made all of you God's own. And when you belong to God that way, then you are as anxious to do good for people as God Himself.[591]

As we give and receive gifts this Christmas, this reminder from the past helps us understand the significance of this tradition—our generosity toward each other is a pale reflection of God's great generosity to us in giving the greatest gift ever conceived.

Korean War Monument in Seoul (National Archives)

North Korean guards on DMZ (National Archives)

Seen by Men

KIM IL SUNG died of a massive heart attack on July 6, 1994, at age eighty-two. The announcement of his death was withheld for thirty-four hours so that North Korean government officials could prepare for the first hereditary succession in the Communist world. Kim Jong Il, the son, came to power amidst the greatest public outpouring of grief ever witnessed.

Jun-sang was a university student in Pyongyang when he heard the news of the great leader's death. All three thousand students and faculty were assembled in a square to listen as a disembodied female voice announced the startling news over a loudspeaker. Immediately, everyone present dropped to the hot pavement and began to wail. Although Jun-sang considered himself a loyal Communist, he curiously found himself unmoved by the announcement and unable to cry. Even as everyone else seemed genuinely grief-stricken by their love for the dead leader, he felt only detachment. Then he was suddenly gripped with fear, as he realized he was alone in his indifference. He also realized that his entire future might be at stake in that moment. He buried his head in his hands and kept his eyes open in a stare until a few tears came. He rocked back and forth, staring and sobbing, blending in with the sea of grief around him.[592]

Jesus would have had great sympathy for people forced to conform publicly in this way, but we can only imagine his attitude toward the system that compelled it. He had little patience with hypocrites and hypocritical behavior. Jesus instructed his followers specifically to shun public displays of righteousness. His concern is not with how we impress others, but with what is in our hearts.

> Be careful not to do your "acts of righteousness" before men, to be seen by them. If you do, you will have no reward from your Father in heaven . . . But when you give to the needy, do not let your left hand know what your right hand is doing, so that your giving may be in secret. Then your Father, who sees what is done in secret, will reward you. And when you pray, do not be like the hypocrites, for they love to pray standing in the synagogues and on the street corners to be seen by men. I tell you the truth, they have received their reward in full. ~Matthew 6:1, 3–5

They Chose God

IN 2001, defectors from North Korea continued to paint a grim picture of religious repression in that rigidly-controlled nation. One woman described how her family would gather under a blanket at night to whisper hymns from memory and offer prayers that, if overheard, could get them killed. *"We were so scared,"* she said. *"If you were caught, you would disappear. We didn't know where you would go, but we knew it was prison or execution."* A couple who had escaped across the northern border explained that their son was caught in China and returned to North Korea. As the woman talked about her son, her grief was apparent. *"He is in prison. I expect he will die in prison."* She explained her own religious upbringing: *"My mother taught me the Ten Commandments, and we memorized hymns. Of course, we could never keep a Bible in the house. The Communist Party would regularly raid the house and go through all the belongings, looking for foreign books. If they found a Bible, you could be executed."*[593]

> I know your afflictions and your poverty—yet you are rich! . . . Do not be afraid of what you are about to suffer. I tell you, the devil will put some of you in prison to test you, and you will suffer persecution for ten days. Be faithful, even to the point of death, and I will give you the crown of life.
> ~Revelation 2:9, 10

Another defector named Soon Ok Lee had spent seven years in a North Korean prison. At the time she was not a Christian herself, but she witnessed how they were treated. *"The torture, and the worst ways of execution were most harsh on the Christians. They didn't give them clothes. They were considered animals. Believing in God instead of Kim Il Sung was the biggest sin in their eyes."*[594] A South Korean minister expressed a sense of futility to Soon Ok Lee about sharing the gospel in North Korea where the most urgent need seemed to be food. She strongly disagreed, citing what she saw in prison: *"I witnessed them being asked to choose God or Kim Il Sung, and they were told they would be released if they chose Kim Il Sung. I saw them choose God."*[595]

Under God

I N HIS Gettysburg Address President Abraham Lincoln said, *"That we here highly resolve that these dead shall not have died in vain, that this nation under God shall have a new birth of freedom, and that government of the people, by the people, for the people shall not perish from the earth."*[596] On February 7, 1954, the Rev. George Docherty focused the attention of his congregation on President Lincoln's

Lincoln Memorial

phrase, *"under God."* With President Dwight Eisenhower in attendance, he made a reasoned and passionate plea for the inclusion of that phrase in the Pledge of Allegiance. After explaining how the nation's fundamental values are based on the Ten Commandments and New Testament, he said,

> This is the *"American way of Life."* Lincoln saw this clearly. The providence of God was being fulfilled. Wherefore, Lincoln claims that it is *"Under God"* that this nation shall know a new birth of freedom. And by implication, it is under God that *"government of the people, by the people, and for the people, shall not perish from the earth."* For Lincoln, since God was in his heaven, all must ultimately be right for his Country.
>
> The only point I make in raising the issue of the Pledge of Allegiance is that it seems to me to omit this theological implication that is inherent within the American way of life. It should be *"one nation, indivisible, under God."* Once *"under God,"* then we can define what we mean by *"liberty and justice for all."* To omit the words *"under God"* in the Pledge of Allegiance is to omit the definitive character of the American way of life.[597]

A bill was introduced in Congress within days of this sermon and signed into law by President Eisenhower on June 14, 1954, incorporating the phrase "under God" into the Pledge of Allegiance. The text for Rev. Docherty's sermon came from the book of Galatians:

There is neither Jew nor Greek, slave nor free, male nor female, for you are all one in Christ Jesus. ~Galatians 3:28

To Honor God

IN WASHINGTON, DC, on June 14, 1954, officials of the American Legion raised the American flag over the US Capitol and led a group of assembled dignitaries in reciting the newly revised Pledge of Allegiance:

I pledge allegiance to the flag of the United States of America, and to the republic for which it stands, one nation under God, indivisible, with liberty and justice for all.

One nation under God

As he signed the bill to revise the Pledge, President Dwight Eisenhower explained the significance of adding the words "under God:"

In this way we are reaffirming the transcendence of religious faith in America's heritage and future; in this way we shall constantly strengthen those spiritual weapons which forever will be our country's most powerful resource, in peace or in war.[598]

Speaking to a group who helped support this change to the Pledge, President Eisenhower later said,

These words will remind Americans that despite our great physical strength we must remain humble. They will help us to keep constantly in our minds and hearts the spiritual and moral principles which alone give dignity to man, and upon which our way of life is founded.[599]

By adding the words *"under God"* to the Pledge of Allegiance, Congress acknowledged God as the Source of authority in this nation, as did our Founding Fathers in the Declaration of Independence: *"We hold these truths to be self-evident, that all men are created equal, that they are endowed by their Creator with certain unalienable rights . . ."*

> Call upon me in the day of trouble; I will deliver you, and you will honor me. ~Psalm 50:15

Final Impressions

IN MAY 2010 Bruce Stone and fifteen other Korean War veterans arrived at the Inchon International Airport, where they were met by Korean officials and escorted to a five-star hotel in Seoul. For five days their hosts showed them the sights of South Korea, including tours of the Demilitarized Zone and war memorials. They attended a formal banquet in their honor hosted by a delegation of veterans and government dignitaries who awarded them Ambassador for Peace Medals and individual letters of appreciation.

> Good will come to him who is generous and lends freely, who conducts his affairs with justice. Surely he will never be shaken; a righteous man will be remembered forever . . . He has scattered abroad his gifts to the poor, his righteousness endures forever; his horn will be lifted high in honor. ~Psalm 112:5–6, 9

Hundreds of other Korean War veterans have participated in revisit programs such as this, funded by the government of South Korea and administered by the Korean Veterans Association of Seoul, as a way of thanking the American and other Allied soldiers who fought for Korea's freedom. Stone was amazed at everything done to make him feel welcomed and honored. Writing later about his visit, he described his final impressions:

> South Korea has come a long way in 60 years. Their cities are very modern and they are the most wired country in the world. Their economy is ranked 14th in the world. Most of the electronic technology we enjoy today is coming out of South Korea. However, I see South Korea as extremely vulnerable. If North Korea were to shoot a few missiles down range into South Korea, the death toll would be in the millions.
>
> The South Korean people and their government will never forget what America and the United Nations did for them in 1950 and for the past 60 years since then. The United States was the biggest contributor of men and materials during the war. The South Koreans know exactly how many men we lost and every man's name is inscribed on the walls of the memorial. They have them all listed by states, so it is easy to look someone up.
>
> It was a great feeling to be in a foreign country where you are respected because you are American. THEY WILL NEVER FORGET US![600]

Homeward Bound

CARL HUGHES was nineteen years old when he set sail for Korea in 1950. He celebrated his twentieth birthday going ashore at Inchon in a landing craft. Assigned to a radio team, he was attached to the 187th Regimental Combat Team during the advance on Seoul and then to other army and Marine units during and after the landing at Wonsan. Having heard the rumor that they would be home by Christmas, he took it hard when someone announced around Thanksgiving that Chinese forces had intervened in the war and were threatening to cut them off from the sea.

> Never again will they hunger; never again will they thirst. The sun will not beat upon them, nor any scorching heat. For the Lamb at the center of the throne will be their shepherd; he will lead them to springs of living water. And God will wipe away every tear from their eyes.
> ~Revelation 7:16–17

Hughes' unit eventually made it to Hamhung to become part of the perimeter defending the port of Hungnam and the evacuation of Tenth Corps. After several days, his team then drew the short straw and was left as one of the very last to board ship. When he finally walked onto the waiting vessel late one night, he found others in his unit waiting up to greet him.

His next homecoming occurred later as he sailed for home on another troop ship. When he arrived at Fort Lewis, Washington, a military band was on hand to give a heartfelt welcome home. He said, "*It was emotional. We were home! I saw more than one grown man wiping his eyes.*"[601] He then had his first stateside meal that he would also never forget: all the steak he could eat accompanied by unlimited milkshakes. A thirty-day leave at home with his family followed.

Returning home after a long separation is always special. We have all had our moments when the journey was over, and we have been reunited with loved ones. Familiar sights and sounds we have missed for too long fill the senses. If such earthly homecomings are special, can we even imagine the ultimate homecoming that awaits each of us? Who will greet us first? What will the heavenly banquet be like? We can only be sure of one thing—this homecoming will surpass every human attempt ever made to describe it.

Freedom on display. The Korean Peninsula at night (Dept. of Defense satellite photo)

Selected Bibliography

Baldovi, Louis, ed. *A Foxhole View: Personal Accounts of Hawaii's Korean War Veterans*. Honolulu: University of Hawai'i Press, 2002.

Berry, Henry. *Hey Mac, Where Ya Been?* New York: St. Martin's Press, 1988.

Blair, Clay. *The Forgotten War*. New York: An Anchor Book, Doubleday, 1988.

Brown, Ronald J. *Counteroffensive: U. S. Marines from Pohang to No Name Line*. Washington, DC: U. S. Marine Corps Historical Center, 2001.

Caldwell, John C. *The Korea Story*. Chicago: Henry Regnery Company, 1952.

Carlson, Lewis H. *Remembered: Prisoners of a Forgotten War*. New York: St. Martin's Press, 2002.

Chancey, Jennie Ethell and William R. Forstchen, eds. *Hot Shots: An Oral History of the Air Force Combat Pilots of the Korean War*. New York: William Morrow, 2000.

Crosbie, Philip. *March Till They Die*. Dublin: Browne & Nolan, Limited, 1955.

Davis, W. J. *Chosin Marine*. San Diego: Self-published, 1986.

Demick, Barbara. *Nothing to Envy: Ordinary Lives in North Korea*. New York: Spiegel & Grau Trade Paperbacks, 2010.

Donovan, Robert J. *Eisenhower: The Inside Story*. New York: Harper & Brothers, 1956.

Drury, Bob and Tom Clavin. *The Last Stand of Fox Company*. New York: Grove Press, 2009.

Gilbert, Bill. *Ship of Miracles*. Chicago: Triumph Books, 2000.

Glenn, John, with Nick Taylor. *John Glenn: A Memoir*. New York: Bantam Books, 1999.

Granfield, Linda. *I Remember Korea*. New York: Clarion Books, 2003.

Hall, Jeannie. *Freedom from Fear*. Knoxville, TN: New Messenger Writing and Publishing, 1995.

Heinl, Robert D. *Soldiers of the Sea*. Annapolis: U.S. Naval Institute, 1962.

Hillman, William. *Mr. President: The First Publication from the Personal Diaries, Private Letters, Papers and Revealing Interviews of Harry S. Truman*. New York: Farrar, Straus and Young, 1952.

Hooker, Richard. *MASH*. New York: Pocket Books (a division of Simon & Schuster), 1969.

Kim, Mike. *Escaping North Korea*. Lanham, MD: Rowman & Littlefield Publishers, Inc., 2008.

Kim, Richard E. *Lost Names: Scenes from a Korean Boyhood*. New York: Praeger Publishers, 1970.

Knox, Donald. *The Korean War: Uncertain Victory*. New York: Harcourt Brace Jovanovich, Publishers, 1988.

Lee, Soon Ok. *Eyes of the Tailless Animals*. Bartlesville, OK: Living Sacrifice Book Co., 1999.

Lewis, C. S. *The Screwtape Letters*. New York: Simon & Schuster, 1996 (first printed 1943).

Maher, William L. *A Shepherd in Combat Boots*. Shippensburg, PA: Burn Street Press, 1997.

Marion, Forrest L. *That Others May Live: USAF Air Rescue in Korea*. Washington, DC: Air Force History and Museums Program, 2004.

Marshall, S. L. A. *Battle at Best*. New York: William Morrow and Company, 1963.

_____ *The River and the Gauntlet*. Nashville: The Battery Press, 1987.

Matthiessen, Peter. *The Birds of Heaven*. London: Vintage, 2003.

Murphy, Edward F. *Korean War Heroes*. Novato, CA: Presidio Press, 1992.

O'Donnell, Patrick K. *Give Me Tomorrow*. Cambridge, MA: De Capo Press, 2010.

Omori, Frances. *Quiet Heroes: Navy Nurses of the Korean War*. Saint Paul, MN: Smith House Press, 2000.

Owen, Joseph R. *Colder Than Hell: A Marine Rifle Company at Chosin Reservoir*. New York: Ballantine Books, 1996.

Paik, Gen. Sun Yup. *From Pusan to Panmunjom*. Washington, DC: Brassey's (US), 1992.

Paschall, Rod. *Witness to War, Korea*. New York: The Berkley Publishing Group, 1995.

Peters, Richard and Xiaobing Li. *Voices from the Korean War: Personal Stories of American, Korean, and Chinese Soldiers*. Lexington, KY: The University Press of Kentucky, 2004.

Rayburn, Robert G. *Fight the Good Fight: Lessons from the Korean War.*: Self-published, 1956.

Rhodehamel, John, ed. *The American Revolution: Writings from the War of Independence*. New York: The Library of America, 2001.

Rice, Douglas. *Voices from the Korean War: Personal Accounts of Those Who Served*. Bloomington, IN: iUniverse (electronic edition), 2011.

Ridgway, Matthew B. *The Korean War*. Garden City, NY: Doubleday & Company, 1967.

Sears, David. *Such Men as These: The Story of the Navy Pilots Who Flew the Deadly Skies Over Korea*. Cambridge, MA: Da Capo Press, 2010.

Sherwood, John Darrell. *Officers in Flight Suits*. New York: New York University Press, 1996.

Soderbergh, Peter. *Women Marines in the Korean War Era*. Westport, CT: Praeger Publishers, 1994.

Terry, Addison. *The Battle for Pusan: A Memoir*. New York: Ballantine Books, 2000.

The History of the Chaplain Corps U.S. Navy, Volume Six, During the Korean War. Washington, DC: US Government Printing Office, 1960.

Toland, John. *In Mortal Combat: Korea 1950–1953*. New York: William Morrow and Company, 1991.

Tomedi, Rudy. *No Bugles, No Drums: An Oral History of the Korean War.* New York: John Wiley & Sons, Inc., 1993.

Venzke, Rodger R. *Confidence in Battle, Inspiration in Peace: The U.S. Army Chaplaincy 1945–1975.* Honolulu: University Press of the Pacific, 1985.

Voorhees, Melvin B. *Korean Tales.* New York: Simon and Schuster, 1952.

Weston, Logan E. *The Fightin' Preacher.* Alexander, NC: Mountain Church, 2001.

Wilson, Arthur W., ed. *Korean Vignettes: Faces of War.* Portland, OR: Artwork Publications, 1996.

Zellers, Larry. *In Enemy Hands: A Prisoner in North Korea.* Lexington, KY: University Press of Kentucky, 1991.

Zimmerman, John D. Oral History Interview by Cdr. H. Lawrence Martin, Naval Historical Collection, US Naval War College, 27–29 July 1981.

Index of Names

Topical Index

440

Notes

1. Tim Lambert, "A Short History of Korea," http://www.localhistories .org/korea.html

2. "Catholicism in Korea: Its Evolution and History," last modified on 29 September 2006, http://asiaenglish.visitkorea.or.kr/ena/SI/SI_EN_3_6.jsp?cid =309625.

3. Jane Lampman, "How Korea Embraced Christianity," *Christian Science Monitor*, 7 March 2007, http://www.csmonitor.com/2007/0307/p14s01-lire.html

4. Paul Backholer, "The First Protestant Missionary to Korea 1865 and 1866," By Faith Media, http://www.byfaith.co.uk/paul200924.htm

5. Ibid. This story has evolved over the ages into different versions. Other accounts can be found at www.Christianity.com/ChurchHistory and in Mike Kim's book, *Escaping North Korea*, 121.

6. Kim, Eun Kook, *Lost Names*, 62.

7. Ibid., 99–100.

8. Ibid., 106.

9. Ibid., 107–110.

10. Ibid., 162.

11. Ibid., 163.

12. Ibid., 175.

13. Harry Truman on 15 August 1950, "Truman's Favorite Prayer," Harry S. Truman Library and Museum, http://www.trumanlibrary.org

14. Ibid.

15. Truman, quoted by Hillman based on an interview, *Mr. President*, 106.

16. Paik, *From Pusan to Panmunjom*, 79.

17. Rear Adm. Thornton C. Miller, "The Chaplains' Attitude Toward Rank," *Navy Chaplains Bulletin*, Winter 1949–50.

18. Caldwell, *The Korea Story*, 153.

19. Toland, *In Mortal Combat*, 208.

20. 2002 Van Fleet Award citation, Horace G. Underwood, The Korea Society, as printed at http://www.koreasociety.org

21. Rear Adm. C. R. Brown, "Our Secret Weapon," *Navy Chaplains Bulletin*, Spring 1950.

22. Harold E. Berger, "The Dangers of the Chaplaincy," *The Lutheran Chaplain*, March–April 1952.

23. Ibid.

24. Ibid.

25. Ibid.

26. Excerpts from the "Address to the Washington Pilgrimage of American Churchmen," by President Truman, 28 September 1951, online by Gerhard Peters and John T. Woodley, *The American Presidency Project*, http://www.presidency.ucsb.edu/ws/?pid=13934

27. "The Bible and Government, Faith Facts," www.faithfacts.org

28. Ibid.

29. M. A. Ditmer, "Chaplains, Use Television," *Navy Chaplains Bulletin,* Winter 1952–53.

30. Robert J. White, "The New Uniform Code of Military Justice, The Navy Chaplain, and Naval Discipline," *Navy Chaplains Bulletin,* Winter 1952–53.

31. Arthur M. Vincent, "Plain Talk and Readable Writing for Ministers," *The Lutheran Chaplain,* Christmas 1952.

32. Ibid.

33. Louis P. Lochner's father was a Lutheran minister.

34. Lochner, "Off Duty," *The Lutheran Chaplain,* January–February 1952.

35. Lochner, "Off Duty," *The Lutheran Chaplain,* March–April 1952.

36. Ibid.

37. Harold E. Berger, "Needs of Others," *The Lutheran Chaplain,* January–February 1952.

38. W. M. Czamanske, "Our Lord's Loneliness," *The Lutheran Chaplain,* January–February 1952.

39. "Tales from the Windy City," *The Chosin Few,* April–June 2011.

40. Medal of Honor citation, Lt. Edward H. O'Hare, as printed in "Medal of Honor, 1861-1949, The Navy," 232, http://www.history.navy.mil/photos/persus/uspers-o/e-ohare.htm

41. Bill Kramer, e-mail to the author, Jan. 25, 2012.

42. Ibid.

43. Military Order of the Purple Heart, http://www.purpleheart.org/

44. Truman, quoted by Hillman based on an interview, *Mr. President,* 97.

45. http://thegatheringplacehome.myfastforum.org,

46. Truman, address at National War College on 19 December 1952, found in "'The Buck Stops Here' Desk Sign," Harry S. Truman Library, http://www.trumanlibrary.org/buckstop.htm

47. Ibid.

48. Soderbergh, *Women Marines,* 34–35.

49. Ibid., 38–39.

50. Keyword search on Dec. 21, 2011, http://www.biblegateway.com, New International Version.

51. "Marine Corps Reassures a Marine's Mother," *The Lutheran Chaplain,* Vol. 12, No. 5, October November, 1951, 11–12.

52. Ibid.

53. Soderbergh, *Women Marines,* 40.

54. Glenn, *John Glenn,* 129.

55. Ibid., 130.

56. Truman, letter quoted by Hillman, *Mr. President,* 34–35.

57. Sung-Gun Kim, "The Shinto Shrine Issue in Korean Christianity under Japanese Colonialism," *Journal of Church and State,* Vol. 39, 1997, accessed at http://www.questia.com/googleScholar.qst?docID=77526112

58. "Cairo Conference Declaration," 22–26 November 1943, as quoted in World War II Database, http://ww2db.com/battle_spec.php?battle_id=68

59. Andrea Matles Savada and William Shaw, eds. "South Korea Under United States Occupation," *South Korea: A Country Study.* Washington: GPO for the

Library of Congress, 1990, accessed at http://countrystudies.us/south-korea/

60. Caldwell, *The Korea Story,* 147.

61. Chester W. Nimitz, "The Threat and the Defense," *Guideposts,"* 1951, quoted in *Navy Chaplains Bulletin,* Spring–Summer 1951.

62. John Adams, letter to the Militia of Massachusetts, Oct. 11, 1798, accessed at: http://www.beliefnet.com/resourcelib/docs/115/Message_from_John_Adams_to_the_Officers_of_the_First_Brigade_1.html

63. Rayburn, *Fight the Good Fight,* 24.

64. Caldwell, *The Korea Story,* 87.

65. Ibid., 99.

66. Truman's First Speech to Congress, Apr. 16, 1945, accessed at The Miller Center, University of Virginia, http://millercenter.org/president/speeches/detail/3339

67. Truman, quoted by Hillman, *Mr. President,* 148–49.

68. Matthiessen, *The Birds of Heaven,* 43, 95.

69. Ibid., 189.

70. Ibid., 192–93.

71. Venzke, *Confidence in Battle, Inspiration in Peace,* 94.

72. Bruce Livingston, interview with the author, April 26, 2012.

73. Lee, *Eyes of the Tailless Animals,* 7–8.

74. Ibid., 113.

75. Ibid.

76. Ibid.

77. Berry, *Hey, Mac, Where Ya Been?* 84.

78. "Desegregation of the Armed Forces," Harry S. Truman Library and Museum, http://www.trumanlibrary.org

79. Berry, *Hey, Mac, Where Ya Been?* 147.

80. Ibid., 148.

81. Ibid., 151.

82. Ibid., 152.

83. Truman, excerpts from the "Address to the Washington Pilgrimage of American Churchmen," 28 September 1951, as quoted by Gerhard Peters and John T. Woodley, The American Presidency Project, http://www.presidency.ucsb.edu/ws/?pid=13934

84. Ibid.

85. Glen Schroeder, "Veterans' Memoirs" Korean War Educator, http://www.koreanwar-educator.org/memoirs/schroeder/index.htm#7

86. Ibid.

87. Joseph Brown, "Veterans' Memoirs," Korean War Educator, http://www.koreanwar-educator.org/memoirs/brown_joe/index.htm

88. Ibid.

89. Truman, "Address to the Attorney General's Conference on Law Enforcement Problems," 15 February 1950, quoted by Hillman, *Mr. President,* 72.

90. Ibid.

91. Rice, *Voices from the Korean War,* 3999.

92. Ibid.

93. Ralph Fly, "Veteran's Memoirs," Korean War Educator, http://www.koreanwar-educator.org/memoirs/fly_ralph/index.htm

94. Ibid.

95. David Ballingrud, quoting Henry Oppenborn, "Korea, the Forgotten War," an Interactive Special Report of the *St. Petersburg Times*, 20 July 2003, http://www.sptimes.com/2003/07/20/Korea/Korea_the_forgotten_.shtml

96. Demick, *Nothing to Envy*, 45.

97. "A Walk Through the Scriptures," *Navy Chaplains Bulletin*, Spring 1950, "All Hail the Power of Jesus' Name," hymn by Edward Perronet and Oliver Holder, circa 1780.

98. Rear Adm. Stanton Salisbury, "The Minister of the Christian Church in the Armed Forces," *Navy Chaplains Bulletin*, Winter 1950–51.

99. Joseph Loper, "Chaplains' Program in RTC at Great Lakes," *Navy Chaplains Bulletin*, Winter 1952.

100. Ibid.

101. Ibid.

102. Leslie F. Brandt, "Your Church Sent Me to You," *The Lutheran Chaplain*, July–August 1952.

103. Ibid.

104. Maher, *A Shepherd in Combat Boots*, 81.

105. Ibid.

106. Wilfred J. Schnedler, "All Clear!" *The Lutheran Chaplain*, Vol. 12, No. 4, August–September 1951.

107. Ibid.

108. Blair, *The Forgotten War*, 45.

109. Toland, *In Mortal Combat*, 18, 26.

110. Ibid.

111. Harry S. Truman: "Statement of the President on the Situation in Korea," 27 June 1950, as quoted by Gerhard Peters and John T. Woolley, *The American Presidency Project*. http://www.presidency.ucsb.edu/ws/?pid=13538

112. Toland, *In Mortal Combat*, 90.

113. Berry, *Hey, Mac, Where Ya Been?* 55.

114. Ibid., 98–99.

115. Venzke, *Confidence in Battle, Inspiration in Peace*, 68.

116. Paschall, *Witness to War*, 34.

117. Ibid.

118. Blair, *The Forgotten War*, 103.

119. Lewis, *The Screwtape Letters*, 37–38.

120. Venzke, *Confidence in Battle, Inspiration in Peace*, 68–69.

121. David Venditta, quoting Cecilia Ann Sulkowski, "Mending Broken Spirits, Shattered Bodies in Korea," *The Morning Call*, Allentown, PA, 5 July 2002, http://www.mcall.com/news/all-ceceliasulkowski,0,5034936.story

122. Lt. Cmdr. A. M. Oliver, "Of One Blood All Nations," *Navy Chaplains Bulletin*, Spring–Summer, 1952.

123. Granfield, *I Remember Korea*, 76.

124. Weston, "*The Fightin' Preacher*," 240.

125. Verses handwritten by Weston in the author's signed copy of his book.

126. Wilson, *Korean Vignettes*, 21.

127. Ibid., 22.

128. Weston, *The Fightin' Preacher,* 222.

129. Chancey, *Hot Shots,* 19.

130. Jorge Sanchez, quoting Albert Provost, "GI Gave Shelter to the Children of War," in "Korea, the Forgotten War: 1950-1953," an Interactive Special Report of the St. Petersburg Times, 25 July 2003, http://www.sptimes.com/2003/07/25/Korea/GI_gave_shelter_to_th.shtml

131. Ibid.

132. Lewis, *The Screwtape Letters,* 32.

133. "The Salvation Army International Heritage Centre," Herbert Arthur Lord, accessed on 12 September 2011, http://www1.salvationarmy.org.ukuki/www_uki_ihc.nsf

134. Ibid.

135. Zellers, *In Enemy Hands,* xvii.

136. Ibid., 33–34.

137. James Lutze on the Korean War Project, quoting from "A Letter Home from Korea: 'Between the Lines,'" originally printed in the *Racine Journal Times,* Racine, WI, http://www.koreanwar.org/html/units/frontline/Racine.htm

138. Gilliland, Burl, "Dozo," www.kilroywashere.org/003-Pages/Burl/Dozo.htm

139. Cdr. W. A. Mahler, "Notes on the Recall Program," *Navy Chaplains Bulletin,* Fall 1950.

140. Voorhees, *Korean Tales,* 122.

141. Terry, *The Battle for Pusan,* 152.

142. Ibid., 151.

143. *The History of the Chaplain Corps, U. S. Navy,* 251–52.

144. Ibid.

145. Tomedi, *No Bugles, No Drums,* 154.

146. John D. Zimmerman, Oral History Interview, 48.

147. Ibid., 49.

148. "Armed Forces Aid Refugee Seminary in Korea," *Navy Chaplains Bulletin,* Winter 1952.

149. David Venditta, quoting Cecilia Ann Sulkowski, "Mending Broken Spirits, Shattered Bodies in Korea," *The Morning Call,* Allentown, PA, 5 July 2002, http://www.mcall.com/news/all-ceceliasulkowski,0,5034936.story

150. Ibid.

151. Bruce Livingston, interview with the author, 26 April 2012.

152. Owen, *Colder Than Hell,* 43.

153. Ibid., 45–46.

154. Maher, *The Shepherd in Combat Boots,* 147.

155. Julia Ward Howe, "Battle Hymn of the Republic," partial verses, first published in 1862, accessed at http://www.cyberhymnal.org/htm/b/h/bhymnotr.htm

156. Heinl, *Soldiers of the Sea,* 544.

157. James Schnabel, "Crossing the Parallel," *United States Army in the Korean War, Policy and Direction: The First Year,* Center of Military History, United States Army, Washington, DC: 1972, accessed at http://www.history.army.mil/books/PD-C-10.HTM

158. Arthur Carl Piepkorn, "The Queen of Holy Days," *The Lutheran Chaplain*, March–April 1952.

159. Maher, *A Shepherd in Combat Boots*, 146.

160. Lyrics by Frederick W. Faber, 1849, music by Henri F. Hemy, 1864, *Faith of Our Fathers*, http://www.hymnal.net/hymn.php/h/830

161. Navy Unit Commendation citation, www.angelfire.com/fl4/stock/images/allhands.jpg

162. Rob Brandon, quoting Lt. Baldomero Lopez, "The Hero from Hillsborough High," *St. Petersburg Times*, 22 July 2003, http://www.sptimes.com/2003/07/22/Korea/The_hero_from_Hillsbo.shtml

163. Medal of Honor citation, Lt. Baldomero Lopez, http://militarytimes.com/citations-medals-awards/recipient.php?recipientid=230

164. George Henderson, www.angelfire.com/fl4/stock/Page9.html

165. Ibid.

166. Ibid.

167. Rear Adm. S. W. Salisbury, "Letter to All Chaplains," *Navy Chaplains Bulletin*, Fall 1950, 3.

168. Tomedi, *No Bugles, No Drums*, 42.

169. Murphy, *Korean War Heroes*, 55.

170. Medal of Honor Citation, Walter Monegan, accessed at http://www.arlingtoncemetery.net/wcmonega.htm

171. George L. Markle, "How Are We Facing Up to Our Task as Chaplains?" *Navy Chaplains Bulletin*, Fall 1951.

172. Berry, *Hey, Mac, Where Ya Been?* 78.

173. O'Donnell, *Give Me Tomorrow*, 68.

174. Owen, *Colder Than Hell*, 79.

175. Brady Dennis quoting Don Ploof, "Of Faith and Fatality," in "Korea, the Forgotten War: 1950-1953," an Interactive Special Report of the *St. Petersburg Times*, 25 July 2003, http://www.sptimes.com/2003/07/25/Korea/Of_faith_and_fatality.shtml

176. Ibid.

177. John D. Zimmerman, oral history interview with Martin, 47–48.

178. Ibid., 51.

179. Ibid., 50–51.

180. Peters and Li, *Voices from the Korean War*, 162.

181. Ibid., 170.

182. Chancey and Forstchen, *Hot Shots*, 48.

183. Knox, *The Korean War: Uncertain Victory*, 19–20.

184. The Salvation Army International Heritage Centre, "Herbert Arthur Lord," accessed on 12 September 2011, www1.salvationarmy.org.ukuki/www_uki_ihc.nsf

185. Ibid.

186. Ibid.

187. "USS Bataan Raises Church Pennant for Burial at Sea," 23 February 2011, Christian Fighter Pilot, http://christianfighterpilot.com/blog/2011/02/23/uss-bataan-raises-church-pennant-for-burial-at-sea/

188. Legal Information Institute of Cornell University Law School, "4 U.S.C. Chapter 1—The Flag," accessed at www.law.cornell.edu/uscode/text/4/chapter-1

189. "Church Pennant History," *Navy Chaplains Bulletin,* Spring–Summer 1951.

190. Harold Voelkel, "Behind Barbed Wire in Korea," originally published in 1953, accessed at http://urbana.org/go-and-do/missionary-biographies/behind-barbed-wire-korea

191. Public Broadcasting System, "American Experience," www.pbs.org/wgbh/americanexperience/features/transcript/warletters-transcript/

192. Robert J. White, "The New Uniform Code of Military Justice, The Navy Chaplain, and Naval Discipline," *Navy Chaplains Bulletin*, Winter 1952–53.

193. Ibid.

194. Paul Noll, "Charles K. House, a Pilot's View of Chosin," *Stories from the Chosin Reservoir,* www.paulnoll.com/Korea/Smith/story-pilots.html

195. Adrienne Lu, quoting Robert Bryson, "A Case of Severe Apprehension," in "Korea, the Forgotten War: 1950-1953," an Interactive Special Report of the *St. Petersburg Times*, 26 July 2003, http://www.sptimes.com/2003/07/26/Korea/A_case_of__severe_app.shtml

196. Ibid.

197. William Shakespeare, "Hamlet," Act III, Scene I, accessed at http://www.enotes.com/hamlet-text/act-iii-scene-i

198. Rayburn, *Fight the Good Fight,* 15.

199. Granfield, *I Remember Korea,* 55.

200. D.C. Everest Area Schools, "Donald Maguire," *Korean War Not Forgotten: Stories from Korean War Veterans,* Wisconsin Historical Society, http://www.wisconsinhistory.org/turningpoints/search.asp?id=1380

201. Ibid.

202. Ibid.

203. The general was recalling a poem by the nineteenth century poet and songwriter Roscoe Gilmore Stott. He said in advance, "I may not quote it correctly."

204. Wilbur S. Brown, "What a Marine Expects of a Chaplain," *Navy Chaplains Bulletin,* Spring 1953.

205. Ibid.

206. Ibid.

207. James Schnabel, "The Invasion of North Korea," *Policy and Direction: The First Year*, Center of Military History, accessed at www.history.army.mil/books/PD-C-11.htm

208. Ibid.

209. Blair, *The Forgotten War,* 349.

210. Toland, *In Mortal Combat,* 282.

211. "US Senate Report 848: Korean War Atrocities," Eighty-third Congress, accessed at http://b-29s-over-korea.com

212. Tomedi, *No Bugles, No Drums,* 59.

213. Paik, *From Pusan to Panmunjom,* 77.

214. Ibid.

215. Rayburn, *Fight the Good Fight,* 92.

216. Paik, *From Pusan to Panmunjom,* 76.

217. "American Fighting Man: Destiny's Draftee," 1 January 1951, Korean War: Weapons and History blog, http://www.rt66.com/~korteng/Small-Arms/1950.htm

218. Ibid.

219. Wilson, *Korean Vignettes,* 65.

220. *The History of the Chaplain Corps, U. S. Navy,* 69.

221. Ibid., 70.

222. Ibid.

223. Maurice S. Sheehy, "A Morning Prayer," *Navy Chaplains Bulletin,* Summer 1950.

224. *Navy Chaplains Bulletin,* Spring–Summer 1951.

225. Peters and Li, *Voices from the Korean War,* 69.

226. Knox, *The Korean War: Uncertain Victory,* 21.

227. Zellers, *In Enemy Hands,* 59.

228. Ibid., 60.

229. Ibid., 217.

230. William Wordsworth, "Lines," *Composed a Few Miles Above Tintern Abbey, on Revisiting the Banks of the Wye During a Tour July 13, 1798,* accessed at http://www.bartleby.com/

231. Edward B. Harp, Jr., "Greetings," *Navy Chaplains Bulletin,* Spring 1953.

232. Roy H. Parker, "Soldiers of God," *The Lutheran Chaplain,* October–November 1951.

233. Harold E. Berger, "Star of Hope," *The Lutheran Chaplain,* Christmas 1952.

234. R. D. Heinl Jr., "A Prayer for the Marine Corps," *Navy Chaplains Bulletin,* Winter 1952.

235. "The Marines Prayer," accessed at http://www.marines.mil/Marines/2012birthdayball.aspx

236. Associated Press, "Korean War Soldier Finally Coming Home," *Lexington Herald Ledger,* 30 March 2012, http://www.kentucky.com/2012/03/30/2132005/korean-war-soldier-finally-coming.html

237. Rayburn, *Fight the Good Fight,* 33.

238. Ibid., 75.

239. Ibid.

240. Al Rasmussen, "P.T.S.D. Symptoms," *The Chosin Few,"* April–June 2011.

241. Birchard L. Kortegaard, "Tech Rep," Korean War: Weapons and History blog, http://kmike,com/TechRep.htm

242. Ibid.

243. Lu, quoting Leroy "Don" Colts, "Korea, the Forgotten War: 1950-1953," an Interactive Special Report of the *St. Petersburg Times,* 27 July 2003, http://www.sptimes.com/2003/07/27/Korea/Trudging_up_the_hill_.shtml

244. Sherwood, *Officers in Flight Suits,* 140–42.

245. Hooker, *MASH,* 157.

246. Ibid., 160.

247. Maher, *A Shepherd in Combat Boots,* 132.

248. Ibid., 134–35.

249. Ibid., 135.

250. Lyrics by George Duffield, Jr. (1818–88) and music by George J. Webb (1803–87), "Stand Up, Stand Up for Jesus."

251. "War Letters," Public Broadcasting System, "American Experience," www.pbs.org/wgbh/americanexperience/features/transcript/warletters-transcript

252. Dr. John W. Raley, "Accentuate the Positive," *Navy Chaplains Bulletin*, Spring–Summer 1952.

253. John F. Kennedy, speech in Indianapolis, Indiana, 12 April 1959, accessed at http://www.quotationspage.com/quote/2750.html

254. Marshall, *Battle at Best*, 125.

255. Martin Kretzschmar, "Korea Revisited," *The Lutheran Chaplain*, December 1951.

256. Harold E. Berger, "Privilege of the Chaplain's Ministry," *The Lutheran Chaplain*, December 1951.

257. Richard W. Stewart, *The Korean War*, "The Chinese Intervention," US Army Center of Military History, last updated 3 October 2003, 6, www.history.army.mil/brochures/kw-chinter/chinter.htm

258. Marshall, *The River and the Gauntlet*, 50.

259. Stewart, *The Korean War*, "The Chinese Intervention," 12, http://www.history.army.mil/brochures/kw-chinter/chinter.htm

260. Toland, *In Mortal Combat*, 281.

261. Paik, *From Pusan to Panmunjom*, 89.

262. Voorhees, *Korean Tales*, 97.

263. "Church Leaders and Involuntary Recall," *Navy Chaplains Bulletin*, Winter 1952.

264. Ibid.

265. Ibid.

266. Peters and Li, *Voices from the Korean War*, 93–94.

267. Paik, *From Pusan to Panmunjom*, 117.

268. William R. Thierfelder, "Fear and Anxiety," *The Lutheran Chaplain*, July–August 1952.

269. Ibid.

270. Toland, *In Mortal Combat*, 257.

271. Voorhees, *Korean Tales*, 137–38.

272. Ibid., 139.

273. Burl Gilliland, "North Korean Shore Batteries," http://www.kilroywashere.org/003-Pages/Burl/Burl-ShoreBatteries.html

274. Dale King, "Two Korean War Veterans Describe Their Experiences," Wisconsin Historical Society, www.wisconsinhistory.org/turningpoints/search.asp?id+1380

275. Linda Lewin, e-mail to the author, Jan. 30, 2012.

276. Ibid.

277. Wilson, *Korean Vignettes*, 91.

278. "A Marine Colonel Speaks on Faith and Religion," *Navy Chaplains Bulletin*, Fall 1951.

279. Abraham Lincoln, quote, accessed at http://thinkexist.com/quotation/sir-my_concern_is_not_whether_god_is_on_our_side/164075.html

280. Venzke, *Confidence in Battle*, 84–85.

281. Wilson, *Korean Vignettes,* 95.

282. Capt. William A. Dickson, diary, 1952, accessed at www.sadlak.com/ Dickson/Diary_1952_Korea.html

283. Raymond Hohenstein, "The Navy Chaplain," *The Lutheran Chaplain,* October–November 1951.

284. Maher, *A Shepherd in Combat Boots,* 125–26.

285. Lyrics by Joseph Mohr (1792–1848); music by Franz Gruber (1787–1863), *Silent Night.*

286. "Chaplain Sobel Takes 'Ark' from Pearl Harbor to Korea," *Navy Chaplains Bulletin,* Winter 1952–53.

287. Jerry Gill, interview with the author, 17 May 2012.

288. Ibid.

289. Owen, *Colder Than Hell,* 129–30.

290. Marshall, *The River and the Gauntlet,* 212.

291. Ibid., 56–58.

292. John McCurry, interview with the author, 20 March 2012.

293. John Craven, "Esprit de Corps 'Was Not an Empty Phrase': A Combat Chaplain Reflects on the Chosin Campaign," November 2000, www .navyleague.org/sea_power/nov_00_11.php

294. Drury and Clavin, *The Last Stand of Fox Company,* 41–42.

295. John Newton (1725–1807), *Amazing Grace,* first and third stanzas, accessed at http://www.hymns.me.uk/amazing-grace.htm

296. John Craven, "A Combat Chaplain Reflects on the Chosin Campaign," http://www.navyleague.org/sea_power/nov_00_11.php

297. Theodore P. Bornhoeft, "The Chaplain's Function in Family Life," *The Lutheran Chaplain,* August–September 1951.

298. S. W. Salisbury, "Christmas 1952," Navy *Chaplains Bulletin,* Winter 1952–53.

299. Ibid.

300. Blair, *The Forgotten War,* 423.

301. Heinl, *Soldiers of the Sea,* 562.

302. Toland, *In Mortal Combat,* 309.

303. Heinl, *Soldiers of the Sea,* 567.

304. Richard W. Stewart, *The Korean War,* "The Chinese Intervention," US Army Center of Military History, last updated 3 October 2003, 24, www.history.army.mil/brochures/kw-chinter/chinter.htm

305. Davis, *Chosin Marine,* 10.

306. Ibid., 45.

307. Ibid.

308. Ibid.

309. Medal of Honor Citation, First Lieutenant Frank Nicias Mitchell, USMC, U. S. Marine Corps History Division, https://www.mcu.usmc.mil/historydivision/pages/Whos_Who/Mitchell_FN.aspx

310. O'Donnell, *Give Me Tomorrow,* 4.

311. Ibid., 137.

312. Omar Khayyam, *The Rubaiyat,* Verse XLIX, AD 1120, accessed at http:// classics.mit.edu/Khayyam/rubaiyat.html

313. Gary Johnson, "Nile H. Marsh, A Forgotten Soldier from a Forgotten War," unpublished article sent to the author, 24 February 2012.

314. Ibid.

315. Ibid.

316. Ray Westbrook, "Cecil McMorris, US Army: A Veteran's Memories," *Stories from the Chosin Reservoir,* www.paulnoll.com/Korea/Smith/story-disaster-1.html

317. Ibid.

318. John McCurry, interview with the author, 29 January 2012.

319. James Dill, "Winter of the Yalu," *Changjin Journal,* December 1982, accessed at http://www.americanheritage.com/content/winter-yalu

320. Ibid.

321. Toland, *In Mortal Combat,* 335.

322. Ibid.

323. Ibid.

324. Ibid., 348.

325. Ibid.

326. Ibid.

327. Ibid.

328. Ibid.

329. Lyrics by Anna Bartlett Warner(1827-1915), 1860; music by William Bradbury(1816-1868), 1862.

330. Rice, *Voices from the Korean War,* 4028.

331. Ibid., 4056.

332. Dill, "Winter of the Yalu," Changjin Journal, accessed at http://www.americanheritage.com/content/winter-yalu

333. Harrell Roberts, interview with the author, 17 May 2012 and 5 June 2012.

334. Ibid.

335. Ibid.

336. Drury and Clavin, *The Last Stand of Fox Company,* 234–35.

337. Walt Hiskett, oral history interview by Paul Zardock, University of North Carolina—Wilmington, http://library.uncw.edu/web/collections/oralhistories/transcripts/807.html

338. Ibid.

339. Heinl, quoting Gen. O. P. Smith, commanding the First Marine Division during the Chosin Reservoir campaign, *Soldiers of the Sea,* 567.

340. O'Donnell, *Give Me Tomorrow,* 166.

341. William M. Hearn, "Psalms at Hagaru," *The History of the Chaplain Corps, U. S. Navy,* 41.

342. Davis, *Chosin Marine,* 104.

343. Don Moore, "One of 'the Chosin Few'" 10 June 2010, http://donmooreswartales.com/2010/06/21/joe-quick/

344. Ibid.

345. Berry, *Hey, Mac, Where Ya Been?,* 101.

346. C. Douglas Sterner "Guam, Summer/Fall 1944," accessed at http://www.homeofheroes.com/profiles/profiles_sitter.html

347. Ibid.

348. Carl Sitter, www.homeofheroes.com/profiles/profiles_sitter.html

349. Medal of Honor citation, Capt. Carl L. Sitter, http://www.arlington-cemetery.net/clsitter.htm

350. Berry, *Hey, Mac, Where Ya Been?*, 102.

351. Medal of Honor citation, Lt. Col. John U. D. Page, http://www.msc.navy.mil/inventory/citations/page.htm

352. Davis, *Chosin Marine*, 113.

353. Ibid., 69.

354. *The History of the Chaplain Corps, U. S. Navy*, 45–47.

355. Paul Noll, "The Real Story," *Stories from the Chosin Reservoir*, www.paulnoll.com/Korea/Smith/story-real-story-01.html

356. Richard W. Stewart, *The Korean War*, "The Chinese Intervention," US Army Center of Military History, last updated 3 October 2003, 25, www.history.army.mil/brochures/kw-chinter/chinter.htm

357. John J. McGrath, *The Korean War* "Restoring the Balance," US Army Center of Military History, last updated 3 October 2003, 4, www.history.army.mil/brochures/kw-balance/balance.htm

358. Ibid., 5.

359. Ridgway, *The Korean War*, 86.

360. Brown, quoting portions of Ridgway's directive, *Counteroffensive*, 7–8.

361. Paul Noll, "Evacuated from Hungnam Harbor," www.paulnoll.com/Korea/Story/story-Korea-asleep-pier.html

362. Noll, quoting Lt. Kevin Kearney, diary, 8 December 1950, Stories from the Chosin Reservoir, www.paulnoll.com/Korea/Smith/story-Chaplain.html

363. Ridgway, *The Korean War*, 102.

364. Noll, "Len Maffioli," *Stories from the Chosin Reservoir*, www.paulnoll.com/Korea/Smith/story-POW.html

365. John Y. Lee, "Silent Night," www.paulnoll.com/Korea/Smith/story-Hagaru.html

366. Gilbert, *Ship of Miracles*, 105.

367. Ibid.

368. Ibid., 115.

369. Ibid., 161.

370. Ibid., 182.

371. Ibid., 178.

372. Ibid., 181.

373. Ibid., 191.

374. Robert Tate, "Veterans' Memoirs," Korean War Educator, http://www.koreanwar-educator.org/memoirs/tate_robert/index.htm

375. Ibid.

376. Rayburn, quoting Psalm 23:4, *Fight the Good Fight*, 45.

377. David R. Hughes, "A Letter to Capt. Flynn," www.koreanwar.org/html/units/frontline/hughes.htm

378. Gilliland, Burl, "Sabotage of Minesweepers in Wonsan Bay," http://www.kilroywashere.org/003-Pages/Burl/Sabotage.htm

379. Glen Schroeder, interviews with Lynnita Sommer (Brown) in 1999–2000, Korean War Educator, www.koreanwar-educator.org/memoirs/schroeder/index.htm#7

380. Ibid.

381. Ibid.

382. Ibid.

383. Davis, *Chosin Marine,* 20.

384. Bill McCaffrey, "Cold: A State of Mind," *Changjin Journal* 01.20.00, accessed at http://bobrowen.com/nymas/changjinjournal.html

385. Pancho Pasqualicchio, interview with the author, May 3, 2010.

386. Robert King, "Images of Orphans Haunt Veteran," "Korea, the Forgotten War: 1950-1953," an Interactive Special Report of the *St. Petersburg Times,* 27 July 2003, http://www.sptimes.com/2003/07/27/Korea/Images_of_orphans_hau.shtml

387. Ibid.

388. Omori, *Quiet Heroes,* 1.

389. Weston, *The Fightin' Preacher,* 241.

390. Truman, excerpts from the "Address to the Washington Pilgrimage of American Churchmen," 28 September 1951, Gerhard Peters and John T. Woodley, *The American Presidency Project,* http://www.presidency.ucsb.edu/ws/?pid=13934

391. Ronald Eugene Rosser, "Veterans' Memoirs," Korean War Educator, http://www.koreanwar-educator.org/memoirs/rosser_ronald/index.htm

392. Ibid.

393. Medal of Honor citation, Richard D. De Wert, http://www.marinemedals.com/dewertrichard.htm

394. Seymour Harris, "Return to Heartbreak Ridge," copyright Hal Barker, www.koreanwar.org/my_html/korea008.htm

395. "Chaplain Austin Writes from Korean Fox-hole," *Navy Chaplains Bulletin,* Fall 1951.

396. Granfield, *I Remember Korea,* 96.

397. Douglas MacArthur, excerpts from Thayer Award speech, 12 May 1962, http://www.au.af.mil/au/awc/awcgate/au-24/au24-352mac.htm

398. Ibid.

399. "Air War Korea," Timothy Warnock, ed., www.airforce-magazine.com/MagazineArchive/Pages/2000/October%202000/1000korea.aspx

400. Jim Givens, "North American F-51D Mustang," http://www.koreanwar.com/KWAircraft/US/USAF/north_american_f51.html

401. William T. Y'Blood, "The Korean Air War," Seventh Air Force, 1 February 2007, http://www.7af.pacaf.af.mil/library/factsheets/factsheet.asp?id=7103

402. "The Korean War," U. S. Centennial of Flight Commission, accessed on 30 January 2012, http://www.centennialofflight.gov/essay/Air_Power/korea/AP38.htm

403. Sherwood, *Officers in Flight Suits,* 49.

404. Ibid.

405. Ibid., 50.

406. Chancey, *Hot Shots,* 32–34.

407. Wilson, *Korean Vignettes,* 13–14

408. Richard Gruber, "Korea," 17 January 1999, http://www.koreanwar.org/html/units/frontline/gruber.htm

409. Silver Star citation, John C. Shumate, http://en.wikipedia.org/wiki/John_C._Shumate

410. Marion, *That Others May Live,* 6.

411. Chancey, *Hot Shots,* 81.

412. Ibid., 82.

413. Sears, *Such Men as These,* 38–39.

414. Ibid., 42.

415. C. Douglas Sterner, "Thomas Hudner and Jesse LeRoy Brown," The Home of Heroes, www.homeofheroes.com/brotherhood/hudner.html

416. Ibid.

417. Excerpts from Medal of Honor citation for Thomas Jerome Hudner, Jr., The Home of Heroes, http://www.homeofheroes.com/moh/citations_living/kc_n_hudner.html

418. Sterner, "Thomas Hudner and Jesse LeRoy Brown," The Home of Heroes, http://www.homeofheroes.com/brotherhood/hudner.html

419. Pancho Pasqualicchio, interview with the author, 19 June 2012.

420. Ibid.

421. Sears, *Such Men as These,* 13.

422. Kenneth Schechter, "Blind and Alone Over North Korea," *Naval Aviation News,* September–October 2004, http://www.history.navy.mil/nan/backissues/2000s/2004/so/blind.pdf. This story, with major modifications, was retold in a movie, *Men of the Fighting Lady* with Van Johnson as Howard Thayer and Dewey Martin as Ken Schechter.

423. Ibid.

424. Ibid.

425. Lou Ives, "Kenneth A. Schechter," United States Naval Aviation: The Brown Shoes Project, http://thebrownshoes.org/AcrobatPDF/SCHECHTER,%20KENNETH%20A.%20%20%20KEN%20%20%205-49.pdf

426. Glenn, *John Glenn,* 134.

427. Ibid., 148.

428. Donald R. Michaelis, Silver Star citation, http://militarytimes.com/citations-medals-awards/citation.php?citation=28953

429. Sears, *Such Men as These,* 89.

430. Comments written by Thomas Moore, Oct. 26, 2010, Korean War Project, www.koreanwar.org/html/units/navy/vf112.htm

431. Diary of Capt. William A. Dickson, 1952, accessed at http://www.sadlak.com/Dickson/Diary_1952_Korea.html

432. Jacqueline Lee, quoting William Chatfield, "I'm a Believer," *Belleville News-Democrat,* Belleville, IL, 30 January 2011, http://www.bnd.com/2011/01/30/1571588/im-a-believer-korean-war-vet.html

433. Chancey, *Hot Shots,* 83.

434. Ted Williams quotation, accessed at http://www.baseball-almanac.com/quotes/quowilt.shtml

435. Glenn, *John Glenn,* 131.

436. President George W. Bush's statement on the passing of Ted Williams, accessed at http://www.baseball-almanac.com/quotes/quowilt.shtml

437. Tomedi, *No Bugles, No Drums,* 159.

438. Sherwood, *Officers in Flight Suits,* 81.

439. Ibid.

440. Chancey, *Hot Shots,* 142.

441. Maj. Richard C. Catledge, "Luke Air Force Base and the Thunderbirds," http://thunderbirdsalumni.com/PDF/Original%20Thunderbirds.pdf

442. Chancey, *Hot Shots,* 144.

443. Andrew J. Birtle, *The Korean War,* "Years of Stalemate," US Army Center of Military History, 13 September 2006, 5, http://www.history.army.mil/brochures/kw-stale/stale.htm

444. Blair, *The Forgotten War,* 910–11.

445. Birtle, *The Korean War,* "Years of Stalemate," 17, http://www.history.army.mil/brochures/kw-stale/stale.htm

446. "First Chapel in Korea for First Marine Division," *Navy Chaplains Bulletin,* Fall 1951.

447. Ibid.

448. Medal of Honor citation for William Henry Thompson, American Armoured Foundation Tank Museum, http://www.aaftankmuseum.com/WMHTHOMPSON.htm

449. Ibid.

450. David R. Hughes, "A Letter to Capt. Flynn," 7 February 1952, accessed at http://www.koreanwar.org/html/units/frontline/hughes.htm

451. Joseph Brown, "Veterans' Memoirs," interview with Lynnita Sommer Brown, 2000, Korean War Educator, http://www.koreanwar-educator.org/memoirs/brown_joe/index.htm

452. Mary Stevenson, 1936. Authorship of very similar stories has also been claimed by Margaret Fishback Powers, 1964, and Carolyn Carty, 1963. The various claims are addressed on http://www.wowzone.com. I have quoted what seems to be the earliest version.

453. Brown, Joseph, "Veterans' Memoirs," www.koreanwar-educator.org/memoirs/brown_joe/index.htm

454. Ibid.

455. Ibid.

456. Albert Gierke, "Sermon Preached at Funeral of Serviceman," March 16, 1952, *The Lutheran Chaplain,* July–August 1952.

457. Carlson, *Remembered,* 145.

458. Ibid.

459. Hall, *Freedom from Fear,* 59.

460. Ibid., 58–61.

461. Col. James Patterson, Testimony given on Crossroads Television, 1985, rerun 11 November 2011. http://100huntley.com/video.php?id=VoYMSLbr48g

462. Ronald Eugene Rosser, "Veterans' Memoirs," interview with Lynnita Brown Sommer, 29 July 2004, Korean War Educator, www.koreanwar-educator.org/memoirs/rosser_ronald/index.htm

463. Medal of Honor citation for Ronald E. Rosser, The Home of the Heroes, http://www.homeofheroes.com/moh/citations_living/kc_a_rosser.html

464. Op. cit. Ronald Eugene Rosser, "Veterans' Memoirs."

465. *The History of the Chaplain Corps, US Navy,* 121.

466. Russell A. Gugeler, "Outpost Eerie," *Combat Actions in Korea,* US Army Center of Military History, 1954, reprinted 1987, accessed at *http://*www.history .army.mil/books/korea/30-2/30-2_18.htm

467. Ralph Fly, "Veterans' Memoirs," Korean War Educator, http://www .koreanwar-educator.org/memoirs/fly/index.htm

468. Ibid.

469. Jacqueline Hames, "Forgotten Fire: Bitter Cold, a Big Gun, Initiative to Spare," Official Homepage of the United States Army, 27 July 2010, http://www.army.mil/article/42897/Forgotten_fire__Bitter_cold__a_big_gun__ initiative_to_spare/

470. Ibid.

471. Peters and Li, *Voices from the Korean War,* 133.

472. Davis, *Chosin Marine,* 50.

473. Samuel "Dave" Chambers, "Veterans' Memoirs: Star of the Sea Orphanage," http://www.koreanwar-educator.org/memoirs/chambers_s_dave/index.htm

474. Venditta, quoting Gene Salay, "So This is What it Feels Like to Die," *The Morning Call,* Allentown, PA, 27 July 2003, http://www.mcall.com/news/all -genesalay,0,1701380.story

475. R. Bruce Wareing, "Veterans' Memoirs: Good Times and Bad Times," Korean War Educator, February 2008, http://www.koreanwar-educator.org/ memoirs/wareing_bruce/index.htm

476. Ibid.

477. Ibid.

478. Rhodehamel, *Writings,* 794.

479. Douglas MacArthur, excerpts from Thayer Award speech, 12 May 1962, accessed at http://www.au.af.mil/au/awc/awcgate/au-24/au24-352mac.htm

480. Arthur Lortie, audio transcript, The Memory Project, http://www.the memoryproject.com/stories/2231:arthur-lortie/

481. Peters and Li, *Voices from the Korean War,* 114.

482. Ibid., 63.

483. Ibid., 64.

484. Tomedi, *No Bugles, No Drums,* 145.

485. David Ballingrud, quoting Norman Parsons, "Korea, the Forgotten War," an Interactive Special Report of the *St. Petersburg Times,* 20 July 2003, www .sptimes.com/2003/07/20/Korea/Korea__the_forgotten_.shtml

486. Dwight D. Eisenhower, "Speech on the Korean Armistice," 26 July 1953, The American Presidency Project, http://www.presidency.ucsb.edu/ws/ index.php?pid=9653&st=&st1=

487. Granfield, *I Remember Korea,* 40–41.

488. Louis P. Horyza, "Home is Where the Howze is," *The Greybeards,* Vol. 25, No. 4, July–August 2011.

489. Ibid.

490. Ibid.

491. Jeffrey Gray, Fact Sheet: "Operations Big and Little Switch," originally in *The Korean War: An Encyclopedia*, Garland Publishing, Inc., accessed at www.nj.gov/military/korea/factsheets/opswitch.html

492. Senate Report No. 848, "Korean War Atrocities," 11 January 1954, accessed at http://www.loc.gov/rr/frd/Military_Law/pdf/KW-atrocities-Report.pdf

493. Toland, *In Mortal Combat*, 255–64.

494. "DMZ-DPRK Tunnels," 7 September 2011, http://www.globalsecurity.org/military/world/dprk/kpa-tunnels.htm

495. Bill Powell, "South Korea's Case for How the *Cheonan* Sank," *Time*, 13 August 2010, http://www.time.com/time/world/article/0,8599,2010455,00.html

496. Volha Charnysh, "North Korea's Nuclear Program," 3 September 2009, Nuclear Age Peace Foundation, http://www.nuclearfiles.org/menu/key-issues/nuclear-weapons/issues/proliferation/north-korea/charnysh_dprk_analysis.pdf

497. "KWVA History in Brief," Korean War Veterans Association, http://kwva.org/brief_history.htm

498. David Venditta, quoting Gene Salay, "So This is What it Feels Like to Die," *The Morning Call*, Allentown, PA, 17 July 2003, http://www.mcall.com/news/all-genesalay,0,4873801,full.story

499. Ibid.

500. Carlson, *Remembered*, 229–30.

501. Rice, *Voices from the Korean War*, 2979.

502. Ibid., 3188.

503. Carlson, *Remembered*, 145.

504. Baldovi, *Foxhole View*, 275.

505. Ibid., 277.

506. Patrice O'Shaughnessy, "Bronx vets get black Korean War hero proper burial at Arlington," *NY Daily News*, 9 November 2008, http://www.nydailynews.com/new-york/bronx/bronx-vets-black-korean-war-hero-proper-burial-arlington-article-1.336079

507. Quintus Horatius Flaccus (65–8 BC), "Horace," *Odes*, Book 3, No. 2, http://www.quotecounterquote.com/2010/10/dulce-et-decorum-est-pro-patria-mori-it.htm.

508. Wilfred Owen, "*Dulce et Decorum Est*," 1918, http://www.warpoetry.co.uk/owen1.html

509. Davis, *Chosin Marine*, viii.

510. Salvation Army International Heritage Centre, "Herbert Arthur Lord," accessed on 12 September 2011, http://www1.salvationarmy.org.ukuki/www_uki_ihc.nsf

511. James Landrum, e-mails to the author, 16 December 2011 and 27 February 2012.

512. Silver Star Citation, Robert S. Durham, Hall, *Freedom from Fear*, 66.

513. Hall, *Freedom from Fear*, 61.

514. Don Childs, "The War I Remember," *The Chosin Few*, April–June 2011.

515. Ibid.

516. Wilson, *Korean Vignettes*, 115.

517. Carlson, *Remembered*, 90.

518. Robert King, quoting Joseph Alaimo, "War Rages On in Body and Soul," Interactive Special Report of the *St. Petersburg Times*, 20 July 2003, http://www.sptimes.com/2003/07/20/Korea/War_rages_on_in_body_.shtml

519. Ibid.

520. "News of His Father Saves a Marine," *The Morning Call*, Allentown, PA, 11 November 1999, http://www.mcall.com/news/all-randolphrabenold,0,1159091.story

521. Charles Malik, "Finding God in the United Nations," Finding God At, http://www.findinggodat.org/the-united-nations

522. Charles Malik, "The World is Waiting," *Navy Chaplains Bulletin*, Winter 1953.

523. Wilbur S. Brown, "What a Marine Expects of a Chaplain," talk given to Navy chaplains, Jan. 15, 1953, *Navy Chaplains Bulletin*, Spring 1953.

524. Granfield, *I Remember Korea*, 23.

525. Ralph Fly, "Veterans' Memoirs," Korean War Educator, http://www.koreanwar-educator.org/memoirs/fly_ralph/index.htm

526. C. Douglas Sterner, "Guam: Summer–Fall 1944," http://www.homeofheroes.com/profiles/profiles_sitter.html

527. Ibid.

528. Donovan, *Eisenhower*, 6.

529. Dwight D. Eisenhower, "Inaugural Address," 20 January 1953, online by Gerhard Peters and John T. Woolley, *The American Presidency Project*, http://www.presidency.ucsb.edu/ws/?pid=9600

530. Library of Congress, "Bibles and Scripture Passages Used by Presidents in Taking the Oath of Office," accessed on 14 December 2011 at http://memory.loc.gov/ammem/pihtml/pibible.html

531. Walt Hiskett, oral history interview by Paul Zardock, University of North Carolina—Wilmington, 25 March 2007, http://library.uncw.edu/web/collections/oralhistories/transcripts/807.html

532. Ibid.

533. Drury and Clavin, *The Last Stand of Fox Company*, 316–17..

534. Chris Vaia, e-mail to the author, Feb. 2, 2012.

535. Ibid.

536. "Loran Stutz Becomes 'Hero' in Son's Eyes," *The Greybeards*, Vol. 25, No. 4, July–August 2011, 22.

537. Ibid.

538. Seymour Harris, posted by Hal Barker, "Return to Heartbreak Ridge," http://www.koreanwar.org/my_html/korea020.htm

539. Letter from the personal files of Ernest Ardente, with permission of his wife, Marilyn Ardente, 16 October 2011.

540. Emil Kapaun, "Second Sunday of Advent (excerpts)," undated, *The Wichita Eagle*, http://www.kansas.com/kapaun

541. "Korean Trade and Business," http://www.seoulkoreaasia.com/trade-business.htm

542. "The Economic History of Korea," Economic History Association, 1 February 2010, http://eh.net/encyclopedia/article/cha.korea

543. Jane Lampman, "How Korea Embraced Christianity," *The Christian Science Monitor,* 7 March 2007, http://www.csmonitor.com/2007/0307/p14s01-lire.html

544. Christopher Landau, "Will South Korea Become Christian?" *BBC News,* 26 October 2009, http://news.bbc.co.uk/go/pr/fr/-/2/hi/asia-pacific/8322072.stm

545. Ibid.

546. Rob Moll, "Missions Incredible," *Christianity Today,* 1 March 2006, http://www.christianitytoday.com/ct/2006/march/16.28.html

547. Ibid.

548. Ibid.

549. From the personal files of Ernest Ardente, with permission of his wife, Marilyn Ardente, 16 October 2011.

550. George Thomas, "Bible 'Balloon Offensive' Floats into North Korea," Christian Broadcasting Network News, 14 October 2011, http://www.cbn.com/cbnnews/world/2011/September/Balloon-Offensive-Invades-North-Korea-for-Christ/

551. Lee, *Eyes of the Tailless Animals,* 151.

552. Ibid.

553. Ibid, 152.

554. Kim, *Escaping North Korea,* 91.

555. Ibid., 92.

556. "Bombing of Korean Air Flight 858," http://www.x-rayscreener.com/?CategoryID=332&ArticleID=161

557. Paula Chin, "A Bomber Repents," *People,* Vol. 40, No. 24, 13 December 1993, www.people.com/people/archive/article/0,,20106989,00.html

558. Ibid.

559. Norbert Vollertsen, "Diary of a Mad Place," 21 January 2001, http://northkoreanchristians.com/norbert-vollertsen.html. Vollertsen has also published a book titled *Inside North Korea: Diary of a Mad Place* (Encounter Books, 2004).

560. Ibid.

561. Ibid.

562. Granfield, *I Remember Korea,* 111.

563. Steve Bousquet quoting Carmine Ranieri Zinn, "Summer of 1953," Interactive Special Report of the *St. Petersburg Times,* 27 July 2003, http://www.sptimes.com/2003/07/27/Korea/Summer_of_1953__far_f.shtml

564. Ibid., quoting Charlie Fuss.

565. Hee Sung Lee, "Veterans' Memoirs: Freedom is Not Free," Korean War Educator, http://www.koreanwar-educator.org/memoirs/lee/index.htm

566. Ibid.

567. Brady Dennis, quoting Dewey Arnold, "Scraps of Love and Loss," Interactive Special Report of the *St. Petersburg Times,* 27 July 2003, http://www.sptimes.com/2003/07/27/Korea/Scraps_of_love_and_lo.shtml

568. Ibid.

569. Ibid., quoting Don Arnold.

570. Kim, *Escaping North Korea,* 124.

571. International Christian University, http://www.icu.ac.jp/en/info/history/history.html

572. M. A. Ditmer, "International Goodwill in Action," *Navy Chaplains Bulletin*, Winter 1952.

573. Kim, *Escaping North Korea*, 124–25.

574. Ibid.

575. Cypert Whitfill, e-mail to the author, 16 January 2012.

576. Col. James Patterson, video of testimony given on Crossroads Television, 1985, rerun 11 November 2011, http://100huntley.com/video.php?id=VoYMSLbr48g

577. Mary Kay Park, video, www.youtube.com/watch?v=5tBt-QqqSvU&feature=youtube gdata player

578. Ibid.

579. Ibid.

580. Frederick C. Proehl, "Life and Light," *The Lutheran Chaplain*, Christmas 1952.

581. Omori, *Quiet Heroes*, 148.

582. Caldwell, *The Korea Story*, 157.

583. Voorhees, *Korean Tales*, 126. The author tells this Christmas story, promising "every word of it is true."

584. Ibid., 127.

585. Peters and Li, *Voices from the Korean War*, 58.

586. This devotional was inspired by the sermon of Rev. Robert Sturdy at Trinity Church, Myrtle Beach, SC, on 25 December 2011.

587. Joseph Mohr and Franz Gruber, "Silent Night," 1818, www.carols.org.uk/silent_night.htm

588. Adrienne Lu, quoting Bob Mills, "All is Calm, All is Bright," *St. Petersburg Times*, 24 July 2003, http://www.sptimes.com/2003/07/24/Korea/All_is_calm__all_is_b.shtml

589. Robert Reichard, "A Desperate Escape as the Chinese Closed In," *The Morning Call*, Allentown, PA, 11 November, 1999, http://www.mcall.com/news/all-robertreichard,0,7052845,full.story

590. Ibid.

591. "An Order of Service for Private Worship," Christmas 1951, published by the Lutheran Church, Missouri Synod.

592. Demick, *Nothing to Envy*, 98–99.

593. Doug Struck, "N. Korean Christians Get Support from South," *Washington Post Foreign Service*, 10 April 2001, http://www.washingtonpost.com/ac2/wp-dyn?pagename=article&node=&contentId=A18300-2001Mar30&notFound=true, accessed at: http://northkoreanchristians.com/secret-christians.html

594. Ibid.

595. Ibid.

596. Transcription of Gettysburg Address from the Lincoln Memorial, http://myloc.gov/Exhibitions/gettysburgaddress/exhibitionitems/Pages/MemorialTranscription.html

597. Sermon by George M. Docherty, New York Avenue Presbyterian Church, 7 February 1954, in an article by Tom Gibb, "Minister reprises 'under God' sermon," 19 August 2002, http://www.post-gazette.com/nation/20020819pledge 0819p1.asp

598. Dwight Eisenhower, June 14, 1954, www.aipnews.com/talk/forums/thread-view.asp?tid=21061&posts=7

599. Dwight Eisenhower, August 17, 1954, message to the Knights of Columbus, www.adherents.com/people/pe/Dwight_Eisenhower.html

600. Earle "Bruce" Stone, "A Most Enjoyable Tour," *The Greybeards*, Vol. 25, No. 4, July–August 2011.

601. Carl Hughes, "Recollection of the 581st Radio Relay Company," http://www.paulnoll.com/Korea/Story/other-Carl-history-4.html

About the Author

LARKIN SPIVEY is a decorated veteran of the Vietnam War and a retired Marine Corps officer. He commanded infantry and reconnaissance units in combat and was trained in parachute, submarine, and special forces operations. He was with the blockade force during the Cuban Missile Crisis and served President Richard Nixon in the White House. As a faculty member at The Citadel, he taught courses in US military history, a subject of lifelong personal and professional interest. He now writes full-time and resides in Myrtle Beach, South Carolina, with his wife, Lani, and their extended family. He is a lay eucharistic minister of the Episcopal Church and has been actively involved in the Cursillo Christian renewal movement and the Luis Palau Evangelistic Association. He has made numerous television and radio appearances nationwide and speaks frequently to church, veteran, and other groups with his patriotic and spiritual message.

For more information about the author, his other books, and speaking engagements, visit: **www.larkinspivey.com**